# MUSICIANS WITH A MISSION

# MUSICIANS
## WITH A MISSION

*Keeping the Classical Tradition Alive*

A N D R E W   L.   P I N C U S

N O R T H E A S T E R N   U N I V E R S I T Y   P R E S S  •  *Boston*

Northeastern University Press

*Library of Congress Cataloging-in-Publication Data*

Pincus, Andrew L., 1930–
Musicians with a mission : keeping the classical tradition alive / Andrew L. Pincus.
p.   cm.
Includes bibliographical references and index.
ISBN 1-55553-516-x (cloth : alk. paper)
1. Musicians—Biography. 2. Music—20th century—History and criticism. I. Title.

ML385 .P55 2002
780'.92'2—dc21
[B]                    2001059190

Designed by Gary G. Gore

Composed in Dante by Creative Graphics, Inc., Allentown, Pennsylvania.
Printed and bound by Thomson-Shore, Inc., Dexter, Michigan.
The paper is Glatfeller Supple Opaque Recycled, an acid-free stock.

MANUFACTURED IN THE UNITED STATES OF AMERICA
06   05   04   03   02      5   4   3   2   1

To the memory of

Arnold Kvam

*musician, mentor, mensch*

# CONTENTS

# OVERTURE

THIS IS A BOOK ABOUT MUSICIANS WHO HAVE DONE MORE than sing their songs, play their instruments, conduct their orchestras, or compose their symphonies. Each has gone an extra mile—in most cases, several extra miles—to assist fellow musicians and advance the art of music. The means may be performing and commissioning new music, teaching, publishing, advocacy, innovative programming, or some combination of those things, but the goal is the same: a search for the renewal of an art form endangered by ossification on the one side and commercialization on the other.

All of these musicians are well known; two, Yo-Yo Ma and Midori, are major attractions on the international concert circuit. None needs to prove himself or herself through acts of charity or valor. Nor, on the other hand, do their good deeds arise out of pure altruism. Like other professionals, musicians have a natural curiosity about what's out there in their field. Knowledge and experience make them better musicians. In music, as in the other performing arts, it takes ego to put your abilities and emotions on the line before an audience. But ego is only the vehicle that gets you to your destination. In addition to healthy egos, generous spirits underlie these musicians' actions.

Alike in their willingness to take chances, the artists have nevertheless followed different paths. Besides commissioning and premiering many works for cello, Yo-Yo Ma has experimented with new media and explored the music and culture of far-off places in Africa and Asia. Phyllis Curtin and the Juilliard String Quartet have been pioneers in the discovery and performance of new music; in so doing, they have served as models for new generations of artists. Gunther Schuller, a leading composer, has headed major academies and founded and operated—partly at his own expense— publishing and recording enterprises that brought music of his fellow composers to light. Robert Spano has devised new ways of programming orchestral music, throwing fresh light on the repertoire and offering hope of renewed concert life. Midori, not long out of childhood herself, has created a foundation and enlisted performer-teachers to bring music education back to the New York City schools.

These musicians have also made significant contributions as teachers. For Curtin, Schuller, and the Juilliard, teaching has been a principal legacy, enabling them to pass along not only knowledge but also the inquiring spirit necessary for a first-rate musician. Each chapter in this volume introduces other musicians who have taken up the teacher's cause or are doing similar work in the field. The Emerson and Tokyo quartets, for example, were trained by the Juilliard. While forging their own identities, these newer groups—both now as established in the chamber music pantheon as the Juilliard itself—have followed the path laid down by their mentors. Like Midori in New York, conductor Michael Morgan has brought music instruction back to the schools of Oakland, California. Both have met with success in an educational area once given up as dying or dead.

Many other musicians could have been given a place in these pages. In addition to his distinguished career as a violinist, Isaac Stern, for example, saved Carnegie Hall from demolition, discovered and assisted many noted musicians (Yo-Yo Ma among them) when they were young, and embarked late in life on a teaching career. But the Stern story is so thoroughly documented—he himself has told it in a recent memoir, *My First 79 Years*—that I felt I could add nothing to the record. Similarly, in the twilight of their careers Leontyne Price and Marilyn Horne have thrown themselves into giving career support to younger singers. Useful as their projects are, I focused on Phyllis Curtin instead because she began teaching while still a star, played an important role in academia, and compiled a distinguished record as a new-music pioneer. Among composers, Philip Glass and Steve Reich have set an example for others not only through their music but also by forming their own ensembles to assure their compositions of a hearing. But Gunther Schuller seems to me to have extended himself far more on behalf of other musicians. He also seems to have more to say as a composer.

Singer and instrumentalist, conductor and composer, soloist and chamber ensemble, male and female, old and young: I have tried to show a broad spectrum of the profession. In addition to a pioneering spirit, one other thread connects the group: an association with Tanglewood. The link is not accidental. Through my coverage of Tanglewood as a journalist and book author, I have followed these musicians' careers over the years. I felt I could better tell their stories than those of artists with whom I was less well acquainted. In the chapter on Robert Spano, for example, I might have changed the emphasis and focused on Michael Tilson Thomas, who is the better known conductor and has been doing innovative programming longer. But it was Spano with whose work I was more familiar.

It is a well-known fact that in helping others, teachers learn more themselves through questioning and reexamining their materials. A similar process takes place in the performance of new music. Learning a new score, especially if it is done in collaboration with the composer, gives the performer insights into the methods used by composers of the past, including the great masters. Beyond that, there is occasionally the thrill of discovery.

Who, today, would remember Count Andrei Razumovsky, an amateur violinist, if Beethoven had not composed the three Razumovsky quartets for him? More recently, Bartók's Concerto for Orchestra and Berg's Violin Concerto, two twentieth-century landmarks, are indissolubly associated with the men who commissioned them, conductor Serge Koussevitzky and violinist Louis Krasner. The opportunity to attach his or her name to a significant piece of music still awaits any musician willing to take the chance. For audiences, too, the possibility of an encounter with a new masterwork always hovers in the wings. Imagine having been at the 1913 premiere of Stravinsky's *Sacre du printemps,* with its attendant riot. And even if there is no discovery, there can still be the pleasure of being taken out of the rut of everyday thinking, doing, and feeling, much as a trip to a new country yields surprise pleasures.

In one chapter Schuller speaks of the cultural illiteracy spawned by television and the other popular media. It is not just coincidence that although Schuller is a champion of jazz, Ma has dabbled in scat and country music, and Curtin sang Cole Porter, none of these musicians has ventured into popular music—not even into the variant called crossover, which blurs the lines between genres. The reason isn't that classical is "good" and popular is "bad"; everybody knows there are good and bad examples of each. Rather, the intersection between classical and pop is a tricky one, and it is a rare musician whose training, skills, and inclinations allow him or her to navigate both streets convincingly. The qualities that have distinguished these musicians in one area lead them away from the other. The distinction is a useful one as classical music tries to hold onto its past while moving into the future. No one strengthens an art by cheapening it.

Music cannot stand still. It needs constant refreshment through new repertoire, new artists, and new ideas. Otherwise it becomes a museum, a place to visit but not to dwell. The artists profiled here love the masterworks of the past. The Juilliard would not be the Juilliard without the sixteen Beethoven quartets, which it has played and recorded repeatedly. Ma goes back again and again to the Dvořák concerto. But Ma, the Juilliard, and the others would serve their audiences (and composers and themselves) poorly if they did not introduce them to the music of their time. That music may prove ephemeral, but there is no way of knowing without singing or playing it. In one way or another all of these artists have enriched the art of music. In so doing, they have also enriched themselves.

I am indebted to more people than I can name for help in making this book. Most of all, I want to thank the musicians themselves, who gave generously of their time amid busy schedules. Gunther Schuller, Samuel Rhodes, and Raphael Hillyer took special pains in providing information and balance. Among others who have been helpful, I should mention Amy Lafave for assistance in research, Clarence Fanto and Jeremy Yudkin for reading parts of the manuscript, and Allison Williams, Brooke Thompson-Mills, Cristin Bagnall, Rawn Harding, and Kristin Champa for their untiring liaison and fact-checking efforts. My editor at Northeastern University Press, William A. Frohlich, offered invaluable assistance in the conception and realization of the book.

Finally, a word about the quotations in the text: Unless otherwise indicated, they come from my own interviews and reporting. I hope I have represented my subjects fairly and given a three-dimensional picture of what they do and why they do it.

# YO-YO MA

*Marco Polo totes a cello*

Yo-Yo Ma as soloist with a student orchestra at
Tanglewood. (Walter H. Scott)

LOOK AT ME, YO-YO MA EXPLAINS. BORN IN PARIS TO CHI-nese parents. Brought up in New York. Mother raised as a Christian, father as a Buddhist. Playing Bach at age four. Harvard graduate. Traveling the world to play concerts. I'm a perfect example of how culture has gone global.

Understand that about the irrepressibly cheery cellist, and you begin to understand why he plays tangos, scat, country, and electronic music; turns up on television and film; goes to Africa to study and perform with the Bushmen; makes videos of Bach with a gardener, a Kabuki actor, and ice skaters; and explores the music and culture of the Silk Road, the ancient trading route between Asia and Europe. It's not enough to be the world's most popular cellist and play the old masters—or the new masters, for that matter. He has to throw philosophy, psychology, cosmology, theology, archeology, and anthropology into the pot. It's as if, following Beethoven's summons in the Ninth Symphony, he wants to embrace the world, or at any rate the part of it that society labels culture. This gobble-it-all approach, this willingness to try anything, infuriates his detractors. Such a gifted musician, they say. Why does he squander his talents on sideshows and trifles?

Ma naturally doesn't see it that way (nor do his legions of followers, many of them young). From one of his many trips to Asia he remembers performing at one of the ancient Buddhist temples in Nara, Japan, near the old imperial capital of Kyoto. The performance, which took place in front of a three-story-high wooden Buddha from about A.D. 800, was "a special event and real privilege," he said.

"So I thought, 'Okay, exotic,' right?" Right. A monk appeared and began talking to him.

"On tatami I'm kneeling down, very formal. I'm scared to death. I'm sweating. What am I supposed to do? Yikes! *What do we talk about?*" Ma wondered anxiously. After the pleased-to-meet-you business he learned the monk had taken a doctorate in Islamic law at the University of Cairo. The talk turned to music and Janos Starker's 1948 recording of Zoltán Kodály's Cello Sonata, a rarity even among music lovers in the West. The holy man was a record collector. Ma's jaw dropped nearly to the ground. Exotic? There went another preconceived notion.

"We think of the exotic as the thing that is far away or the thing that is mysterious or the thing that we're afraid of," Ma reflected. But because of globalization and emigration in the late twentieth century, "we find the other probably as our neighbor sooner than we need to travel ten thousand miles" to find him.

Onstage, playing the Dvořák Cello Concerto, say, or Strauss's *Don Quixote,* Ma looks like a man enraptured: eyes shut, head thrown back, bow arm plunging, smile creasing his lips, glasses glinting in the overhead lights, glances thrown backward now and then at a partner in the orchestra. The world sees a superstar cellist. But this cultural icon, immortalized in Rolex watch ads as well as videos and Grammy-winning compact discs, is like Socrates, with the concert stage as his agora. He sees connections— between Bach and a garden, for example—where others only hear music and see flowers. Or like Plato, he wants to know the meaning behind all those shadows dancing on the wall of the cave. Many of his thoughts turn into questions: What is Bach trying to say in this passage? What can others bring to this music that I can't bring by myself? How do other cultures deal with these issues? How can I find what brings us together as people rather than what drives us apart?

Ma and his wife, Jill Hornor Ma, are Episcopalians. They attend the non-denominational Harvard Memorial Church in Cambridge, Massachusetts, where he went to college and they now live. To an observer everything about him is ecumenical. Idealistic and trusting—sometimes naively so, it seems—he is both of this world yet somehow apart from it, as if walking in ether. Ma says he'll never be completely mainstream; the country is too culturally diverse, and so is he. So he'll do commercial things, like touting watches or appearing in a popular television series, to bring people to music. He loves doing it "because it's not normal. It's not exotic." It doesn't set him and classical music apart as something strange or foreign—something people have to be dragged to against their will.

Seemingly wreathed in sunshine wherever he goes, Ma still looks like a Harvard student, even in his midforties. Like Leonard Bernstein in his omnivorous erudition, Ma still carries a Harvard student's intellectual baggage, too. An optimistic, idealistic outlook shows in his playing. It is soulful, questing, and tonally lustrous, touched sometimes by sorrow but unscarred by the darker states of tragedy or angst, which seem to have passed him by. In this it is unlike the earthier style of the other leading cellist of the late 1900s, Mstislav Rostropovich, or the more rigorous playing of Janos Starker, another exemplar. Or, to take renowned cellists from an earlier era, the volcanic force of Jacqueline du Pré or the philosophical gaze of Pablo Casals. Yet Ma shares with Casals a belief that music is something more than producing beautiful sounds for a roomful of people. As Casals put it in 1973 in *Time* magazine, "I am a man first, an artist second. As a man my first obligation is to the welfare of my fellow men. My contribution to world peace may be small. But at least I will have given all I can to an idea I hold sacred."[1]

"I'm always struggling to think about what I do—play the cello, play a limited repertoire from a certain time period—and [about] . . . the things that we claim to be universal values," Ma said. Yet, because the world wants to put music and larger values into separate compartments, "there's a divide between the perception and the knowledge I've gained from what I've done." The more he learned about Bach, Ravel, or Debussy, the more he realized that, like political or geographical boundaries, cultural boundaries are porous. In geography, he said, these porous boundaries lead to the edge effect, in which the greatest richness in diversity lies at the meeting of differing ecosystems. "That's when all the interesting stuff happens. It's not at the center of greatest density. It's not at the center of each system. So I'm thinking if that happens in nature, if it happens in biology, culture is a form of biology." And so he'll go to the boundaries, making connections between music and other phenomena.

Pianist Emanuel Ax, Ma's longtime recital partner, describes him this way: "If someone said, 'I'm reading Hegel and then I'm going out for pizza tonight,' Yo-Yo would find a way of connecting Hegel and pizza. I always think that's the most exciting thing about spending time with Yo-Yo—that everything is affected by everything else, and his intellect is really very wide ranging. You'll never find him saying that 'this is culture and this is something else.' Culture is everything. And everything he does, he does with passion and involvement."

So close are Ma and Ax in outlook, so beloved has their brand of civilized passions become for a quarter of a century on the concert circuit, that when they played a twenty-fifth anniversary recital in New York's Avery Fisher Hall on December 1, 2000, Bernard Holland threw up his hands and said in the *New York Times,* "The elegant soulfulness of both these players has been dissected so many times that there is little I can add here." Nevertheless, Holland did add, "In a field with more than its share of jealousy, backstabbing, and mean-spiritedness, these are two genuinely decent human beings."[2]

The Silk Road Project was Ma's big venture into connection-making as the century turned. While keeping up a busy concert and recording schedule, he conceived, planned, and is directing the four-year effort to create new works and re-create traditional music from along the four-thousand-mile, ancient caravan route between Japan and the Mediterranean.

Sixteen commissions to composers from Silk Road countries—China, Mongolia, Iran, Uzbekistan, Tajikistan, and Azerbaijan—would produce new music, much of it mixing the instruments and styles of East and West. Three commissions to composers living in the United States but with Asian or Middle Eastern backgrounds or philosophies would produce cello-orchestral works on Silk Road themes for Ma to perform. A two-year series of festivals featuring Ma and the Silk Road Ensemble would range across the United States, Canada, Europe, and Asia. Its centerpiece would be the Smithsonian Institution's Folklife Festival on the Mall in Washington in the summer of 2002. Four hundred musicians, artisans, and others from contemporary Silk Road cultures, including émigrés living in the West, would take part in the celebration on the Mall. An international team of scholars, artists, and others would connect the music to broader cultural exchanges along the route. Educational activities would include a documentary film, classroom programs, school and neighborhood concerts, and an interactive Web site.

The Silk Road, like culture and commerce elsewhere in the world, was going global, and Ma was its Marco Polo. In a formal statement he summed up his goals for the project as well as his personal mission:

> In the course of twenty-five years of performing in different parts of
> the world, I have become increasingly intrigued by the migration of
> ideas among communities. In my musical journey, I have had the op-
> portunity to learn from a wealth of different musical voices—from
> the immense compassion and grace of Bach's cello suites, to the an-
> cient Celtic fiddle traditions alive in Appalachia, to the soulful
> strains of the *bandoneón* of Argentina's tango cafés. . . .
>
> Throughout my travels, I have thought about the culture, reli-
> gions, and ideas that have been influential for centuries along these

historic land and sea routes, and have wondered how these complex interconnections occurred and how new musical voices were formed from the diversity of these traditions. How did a *biwa*, a medieval Japanese stringed instrument, become decorated with Persian designs and African gemstones, for example; how did ancient Roman glass influence objects made in Kyoto; how did such string instruments as the Arab *oud,* Chinese *erhu,* and Indian *sarangi* come to influence both East and West?

We live in a world of increasing awareness and interdependence, and I believe that music can act as a magnet to draw people together. Music is an expressive art that can reach to the very core of one's identity. By listening to and learning from the voices of an authentic musical tradition, we become increasingly able to advocate for the worlds they represent. Further, as we interact with unfamiliar musical traditions we encounter voices that are not exclusive to one community. We discover transnational voices that belong to one world.

This fusion of musical styles is called crossover, in its more popular, commercial form. Popular and classical, Western and Eastern, they're all one in this globalized, hugger-mugger vision. Pop stars go classical, classical stars go pop, the world goes round; hey, aren't we having fun. But Bach is Bach, Ma's detractors say. He doesn't need help from gardeners and ice skaters. Leave the Silk Road to the anthropologists and play your cello. As the *London Telegraph* put it, Ma is so crossed over that he's in danger of becoming crossed out.[3]

Naturally, Ma doesn't agree. Neither do his legions of admirers, old and young.

Look at the Web and you'll find sites filled with Yo-Yo fan talk, much of it by the adoring young. There's Roger Chang, for one. An amateur cellist, he devotes an entire Web site to an enchanted visit he paid to Ma during the summer of 1996, when he was a Massachusetts Institute of Technology student.

Chang had journeyed to the Wolf Trap performing arts center in Vienna, Virginia, near Washington, to hear his idol play the Dvořák Cello Concerto with the National Symphony Orchestra under Leonard Slatkin. He sat in the front row and found the performance "outstanding." After a solo encore, a movement from Bach's Third Suite for Unaccompanied Cello, Chang rushed backstage during the intermission. So did a lot of other people. Chang waited forty-five minutes, until an usher allowed him into the dressing room. Greeted by Ma, he proffered his copy of the Dvořák concerto's solo part for an autograph; when it came back with the treasured signature, it also carried the exhortation "Enjoy!" Meanwhile other fans, mostly of Chang's age, crowded in.

"They were mostly eager young cellists wanting to see their musical inspiration," Chang wrote. "I asked one of the people if they would take a picture of me and Mr. Ma together. A girl my age agreed and snapped a picture of Mr. Ma and I. She then took a picture of the entire group of people in the backstage area with Mr. Ma. Soon after, Leonard Slatkin joined us. Mr. Ma put on an arm brace and I asked him what had happened. 'Oh, the conductor bit me for not practicing,' he said jokingly. He then said, 'I have tendinitis. All that playing really puts a lot of strain on my arm.' I then said he played beautifully nevertheless and he shook my hand once more."

If Mr. Ma weren't a cellist, Chang went on, "I wouldn't be playing the cello anymore. . . . What he has done to make classical music popular alone surpasses what dozens of other musicians combined have done." Chang hung the picture of himself with Ma in his dorm room "to remind me of that night forever." He reported nearly sixty thousand visits to his site through the year 2000.[4]

Confirming Ma's appeal to young people, the Bis-Quits, a Tennessee rock band, recorded "Yo-Yo Ma," a Chuck Berry–style song, in the 1990s. The cellist plays to the little kids, too. In the late 1980s he appeared as a guest on *Sesame Street* and *Mister Rogers' Neighborhood,* sometimes with his young son, Nicholas. In 1999 he did a turn on the cartoon series *Arthur,* where the animation turned him into a floppy-eared giant bunny rabbit wearing spectacles and clutching his cello.

In a talk to a group of Tanglewood patrons in 2001, Ma said his appearances on the children's shows were among the things he was proudest of having done:

> I did that because I was asked to. I said yes because at that time I had young children. And I'm proud to say that I helped Elmo [a character on *Sesame Street*]. I knew Elmo before he became a superstar and while he was learning the violin [according to the show's plot]. He was not too good at it. He was playing a scale and *na-na-na-na-neh* [here Ma imitated the scraping of a violin going up the scale]. He couldn't quite get to that last note. I helped him through his prob-

lem. What I did was, by being Elmo's friend, I actually entered into the world of the child that was watching the show. They don't come into my world. I went into their world. And what then happened is that years later I actually have young people coming to concerts, sitting through a two-and-a-half-hour boring recital, you know, waiting half an hour, forty-five minutes backstage, wanting to just tell me about it. Whatever they had to say, they had the patience really to go through all of this because someone entered their world. It's not about us. It's about how we connect to others.

Virtual communication is another avenue to the young in this global era. In February 2000 Ma went online live on the Barnes and Noble Web site to promote his recent compact discs, *Solo* and *Simply Baroque,* by keyboard and mouse. Though the implicit goal was to sell recordings, the questions, respectful and earnest, elicited answers in kind.

Mutsumi Sato of London wanted to know where Ma got his "strong spiritual energy" when he performed. Did he practice yoga or tai chi? Ma replied:

I do breathing exercises just to calm down. But again music involves the imagination, and I think in our imagination we use all of our senses—verbal, visual, aural, sense of touch—and then we have our emotional memory. We have the sense of proportion. All of that is part of our imagination, as well as the tremendous feeling of love. It is the combination of the abstract and real, the memory of the past and being very much in the present. All of that become[s] part of what creates a voice in music.

From Moab, Utah, Jane Brown wanted to know whom Ma considered the great cellists of the twentieth century, and which of them had inspired him.

I think my cello teacher Leonard Rose was one of the kindest people I have ever met, very gentle. I love his playing, because it has such integrity and soul. I love the beauty of his sound, which you can tell is something that has been crafted with great care over a long period of time. Pablo Casals: I admire him because every tone he made seemed to have been sculpted. I really feel that the materiality of the sound that he would carve out and the strength of his voice was not just great music-making but the product of a tremendously strong character. I like Jackie du Pré in the sense that I thought she was a force of nature; everything she did was like a volcano, everything was filled with passion—an overwhelming force of nature. The great cellist Mstislav Rostropovich I admire for changing the landscape of the cello by asking so many composers to write for him. Through his work and their works he added considerably to the cello repertoire.

From California Jason (no surname given) said he found it difficult to get through the Ma-Ax recording of Brahms's cello sonatas "without having a huge emotional response to the music (such as tears at times)." Did Ma have the same feeling when playing it?

I think that Manny and I have a great affection for Brahms's sonatas. If Mozart had this ability to describe the divine, and Beethoven could describe the heroic, then Brahms had this great ability to describe humanity—humanity really grappling with life—and I think a lot of the music we feel close to describes us in our very human efforts to deal with both our daily questions in life as well as the bigger problems.

The conversation ended with Ma tapping out a message of thanks to his interlocutors and describing the virtual format as "a fascinating way to respond."[5]

More conventionally, Ma sometimes gives classes—they're not always master classes—in conjunction with his concerts. In January 2001 he visited Dartmouth College for one of his first concerts with the Silk Road Ensemble, the East-West group that he formed to play the Silk Road music. While at the college, he went before a Music 1 class to discuss his career and how it led to far-off Asia.

The session takes place in a modern lecture-recital hall, away from public view. Ma stands in front of a piano on the stage, holding his cello ready at his side. He is not a polished lecturer, unlike the pair of Dartmouth faculty members who act as his interlocutors. He gropes for words, fills in the blanks with talkative hands, and lets his voice drop at times to near-inaudibility. But, dressed conservatively in a dark jacket and slacks—the fifty or so students before him are arrayed in boots, baggy pants, and ski gear—

he establishes quick rapport through his boyish charm. After the introductions he begins his part of the class by playing Mark O'Connor's "Appalachia Waltz," a nostalgic, folklike solo tune that he has been championing in concert and on records.

The rest of the hour goes like this:

How old is this old-sounding music? he asks. Nobody even guesses. Four years old, he says. How is it like the early American Baptist hymn the class has been studying and has sung to start the hour? Both are based on drones, a young man in a backward-facing baseball cap volunteers. Exactly. The drone is "such a powerful thing that it exists absolutely everywhere," Ma explains. And while "Appalachia Waltz" draws on many traditions, "it's just a wonderful piece of music."

Ma tries to engage the class in further dialogue. Only a few students respond, but those few make perceptive comments. It's still early in the morning for me too, he jokes. (It's after ten o'clock.) Dartmouth ethnomusicologist Theodore Levin, one of the discussion leaders—he's on leave to serve as executive director of the Silk Road Project—jumps in. He points out the conflict facing the Silk Road countries. How do they maintain a sense of community through a musical tradition while the age of the Internet insists on linking that tradition to the rest of the world? He addresses Ma: your life also embodies those opposing forces. How do you reconcile them in your work?

My father was a composer, violinist, and educator in Western music, Ma replies, and "those sounds were certainly in my head when I was growing up." But it wasn't until he went to Harvard as an undergraduate that he "suddenly was exposed to many different worlds that I didn't know about or had just heard a little about." His desire for more knowledge led him to courses that ranged far afield from music. An anthropology course was especially stimulating, leading to later musical explorations in both Africa and Asia. He commends a liberal-arts education to the liberal-arts audience. For him it determined the course of the next twenty-five years, up to that very moment. In all that time "I've been doing pretty much all the things that I first thought about in college," he explains.

Warming to his subject, he says he doesn't "generalize" about the music he plays. He doesn't, that is, put American and European music—or Western and Eastern music—in different compartments. Bach, Schubert, and Brahms, he explains, are very different composers. They can't be played as if they come out of the same milieu. Music is "not about a joint tradition, it's not about an economic community and culture. It's really about totally different people fighting for their voice to be heard."

The National Endowment for the Arts has a budget of $99 million for the entire country, he says. A few years ago the city of Berlin alone allotted $1.2 billion for the arts in a single year. Although private support makes up the difference in the United States, the two funding approaches reflect different beliefs about the role of culture.

"You cannot be, I think, an elitist classical musician in America," Ma declares. Concert donors and sponsors expect the soloist to go to their parties and show appreciation. In Europe you can refuse. In the United States "if they don't care about what you do and there's no connection made, you're out of a job." The American way is better—for an American, anyway. "Because you come across so many different types of people all of the time, you get a slightly more open outlook," Ma says.

Ma has brought Wu Man, a soft-spoken young Chinese-American woman, to the class with him. She plays the *pipa,* a short-necked Chinese lute. Together they play a modern setting of a traditional Chinese love song. The arrangement is by Bright Sheng, a Chinese-American composer, Silk Road collaborator, and friend of Ma's. Wu Man proves as fluent on the *pipa* as Ma is on the cello.

Did you like it? Ma asks the class when the run-through is over. How do you think the performance might be improved?

The braver students throw out a few suggestions about phrasing and emphasis—a longer line here, a diminuendo there. The musicians try out each idea in turn, sometimes offering alternative possibilities. The suggestions snowball as the students realize they are being taken seriously. After the class has worked through the piece, the musicians play it again, adopting the improvements.

What do you think? Ma asks, still clutching his cello. The class voices its approval; the performance sounds better. He agrees. He likes it better this way, too. He thanks the class for its help. He has turned passive listeners into active participants in the creative process.

To conclude the hour, Ma returns to the Chinese song. He demonstrates how the music, with its distinctive Chinese tang, would sound if he played it in a Western style on his Montagnana, "a very expensive instrument" capable of many nuances. He'd feel "dirty" doing it that way, he says. The Montagnana has "incredible tones and growls, but it doesn't work in a young woman's love song." With Wu Man he plays the piece again, now echoing the sinuous twists and turns of the *pipa*. The music sounds more plaintive, more Asian. More Asian still were the sounds he elicited in the public concert the night before on the *morin khuur*, the boxy Mongolian two-stringed fiddle, which he learned to play for the Silk Road Project. That instrument, held between the knees like a cello, has a carved wooden horse's head as a decoration on the neck—appropriate, Ma told the concert audience, for a musician whose last name, *Ma,* means "horse" in Chinese.

In a different kind of educational endeavor, Ma took part in the 2000 World Cello Congress at Towson State University in Maryland, which brought together six hundred musicians from forty-five countries. He managed to carve out time to lead a "children's cello party" for an ensemble of eight students, ages seven to twelve. In a report headlined "For He's a Jolly Good Cello," John Pitcher of the *Washington Post* set the scene with this description of Ma's entry into the concert hall:

"A singular phenomenon in the classical music world, Ma is a bona fide celebrity who draws about as much attention at a cello expo as Bill Gates does at a Microsoft convention. Entering the building with a blue cello case strapped to his back, he is instantly recognized by a throng of enthusiastic well-wishers, autograph seekers, and photographers. He doesn't so much walk to his master classes as he is swept along in the wave of the crowd, shaking hands and exchanging pleasantries all the way with the ease of a politician on the campaign trail."

To avoid distractions, Ma and the expo organizers closed the children's class to the public. Even parents had to watch on a large video screen set up in the nearby concert hall. Only the ensemble's conductor-teacher, John Kaboff, remained in the room.

A group of four older children go first. With Kaboff conducting, they play a serenade by Georg Goltermann, carefully rehearsed over the course of a year. At the end Ma offers corrections. "That was so beautiful," he says, "but this time I want to see what happens when all of the energy is coming from you." The second time through, the performance comes to life. The same thing happens when the younger group of four takes its turn and plays the song "Long, Long Ago."

"I think their teacher did a fantastic job in getting these kids to the point where they can fly on their own," Ma tells the reporter. "Moving to a new performance level is always exciting because it involves a different kind of thinking. It's the kind of experience that really makes a musician feel alive."

Kaboff says, "I was really amazed at how their playing level rose. The kids learned to use their eyes and ears in a way that made them sound much more musical and together."[6]

Why does Ma do it? Why does he go online, get turned into a funny bunny, and join in cello parties for kids? The real work of teaching, as he readily admits, is done by people like Kaboff, drilling students day in, day out on the fundamentals of performance. Master classes at best supply another point of view and an incentive to try harder; at worst they become a star show and distraction from the business of learning.

For Ma the appearances become another way of making connections with students, concertgoers, moviegoers, whoever, wherever. If making connections means sitting with legs sprawled, arms akimbo, and a goofy smile on his face in a Rolex watch ad, okay. ("Yo-Yo Ma says the 1712 Stradivarius he plays is 'like a great Bordeaux,' while the 1733 Montagnana is 'earthier, like a Burgundy,' " the ad copy reads. "About a third instrument, his Rolex, he says, 'I just love it. You can use it for any occasion.' " He says he got a free Rolex for doing the ads. You can believe him or not that that was the entire fee.) If making connections means playing in a hospital, squeezing in a talk just before a concert, or playing a movement from Bach at a fictional president's soiree in the popular television series *The West Wing,* that's okay, too. His aim is to avoid confining himself to a ghetto of music lovers, which he says "is the worst thing that can happen."

The novelty of the name Yo-Yo has probably worn off, but for the young the novelty of a slightly goofy adult who acts like a kid while making music like a god remains. Roger Chang said it: he's not like the television celebrities who seem like nice guys on the screen but turn out to be monsters in life. When he puts on his arm brace, ha ha, it's because the conductor bit him for not practicing. No, he really has tendinitis, Roger. And now you know his secret.

Ma holds no regular teaching affiliation. A residency of a few days most summers at Tanglewood's school for advanced studies is the closest he comes to a teaching schedule. But with its outstanding faculty, he says, Tanglewood doesn't need more coaching power. Ma would rather talk to the students, planting such thoughts as the ideal taught by the school's former artistic director Leon Fleisher: a rounded musician must encapsulate within himself or herself the composer, performer, and audience. The combination becomes reflexive, habitual—"like a muscle," Ma says. With every group of listeners he addresses, he tries to "just take them through what the thinking process is, how you deal with the hall as an instrument, how you make it friendly, how you think of a release [from a note], or what questions they have."

Ma may, as he claims, never be completely mainstream, but he bears the mainstream's trappings of success: the celebrity, the ample lifestyle, the fees that, except for an occasional benefit, price him out of the range of anyone who is not a major concert presenter. In 2001 his fee was reported to have risen to $75,000 per concert, which would add up to earnings of about $3 million a year, not counting royalties from audio and video recordings. The price range is not unusual for a musician of his prominence. His management agency—the giant ICM Artists corporation—probably dictates the concert and fee schedule to some extent. But the pricing, and his maintenance of two substantial homes, one in Cambridge and the other, recently built, in the Berkshires, leaves him open to the criticism that he does it mainly for the money. Yet he is generous in giving benefit concerts for orchestras, educational programs (including Midori's; see page 233), and other causes he favors. It's likely that he also puts some of his money into his far-ranging projects, such as the Silk Road venture.

Wherever the income goes, whatever the critics may say, Yo-Yo Ma remains an idealist. For him the payoff is the response of kids like Mutsumi Sato, who feel the spiritual energy and want to know how they can get a piece of it.

Charisma, it's called: the aura that makes a musician (or politician or preacher) stand out in a crowd. Whether it's from nature, nurture, or both, some have it and some don't. Cellist Lynn Harrell is comparable to Ma in musical abilities but has never caught on with the public to the same degree. (Is this fair? Probably not.) At an opposite pole are stars like tenor Andrea Bocelli, whom the public rushes to embrace more for their personal appeal—in Bocelli's case, his ex–pop star status and courage in making a career in spite of blindness—than for their musical abilities, which may be modest. (Is this fair? Certainly not.)

Ma's particular charisma has conferred on him an aura of saintliness, a quality that no one would attribute to Leonard Bernstein, for example, or to others in the current crop of superstars, such as Luciano Pavarotti. In a *Harvard Magazine* profile of Ma, conductor David Zinman, a frequent partner in concerts and recordings, actually compared him to a saint with healing powers: "People are always bringing babies to him to be kissed and pushing folks in wheelchairs. I asked him once if he was planning to raise the dead."

In the same article, composer-conductor Leon Kirchner, Ma's mentor at Harvard, recalled the time his wife was dying and Ma played one of the Bach suites at her bedside in the hospital. (For Kirchner Ma brought "a beautiful little silver flask filled with wonderful Scotch.") Ma returned with his cello on another day. As Kirchner describes the scene, "Gert, who had been having an astonishing penchant for pickles, was not quite there. So I said, 'Gert, Yo-Yo is here. Do you want pickles or do you want Yo-Yo?' She said, 'I want pickles.' The next thing I knew, Yo-Yo left his cello and took off. He came back thirty minutes later with about six jars of pickles, all different kinds."7

On the afternoon before a concert with the Pittsburgh Symphony Orchestra, Ma offered to perform solos in a home for the elderly during his one free hour in the day. That night the orchestra had to install temporary seating for eighteen residents of the home who, smitten by their visitor, insisted on coming to the sold-out concert.

In 1999 conductor-pianist Daniel Barenboim and Ma led an intensive three-week workshop in Weimar, Germany—home of Goethe, Schiller, the Weimar Republic, and Buchenwald, and Europe's official Culture City that year—for seventy-eight Arab and Israeli musicians between the ages of eighteen and twenty-five. Ma, Barenboim, and first-desk players from the Chicago Symphony Orchestra and Berlin Philharmonic, both of which Barenboim regularly conducts, gave daily master classes. Ma and Barenboim also led political discussions about the short-lived Weimar Republic, its descent into Buchenwald genocide, and Palestinian-Israeli tensions, with their troubling overtones of anti-Semitism.

"We didn't know what would happen," Ma recalled; "we found that after twelve hours of rehearsal, at night they would be playing dance music and dancing—the Iraqis, the Israelis, the Egyptians. They partied!" They all used e-mail and worried about the same issues. They got along! The classes, talks, and parties culminated in a concert in which Ma played the Schumann concerto with an orchestra made up of workshop members under Barenboim's direction. On the same program, an Israeli and a Palestinian were the soloists in Mozart's Concerto for Two Pianos. It will take more than three weeks of music and talk to bury ancient hatreds. But three weeks with an idealist whom both sides can look up to is a start.

Six years older than Ma, Emanuel Ax fell under his spell at the Juilliard School in the late 1960s, when Ma was in the precollege division. To earn money—Ax remembers it as three dollars an hour—he was working as a studio accompanist for three of the school's celebrated string teachers, violinists Dorothy DeLay and Oscar Shumsky and cellist Leonard Rose. One day Rose mentioned an outstanding Chinese student of his. There were few Asians at the school then, unlike today, when they make up a sizable minority. An Asian cellist was hard enough for Ax to believe. But the name, Yo-Yo Ma—was that somebody's idea of a joke? When Rose urged Ax to hear this student in a recital in Carnegie (now Weill) Recital Hall, Ax decided to see what the fuss was about. It was no joke, Ax found. It was, in fact, "unforgettable," he said, "just an incredible exhibition of cello playing."

A couple of months later, as Ax remembers it, he encountered Ma in the school cafeteria. They kept running into each other and struck up a friendship. Then they spent the summer of 1973 together at the Marlboro Music Festival in Vermont and, as professionals, wound up under ICM Artists' management. After a while it just seemed natural that they would make music together. Their first concert was a benefit for a youth orchestra run by Ma's father in New York. Their first program for pay took place in 1975 at the Caramoor Festival in Katonah, New York. Twenty-five years later they were limited in their collaborations by their individual schedules, but they still got together every year for concerts, tours, or special projects, such as a cycle of piano quartets with violinist Isaac Stern and violist Jaime Laredo.

In some ways Ma and Ax are at opposite poles. If Ma seems like a perennial Harvard student, still breathing Cambridge's rarefied air, Ax seems more down to earth (or macadam) as a New Yorker. He can also do a pretty fair turn as a comedian and once played straight man to Garrison Keillor on his *Prairie Home Companion* radio show. Ma will try nearly anything musical, short of pop. Ax plays a good bit of contemporary music, but follows a more traditional concert career. The glue that has kept them together, Ax said, is that they get along well and are alike in their approach to music. "And what I mean by that is that we're both willing to try many, many possibilities and don't like to adhere to one way of doing things," he explained. After exploring the possibilities during rehearsals, in Ax's words, they "sort of leave it in the lap of the gods as to which way will happen at the concert. It's not that we don't work hard. We do work hard. But I've always felt, and I think Yo-Yo and I agree on this, that a piece of music like a Brahms or a Beethoven sonata or concerto is just too rich in possibilities to ever be encompassed by any one performance. And I refuse to be tied down to 'I feel this way about the piece' because there are many ways I feel about it, and I'd like the possibility of trying them all."

The decision on which way to go with a piece—faster or slower, more aggressive or relaxed—often won't take place until just before they walk out onto the stage. As the performances evolve, Ax said, "I think sometimes we come full circle. We do things that we haven't done for a very long time and we find ourselves coming back to the way we used to do them. But that's all fine. That's part of the fun."

Ma's parents first gave him the Western name Ernest but it didn't seem to fit. Yo-Yo Ma, their second choice, translates from the Chinese as "Friendship-Friendship Horse." It is a generational name. Following Chinese custom, the name of his sister, a violinist and pianist four years his senior, also represents the written character for friendship assigned to their generation. She is Yeou-Cheng.

An interest in Western music ran in the family. The paterfamilias, Hiao-Tsiun Ma, who died in 1991, was musicologist (with a Ph.D.) and violinist on the faculty of Nanjing University. He left China in 1936 to study further in Paris. His wife, Marina, a soprano, studied theory under Hiao-Tsiun before emigrating in 1949. Reunited in Paris, they were married there, and there both children were born. Hiao-Tsiun started Yo-Yo on the cello at four and soon had him playing and memorizing the unaccompanied Bach suites. Looking back on the experience in a *New Yorker* profile, Yo-Yo said, "This isn't 'practicing'; it's contemplating. You're alone with your soul."[8] He first played in public at Paris University when he was five. His sister was his accompanist.

When Yo-Yo was seven, the family moved to New York. Violinist Isaac Stern, who had discovered Yo-Yo in Paris through a luthier friend, lent assistance (as he did for many another promising émigré musician). While Yo-Yo was studying at various private schools, his father taught music and founded the Children's Orchestra of New York.

When Yo-Yo was nine, Stern arranged for him to study with Leonard Rose. In the *New Yorker* Ma described himself to author David Blum as "a pipsqueak kid and overwhelmingly shy" at the time. He was afraid of Rose, and he would try to hide behind his cello during lessons. Expected to be as obedient as a Chinese but as outspoken and independent as an American, he became disorganized and withdrawn. "My conflict was apparent to Pablo Casals, to whom I was presented when I was seven," he told Blum. "I don't remember what he said about my cello playing, but he did suggest that I should be given more time to go out and play in the street."[9]

In the winter Ma studied with Rose in the Juilliard School's precollege division. Summers he spent at other proper musical addresses: violinist Ivan Galamian's Meadowmount camp in the Adirondacks of New York and pianist Rudolf Serkin's Marlboro Festival, where he put in four years. By then he had long been out on the concert circuit, having performed at age seven in a televised concert in Washington led by Leonard Bernstein (and attended by President and Mrs. Kennedy). At fifteen he played his Carnegie Recital Hall program and was a soloist with the San Francisco Symphony.

Here the story departs from the child-prodigy script. Ma won a competition at age five, but lost the few he entered after that, including three auditions to play in Bernstein's Young People's Concerts with the New York Philharmonic. To this day he disdains competitions and refuses to serve as a judge. He thinks they reward cookie-cutter winners and harm performers equally talented but more individualistic. He has often likened the years between fifteen and twenty to an "emotional bank account" on which you must draw the rest of your life. You can play a lot of concerts or you can open yourself to learning about the world around you, he says, and thus about yourself. But you can't do both.

Instead of following the usual conservatory-competition route, Ma went to Columbia University for a semester and then, quitting Columbia, entered Harvard in 1972. By his own admission he was often drunk, would miss or be late to rehearsals, and crashed cars more than once. "All I was trying to do was to be accepted as one of the guys and not be considered a freak," he told Blum.[10] But his talent was unmistakable, and the steadying influence of his teachers and his sister, who was studying at Radcliffe in preparation for medical school and becoming a pediatrician, helped to pull him through. After a freshman year in which he played thirty concerts in the United States and abroad, he—or perhaps his father—had sense enough to confine his out-of-town performances to one a month for his last three Harvard years.

Leon Kirchner and Luise Vosgerchian were Ma's principal teachers at Harvard. Kirchner, whose performance and analysis course was the first at Harvard to give course credit for performance, became the gifted but wayward student's mentor. "I *was* a severe critic," he told Janet Tassel in the *Harvard Magazine* profile of Ma, "but only because even then I was in awe of him. I was always telling Yo-Yo that he didn't have the true center of his tone yet. Meaning there was something more spiritual, the center of his person, of his being, that was not coming through yet." Mstislav Rostropovich made the same observation on hearing Ma play in a 1976 master class at Harvard, Kirchner recalled. "The audience was not happy with this criticism of Yo-Yo but they didn't understand that Rostropovich too recognized that here was something very different, something worthy of the deepest criticism. It wasn't long afterwards that he invited him to play in Washington. Needless to say, Yo-Yo has long since found that center."[11]

At Harvard, Ma concentrated on literature, language, fine arts, and science courses rather than on music. Dostoyevsky became a passion. Ma would call up friends in the middle of the night to hold forth about his discoveries. He was even more influenced by anthropologist Irven DeVore, an authority on the Kung Bushmen, hunter-gatherers who live in the Kalahari Desert, on the border between Botswana and Namibia in southwest Africa. Learning about the diversity of civilizations and coming to grips with the diverse strains in his own makeup, Ma felt he would someday have to go to the Kalahari and know the Bushmen for himself. He finally made the trip for a television documentary in 1993.

While he was a student, Ma was conducting a long-distance courtship of Jill Hornor, a violinist. Though Ma's imminent marriage to a Westerner caused a temporary strain within the Chinese family, their wedding took place in 1978. Their son, Nicholas, was born in 1983, and their daughter, Emily, in 1985.

At the time of his marriage, Ma was playing as many as 150 concerts a year and was always on the brink of exhaustion. Tensions would build up at home. By the time he had recovered from the stresses of one tour, it was time to leave on the next. The birth of Nicholas brought a realization. In the *New Yorker*'s 1989 profile Ma said: "Fame and success are always being dangled before you. You can easily become a slave to your desire, become an addict. But you have to choose your drugs carefully. I have yet to find something that beats the power of being in love, or the power of music at its most magical. So if someone suggests adding just one more concert at the end of a tour—it's always just one more—you just have to say no."[12]

Unlike violinists and pianists, cellists do not enjoy a lifetime's supply of great music. (Probably for that reason, there are fewer solo cellists than violinists or pianists.) Mozart wrote twenty-seven piano concertos; Beethoven wrote five. Mozart wrote five violin concertos; Beethoven wrote one. Neither composer wrote a concerto for cello, though Beethoven left five cello sonatas and a concerto for violin, cello, and piano. By contrast, the standard concerto repertoire for cello pretty much begins and ends with the Dvořák,

Schumann, and Elgar concertos, the two by Haydn, Brahms's Double Concerto (for violin and cello), Strauss's *Don Quixote* (for viola and cello), Tchaikovsky's Variations on a Rococo Theme, and Bloch's *Schelomo*. A step down on the ladder there are concertos by Boccherini, one each by Prokofiev and Lalo, and two each by Saint-Saëns and Shostakovich. The solo and duo works begin with the six Bach suites, Beethoven's five sonatas, two by Brahms, Schubert's *Arpeggione* Sonata (not really for cello, but for an obsolete six-stringed instrument), a sonata by Debussy, and works by Ravel, Prokofiev, and Britten. An inexhaustible supply of chamber music for larger combinations, which Ma also plays, is available.

For the first fifteen years of his post-Harvard career, Ma pursued a fairly conventional concert and recording life with this repertoire. Adventurous even then, he embellished them with commissions—by 2000, he figured, more than a hundred commissions dating back to his Harvard years. But with his roving mind, it was probably inevitable that even a larger repertoire would not have kept him on a standard track.

The recordings partially chart the course that Ma's career took in the 1990s. Early on, scat singer Bobby McFerrin introduced him to improvisation—"a terrifying as well as exhilarating experience," Ma recalled in the liner notes for their compact disc, *Hush*.[13] Soon after, he teamed with country fiddler Mark O'Connor and pop-classical bassist Edgar Meyer. They made two crossover albums, *Appalachia Waltz* (the title is borrowed from O'Connor's tune of the same name) and its sequel, *Appalachian Journey*. The latter also featured folksingers James Taylor and Alison Krauss.

It took Ma a year of coaching by O'Connor and Meyer to master the Nashville style. In a feature article on Ma in the *New York Times* O'Connor recalled, "Yo-Yo said that whatever we did, he wanted to be stretched. So we came up with some really great fiddle material that we hoped would challenge him. It was amazing to see him process this intellectually and make it work on his instrument. It has been quite a transformation."[14] Quite. Ma began to play "Appalachia Waltz" as an encore after the Bach suites. It also turned up in his Dartmouth class.

Other travels outside the mainstream included an exploration of Astor Piazzolla's tango-driven music, leading to a concert tour; a recording, *Piazzolla: Soul of the Tango;* and a soundtrack for the film *The Tango Lesson*. He also performed on the soundtracks of *Immortal Beloved* (a Hollywoodized biography of Beethoven), *Liberty!* (a Public Broadcasting Service documentary series about the American Revolution), and *Crouching Tiger, Hidden Dragon* (the acclaimed Chinese martial-arts feature directed by Ang Lee).

For the *Strictly Baroque* album Ma "retrofitted" his Stradivarius to play Boccherini, Bach, and other eighteenth-century selections—some in transcriptions—with the period-instrument Amsterdam Baroque Orchestra under Ton Koopman. The compact disc evoked a sour response in the *New York Times,* where Michelle Dulak accused Ma of "slumming. He is enjoying the thrill of hanging out with the musical equivalent of 'fast company' without the dreary necessity of having to go home to its cramped apartment."[15] Translation: he wants to enjoy the pleasures of baroque music and period-instrument performance without the effort of learning the literature and style.

Rushing to the defense in a letter to the editor, Emanuel Ax replied, "Mr. Ma's entire attitude is based on exactly the opposite view: that making music in a serious way, with devotion and care, is never slumming, be it in a concert of Beethoven and Brahms or a country music performance."[16] For the prosecution, violinist Stephanie Chase, noting "blatant anachronisms" in a photo of Ma's cello and bow, fired off a letter terming the result "neither 'authentic' nor modern but some strange amalgamation. It resembles the many other crossover strategies so shamelessly promulgated by record companies and presenters."[17] Slumming or not, anachronistic or not, commercial or not, most of these albums traveled to the top of the charts.

Another album, *Solo,* launched Ma on the Silk Road journey. Chosen to illustrate the idea of how culture travels yet maintains its roots, particularly in the Silk Road areas of Eastern Europe and Asia, the contents range from "Appalachia Waltz" by Mark O'Connor (again) to *Seven Tunes Heard in China* by Bright Sheng (the Chinese-American composer who would become central to the Silk Road Project), *The Cellist of Sarajevo* by David Wilde (a meditation on a fatal bombing of civilians in the war-torn city), the Suite for Solo Cello by Alexander Tcherepnin (a Russian who spent time in China and taught Ma's father), and Cello Sonata by Kodály (a Hungarian strongly influenced by folk music). The recording was inspired by Ma's 1999 visit to the Zen garden of the Ryoan-ji Temple in Kyoto. Ma discovered that a visitor must wander about to take in the whole, and even then finds it only from different perspectives. In the liner notes Ma explains:

"It's interesting to find music that's wandered a lot. But no matter how much one absorbs by wandering, there's always going to be a piece missing, and that's the piece that comes from having roots. The best that music can do is to show both. It's the balance between them that will create something meaningful, because ultimately that's what we are struggling with forever [wandering and maintaining roots]. It's the human dilemma, and at the same time, it embodies a continuing human spirit."[18]

He was finding connections again.

In addition to making recordings, Ma was keeping up a busy concert schedule with the major orchestras and such classical partners as pianists Daniel Barenboim, Peter Serkin, and Christoph Eschenbach and violinists Isaac Stern and Pamela Frank, always with Emanuel Ax as his regular recital partner. Many of these programs included his commissions and other new music; others remained true to the old standbys. A 1995 performance of Schubert's popular *Trout* Quintet, with Pamela Frank, violist Rebecca Young, double-bass player Edgar Meyer, and Ax, led to a recording of the *Trout* with the same ensemble, along with Schubert's *Arpeggione* Sonata with Ax. The liner notes claim that Ma's "urge to *communicate* with every musician in the orchestra as well as every member of the audience is so deeply felt that one wonders if he isn't going to jump out of his chair in the middle of the cadenza and invite everybody over to his house for a barbeque."[19] Young doesn't jump out of her chair, but the cover photo of the five musicians does show her playing barefoot in a tree above a white-suited Ma. Fortunately, the performances live up to the marketing hype.

On the high-tech side, one of Ma's experiments was to premiere *Begin Again Again . . .* by Tod Machover, a cellist himself and director of the Media Laboratory at the Massachusetts Institute of Technology (M.I.T.), in Cambridge. Hooked up to a computer-synthesizer by an electronic glove, sensors, and wires, Ma switched between his Stradivarius and an electronic cello while the composer presided at the console. Designed by Machover, who called it a "hyperinstrument," the space-age cello was cellolike in shape but flat like an electric guitar. Sometimes shrieking, sometimes purring, the synthesizer echoed and answered Ma's sounds and physical gestures through ten variations on a theme. Ma played the piece in concert only a few times. He said it was an interesting prowl into a new area but not entirely satisfying as music.

It's rare for a soloist to play in every work on an orchestral program. Different as they are in other ways, Ma and Mstislav Rostropovich are alike in being among the few musicians who will put themselves on the line to that extent. Rarer still is an entire program made up of three new concertos, all played by the soloist for whom they were written. In 1996 Ma made a triple-header of three concertos commissioned by or for him. With the Philadelphia Orchestra, under David Zinman, he played all three on a weekend's programs and recorded them concurrently. (A third of a concert just isn't enough for Ma. When he plays only a single concerto, usually on the first half of a program, he'll often slip into the back row of the orchestra's cellos to play along in the second half. He likes the different perspective of being part of an orchestra.)

The three Philadelphia concertos have little in common except an attraction to violence. Two are explicitly concerned with death. Music for Cello and Orchestra by Leon Kirchner, Ma's Harvard mentor, goes through a fierce struggle between the solo instrument and orchestra, only to subside into a Bach-like sense of repose. Richard Danielpour's Concerto for Cello and Orchestra grew out of a dream in which he witnessed an oracle, the bearer of ill tidings, sentenced to death by an angry assembly. In a program note Christopher Rouse describes his Violoncello Concerto as "a meditation upon death—the struggle to deny it, and its ultimate inevitability."

Ma premiered this sometimes angry assembly of concertos with different orchestras: the Danielpour with the San Francisco Symphony, the Kirchner with the Philadelphia Orchestra, the Rouse with the Los Angeles Philharmonic. The collective performance took place in Philadelphia in early January 1996. The recording sessions were scheduled to run in a studio in Collingswood, New Jersey, about ten miles to the east. The three composers were on hand, as were Maurice and Lillian Barbash, who had commissioned the Kirchner piece as a fortieth-anniversary gift to themselves and the world.

The studio sessions began comfortably enough with the Danielpour, which was recorded on a Saturday between the Friday and Saturday night concerts. Early on Sunday a two-foot blizzard began to bury the East Coast. The Monday sessions had to be canceled, and the Tuesday sessions became iffy. Zinman worried that the project might have to be postponed for years, or never get done at all. But on Tuesday, after holing up in Philadelphia hotels for two days, Ma, Zinman, Kirchner, and the Barbashes drove to New Jersey to complete the project. Zinman, in a diary printed in the liner notes, tells the rest of the story:

The ride to the studio is slow—there are still masses of piled-up snow but we get there on time. Most of the orchestra is there already, a small miracle in itself, considering that they live all over the metropolitan area. We start to record the Rouse only five minutes behind schedule. Yo-Yo outdoes himself. He shows no sign of fatigue, is smiling and patient, caring and loving to all. The Barbashes arrive to root for the Kirchner. We all want this to go well, because this is the work that started the whole project and Yo-Yo especially wants to please Leon, his former Harvard professor. We dig in. Yo-Yo transcends himself. The takes are magical in their beauty. Leon is thrilled, as are we all. And then it's over. We hug, give utterance to our thanks, say our goodbyes. As we ride back to Philadelphia, I breathe a quiet sigh of relief. Another crisis averted. Another victory for American music.[20]

Beyond the chauvinistic boast, it is true that no other American cellist—and probably no single American musician—has been responsible for the birthing of so many works in so many genres and idioms. The record may be matched, in fact, only by the Juilliard String Quartet's much longer history of commissions. Together, Ma and Rostropovich have greatly expanded the solo cello literature, at the same time giving many composers support and exposure. Other American recipients of Ma's commissions are Stephen Albert, William Bolcom, John Corigliano, David Diamond, John Harbison, and John Williams. All steer a middle course between twelve-tone complexities and minimalist simplicities; most were well-established composers before Ma commissioned them. Among Ma's more experimental composers are H. K. Gruber, an Austrian better known in the United States for his clownish exploits in music, and Tan Dun, a Chinese émigré in the United States who tries to bridge the two cultures in his compositions (and figures in the Silk Road Project).

As is usual with commissioned concertos, most of these composers wrote with Ma's sound and personality in mind. His fellow Cantabrigian John Harbison, who teaches at M.I.T., did some of the composing with Ma's participation. Ma would read through the sketches while Harbison played the orchestral part at the piano. To see the pages on the piano's music rack, Ma would play standing up behind the composer—a rare position for a cellist.

Funded by a private foundation, a donor, and the National Endowment for the Arts, the Harbison concerto was jointly commissioned for Ma by the Boston and Chicago symphony orchestras. It premiered in Boston in 1994.

Because the idea came from the soloist rather than an orchestra, Harbison put more emphasis on the soloist than he has in other concertos. The result is a work unusually rich in lyricism and warmth, yet unmistakably of its time. Christopher Rouse's concerto, by contrast, is a threnody on the death of several composers to whom he was close, especially William Schuman. The solo cello is only an actor in a drama that ends when the orchestra is "bitten" or "stung"—the words are Rouse's—to death by the hissing and rattling of wooden percussion instruments.

In 2001 Ma premiered the Cello Concerto by the ninety-two-year-old Elliott Carter, the dean—and probably the most formidably complex—of American composers. The single-movement work was commissioned for Ma by the Chicago Symphony Orchestra, which, under conductor Daniel Barenboim, joined him in the premiere. The commission resulted from an earlier encounter at a Chicago Symphony concert. In a newsletter issued by Boosey and Hawkes, Carter's publisher, the composer recalled having gone backstage to see Barenboim and Ma, who was also on that program. While Ma was warming up in the green room, Carter asked him, "Why don't you play my Cello Sonata?" To Carter's astonishment, Ma "proceeded to play the cello part from memory!" Ma went on to give several performances of the sonata with Barenboim as the pianist, impressing Carter with his "extraordinary sensitivity, subtlety of expression, and beautiful sound." Carter proposed the Cello Concerto commission to Barenboim, and both Barenboim and Ma accepted.[21]

Reviewing the premiere in the *New York Times*, Bernard Holland was struck by the technical difficulty and the gray, February-like chill of the work. The "almost uninterrupted cello line is rapid-fire intricacy that leaps from meter to meter," he wrote. Ma's performance, however, was "extraordinary." On the same program, Ma was the soloist in Max Bruch's *Kol Nidrei*, performed in memory of violinist Isaac Stern. Bruch's music had a "fragile sensitivity" that Ma also captured masterfully, Holland said.[22]

John Williams is a composer from a more unlikely milieu. Though he pursues a career as a composer and occasional conductor of serious concert music, he is best known as the multiple Oscar- and Grammy-winning creator of scores for such films as the *Star Wars* series. His association with Ma began when they performed the Elgar concerto in 1993 at Tanglewood, with Williams conducting the Boston Symphony. They took such a liking to each other that Williams proposed a concerto. Ma agreed and they premiered the work the following summer, again with the Bostonians, as part of the gala program inaugurating Tanglewood's Seiji Ozawa Hall. Every day for a week before the performance, Williams would drive to Ma's rented house near the festival grounds and spend four hours going over the score with him. In a program note Williams said, "From the moment I first heard him play, I aspired to write something that might express the exuberance, vitality, and especially the lyrical expression that are the essence of this remarkable man." The resulting work has the lush melody and orchestration of Williams's film scores.

An even more unlikely choice for a commission than Williams was Hugh Downs, the television personality. His association with Ma began in 1990, when Downs served as host for a Ma concert in the *Live from Lincoln Center* series. Discovering that Downs was a closet composer, Ma issued a challenge: if he'd write an orchestral piece, Ma would play it. Downs proceeded to compose *Windows for Cello and Orchestra*. In 2000 Ma premiered it with the Saint Louis Symphony, which had played a Downs piece before; Jahja Ling conducted. Downs told ABC News that the ten-minute piece "moves from chaos to serenity, and the theme I tried to convey is that life builds order out of chaos."[23]

Ma said he loved performing the piece because music works best when it has a society of dedicated amateurs, like Downs and the Barbashes, the donors of the Kirchner commission, around it. But he doesn't pretend that all this commissioned music will enter the repertoire. If only one work in ten makes it, he believes he'll have done well. He also thinks the violence in the Danielpour, Kirchner, and Rouse concertos has a positive side. They show an awareness of a meaningful past (as in Kirchner's allusions to Bach) and hope for a way out of violence. If there was no hope, he asks, why compose? Writing music becomes a shout across a chasm, one person telling others—mostly unseen—that something out there is worth saving.

The Dvořák concerto is a cellist's bread and butter, beloved by audiences everywhere. Ma doesn't play it often. Because of his other activities, he said, he doesn't perform much with orchestras at all anymore. And since he doesn't perform the Dvořák often, "every time I play it it's fabulous, just incredibly exciting to do. The more I go away, the more I come back and have fresh ears." Recent performances have been unusually free in their liberties with tempo and phrasing; the music seems almost improvisatory in its alternations between fiery and soulful states. Although some orchestras are receptive to new music, Ma finds that most prefer standard works, like the Dvořák, partly because of audience preferences but partly too because of limits on rehearsal time. But Ma gladly plays the standards "because there's a reason why they're standards."

Even with the standards there can be an unusual twist. When Ma recorded the Dvořák concerto with Kurt Masur and the New York Philharmonic in 1995, he paired it with the Concerto no. 2 by Victor Herbert, the operetta composer. Usually thought of (if thought of at all) as a faded relic of the past, the American work, Ma pointed out, is contemporary with Dvořák's. In fact, the two composers were colleagues and friends in the 1890s during Dvořák's New York years. Besides, Ma said, he just likes to play the Herbert.

Ma is a moneymaker for his record company, Sony Classical, which promotes him heavily and backs him in some of his more experimental and controversial ventures, such as his television and videocassette series of Bach's unaccompanied cello suites performed with artists from other disciplines. By 2000 Sony had put out fifty Ma albums, including thirteen Grammy winners, along with two Emmy-winning videos. Many of the compact discs made it onto the *Billboard* chart of classical best-sellers, often staying in the top fifteen for weeks or months at a time; sometimes as many as four albums were on the list at once. Some things are more bankable than others, though. The popular albums—*Hush, Appalachia Waltz, Soul of the Tango*—help to support Ma's taste for such arcana as a disc of three commissioned concertos. But if you're a record company, it doesn't hurt to have a superstar in your fold.

Ma's travels during the 1990s took him to far-off places, and not only to play music. The 1993 trip to the Kalahari Desert represented unfinished business from his Harvard years. Remembering his anthropology classes with Irven DeVore and the films they watched about the Bushmen, he felt the pull of the ancient culture. He especially recalled a blind musician playing and singing in one of the films, *Bitter Melons*. The music was so haunting that there was no escape. He finally had to go, hear, and see for himself. As he says in the hour-long film that resulted, *Distant Echoes: Yo-Yo Ma and the Kalahari Bushmen,* the trip became a personal quest. He wanted "to find out where their music comes from, why they play it, and whether I would find any common ground between us."

When the film was just an idea, Ma kept talking it up until an independent television producer in England, Skyline Productions, agreed to make a documentary. Experts whom Ma consulted, including Richard B. Lee, who eventually served as his interpreter, warned him that many things had changed since the films he had seen at Harvard, which dated from the 1950s. There had been the West African war, in which many Bushmen were used as guides and exposed to outside influences (and which made Botswana unsafe for travel). Ma remembers being told, "Don't be romantic about it. This society has changed. The lands have been appropriated. They now live in villages as opposed to being hunter-gatherers." Because of the war, the expedition would have to remain on the Namibian side of the border. It would be an investigation of music's place in Bushmen society.

As the film begins, a single-engine plane leaves Ma standing alone on a landing strip in the middle of the desert. He is afraid—afraid of snakes, afraid of dying in a strange land, but also afraid that he might be looking for something that doesn't exist. "I am not a musicologist, I am not an anthropologist, I am not a poet," he muses in a voice-over. "So what am I doing? I think what really made me go for it is a sense that . . . the role of a musician is to explore the human psyche—all emotions, good, bad, terrible, fears, evil. And I think that it's all part of one's education as a musician and in life to go find out." Whether he succeeds or fails, he will have learned something about himself.

He listens to old men play their instruments, made of such everyday materials as bones, sticks, and an oil can, and tries to play them himself. He tries to notate their music, which has no written tradition. He's all thumbs. The villagers, sitting in a semicircle on the bare earth in a motley array of African and Western garb, laugh at him. His face is boyish, clean shaven, innocent; the men around him are snaggletoothed, furrowed, grizzled. They speak rapidly in a mixture of words and clicks; he is hesitant, groping for words. At his urging the musicians try his cello and children play recorders and whistles he has brought. He plays some Bach on the cello for the group. It doesn't sound right. He reflects:

"I felt a little awkward about playing my instrument in front of these people. It has such a booming sound, more appropriate to the concert hall than to this intimate setting where music is not performed. It just happens. Bach sounds so young here. Three-hundred-year-old music is old by my standards, but compared with the Bushmen's cultural history, it's little more than an instant."

He watches the trance dance, an ancient ritual in which the villagers sing, clap, and dance—sometimes for hours—until one of the men falls down in a trance. He becomes the shaman who will perform cures on others. Wall paintings show the dance to be forty thousand years old, which would make it one of the oldest rituals known to man, Ma says. Villagers travel from miles around to take part. In the darkness the men dance around a fire with rattles on their legs. Clapping and singing in a circle around the fire, the women direct the action. Sitting in their midst, firelight flickering in his face, Ma claps and sings along with the women as the intensity mounts. Finally one of the dancers collapses on the earth in a fit of trembling and shaking. The village has found its healer.

On the last day of his visit, Ma threw a party. He had a cow slaughtered, and invited the villagers to the feast. Ma made a speech thanking them for their help, and to show his appreciation, he prepared to play the Kodály Sonata for Cello, folk-based music that he had spent months learning for the occasion. But the Kalahari is not Carnegie Hall. Before Ma could start on what back home would have been a singular musical event, the head villager made a speech thanking him for coming and set the village musicians to playing for the departing guest. Kodály was forgotten. The scene didn't make it onto the film but sticks in Ma's mind as one of the funny yet revealing moments of the trip.

Ma and his camera crew spent two weeks in the desert, interviewing residents of twelve villages. The film was shown on English and French television but was not widely seen in the United States, where the Ovation cable channel premiered it in 1996. For Ma the Bushmen's trance dance was the big revelation. Back in Cambridge, he described it as "essentially their religion, music, culture, and medicine all in one thing" and as "the giving away of something that is more than yourself." He said, "It changed my life. This is what the Beethoven Ninth is about. You get to the same place, the brotherhood of man." It takes longer in the trance dance, but the end result is the same.

The Kalahari became a part of him, something his thoughts go back to nearly every day. It reminds him of the rhythms of nature. Until agriculture came along, we were all hunter-gatherers, he noted. We all have those old instincts and rhythms inside us. When he looks at lakes, mountains, and geologic formations, he sees a connection with music. In music as in nature, "we deal with rhythmic possibilities and rhythms that we can perceive, rhythms that we can't perceive because they're too small, and rhythms and cycles that are much larger than our own life cycle. Anything to do with nature deals with all those cycles all the time." And from nature, as the Bushmen showed, comes music—just one more connection in this cellist's ecumenical mind.

After his return from the Kalahari, Ma was soon at work on another television project. Five years of planning and filming went into *Inspired by Bach,* six hour-long programs based on the composer's six cello suites. Ma performs these unaccompanied works, each about twenty-five minutes long, with six partners whose normal business takes them almost as far from the world of Bach as the Kalahari.

For the first suite, Ma and garden designer Julie Moir Messervy create a garden in downtown Toronto. They explain that before they arrived there, they had become entangled in a bureaucratic maze that made it impossible for them to build the garden in the business district of Boston, their first-choice location. Ma and Messervy then take viewers through the steps in the approval, design, and building of the Toronto project, with Ma playing before civic groups to sell them on the idea. The finished garden becomes a kind of urban oasis or retreat from the surrounding bustle. The six Bach movements evoke what Messervy, in a liner note, describes as the "magic lands" that were in her thoughts as she designed the garden. The prelude becomes "an undulating riverscape," the allemande "a forest of wandering squirrel trails," the courante "a swirling path through a wildflower meadow," the sarabande "a deep, dark fern dell," the minuet "a formal parterre garden of flowers," and the gigue "giant grass steps that dance you down to the outside world."[24]

The process is similar in the five other films: talk about the project is interwoven with the project itself. Ma is at various times a presence front and center, shadowy, or unseen. He interrupts his performances for conversations about Bach's meaning and for trials of his partners' ideas about the music. Like a leitmotif, there are recurrent shots of Ma playing on a traffic island, surrounded by streams of cars and pedestrians passing him by without heed, in the middle of what appears to be Times Square. The point apparently is that Bach is not something apart from life but part of the ceaseless flow of life itself.

For the second suite, film director François Girard creates a fantasy of dark, ominous, computer-generated images based on prison designs by the eighteenth-century architect Giovanni Battista Piranesi. Ma appears to play in a dungeon. For the third suite, Mark Morris choreographs a new dance, *Falling Down Stairs,* and performs it with his company, which actually does spill downstairs onto the stage.

Sarabande, the stately dance at the center of each suite (and much other eighteenth-century music), becomes the guiding idea of director Atom Egoyan's treatment of the fourth suite, with Ma himself as the central figure. For the fifth suite Kabuki actor Tamasaburo Bando creates a dance, *Struggle for Hope,* that seeks to transcend the differences between East and West, classical and modern, male and female. Ice dancers Jayne Torvill and Christopher Dean are more specific in *Six Gestures,* their response to the sixth suite. They create a movement-by-movement scenario consisting of "Looking Upward" (the prelude), "Looking Inward" (the allemande), "Hands and Feet Working" (the courante), "Hand Stroking the Face" (the sarabande), "Mannered, Courtly Gestures" (the gavotte), and "Flight, Rebirth" (the gigue).

Produced by Rhombus Media of Toronto in association with Sony Classical, the six programs were shown in 1998 on PBS stations in the United States and on Canadian, European, and Japanese television. They were also released on Sony home video. At the same time Ma rerecorded the suites on a pair of Sony compact discs, which superseded his long-playing-record version of twelve years before. In an introduction to the audio set he said:

"All of the artists with whom I have worked [in the video project] have stretched the limits of their art forms, just as Bach stretched traditional limits when he wrote polyphonic music for what is essentially a single-line instrument. Each collaboration has transformed my understanding of the suite and how to play it. The project, in which Bach's music inspired dance, film, and garden design, has been one of the most exhilarating experiences of my life."[24] The new audio versions, he added, "reflect what I have learned in working with artists from other disciplines."

Exhilarating as the collaborations may have been, they were also trying. The problems ranged from unsympathetic Boston officials to the inability of Ma and Tamasaburo Bando to understand each other's language. François Girard wrote in the liner notes that "what appeared to be a simple cinematographic project turned out, almost accidentally, to be much more complicated, a major occasion for experimenting with diverse media, sophisticated recording technology, and computer-generated images." Mark Morris needed a year before he could agree to participate. He said:

"I've known the Third Suite for much of my life and had never considered choreographing it. . . . I had doubts about the idea of laying more opinions onto what already existed. But the liberating part was that we didn't actually have to agree on everything—we didn't have to share an exact point of view with this music. We knew that if we were relatively honest, at the very least something might happen that wouldn't be a terrible crime. Thankfully, mercifully, it turned out to be beautiful and a great deal of fun."

Barbara Willis Sweete, the director for the third suite, had to overcome both artistic and technical doubts posed by Ma's conception: "I was reassured by his notion that this music, great as it is, can thrive on being interpreted by infinite numbers of creative artists, whether they be musicians, dancers, or even filmmakers—and that even with all of these interpretations, only aspects of what this music is describing can ever be grasped. . . . For me, the key was to find the balance between making a visual presentation of the music and participating in the 'dance' through the choice of camera moves, angles, frame sizes, and editing."

Critical response to the television series was lukewarm and sometimes hostile. Reviewers liked some of the visual images but found the connection with Bach tenuous and distracting, even pretentious. Leon Kirchner termed the visual overlay "baloney, unworthy of a supreme musician like Yo-Yo. I told him he should have saved a suite for Tiger Woods." Also in *Harvard Magazine* Christoph Wolff, dean of the Harvard Graduate School of Arts and Sciences and a leading authority on Bach, found much of the project "embarrassing." When he listens to the cello suites, he said, "especially the intricate sections that are so sophisticated, I close my eyes. Yo-Yo also closes his eyes. I think that is what a serious musician and listener does naturally. Visuals are at best distracting."[25]

Ma traced the origins of the project back to a 1991 symposium in Boston on Albert Schweitzer, the Bach scholar, organist, theologian, and missionary physician (and, of course, a public figure like Ma). As a panelist expected to speak on the performance of Bach, Ma had to rethink his views on the composer in the light of rereading Schweitzer. He was especially struck by Schweitzer's descriptions of Bach as a pictorial composer. (The cantatas are particularly rich in imagery.) Other speakers at the Boston program included a child psychologist, social workers, and a spokesman for the homeless. Listening to the discussions and thinking of the impossibility of reaching bottom in a composer as profound as Bach, Ma realized "how basically we're all involved in trying to do something impossible. You can't cure all people. You can't solve the homeless situation. You can't find absolute justice. Essentially none of our work is totally solvable. But it is totally meaningful and we are in fact energized by seeing what each other's work means."

The next year, in conjunction with a marathon performance of all six suites in a single evening at Tanglewood, Ma took part in a weekend conference entitled "The Spiritual Beauty of Bach." It was presented by the Berkshire Institute for Theology and the Arts, of which Ma and his wife are directors. One of his fellow panelists was Jaroslav Pelikan of Yale University, author of *Bach Among the Theologians*. To hold his own in such company, Ma again had to reexamine his understanding of Bach.

Out of the Berkshire program came the further realization that in attempting to create polyphonic music on an instrument capable of playing only a single melodic line, Bach was "trying to describe the unknown." At the same time, perhaps thinking of his own early experiences, Ma realized that the music could be a source of comfort, "a healing thing for people going through tough times." In the end the text becomes larger than the performer; it is too big for any one musician to encompass all of its meanings. "I can't own it," Ma realized. "And so I thought, 'I can spend all my life playing it and I can just report my experience or my knowledge of it.'"

So why not expand that experience and knowledge by drawing on the experience and knowledge of others—in effect by making polyphonic performances of music written for a single performer? That led to the idea of the Morris and Torvill-Dean dance collaborations, both with artists whose work Ma had admired for many years. That in turn led to the idea of doing all six suites with partners from other disciplines. Putting the performances on film, Ma said, gave them a permanence lacking in a concert rendition, which is given once and vanishes into the air. The Toronto garden lives on as a three-acre community refuge. Ma says, "I'm really proud of that. I'm proud of very few things that I've done. I'm really proud of that because it's living, it's being nurtured by the residents, a school is there, the National Ballet is right there next door, and kids go and play there. It's like a concert hall without walls. It's a place where things happen because people want them to happen, and that's my paradigm for culture. I can actually go see it. It's alive. It's not ephemeral. And it was really difficult to do."

The Morris and Torvill-Dean dances also live on, as repertory items for the performers. Morris's choreography has become in effect a living text, Ma said. The dance gestures show him how to play the music. Instead of notation in traditional form, he sees action in three dimensions, providing energy, timing, and inevitability. The collaboration led to two others with Morris, *Rhymes with Silver,* to music by Lou Harrison, and *The Argument,* in which Ma performed Schumann's *Five Pieces in Folk Style* onstage while Mikhail Baryshnikov, Marjorie Folkman, and other dancers enacted fights between three pairs of lovers.

Even with all his experience in working with other musicians, Ma said, he learned valuable new lessons about collaboration from the directors of the six films: "I'm not saying that these films are the greatest ever. But personally it was another college education. It was such a steep learning curve. What I learned is that collaborations are really difficult. It's hard for groups of people to trust one another. It takes a long time to get inside something, which is the first thing that has to happen in an artistic union—you have to jump in. You can't look at it from the outside and say, 'Okay, I will analyze it.' It doesn't work. You need to work to start it and then there's an internal logic that starts to happen. There's always a breaking point where things can start falling apart and you have to have a leap of faith."

Ma's next big leap of faith landed him in the footsteps of Marco Polo on the road to Cathay. He founded the Silk Road Project. This many-sided undertaking was an "obsession" growing out of "many different kinds of beginnings." First, of course, were his own beginnings as a Chinese-American who had grown up in differing cultures and fallen under the spell of anthropology. A more specific catalyst was a trip to Jordan in 1994 at the invitation of King Hussein and Queen Noor. Ma had met them in Israel on October 27, the day after the signing of the peace treaty between Israel and Jordan. He was there to play concerts, and the royal couple was there to make peace. They invited Ma and a few other guests to join them on a sightseeing trip to the Jordanian cities of Petra and Aqaba. Ma accepted and was "awestruck" by how the cliffside city of Petra had been carved out of stone. On the way back to Tel Aviv, the queen asked him to give a master class at the conservatory in Amman, which came under her patronage.

Again Ma accepted. In Amman he heard Jordanian students struggling to master their Western instruments and answered their questions. "What came out from every single kid was such poetry, such deep feeling for what they wanted to say, I was really taken aback. So I logged on to the thought that one day I've got to do something in this area." The Arab-Israeli sessions in Weimar were the first "something" to result.

Another landmark in Ma's Silk Road pilgrimage was the book *The Hun-*

*dred Thousand Fools of God: Musical Travels in Central Asia (and Queens, New York)* by Theodore Levin, the Dartmouth ethnomusicologist who joined him during his visit to the college. The book recounts the struggles of Muslim, Jewish, Sufi, and other musicians in the former Soviet republics of Uzbekistan and Tajikistan (these musicians are the "fools of God") to keep their traditions alive despite the efforts of Communists and nationalists to co-opt them for political purposes.

For a musician on a lifelong safari, this was another Kalahari, too tempting to pass up. His curiosity piqued by Levin's descriptions of the many kinds of music in a faraway part of the world, Ma wanted to experience "all this fantastic music" for himself. He was also fascinated by the diaspora that Levin described: since the collapse of the Soviet Union many musicians from those countries were living in the United States. (Jewish musicians who had emigrated from the ancient city of Bukhara to Queens led Levin to that unlikely musical destination.) Other immigrants, meanwhile, were coming to the States from China, Korea, Vietnam, Thailand, and other parts of Asia, much like the waves of immigrants from Europe a century before. Why did they leave? Was it voluntary? What did this exodus mean for their music? For Western music?

Ma also pondered the case of Astor Piazzolla, the tango-obsessed Argentine composer whose music he had performed in concert, on recordings, and on film. Why had Piazzolla left Argentina several times, living in New York and Paris, only to return to Buenos Aires, where his music was reviled for its foreign influences? Is it ever possible to cut yourself off from your origins?

Amid these speculations Ma's curiosity was further whetted by Elizabeth ten Grotenhuis, a Boston University specialist in Japanese and Asian art history. She told him how the Silk Road had been the link between Rome and Kyoto for two thousand years through the fourteenth century A.D. (Marco Polo was one of its latter-day travelers.) She also said that only recently had scholars joined to study the road and its culture from an interdisciplinary point of view rather than as anthropologists or other specialists.

A twelfth-century mandala from Japan showed the signs of the zodiac as recorded by astronomers in the West: how did they get there? That kind of question was an open invitation for a perpetual culture-crosser and question-asker like Ma. In 1998 he convened a conference to plan a multidisciplinary study of the route, based on its music. Levin was hired as executive director. A board was formed and seed money was provided by Sony

Classical, which planned to record the commissioned pieces. Major funding also came from the Aga Khan Trust for Culture, the Ford Motor Company, and other big players on the international cultural scene.

It was decided that a two-year series of Silk Road festivals would begin in the summer of 2001. The first would be at the Schleswig-Holstein Music Festival in northern Germany. Others would follow in the United States, Canada, Europe, and Asia, with the Smithsonian Folklife Festival on the Mall in Washington in the summer of 2002 as a focal point. The project would link its work with that of the presenting organizations, which included research groups and museums as well as musical sponsors.

In the autumn of 1999 Levin traveled in Azerbaijan, Uzbekistan, and Mongolia, choosing composers for commissions. Bright Sheng, Ma's Chinese-American composer-friend, recommended composers from China. An advisory board made the final selection of sixteen from among forty composers under consideration. They would write for small ensembles, mixing Asian and Western instruments and styles according to their own predilections. Three other composers with Silk Road connections would write works for symphony orchestra with Ma as soloist: Richard Danielpour, an American from an Iranian family who had already composed a concerto for Ma; Peter Lieberson, an American whose music reflects his studies in Buddhism; and Tan Dun, a Chinese-American who freely mixes Asian and Western elements, sometimes in theatrical fashion. Dun planned a multimedia concerto, *The Map,* with a video component showing folk musicians from along the trade route. Music by such Western orientalists as Rimsky-Korsakov *(Scheherazade)* and Mahler *(The Song of the Earth)* would complement the new orchestral works. Ma would learn Chinese and Mongolian instruments and play them in the Silk Road ensembles. Though initially planned to climax in 2002, the project was left open-ended so that other sponsors could pick it up, with or without Ma.

The Silk Road was actually not one road but a network that crisscrossed Eurasia and ended on the eastern coast of the Mediterranean. At its height the route extended from China and Japan through the central Asian cities of Kashgar, Samarkand, and Bukhara to Persia, Turkey, and Greece. In a summary prepared for project participants, ten Grotenhuis listed gunpowder, the magnetic compass, the printing press, silk, mathematics, and ceramic and lacquer crafts among the inventions that migrated to the West along the route. Musical instruments and forms traveled in both directions. The European oboe and clarinet seem to be derived from the Persian *mizmar.*

Cymbals came to China from India, and Chinese gongs traveled the other way, to Europe.

The Silk Road Project coincided with a flowering of interest in "world music" in the United States. But there was a difference: the world-music trend was fed by a wave of immigrants, especially from Asian and Hispanic countries, and an emphasis on multiculturalism on campuses, in the other arts, and in the big cities. Whatever the music's origins, the product that poured from concert stages, recordings, and radio was primarily a branch of popular music, profitably marketed as such by concert presenters and record companies. Ma and the Silk Road Project, by contrast, sought to preserve and enlarge upon folk and classical traditions. No one would mistake the more complex sounds—often elusive to Western ears—of the Silk Road pieces for the pleasantries of such pop attractions as Cuba's Buena Vista Social Club.

There was a need for exploration beyond scholarly curiosity or Marco Polo–style expeditions. In the Kalahari Ma had worried about the possible disappearance of native traditions as young people discovered the temptations of money and city life. Similar processes were at work in Asia.

Just as Levin served as an advisor on central Asia, Bright Sheng became Ma's emissary to China. In the summer of 2000 he traveled ten thousand miles along the Chinese parts of the Silk Road to interview residents, tape their music, and take photographic slides. He discovered that American pop culture had seized the imagination of the young, threatening traditional Chinese music—whether folk or classical—with extinction when older generations died off. The Silk Road Project had a job to do: celebrate this music and present its native performers while they were still alive.

Unlike Ma, who had never lived in China, Sheng had spent twenty-three years there, including the years when the Cultural Revolution made playing Western music a crime punishable by internment in a work camp or death. Born in Shanghai in 1955, the same year Ma was born, Sheng put in seven years in a folk music and dance troupe in Qinghai province, in western China, instead of the manual labor that was the fate of many artists, writers, and intellectuals during the Communist campaign to instill ideological purity. He was twenty-two when the Cultural Revolution ended and he could return to Shanghai. He had been so taken with the folk music of Qinghai that when he went back to the Shanghai Conservatory to study composition, he began mixing the musical instruments and languages of East and West.

The idea was far from new. Debussy and Ravel had been influenced by the sound of the Javanese gamelan, a gong and xylophone orchestra, on hearing it at the 1889 World Exposition in Paris. Tinges of the Orient run through the work of both French composers. Japan opened itself to Western music with the Meiji Restoration of 1868; German immigrants brought the Western tradition to China around the same time. By 1950 a Japanese composer like Toru Takemitsu could fashion an original musical language out of the resources of both worlds. Before Sheng, other composers in the United States, such as Lou Harrison and Philip Glass, were also looking in both directions.

Sheng continued to refine his style upon settling in New York in 1982 and studying composition at Queens College. It was in New York a year later that he and Ma first met. Sheng served as a page turner for Ma, Ax, and violinist Yong Uck Kim at a trio concert. Ma "was a star already but he was very nice to me and his music really made a big impression," Sheng recalled. He doubts that Ma remembered him when they met again a few years later, but with so much in common, cellist and composer became friends.

Sheng's first composition for Ma, written in 1995, was *Seven Tunes Heard in China,* which became part of Ma's Silk Road compact disc, *Solo.* In the liner notes Sheng says that he followed Bartók, Kodály, and Stravinsky in using folk materials not merely for color or atmosphere, their customary role in the Western classical tradition, but to "convey the roughness, the savageness of this music."[26] For Ma, Sheng next composed *Spring Dreams,* a concerto for cello and the National Traditional Orchestra of China. For Ax he wrote *Red Silk Dance,* a Silk Road–inspired concerto for piano and symphony orchestra. Drawing on some of the material he picked up during his return trip to Qinghai for the Silk Road Project, Sheng then began work on a concerto for Ma, Ax, *suona* (a reed trumpet that has the same ancestor as the oboe), *sheng* (the Chinese mouth organ), and symphony orchestra. It was scheduled for a 2003 premiere with the New York Philharmonic.

The trip to China on behalf of the project was also a sentimental one for Sheng. Though he had been back to Shanghai and Beijing many times since emigrating to the United States, this was his first time back in rural Qinghai, which became the first stop on his Silk Road tour. In an e-mail diary sent back to his publisher, G. Schirmer, Inc., he reported:

It has been overwhelmingly emotional for me to come back to Qinghai after an interval of twenty-two years. My heart started pumping crazily as soon as our plane reached the border of Qinghai. When I left here twenty-two years ago, in a way I was escaping a self-imposed exile, and I sensed jealousy from many of my colleagues and friends. So I wasn't quite sure how I would be received here. They received me with open arms!

The lifestyle here has changed dramatically in twenty-two years—life is much better, and I could even see myself living here now. All my friends have their own rather nicely furnished apartments, and food is abundant everywhere. I was very happy for them. Whatever disagreements we had before, it is certain that time has washed them away. We really missed each other.

Sheng traveled mostly by car but twice switched to horseback to reach remote mountain settlements. He was accompanied by a driver—a necessity under Chinese regulations—and a guide. Discoveries rained on him right and left. At a puppet show in Qinghai, he was treated to a meal that featured liquor, brick tea with salty milk, and pancakes stuffed with a paste of garlic and ground poison ivy. "After we were half-drunk," he reported to Schirmer, "they set up a stage in the courtyard and gave us a fantastic show." In Gansu, a north-central province, he visited the Dunhuang Caves, a Silk Road way station in the middle of the Gobi Desert. Buddhist and Taoist monks and nuns had lived in the more than one thousand caves, and artists had adorned the walls with religious murals and pictures. Dating from A.D. 400 to 1900, the painted scenes show performing musicians and dancers. "They took my breath away—what a way to trace the evolution of instruments and performance practice!" Sheng excitedly e-mailed back. "Suddenly I realized that since the Tang dynasty [A.D. 618–907] was so powerful militarily and economically, maybe it was inevitable that, like the United States today, its influence and penetration just embraced and absorbed other cultures, turning them into its own."[27]

Sheng taped forty hours of performances by folk musicians and bought another sixty hours' worth of folk tapes and compact discs to provide material for study and to help with the choice of festival performers. He returned to the question of cultural hegemony in a report written for the 2002 Silk Road issue of the Smithsonian Institution journal *Asian Art and Culture,* which would appear in conjunction with the Smithsonian Folklife Festival. Now it was not Chinese military and economic power that was engulfing other cultures, but American pop songs and television. In his conclusion Sheng wrote:

The influence and attraction between powerful Chinese empires and their surrounding countries were very much like the present-day relations between the United States and the rest of the world. Everywhere during my trip, I was overwhelmed to discover that American pop culture reached almost every corner of this remote area. In many of the small villages, I saw American soap operas on television, and in each town I could find street vendors selling pirated tapes of American pop songs. Still, I do not believe that someone is pushing the globalization of American pop culture there. Instead, for better or worse, I could feel a natural attraction to American culture. In turn, American culture itself has been enriched deeply because of its diversity and inviting environment. As a result, what defines American music today is exactly this melting-pot effect— from European classical music to jazz, folk, pop, new age, Asian, and African music. This multiculturalization makes it possible for composers like Lou Harrison and myself to have an audience.

The problem was the obverse of the one Levin had encountered in other Silk Road countries. There, religious and political pressures were uprooting cultural traditions. Here, American pop was doing it. Regardless of where the pressures were coming from, the effect was the same. The American melting pot might be beneficial for composers like Sheng and Lou Harrison, but as Levin said, how do you preserve traditions and a sense of community at a time when the influences of television, movies, recordings, and now the Internet are speeding across the globe? Indeed, Ma sometimes describes the Silk Road as the Internet of antiquity: the link between the music, culture, religion, and commerce of diverse regions. The contradictions—the clash between cultures—that he struggled with early in his life he later embraced in the larger world. In his fascination with the links he was forging with antiquity, was he becoming a fool of God or, as others said about Gunther Schuller, who also explores music from many cultures, just a fool? (See page 135.)

On a sun-splashed July day in 2000, a bus from New York rolls up to Tanglewood's main gate, and out pour fifty-eight musicians from Azerbaijan, Uzbekistan, Tajikistan, Mongolia, China, Iran, New York, and other exotic places. Among the tired, slightly dazed travelers are some who speak no English and have flown twenty-four hours to get to New York. As they step off the bus, Ma is there to greet each with a handshake or welcoming hug. A contingent of Silk Road Project functionaries and thirty host families stand nearby, ready to assist. After two years of planning, the first conclave of Silk Road composers and performers is about to begin.

Like others, pianist Joel Fan emerges from the bus into Ma's embrace. Fan, a resident of New York, tells Ma he has been talking to an Iranian on the way up and is excited about meeting with so many different musicians and learning about their cultures.

"Whatever you learn, you have to teach me because I start from ground zero," Ma jokes.

After the greetings the visitors stroll to a tent set up in Tanglewood's formal gardens for an American-style lunch of sandwiches, watermelon, and cookies spread upon picnic tables. Standing on a bench, Ma tells the assembled musicians and hosts why he has chosen Tanglewood, the summer home of the Boston Symphony Orchestra, for the gathering: "This is a very special place because for many, many years some of the most wonderful music was made and created here." At the tables the visitors and their new families get acquainted, often struggling with language and searching for topics of mutual interest. Ma, Levin, and Sheng circulate through the crowd, asking if everybody is okay and helping to make connections. Dress is casual all around; sports shirts and jeans or khakis seem universal. After lunch another culture shock awaits. At a pond across the nearby mountain, the visitors are the townspeople's guests for an old-fashioned New England beach party.

A strong bond with Tanglewood has brought Ma there. As a soloist, recitalist, chamber player, and occasional teacher, he is a regular visitor to the festival, with its parklike lawns overlooking a scenic lake in the Berkshire Hills of western Massachusetts. Few other outsiders, and probably not many insiders, could have persuaded a tightly scheduled festival and school to open their rehearsal studios to fifty-eight strangers for nine days. Sheng is a graduate of the school, where he—along with a small army of other composers, conductors, singers, and instrumentalists—became a protégé of Leonard Bernstein.

During the nine days at Tanglewood, the musicians rehearse both traditional music and the sixteen commissioned pieces from Silk Road countries. The group is evenly divided among residents of Asia and the United States, but about half of the Americans are immigrants from Asia—part of the wave of Asian immigrants described in Levin's book. The non-Asians were chosen for their skills on Western instruments that the Asian composers would use. All sixteen of the commissioned composers are present. Seven are from China, three from Uzbekistan, two each from Azerbaijan and Mongolia, and one each from Tajikistan and Iran. One Chinese composer is living in New York and one in Germany. The others come from Shanghai or Xi'an.

In a conversation amid the hubbub in the tent, Levin says the project sought "music that, while rooted in the tradition, was written in a language that would be accessible to an audience anywhere in the world." It proved surprisingly easily to choose composers whose earlier work "spoke to us" in that fashion, he says. Sitting in on the chat, Ma says the composers are well known and often performed in their home countries.

The Tanglewood sessions are closed to the public, but two workshop readings, one on each of the last two days, present the commissioned works in concert format. Though the programs are supposedly open by invitation only, a throng squeezes into every seat in a chamber-music hall and stands two and three deep along the walls. Other listeners and curiosity seekers overflow onto benches and lawns outside the open-sided wooden building.

Some of the sounds fall oddly on Western ears. The music goes from delicate chiming to thunderous eruptions, sometimes within a moment. One of the more striking pieces is *Legend of Herlen* by B. Sharav, a Mongolian. Over an ensemble made up of the *morin khuur* (the whining Mongolian two-string fiddle that Ma later learned to play), three trombones, percussion, and piano, a woman narrates the tale of the Herlen River in a series of unearthly, singsong vocalizations called the *urtiin do,* or Mongolian long song. *Dervish,* by Franghiz Ali-Zadeh of Azerbaijan, also employs a voice— in this case the composer's—to recite the story of a Sufi dervish skinned alive because of his beliefs. *Moon over Guan Mountains,* by Zhao-Jiping of China, the composer of scores for such movies as *Raise the Red Lantern* and *Farewell, My Concubine,* portrays a nocturnal Silk Road scene in instrumental form, using a *sheng, pipa* (Chinese lute), cello, and *tabla* (the Indian drums). At first quiet and atmospheric, the music becomes rhythmically charged and then, in A-B-A form recognizable in the West, subsides back into the stillness of the opening.

Ma was also the featured attraction at the Boston Symphony's season-opening concert, which coincided with the Silk Road visit. With Seiji Ozawa conducting, he played the Cello Concerto in C by Haydn and the Double

Concerto for Cello and Double Bass by Edgar Meyer, his occasional partner in both classical and country music. Meyer was also a soloist in his own work.

The Concerto in C, unlike Haydn's Cello Concerto in D, is an undistinguished work, which Ma nevertheless enlivened with endlessly inventive alterations in tempo, dynamics, and phrasing—now swooping or pushing ahead, now sighing or pulling back. The adagio took on a dreamlike air, verging on a trance. It was not Haydn for those who found the liberties of Ma's baroque album "slumming." The Meyer work proved a lightweight affair notable for its unusual pairing of solo instruments from the lower end of the string section. If the repertoire was less than top-drawer, the evening, complete with a gala dinner for well-heeled patrons, drew a crowd. Ma's mere presence on a program guarantees that.

Ma and a small ensemble took some of the Silk Road pieces on a short tour during the winter in preparation for the festivals beginning the following summer, of 2001. The Dartmouth program was typical. It included *Legend of Herlen* and *Moon over Guan Mountains* along with *In Habil's Style*, a 1979 work for cello and piano by Ali-Zadeh, the Azerbaijani composer of *Dervish*. The programming also held up a different kind of mirror to East and West. After intermission came *Five Finnish Folk Songs*, composed in 1977 by Michio Mamiya of Japan, and Ravel's 1914 Piano Trio, a chamber music staple from France. The program notes, partly written by Levin, said the intent was to show that the connections between East and West were not linear but "exquisitely circuitous."

Written for cello and piano, Mamiya's work grew out of his travels to Finland to study the music of the Lapps. (There is a precedent for Ma's trip to the Kalahari here.) Japanese modernism, Finnish folk music, and French Impressionism combine in a work that the notes characterized as "not only cross-cultural but cross-chronological." The Ravel trio contains only passing references to Asia, but that was enough to get the piece on the program as an example of the continent's influence on his music—also as something familiar to give a Western audience a pleasant dessert.

Ma performed in all five works, switching to the Mongolian *morin khuur* for Sharav's *Legend of Herlen*. He also acted as an amiable master of ceremonies, introducing each piece and his fellow musicians. G. Khongorzul, a Mongolian woman in an elaborate red native costume crowned by a towering white headdress, vocalized the *Legend of Herlen* long song and a solo encore. The sellout audience listened to everything in fascination, partly because of the eclectic program but also because of the celebrity artist who directed the road show.

As a further prelude to the festivals, in March 2001 Ma and the New York Philharmonic premiered two Silk Road works: *Blue as the Turquoise Night of Neyshabur,* a chamber piece by Kayhan Kalhor of Iran, and Richard Danielpour's Cello Concerto no. 2, *Through an Ancient Valley.* Music director Kurt Masur conducted the Danielpour concerto, pairing it with Rimsky-Korsakov's tales of the Arabian nights in *Scheherazade.* Kalhor played the *kamancheh,* an ancient bowed instrument from Persia, in his own work, which also employed Ma's cello, six Western stringed instruments, and other Iranian instruments. The *kamancheh* was similarly matched with the solo cello and ancient instruments in the Danielpour concerto, the two solo instruments engaging in a kind of East-West dialogue. Geography provided another connection between the Silk Road works. Danielpour's "ancient valley" is an actual place in what was once Persia, while Kalhor's Neyshabur, a center of trade and culture in that Persia, still exists as a city in Iran.

Ma and the Silk Road Ensemble made their first foray abroad in August 2001 to perform at the Schleswig-Holstein Festival in Germany. Pressing ahead with plans to tour in Asian countries despite political and religious strife that might make travel risky for foreigners, he and the ensemble planned a trip to Tajikistan and Kazakhstan in October 2001. Tan Dun discounted such dangers where Ma was concerned. In *Harvard Magazine* the Chinese-American composer likened him to "one of those ritual dancers who pass through fires"—an apt metaphor for someone who had participated in the Bushmen's trance dance by firelight.[28] Nevertheless, the September 11, 2001, terrorist attacks on the World Trade Center and the Pentagon, followed by the war in Afghanistan, forced a postponement of the Asian trip. There are some cultural divides that even music cannot bridge.

To hear Ma play Bach's cello suites is, in Blake's words, to see the world in a grain of sand and hold eternity in an hour. The crowds fill the hall as they do to hear him in the big concertos. But he sits alone on the stage, eyes closed, the still center of forces that flow outward from him and inward to him. The dance forms of the individual movements are left behind. What remains is pure and refined, like an elixir. The courantes bound and leap, gazelle-like; the sarabandes flow in timeless lines. Casals once said, "The written note is like a straitjacket, whereas music, like life itself, is constant movement, continuous spontaneity, free from any restriction."[29] So it is here.

Ma is one of the few musicians who talk regularly and unashamedly of spirituality in music. In his *New Yorker* interviews with David Blum, he spoke of a need for idealism and a belief in the soul and God in order to play Beethoven: "Beethoven thought that through his music he could change the world. Today, rock musicians are virtually the only ones who believe that. Beethoven believed that there is a soul. Today, most people don't believe that there is a soul. Although he wasn't religious in a traditional sense, Beethoven believed in God. Today, most people don't believe in God. When you perform Beethoven, you have to transform yourself and commit yourself. You have to believe that God exists, that there's a soul, and that you can change the world."[30]

Blum, who was a conductor as well as a writer, recalled a 1988 performance by Ma and Ax of Beethoven's complete works for cello and piano. It reminded him of the postscript to Beethoven's *Heiligenstadt Testament*. Bemoaning his deafness, Beethoven cries out to heaven: "O Providence—do but grant me one day of *pure joy*—For so long now the inner echo of real joy has been unknown to me—Oh when—oh when, Almighty God—shall I be able to hear and feel this echo again in the temple of Nature and in contact with humanity—Never?—No!—Oh, that would be too hard." Blum heard the same profound yearning in the performance of the slow movement of Beethoven's last cello sonata, the fifth. As Ma and Ax play, he wrote, the melody "embraces them in its gentle folds of purity and devotion. They are eavesdropping on the soul of the composer. Time and space lose their particularity. A spirit, set free from the past, tends us with its power of consolation."[31]

Others ponder the mysteries in everyday terms. In *Gramophone* Philip Kennicott described Ma as "the perpetual prodigy, not just because he displayed an eerie technical mastery and musical maturity at an early age, but because he still plays with the intensity and abandon of a young man new to his powers. . . . He garners again and again that strangest of reviews, in which critics ponder the existential possibility of music that is *too* beautiful."[32]

(Not everything is perfect and beautiful, of course. There was the Carnegie Hall recital in 1991 when Ma played all six Bach suites in a single night for the first time. After a postconcert celebration, he returned to his in-laws' apartment at three A.M. on that frigid January night, only to find himself locked out. Unable to rouse anyone by knocking, he rolled up his overcoat as a pillow and tried to sleep on the hallway floor. After a 1999 concert in Carnegie Hall he forgot to retrieve his Montagnana from the trunk of the taxi that took him back to his hotel. The New York police found the missing instrument after a three-hour search and returned it to him the next afternoon. Ma became one of the celebrities who recorded messages played in the city's cabs to warn passengers to take their belongings with them.)

Most critics, like Blum and Kennicott, adopt reverential tones to describe Ma's playing. In a rare breach of etiquette, Michelle Dulak went after him like a hornet in her *New York Times* critique of his *Simply Baroque* album, beginning with the title, which she labeled "inane." Besides quarreling with his notions of a "retrofitted" cello and baroque style, she rejected his whole taste-of-this, taste-of-that approach to genres and styles. Contrasting Ma's dip in the baroque waters with the "bizarre, voluntary handicaps of hardware and tuning" to which early-music specialists submit themselves, she asked: "But then, why bother with the 'why' when you can present 'early music' as just another off-beat, alternative musical culture? There is a kind of easy broad-mindedness here that is somehow worse than forthright hostility. At least the snide dismissals of historical performance by some of Mr. Ma's colleagues in the mainstream firmament stem from conviction, even passion; here, all the professed good vibes have a condescending ring. The image that springs to mind is of the explorer among the gentle natives."[33]

The last remark pointedly recalls Ma's explorations among the Bushmen.

Another critical squawk greeted the Silk Road Ensemble's debut at the Schleswig-Holstein Festival in Germany. On the online site andante.com, Ken Smith observed, "Ma has certainly traded on trust in The Project, as the Silk Roadies uniformly call it. Only a star of his stature—with management like ICM, a record label like Sony, and a circle of highly placed friends and professional associations—could have generated solid artistic momentum from such a pie-in-the-sky premise." Smith nevertheless conceded that the Schleswig-Holstein performances "came alive with both flavorful idioms and a truly collaborative chamber music spirit."[34]

If most scribblers of the press won't commit such lèse-majestés, practicing musicians, who love to gossip and grouse among themselves in the sanctity of the living room and dressing room, accuse Ma in private of selling out. The Bach circus, the Silk Road caravan, the country shtick, the television and movie stuff, the superstar fees and life, the wristwatch ads—he's gone commercial, they say. What a waste. Ma furnished them with further ammunition at the televised 2001 Academy Awards ceremonies, teaming, amid Hollywood hoopla and glitz, with violinist Itzhak Perlman in music from Tan Dun's Oscar-winning score for *Crouching Tiger, Hidden Dragon*. Even Emanuel Ax will kid him, saying in jest, "It's wonderful playing with you but now I'm going to practice some important repertoire, like the Beethoven piano sonatas."[35] When Ma puffs Hollywood's ego or plays fluff like the Meyer concerto, there seems an element of truth in the joke. Still, those who know him best, like Ax, insist that Ma is 100 percent sincere, and there seems little reason to doubt them.

So the Bach thing seemed circuslike and pretentious. So the Silk Road Project may not produce any enduring music. So Ma doesn't have the qualities that make Rostropovich, Starker, du Pré, and Casals who they are or were. The problem—if there is a problem—may not be that he has gone commercial, but that he is still that two-culture kid from Paris trying to discover where he fits in. Or, like the Harvard student, he wants to show that being gifted does not make him some kind of freak.

In her book *My Son, Yo-Yo,* Marina Ma recalls some lines that he penned in his youth:

"My parents taught me to believe in the soul,/In that something extra, in the beauty that/Is in human nature."[36]

Mutsumi Sato, Ma's online interlocutor from London, asked where the spiritual energy came from. It comes from the imagination and love, Ma replied. "It is the combination of the abstract and real, the memory of the past and being very much in the present." Are these the mouthings of a naïf or the deeply rooted beliefs of a philosopher-musician? It is the same with the playing. Where some hear a desire to please or smell money, others hear eternity clasped in an hour.

Right or wrong, Ma is himself, and to be less would make him less of an artist, not more. "What passion cannot Music raise and quell!" Handel cries (to words by Dryden) in his *Ode for Saint Cecilia's Day,* celebrating music's patron saint. The passions are many. Ma's playing, still reflecting wide-eyed wonder at human nature and the unlimited possibilities in the world around him, reaches the heights by its own silken road.

# PHYLLIS CURTIN

## *The eternal feminine draws us on*

Phyllis Curtin teaches a student about breath control. (Eugene Cook)

*Going to heaven!*
*I'm glad I don't believe it,*
*For it would stop my breath,*
*And I'd like to look a little more*
*At such a curious earth!*

—EMILY DICKINSON,
"Going to Heaven!" (set by Aaron Copland
in *Twelve Poems of Emily Dickinson*)

WHEN PHYLLIS CURTIN RETURNED TO LA SCALA AROUND 1960 to sing Fiordiligi in Mozart's *Così fan tutte,* one of her signature roles, a company pooh-bah proudly presented her with a list of other roles the fabled house in Milan would like her to do. To his annoyance she refused the whole lot. She had a year's bookings with major American orchestras. They were as important to her as La Scala, and she couldn't break her word.

"What *is* all this stuff?" she recalls his snarling when she showed him her date book. Meanwhile, another La Scala chieftain pointedly asked the glamorous soprano why she always traveled with her husband, photojournalist Eugene Cook. Couldn't she come alone sometime? It wasn't Mozart this gentleman had on his mind. Curtin was a brunette beauty in her thirties (she was a silver-haired beauty when she retired from singing in her sixties), but she didn't play the games that singers sometimes play to get ahead. And that was the end of her La Scala career.

The story tells a lot about Curtin, who had fame enough as a singer, but who in a sense is most famous in musical circles for not being more famous. Whether at La Scala or in a high school auditorium on the former Community Concerts circuit, she kept to the high road. She sang only what she wanted to sing, and much of that music was new and by Americans. Her legacy lives on not only in the roles she created, such as the Tennessee hill country heroine of Carlisle Floyd's *Susannah,* but also in the legion of students who have come out of her classes at Tanglewood, Yale, and Boston University. Many teachers inspire gratitude and loyalty among their protégés; Curtin inspires discipleship. Many singers give master classes or become teachers on retirement; Curtin began teaching in the prime of her career and never stopped.

Audiences still crave their Pavarottis and Domingos, their Callases and Tebaldis, and new stars and wannabes will come along to satisfy, or try to satisfy, the need. Opera is thriving, but the song recital is on life support except among a relatively small band of aficionados. For better or worse, the art of singing is not what it was, just as audiences are not what they were. But whatever the singers' failings—and Curtin and others criticize them for being more interested in the sound of the voice than what the voice is saying—a breed of singer has emerged to whom a new opera or song cycle is as natural as Mozart or Verdi. Many of these singers, such as Dawn Upshaw, Sanford Sylvan, and Lisa Saffer, have come out of Curtin's classes. Knowingly or not, others have taken her career as a model. Performing new music is no longer the mark of a specialist. Slowly, because of musicians like Yo-Yo Ma, Curtin, the Juilliard Quartet, and their progeny, audiences have also come to accept new music—not all of which, by definition, will be lasting or even good—as part of their diet. They, the repertoire, and musicians themselves are reinvigorated by the comfortable mingling of the old and the new.

Here's another story, unblushingly told by Beverly Sills in her autobiography, *Beverly*. For thirteen years Curtin had been the New York City Opera's leading singer, if not in name, then in the roles she sang. Then came the 1966 opening of the State Theater at Lincoln Center as the company's new home. Curtin was cast as Cleopatra, the female lead, in the inaugural production, Handel's *Julius Caesar*. Because she had also been singing at the Metropolitan Opera next door for three years, Sills decided, "as a matter of principle," that a City Opera regular—namely Beverly Sills—should be the Queen of the Nile. As she tells the tale, she burst into the office of general director Julius Rudel and demanded the role for herself. If she didn't get it, she roared, she would hire Carnegie Hall for a recital featuring Cleopatra's arias—"and you're going to look sick."[1]

Rudel caved in. And that, but for a single guest appearance in 1976 as the Countess in Mozart's *Marriage of Figaro*, was the end of Curtin's City Opera career. The *Figaro* was also her farewell to any opera stage.

"We did stay friends," Sills says sweetly. "Phyllis is quite a lady."[2] Curtin, who with her City Opera colleagues had banded together to save the company when it was near financial collapse in the mid-1950s, didn't quite see it that way. It was a stab in the back, she tells Peter G. Davis in his book *The American Opera Singer*. "I was so stunned! After my life at the City Opera, which had always been so successful for me and the company, I simply couldn't believe that my family would do that to me . . . I lost a stage, and a stage I believed in."[3]

Recounting the incident, Davis says, "Curtin would surely have sung a distinguished Cleopatra, but Sills sang a sensational one."[4] The distinction is a useful one. Sills, who on her retirement from the stage went on to become general director of City Opera and then chairwoman of Lincoln Center, had the diva's gilding that Curtin, who became a teacher and dean of the Boston University School for the Arts, never sought. Although Curtin had a busy opera, orchestral, and recital career, achieving renown in the United States and Europe in such roles as Fiordiligi, Violetta in *Traviata,* Ellen Orford in Britten's *Peter Grimes,* and Salome in Strauss's shock opera, it was for artistry and musical curiosity that she commanded respect. Davis sums up the critical consensus: "Her voice may have lacked the immediately identifiable timbral characteristics that all the greatest singers have, but its intonational purity and attractive silvery sheen adapted to an amazing variety of styles and the secure technical base of her method never deserted her, right up into her mid-sixties."[5]

Ned Rorem, who wrote the song cycle *Ariel* for Curtin and whose music Curtin championed, makes the point in a more idiosyncratic way in his book *Settling the Score.* Drawing a distinction between music that appeals to the viscera and music that appeals to the intellect, he says Joan Sutherland "is a dumb singer of dumb music. Sills is a smart singer of dumb music. Curtin is a smart singer of smart music." In other words, "Sills is intelligent about analyzing that which requires no analysis, but at least her diction and stage action are cleaner than Sutherland's. Curtin is more 'important': she knows what she's up to in scores that ask that she know what she's up to."[6]

Things have changed since Phyllis Curtin was born Phyllis Smith in Clarksburg, West Virginia, a town of about thirty thousand inhabitants, on December 3, 1921. (Curtin was the name of her first husband, Philip Curtin, a history professor at Johns Hopkins, whom she divorced after nine years.) When she was starting out in the 1940s and 1950s, there were few opportunities for young singers. Now, she observes from the perspective of motherhood, retirement, widowhood, and half a lifetime of teaching, they have a veritable banquet they can choose from: competitions, university programs, regional opera companies, major companies' young artist programs, and festivals small and large.

Looking back, Curtin believes that today's greater possibilities have led, paradoxically, to a narrowed professionalism. Singers were more individualistic in her day. "I'm concerned about it with the young singers that I see. By now with so many opportunities for auditions—some are just for money, some are for summer programs, some are for travel abroad, all kinds of things—there is a great compulsion with all the young people to be sure they're singing what *they,* whoever *they* are, want to hear. And the whatever-they-want-to-hear idea seems to me to reflect a kind of general idea esthetically about what singing is now. In other words, beautiful tone—big, lovely voices—seems to be the big standard. We always hear about the *voice.* We almost never hear about what the voice is doing, or why it's doing it." Verdi, she says, insisted that the music must express the word. He didn't make a point of beauty of tone.

That, at any rate, is the professional view. Curtin gave the idea a more personal and philosophical turn in the 1988 University Lecture at Boston University, where since 1983 she had been serving as dean of the School for the Arts and professor of voice. Established in 1950, the annual University Lecture is given by a distinguished faculty member, who presents his or her research to the public. A singer, of course, is not a researcher in the everyday sense. So in a talk titled "Views of Life and Education Gleaned from Performance," Curtin described how a singer uses understanding, intellect, musicality, and imagination to communicate the work of others to an audience.

"So it has been," she said, "that I have lived in the psychology, philosophy, religion, romance, [and] society of artists of the past three hundred years and in the world of the twentieth century, occasionally and excitingly, as a collaborator or catalytic agent." Picking up the theme later in the talk, she went on: "The best of us musicians bring the scholar's information and precision to our work, but without the artist's wonder it is for nothing in the performance. Then the music and the text must leave the page, alive and persuasive. Emotion and imagination are the crucial ingredients. There are musicians who have a genius for revealing the very heart of a work, for exposing meaning and beauty that we never knew were there. It is inexplicable. A fundamentally nonverbal intelligence leads. Finding ways to feed and draw on that intelligence in myself has been of compelling interest to me through the years of performance."

It is indeed inexplicable, as any serious musician or concertgoer can attest. Yet it is a gift that has informed Phyllis Curtin's life as performer, teacher, and member of the human race.

In a way, that hot-eyed manager at La Scala was only following the script, because Curtin's story is tied up with that of Susannah, the object of desire in Carlisle Floyd's opera. Homespun, folksy, and mostly tonal in style, *Susannah* is adapted from the story of Susannah and the Elders in the Old Testament Apocrypha. In the opera the eighteen-year-old heroine is an orphan brought up in the Tennessee hills by her older brother, Sam Polk. Looking for a baptismal site, the church elders from town stumble upon her as she is bathing naked in a secluded creek near her cabin. They denounce her to the Bible-thumping preacher, the Reverend Olin Blitch, who is leading a series of revival meetings. New in town and lonely, he seduces her during a visit to her home to seek her repentance. Although the reverend inwardly repents his sin, Sam kills him with a shotgun blast and flees into the mountains. Susannah is left to face an outcast's life by herself.

Curtin is no outcast. But like Susannah and Floyd himself, she came out of the small-town South and knows its ways. And Susannah is the role she created and set the standard for in what, along with Douglas Moore's *Ballad of Baby Doe* and the works of Gian Carlo Menotti, became one of the most popular American operas.

It was partly because of Curtin's City Opera successes that Floyd, then a twenty-eight-year-old piano student at the Aspen Music Festival in Colorado, approached her with the unpublished, unperformed score of *Susannah* in 1954 at Aspen. "But more specifically," Floyd recalled, "I knew of her from a friend of mine who had been at Aspen the previous summer and said what a wonderful new soprano they had. Those two things combined to pique my interest. Of course, being a kid basically, with no professional connections to speak of, I simply took the bull by the horns and called her up and asked to see her."

Born in South Carolina and unknown as a composer, Floyd was teaching piano at Florida State University at Tallahassee. In Aspen he was staying in a dormitory, and since the thirty-two-year-old Curtin enjoyed faculty status and had a small house, she invited him to her place to read through parts of the score. He outlined the story and sang Susannah's two arias, "Ain't It a Pretty Night" and "The Trees on the Mountains," accompanying himself at the piano. He was prepared to go through the rest of the opera, but the two arias were all Curtin needed. *Susannah,* which went on to achieve repertory status—a rarity for an American opera—became the first of three operas she premiered for him.

"Everything about this piece just felt at home to me," she said. "Maybe it was the locale—my growing up in West Virginia, this being the hill country of Tennessee. They're not all that different. I just took to this piece right away."

At Curtin's suggestion Floyd showed the score to baritone Mack Harrell, who was also in residence at Aspen. A native Texan, he too knew the rural milieu and was impressed by the piece. He became the Blitch against Curtin's Susannah when Floyd obtained a 1955 world premiere at Florida State.

Attempts to get a New York premiere ran into a wall of indifference. Curtin and Floyd auditioned the opera for Joseph Rosenstock, then City Opera's director, and several other producers. Curtin sang all the roles and the chorus's part as well, Harrell occasionally joining her. Floyd is grateful for "the enormous service she did the opera and me in auditioning it to anybody who would listen." But the producers dismissed *Susannah* as being of only regional interest—and, in one instance, as "no boy meets girl."

Harrell played another card. One of his neighbors in Larchmont, New York, was conductor Erich Leinsdorf, who was then beginning what turned out to be a mostly unsuccessful one-year reign at City Opera, replacing Rosenstock. Harrell arranged for a meeting in Leinsdorf's house. He and Curtin spent an afternoon singing *Susannah* for the conductor. Curtin isn't sure whether it was Leinsdorf or his wife who wound up liking the piece. In any event, it had its City Opera premiere in 1956, eighteen months after the world premiere, with Curtin as the heroine and Leinsdorf conducting. The work won the New York Music Critics' Circle Award and an invitation for City Opera to reprise its production at the 1958 Brussels World Fair. There Curtin scored her first international success.

As chance would have it, Harrell was not available to be the City Opera Blitch, and Norman Treigle took over the role. Curtin said the two men, both lifelong friends of hers, were strikingly different in physical appearance and sang the part in different but equally compelling ways. From them she learned that "everybody has to be his own Rigoletto or his own Olin Blitch or her own Susannah."

The opera, Curtin said, scandalized an "astounding" number of clergymen in far-off places, and many wrote to newspapers to denounce it. Yet *Susannah,* she said, is "the least scandalous of all operas." The evil is not in what Susannah does—she has been bathing in the creek all summer when the elders come to look it over—but in the elders' minds. The story and music, at any rate, struck a responsive chord among opera givers and operagoers, not normally species that welcome anything later than Puccini or Strauss. By the time the work received its Metropolitan Opera debut in 1999, it had had more than eight hundred performances around the world. Curtin herself sang in about thirty productions until the late 1960s, when, deciding she was too old to play a teenager's role, she reluctantly gave it up.

Buoyed by the opera's success, Curtin asked Floyd to write a concert aria that she could use in a New York recital she had planned. She confessed that she had no money to pay for a commission. Grateful for her service in *Susannah,* Floyd nevertheless responded with a *Wuthering Heights* scena and aria. He chose the scene in which the love-smitten Heathcliff flees after overhearing Cathy say she could not possibly marry him (though she loves him) because he is below her in social standing. Floyd set out with no intention of writing an opera. He simply picked a standard audition piece for actresses and made it his text.

Curtin took the aria to Joseph Regneas, her teacher, with Floyd as her pianist. Forgetting that the composer was present, Regneas delivered his verdict after their reading: "Whoever wrote that piece certainly doesn't know anything about the human voice." Likewise the sun rises in the west. The aria made such an impression at the recital, Floyd remembers, that several opera directors in the audience went backstage afterward to ask Curtin about the rest of the opera.

There was, of course, no rest of the opera. But John Crosby, then director of the year-old Santa Fe Opera, was impressed enough—with a little prodding from Floyd's publisher, Boosey and Hawkes—to ask for a complete *Wuthering Heights.* Floyd kept saying, "No, no, I'm not interested in doing the whole opera, that whole book." He "knew it would be a problem, which it certainly was." Boosey and Hawkes then prodded Floyd, who finally accepted the commission. It was the only time, he recalled, that he wrote an opera—and he has written a dozen of them—to a prescribed text. The premiere, with Curtin as Cathy and the Heathcliff-Cathy scene installed in the second act, took place in 1958 in Santa Fe. *Wuthering Heights* went on to attain popularity, second only to that of *Susannah* in Floyd's oeuvre.

On a Ford Foundation grant in 1962, Floyd wrote a third opera, *The Passion of Jonathan Wade,* for Curtin. Also premiered by City Opera, it is set in Columbia, South Carolina, in the years just after the Civil War. Jonathan Wade is a Union Army colonel who falls in love with and marries the war-widow daughter of an honorable South Carolina judge amid Reconstruction-era turmoil. At the opera's end Wade pays with his life for his passion both for the widow and for justice. The opera was not a success, and Curtin, who took the role of the widow who becomes Wade's wife, concedes that even after a revision it is uneven in quality.

The Floyd-Curtin collaboration also produced two concert works with orchestra: *The Mystery* (1960) and *Flower and Hawk* (1972). Supported by a Ford Foundation grant to Curtin, *The Mystery* is a cycle of five songs setting poems by the Chilean Nobel Prize–winner Gabriela Mistral. The songs, sung in English translation, follow a mother from her discovery that she is carrying a child through the birth and a closing lullaby. The Ford Foundation also paid for three premiere performances. The first was by the San Antonio Symphony. The Louisville Symphony, the next in line, made a recording. When it was the Pittsburgh Symphony's turn, Curtin recalls, conductor William Steinberg offered a biting, if kindly intended, reaction: "That piece was old-fashioned when I was in knee pants."

*Flower and Hawk,* a monodrama, casts the soloist as Eleanor of Aquitaine, who is imprisoned by her husband, King Henry II, for plotting with her sons to overthrow him. Taking liberties with the historical accounts, Floyd has Eleanor summon up memories of her past to amuse herself and keep from going mad in the castle where Henry holds her captive for eighteen years. Staged by Frank Corsaro with a small set and Curtin in costume, the fifty-minute work was commissioned and premiered by the Jacksonville (Florida) Symphony. It gave performances in Jacksonville, the Kennedy Center in Washington, and Carnegie Hall in New York.

Floyd remains indebted to Curtin. Having heard many Susannahs over the years, he is impressed that "so few really stand out." Curtin left an indelible stamp in "the way she appeared, what she looked like, and her physical presence onstage, and the terrific dramatic intensity she brought to it."

It wasn't just a matter of voice and stage smarts. Curtin grew up in a place and time when music was still a vital force in the family, school, and community. Her mother was a church organist, her father sang in a church choir (it was a different church), and the Clarksburg schools offered a lively music program with a glee club and instrumental ensembles. Her father had a good tenor voice and remained a chorister until well into his sixties. Curtin sang in the junior choir in his church but "didn't think anything about it." She also studied dance and the old-fashioned art of elocution—she remains a compelling public speaker—and took part in plays.

When Curtin was seven, a friend of her mother's passed along a child-sized violin that the friend's son had outgrown. Curtin went to the town's violin teacher, a Mr. Kember, for lessons. Discovering that she had a good ear and natural aptitude, he let her go her way without much formal direction. She learned to read music on her own and was good enough to play second violin in the faculty string quartet when, at fifteen, she went away to Monticello Preparatory School in Alton, Illinois. She also continued to perform in modern dance productions and plays. When her Monticello violin teacher left toward the end of her time there and the new teacher didn't seem to care what she did, she dropped the instrument. "And the curious thing is," she recalled, "it didn't cause me any pain at all." All this time she had been singing in school glee clubs as well as the church choir, but didn't think about singing as a calling or passion.

As a student at Wellesley College, Curtin continued singing with a glee club and choir. When it turned out that she had two seminars on the same night as choir practice, however, she gave up choir. Now she missed her music. After considering a return to the violin, she decided to take singing lessons. But in the grand manner of academe, the dean set up so many course requirements that Curtin, on her own, simply walked over to the music building and looked up the voice teacher. Thus did Olga Averino enter her life.

An émigré Russian soprano, Averino had gone through the Moscow Conservatory as a pianist. She sang regularly with the Boston Symphony Orchestra under Serge Koussevitzky and performed new music by Ravel, Rachmaninoff, Schoenberg, and Berg. Unconcerned about institutional niceties, she took Curtin on—never mind the course requirements. Curtin recalls her as "an iconoclast from the first day of her life" and the most interesting woman she has ever met. "I probably practiced ten minutes a day, if that, but I was having the most marvelous time finding all this terrific song literature." One of her first discoveries was Fauré, who remained a favorite for life.

For a political science major, music still seemed something you did for pleasure rather than a living. Graduating in 1943, at the height of World War II, Curtin felt the call of country and conscience. She took a job with the War Production Board in Boston. Working six days a week at arranging supplies for electric, gas, and water utilities in the Northeast left her bored for the first time in her life, and with little energy for practice. (If all the lights in New England went out, her father told her, he'd know why.) When the board, under one of President Roosevelt's dollar-a-year men, ran out of inventory, Curtin felt she could honorably leave government service. Staying on in Boston, she supported herself by singing in a Congregational church and Temple Israel. Meanwhile, she pursued studies with Averino and with Boris Goldovsky at the New England Conservatory.

During the week Curtin taught music to children from nursery school to sixth grade at a suburban day school. At each level she improvised games and stories to get her pupils' interest. For the older children she put aside the assigned songbook, which she found bland, and had the class sing Schubert songs that she translated into English. The tales of the trout and the miller's wheel fascinated the children, and she moved on to Mozart, Brahms, folk songs from the hollows of her West Virginia, and ultimately Mussorgsky's *Songs of the Nursery*. The last had a long list of funny-sounding names for uncles, aunts, a scary beetle, a hobbyhorse, and other figures to appeal to childhood fancies. In the year's final class, the children chose to sing the classicists' songs and never mind the school songbook. A teacher was born.

In 1946 Curtin spent the first of three summers at Tanglewood in the pioneering opera program run there by Goldovsky. It was the same heady summer, the first after the war, that Tanglewood was reopening and Goldovsky began changing the face of opera with his teachings and productions there. Across the state, in Cambridge, the Juilliard Quartet was getting its start. Aaron Copland was the country's leading composer (he was also teaching at Tanglewood), but a new generation of composers, including Gunther Schuller, was emerging. New energies were released, new ideas were in the air. Curtin got her first taste of opera that summer as one of the bawdy "nieces" in the American premiere of Britten's *Peter Grimes,* conducted by the young Leonard Bernstein in the Goldovsky program. Curtin immersed herself in the secondary role, getting to know the whole opera so thoroughly that when she sang the role of Ellen Orford, the female lead, in the Britten year at the 1968 Edinburgh Festival, "every note was firmly in my mind after but two days' study."

There were good singer-actresses before the Goldovsky era. Risë Stevens, for example, was a steamy, vocally opulent Carmen. But the defining style, insofar as there was one, was stand and deliver, often by bulky ladies who looked little like a young Isolde, Violetta, or Carmen. In *The Glorious Ones* Harold C. Schonberg catches the manner in his portrait of the great Wagnerian soprano Kirsten Flagstad:

"A large-sized but not stout woman in her early years at the Metropolitan Opera, Flagstad conquered with her voice and instinctive musicianship rather than with temperament. She never was much of an actress; but at least she had the good sense not to make a fool of herself by indulging in excessive gesture or movement. . . . For the most part she stood solidly and stolidly where she was planted, throwing her head back and emitting cascades of glorious sound."[7]

In the postwar 1940s and 1950s, a new style of singer-actor emerged. The way was heralded by Maria Callas, *La Divina,* whose incendiary stage manner, flights (sometimes wild) into the vocal stratosphere, and scandalous personal life inflamed audiences to new heights of idolatry. But Callas was one of a kind. More typical were Curtin, Beverly Sills, and Marilyn Horne, along with Curtin's fellow Goldovsky graduates, such as Leontyne Price, Shirley Verrett, Sherill Milnes, and Frank Guarrera. Young and physically attractive, they combined vocal and dramatic skills, becoming Carmens and Josés, Violettas and Alfredos, who looked and moved like lovers.

Goldovsky became a lifelong influence on Curtin. At a time when opportunities for opera training were few, she and her fellow students acquired from him what she later described in an essay as "attitudes and skills that produced opera directors, conductors, and singers who were welcomed on operatic stages across the country and abroad. Boris Goldovsky began the training of performers who are musically secure, theatrically skilled, and always aware that the musical score is the primary director in the realization of the character, of the scene."[8] Also from Goldovsky she learned a lifelong preference for opera in English for English-speaking audiences, no matter who the composer. And no supertitles, please.

The future Salome, Violetta, and Ellen Orford returned to Boston in 1948 after marriage to Philip Curtin and two years at Swarthmore College, where he was finishing his war-delayed undergraduate studies. She rejoined Goldovsky as a performing member of his New England Opera Theater while her husband worked toward a doctorate at Harvard. A quick learner, she also performed concert works by young Boston composers, including Lukas Foss, Daniel Pinkham, Irving Fine, and Yehudi Wyner, at Harvard concerts. (Hers were "the first and last performances" of many of these works, she says.) She still had no goal in mind. "I just kept wandering in and sort of adjusting my life so that I could study more or do more, and in that way I felt, without really making up my mind, inevitably drawn into a life in singing."

She returned to Tanglewood for two more summers, now taking principal roles in two Tchaikovsky operas under Goldovsky's direction: Tatiana in

*Eugene Onegin* in 1948 and Lisa in *Pique Dame* in 1951. Listening to her friends and fellow students, who included David Lloyd, James Pease, and Ellen Faull, convinced her that she had serious gaps in her technique. Dissatisfied, she went to their teacher in New York, Joseph Regneas—the first American to sing Hans Sachs in Wagner's *Meistersinger,* she recalls—for further study. Even the realization that she could do better marked her as outstanding in Goldovsky's eyes. "That's where she showed how superior her mind is," he said in *Opera News.* "Most people tend to ride their strengths. Phyllis was the rare kind who worked tirelessly on her weaknesses."[9] Regneas, with whom she studied off and on for three years, gave her the sound and technique that kept her singing into her sixties and became the bases for her own teaching later.

Curtin made her New York recital debut in 1950, and her City Opera debut in 1953, singing three roles in the American premiere of Gottfried von Einem's *The Trial.* Her appearance in the now-forgotten opera attracted the attention of not only critics but also Eugene Cook, a photojournalist and opera buff who was in the audience. Struck by the beauty on the stage and the oddity of the Kafka-inspired opera as a debut vehicle, he traced her through her agent and photographed her for *Life* magazine in a 1953 *Salome* at City Opera. The assignment was truly for life. They were married in 1956, had a daughter, Claudia—their only child—in 1961, and remained inseparable until his death in 1986. Fluent in Italian (he came from an Italian family and looked like Arturo Toscanini), he became her counselor, photographer, press representative, and unofficial manager as well as consort.

In the following years at City Opera Curtin sang all the principal Mozart heroines, Alice Ford in both Verdi's *Falstaff* and Nicolai's *Merry Wives of Windsor,* Giulietta and Antonia in Offenbach's *Tales of Hoffmann,* Rosalinda in Strauss's *Fledermaus,* and Salome in the opera of the same name, which became one of her principal roles in both New York and Vienna. Over a thirty-one-year career she sang eighty roles in all. She made her Metropolitan Opera debut in 1961 as Fiordiligi in Mozart's *Così,* returning as the Countess in his *Figaro,* Violetta in *Traviata,* Alice Ford in *Falstaff,* Ellen Orford in *Peter Grimes,* Eva in *Meistersinger,* Rosalinda in *Fledermaus,* Donna Anna in *Don Giovanni,* and *Salome.* Even before the Met debut she was singing in Vienna and at the Teatro Colón in Buenos Aires. Her other stages included La Scala, Frankfurt, and the Glyndebourne Festival in bucolic England.

In Geneva she sang in the world premiere of Darius Milhaud's *La mère coupable,* in which Beaumarchais's Rosina—already given memorable utterance in both Mozart's and Rossini's *Figaro* operas—reappears. Curtin thus made the circuit of the three Rosina roles. At Milhaud's request she also sang the United States premiere of his *Médée.* She appeared with the NBC Opera both on television (Fiordiligi in *Così* and Fiora in Italo Montemezzi's *L'amore dei tre re*) and on tour (as the Countess in *Figaro* and Cio-Cio-San in Puccini's *Madama Butterfly).* She was Thérèse in the first United States performance of Poulenc's *Mamelles de Tirésias* and Cressida in the New York premiere of William Walton's *Troilus and Cressida.*

Opera was only half of a career that led repeatedly to concert and recital halls. Curtin's orchestral repertory encompassed Bach's passions, cantatas, and oratorios; Beethoven's Ninth Symphony and *Missa Solemnis;* works by Handel, Haydn, Rossini, Brahms, Fauré, Verdi, Bruckner, and Poulenc; Wagner's *Wesendonck Songs,* Strauss's *Four Last Songs,* Ravel's *Shéhérazade,* Stravinsky's *Les Noces,* Schoenberg's *Erwartung,* Frank Martin's *Golgotha,* and Villa-Lobos's *Bachiana Brasiliera* no. 5—a compendium of human experience, from the earthly to the divine. In the 1963–64 season alone she sang fifty-six orchestral engagements. The orchestras included Boston, Cleveland, Detroit, Los Angeles, Philadelphia, Pittsburgh, and Minneapolis. She sang in the American premiere of Shostakovich's death-haunted Symphony no. 14 with the Philadelphia Orchestra under Eugene Ormandy, and in the early 1970s substituted at the last minute in two monumental works, Schoenberg's *Gurrelieder* (under Seiji Ozawa) and Beethoven's *Missa Solemnis* (under Leonard Bernstein), with the Boston Symphony at Tanglewood.

"I adore that part of Tove. It never really left me," she said of the fated heroine in Schoenberg's opulent late-romantic work. But she sang it only twice after Tanglewood, in Los Angeles and Milwaukee. Because of the work's gargantuan length and performing forces, it is rarely done anywhere.

Curtin had her own conception of many of her operatic heroines. In Mozart's *Figaro,* going against convention, she portrayed the Countess as a young rather than going-on-forty woman, hurt by her husband's skirt-chasing and still longing for love. Similarly, she depicted Salome as a passionate young girl, not the usual harlot. In the liner notes for a recording including a 1968 concert performance of the opera's final scene, Curtin writes:

"I was assigned this opera in my second season at New York City Opera. I knew the play [by Oscar Wilde] long before I even thought of being a singer. I was too inexperienced to be daunted by the assignment and absolutely thrilled with the prospect of living in her. There is no doubt in my mind that she launched my career. While I sang the opera in several places, it was part of my regular repertoire in Vienna. Having danced as a young girl and until I was about twenty, I found it wonderful to stay in acceptable condition for the dance [of the seven veils]. After I stopped singing the opera, the final scene remained a staple in my orchestra repertoire."[10]

It was in 1961, during her Salome heyday, that Curtin gave birth to her daughter, Claudia. Curtin sang the role well into her pregnancy, until "one day when I woke up and couldn't fasten my skirt and took a good long look in the mirror, and I decided, 'That's it.' " Her lower register, however, was strengthened by the pregnancy—perhaps through hormonal changes, she thinks.

Soon afterward Curtin gave up regular work in Europe. She refused to leave Claudia at home, and she and Gene, her husband, found frequent travel with the baby interfered with family life. Vienna didn't assign her to a *fach,* or specialty, as American houses sometimes do with singers. But she wearied of the European way, in which a leading singer can simply drop in and do a role without rehearsal—without even going over it with the conductor. She remembers a *Don Giovanni* in Vienna when, just before the performance, there was a knock at her dressing-room door. A man stuck his head in. He was Joseph Keilberth, the evening's conductor.

Introducing himself, he said, *"Guten Abend.* Keilberth." She said, *"Guten Abend.* Curtin." He asked if she made a cut in a certain place in the score. She said she didn't. That was it—no plan, just go on cold. The next time she saw him, she was onstage and he was in the pit. She was Donna Anna. Her Don Giovanni was Eberhard Wächter. The first time she laid eyes on him, he was grabbing her and pulling her onto the stage in their Act I entrance after the rape (or attempted rape) in Anna's room.

Who needs introductions? Hurried onto the stage in a Stuttgart *Traviata,* Curtin sang Violetta against the Alfredo of the now-legendary Fritz Wunderlich. She never realized who he was until years later. (But then neither does Donna Anna recognize Don Giovanni until later in the show.)

For a glamorous young soprano, the system also created hazards with leading men. As Violetta to an unfamiliar Alfredo, Curtin would give him her "warmest, most available look." If he looked embarrassed and turned aside a little, she knew, "Well, I have to carry this evening by myself." If, on the other hand, Alfredo got "a real eager look and pawed the ground, sort of," she knew the problem "would come after the opera." It was "pretty much a perfect analysis," she recalls. "That's how it worked."

Curtin never made it big at the Met. General manager Rudolf Bing, she recalls, liked her as a lunch partner and as the flighty Rosalinda in *Fledermaus*. For the big Italian roles he imported Italian sopranos, no matter how good or bad.

Whether under contract or not, Curtin said, she would often be called to step into *Traviata* when one or another Violetta from Italy had to be sent packing because she was inadequate in the role. Even under contract, Curtin would get only about three of the season's *Traviatas* (there were usually about twelve in all), and those were late in the run, when the cast was mostly made up of substitutes. One year she asked Bing for more, even offering to sing her scheduled performances gratis if he'd pay her for the substitutions.

"Oh, my dear, no," she recalls his saying. "Of course, you're the finest Violetta we have but I can't give that to you. You're not Italian." It didn't even help that Franco Corelli, who had sung *Tosca* with her in California, told Bing she was the best Tosca he had ever died for in the opera. "Well, you'll never sing it here," Bing told Curtin. "You're not Italian." The closest she ever got was a weeklong run of *Toscas* in the Met's New York parks program, often a testing ground for unknown singers. American singers were for the house across the Lincoln Center Plaza, City Opera. Or for the rapidly growing regional opera circuit.

Since she was not a star in Bing's mind, Curtin said, she always went into productions that had been staged for other singers. Despite some great moments, such as singing Ellen Orford against Jon Vickers's monumental Peter Grimes, she said, "I had much better operatic experiences in every other house I was ever in." She "just got tired" of the Met treatment. "It wasn't opera to me." She quit the house in the mid-1970s, about the time she began teaching at Yale, and doesn't even remember the last opera she sang there.

If Bing was an indifferent Alfredo to this Violetta, composers weren't. Carlisle Floyd was only one in a line of musical suitors. She sang with Aaron Copland as her partner at the piano, often in his *Twelve Songs of Emily Dickinson*. In Vivian Perlis's Copland biography, Curtin recalls first trying the *Dickinson Songs* in 1951–52, when Copland, then the Charles Eliot Norton

Lecturer at Harvard, gave the still-new music to her. It took her fifteen years before she felt her voice had developed enough to do them justice.

"I had never liked Emily Dickinson," she told Perlis. "I used to read her and get very exasperated. I didn't like her personality—I thought she was unnecessarily quirky and coy. But as soon as I could sing Aaron's songs, I began to understand Emily Dickinson!" After doing the songs hundreds of times, she decided, "If anybody ever sent Emily Dickinson's 'Letter to the World,' it's Aaron Copland. It was Aaron who found the musical voice for Emily Dickinson, and the times when I sang them best, I had the feeling that she was speaking."[11]

Popular with recitalists today, the Dickinson songs were not well received at first. Audiences and critics missed the folksy Copland of the *Appalachian Spring, Rodeo,* and *Billy the Kid* ballets, composed during the previous decade. But Curtin recalled that neither the songs nor she had ever received a bad review in the many times she sang them. On the rare occasions when she tried new interpretive ideas, Copland accepted them with good grace. Once, when she muffed a note in rehearsal, Copland looked up from the piano and said, "Do that again." She did, and he said, "I kinda like it that way. Sometimes I find my best music on other people's pianos." It was, she recalled, "a sweet little exchange."[12]

Curtin preferred Copland's piano version of the songs to the orchestral settings he made later for eight of them, just as she preferred Alban Berg's *Seven Early Songs* with piano rather than with orchestra. But she sang both versions of both works. She remembers a 1972 performance of the Dickinson songs at Tanglewood with Copland conducting the Boston Symphony. During the rehearsals they had to sit through Charles Wuorinen's Violin Concerto, a defiantly dissonant, amplified work. "It was so loud I thought I would lose my mind," Curtin recalls in Perlis's book. "I finally said to Aaron, 'I can't sit here and wait. I don't think I'll be able to hear when it gets to be my turn.' Aaron kind of giggled and said, 'This is the first time I have ever felt like a nineteenth-century composer.' "[13] There is new music and there is new music.

With Lukas Foss on the podium or at the keyboard, she sang his thorny *Time Cycle* and quirky *Thirteen Ways of Looking at a Blackbird,* as well as other works. But the "most amazing" of her many performances with him as a conductor took place when he was director of the Buffalo Philharmonic. She was the soloist in Berg's *Seven Early Songs* and the "Liebestod" from Wagner's *Tristan und Isolde.*

Curtin at first refused to sing Isolde's music, which is usually the province of sopranos with heavier voices. "You know, Lukas," she recalls having said, "I don't have anything to give to that piece of music." But he persisted, reassuring her that the death scene's overall dynamic level was low. She finally gave in, taking Kirsten Flagstad's celebrated performance as a starting point. The performance went off well, she felt. "That was a wonderful experience and I learned so much from it about thinking and imagining." But she never sang the role again.

After Floyd, the composer whose name is most closely linked with Curtin's is Ned Rorem, the Francophile Pulitzer Prize–winner especially noted for his songs. Their association began in 1946, when both were students at Tanglewood. Though they barely knew each other then and did not work together for another twelve years, Rorem remembers being impressed by her in the 1946 *Peter Grimes*. "At twenty-two I was ripe for her unusual (even more unusual today) admixture of a nectarine sound with a sharp-as-ice diction," he wrote in the liner notes for the compact-disc release of a 1969 recital she sang in Boston, with him at the piano. Praising her as "the most *intelligent* soprano I've ever known," he went on, "Throughout her career, her delicious voice has never been used for its own sake rather than as a medium to impart the sense and feel of a text. For her—rare creature—the composer comes first."[14]

There is a long tradition of composers writing for specific voices, just as they have for pianists, violinists, and other performers. Mozart did it, for instance, for the English soprano Nancy Storace, who became the original Susanna in his *Figaro*. Richard Strauss did it for his wife, Pauline de Ahna, and Britten wrote for his lover, Peter Pears, whose voice, preserved on recordings, defines the sound of Britten's tenor roles even today. More recently, many composers wrote for Bethany Beardslee and Jan DeGaetani, a pair of revered American singers. DeGaetani, who died in 1989, was in fact a singer whose career in many ways paralleled Curtin's. Though she never sang opera, she ranged freely and with a pure tone through new music and old. While Curtin became a fixture at Tanglewood, DeGaetani filled a similiar role at Aspen. Among the few predecessors in a do-it-all approach to the repertory, Jennie Tourel and Eleanor Steber enjoyed major careers.

A landmark in the Curtin-Rorem partnership was *Ariel*, his 1971 setting of five tormented poems by Sylvia Plath for soprano and piano. All five are characterized by angular leaps that match the poetry's fascination with madness and death. The last song, "Lady Lazarus," which Rorem marks "fast and frantic, but mechanical," rises to a suicidal frenzy, calling on all of a singer's vocal and emotional resources. Few singers would essay it, and fewer still succeed.

*Ariel* was born partly out of desperation. Curtin had a recital coming up at the Library of Congress with clarinetist David Glazer and pianist Ryan Edwards, her regular accompanist. After Schubert's *Shepherd on the Rock,* the repertory for clarinet, piano, and voice thins out quickly. Seeking variety, Glazer had programmed a group of songs with clarinet and piano accompaniment by Ludwig Spohr, a contemporary of Beethoven's. Curtin found them just too "awful" to contemplate. Lacking money to commission a new work, she called Rorem and pleaded, "Ned, somewhere in one of those marvelous boxes of yours you must have a piece for clarinet, piano, and voice." He didn't, but out of friendship he wrote one for her. Premiered at the Library of Congress, *Ariel* was later recorded by Curtin, Edwards, and clarinetist Joseph Rabbai.

For two decades through the 1970s, Curtin and Rorem teamed in recitals across the country. The programs—"half me and half 'them' [other composers]," Rorem recalls—revived the nineteenth-century tradition of a composer as accompanist. The idea that the composer knows best about his own music, Rorem remarked in the notes for their recital disc, is a presumption. "I like to think that I learned as much about performance from Phyllis as she from me. If what I composed came first, she, as interpreter, literally had the last word."

Curtin pioneered the recital with songs in English; it did not happen easily, however. In the mid-1960s, reasoning that English was her mother tongue and that of most of her American audiences, she decided to take the plunge. Her manager and the concert presenter were aghast. They promptly vetoed the idea, insisting on a "regular" recital program, meaning mostly German. She reluctantly complied, although, as she puts it, her regular programs even then "were not very regular." But the idea of singing in English continued to lurk in the back of her mind.

Meanwhile, songs in Spanish from Latin America caught her interest. She included a few in a demonstration recital she sang for managers and sales agents at Columbia Artists Management, which represented her and sent her out to cities, towns, and campuses across the country on its then-thriving Community Concerts circuit. Her Columbia manager told her to forget it—nobody had ever heard of the stuff. She went on to sing and record the repertory anyway. In fact, she fought management "all the way through" except on the English-language issue, which she had put aside. That changed when, at Columbia's urging in the 1960s, she sang a "regular" recital in Myrtle Beach, South Carolina, seemingly a cultural backwater. A woman who had been in the audience came backstage afterward and said she was disappointed because she had read so much about Curtin's unusual repertory.

"So that did it," Curtin decided. "I never gave in one more time." She would mix American, Latin American, and standard repertory on her recital programs, sometimes performing an all-English section after intermission. These would often include Copland's *Dickinson Songs* and pieces by Britten, another favorite. Berg also figured regularly in the programs.

With Ryan Edwards she would come up with programs linked by themes. The connections among works were sometimes so subtle as to go unrecognized by audiences, but they fired the performers' imaginations. An all-Schubert group opened and closed with his two *Suleika* songs, which address the east and west winds, the east bearing a message from the beloved, the west carrying a message back. In between came other Schubert love songs, all marked in slow tempos but varied in mood and degrees of slowness. A *"du bist"* group consisted of German songs beginning with that whispered or rapturous praise of the beloved's qualities, and an Ophelia group offered selections by Strauss and Berlioz. There was a program about women, ending with Fauré's *Chanson d'Eve*—all this from what Curtin calls "an endless repertory of marvelous music."

In recitals Curtin drew the line at operatic arias, which she would do only as encores. Asked to put arias on a program, she would reply, "No, because this is a *song* recital." Finally Columbia, the colossus of musician management agencies, stopped bothering her about programming. Instead, Columbia just didn't push her as much as it did its more pliant or starry songbirds, although she attracted large audiences. For years, she said, she was actually the agency's busiest recitalist, feted as such with a big party at the Saint Regis Hotel in New York. As at the Met, she didn't fit into the proper niche.

Though Curtin taught briefly at Aspen during her four years there in the 1950s, she had been teaching in one form or another since she was nine. When she took dancing classes as a girl back in Clarksburg, she would instruct her best friend in what she had learned. She found that after explaining a step, she could do it better herself. But it was not until 1964, when she was in midcareer, that she began the series of seminars that made Tanglewood a summer mecca for aspiring singers and led eventually to full-time positions at Yale and Boston Universities.

The spark was lit in 1963, when Curtin was at Tanglewood to sing in the American premiere of Britten's *War Requiem*. It was a solemn and major occasion. Britten had only recently composed the pacifist work for the consecration of the new Coventry Cathedral in England, built beside the ruins of the original edifice, which had been destroyed by German bombs during World War II. Erich Leinsdorf, who was to conduct, had just become director of the Boston Symphony Orchestra. One of his first acts at Tanglewood was to abolish Goldovsky's opera department, which he considered a fiefdom unto itself. The dozen or so vocal students were left with nothing to do.

Out of desperation Harry Kraut, then administrator of the Berkshire (now Tanglewood) Music Center, the festival's school, asked Curtin to meet with the group and *do* something. "I don't know what to do—maybe just talk about singing," the baffled Curtin replied. For a week she talked and taught. The experience so pleased her and the Boston Symphony management that she returned the next year for what became a summerlong series of celebrated seminars. She and her husband bought a white colonial house at the end of a dead-end dirt road in Great Barrington, about ten miles south of Tanglewood. Thirty-three years later it became her retirement hideaway, from which she would emerge for her summer rigors at Tanglewood.

Accorded the title of artist in residence, Curtin became a Tanglewood adornment both on the stage and in the studio. With the Boston Symphony, she ranged through repertory from Bach's *Saint Matthew Passion, Magnificat,* and B Minor Mass and Beethoven's Ninth Symphony and *Missa Solemnis* to Mozart's *Così* and *Requiem,* Ravel's *Shéhérazade,* and the final scene from Strauss's *Salome,* in addition to Britten's *War Requiem* and Schoenberg's *Gurrelieder.* In recital her repertory was equally catholic, going from Russian songs and Schoenberg's *Pierrot Lunaire* to standard lieder and Cole Porter.

The early years were a scramble as Curtin tried to keep up a performing career on the outside while meeting her obligations in the barnlike spaces that serve as classrooms at Tanglewood. She remembers the summer when she was singing *Tosca* in the Met's New York parks program. Through the weeklong series of performances, she would teach her class at Tanglewood, drive to New York, get made up, sing the opera, drive back, and get up to meet her next morning's class.

"That's what it was to be young, strong, and healthy," she recalls. Her husband was her chauffeur.

Every singer must learn to die twice, Joseph Regneas, Curtin's teacher, had warned her. Before the cessation of heart and lungs comes the time—usually in a singer's late fifties—when the voice frays and public performance becomes an embarrassment. For a time in the 1970s, Curtin was able to stave off the first death by giving up opera and devoting herself to the song literature. As she edged toward retirement, she sang a final Tanglewood recital in 1978, typically, for her, pairing song cycles that told stories of women: Schumann's *Frauenliebe und Leben* and Fauré's *Chanson d'Eve*. Her students continued to carry the banner for her, giving weekly recitals—usually four to six singers to a program—that offered a repertoire as diverse as her own. After a 1984 recital at the Castle Hill Festival in Ipswich, Massachusetts, she decided enough was enough and gave up the whole lot, except for occasional private recitals as benefits. She was sixty-three years old, well beyond the age when most singers have called it quits, or should have. But even before then she had been thinking about teaching as an extension of her career. When Philip F. Nelson, then dean of the Yale School of Music, called in the early 1970s, she was ready to listen.

It wasn't as if Yale was the first to ask. Before Nelson's call she had turned down the Juilliard School and Indiana University, among others. She rejected the conservatory route "because I like other things in my life and I think other things ought to be in singers' lives so they have more to sing about." Yale's offer to head its voice department was different. She would be in a liberal arts environment.

Nelson had worked at Harpur College (now the State University of New York at Binghamton) before Yale, and he felt that "the artist is an uneasy guest in the house of intellect," where committees and curriculum take precedence over performance. To tip the balance, he brought the Guarneri String Quartet to Harpur for a performing as well as teaching residency. When President Kingman Brewster summoned Nelson to Yale in 1970, one of his first assignments was to revitalize the School of Music, which confers graduate as well as baccalaureate degrees in performance and composition. Thinking of the Guarneri, Nelson decided he needed someone of international reputation to head the vocal and operatic program. And Curtin, "a marvelous artist, a marvelous human being, somebody whose outreach extended in many, many directions," was just the person to do it.

A yearlong series of meetings took place at Curtin's New York apartment. When, finally, the time seemed right, Nelson declared that Curtin and her husband belonged at Yale. "They both looked at me," Nelson recalls, "and said, 'I think you're right.'"

Curtin took up her first full-time academic position in 1974. For the first year on the job, she commuted from New York. But then she left the Met, and it made sense to move to New Haven and make that her base for travel. In 1979 she took on the additional duties of master of Branford College, one of Yale's undergraduate residential colleges. Nelson said it was her popularity with students that led to the appointment. Only the second woman to hold such a job, she learned the fine art of dealing with rowdy parties as well as the civilities of hosting weekly teas—some with talks by visiting dignitaries—in the master's apartment. (If Curtin was the master of Branford, the joke went, what was her husband?) She also supervised extracurricular activities, which took her into the realms of the drama club and intramural football.

Curtin remained at Yale until 1983. Through her "magical name," Nelson said, she attracted many fine musicians, such as Joseph Silverstein, concertmaster of the Boston Symphony, to Yale to teach. She herself taught ten or twelve vocal students a year and oversaw operatic productions. "She was an extraordinarily seminal person," Nelson said. "Quite apart from her artistry, her contributions were wonderful. The students loved her, the faculty loved her; everybody loves Phyllis."

The Yale years also brought a new specialty as Curtin phased out more and more of her former repertory. With a pair of well-known jazz players on the faculty, bassist Willie Ruff and pianist Dwike Mitchell, she began giving cabaret-style Cole Porter benefit programs, proving that a woman in her fifties and sixties could be a smoldering torch singer. But after a time she came to feel that she was getting little institutional support or money from President A. Bartlett Giamatti, who replaced Brewster in 1978 (he eventually left Yale to become president of baseball's National League). On the contrary, she said, while Giamatti was clutching the purse strings and was conspicuously absent from student concerts and opera productions, she and her Ruff-Mitchell combo were out raising money for Yale. Nelson, who left Yale in 1980 because of Giamatti's policies, confirms Curtin's complaint. Giamatti "didn't seem to understand what we had tried to put together," he said. Four other deans (out of ten) left at the same time and for the same reason, according to Nelson.

So it happened that Curtin was almost ripe for the plucking when John R. Silber, the fiery president of Boston University, philosophy and legal scholar, and political conservative, decided he wanted her as the dean of Boston University's School for the Arts.

Silber is not the kind of man who takes no for an answer. But no is what Curtin told him when, on the recommendation of baritone Mac Morgan, an old colleague of hers who had joined the B.U. faculty, he first called in 1980. Since she wouldn't go to Silber, he went to her, meeting her for lunch in New Haven. Curtin, not yet wholly disenchanted with Yale, gave him a dozen reasons why she couldn't move. Silber wouldn't budge. He even had his daughter Judith, who was taking a doctorate in music at Yale, put in a word on his behalf at a concert.

Silber had first met Curtin when he sat in on some of her master classes at Tanglewood, where Boston University runs a training institute for high school–aged musicians. (Tanglewood's own students are older, ranging in age from about eighteen to thirty.) He discovered what many another visitor and musician had already observed. Her classes, he recalled, "were truly remarkable occasions. The thing that was striking was that the persons she was coaching and working with were singing better by the end of the lesson than they were at the beginning. You could actually hear the improvement. It was a convincing demonstration of her capacity as a teacher. It was unavoidable. You could just see it. Then I had the opportunity of meeting her and talking to her, and became well aware of her extraordinary intellect. She is not only a gifted artist but a very intelligent, learned person. She has a first-class mind, and she has educated herself over broad ranges of subjects, which she wouldn't need to know perhaps in order to be a musician."

Silber was also impressed by Curtin's standing as an interpreter of new music. It didn't matter that her only administrative experience for a deanship was heading a department at Yale. He would see to it that she had assistants to handle business matters, including finances, for which she told him she had no head. What he was looking for, he said, was not a bureaucrat but a leader with vision, taste, intelligence, and artistic discrimination.

"Beyond that," Silber discovered, "my God, that woman is charming!" She "could have been the inspiration for what Goethe had in mind [in *Faust*] when he said, 'das ewig-Weibliche zieht uns hinan' [the eternal feminine principle draws us onward]." The fearsome scholar-president and (later) candidate for Massachusetts governor was smitten.

In the end Silber played the husband card, inveigling Gene Cook to come to B.U. to teach photography in the communications school. Then he told Curtin that as a family-values man, he felt obliged to bring her to Boston too because he felt "guilty about having split this family apart." The approach was ridiculous, and both Silber and Curtin knew it. But he thinks it was just cunning enough to turn the tide. After three years of courtship, Curtin gave in.

"It was at least a surprising approach," he recalled, savoring his ploy.

At B.U.'s School for the Arts, Curtin was in charge of a faculty of about 170 and an enrollment of about 900 in a school that grants baccalaureate and graduate degrees in theater and visual arts as well as music. In addition to overseeing hirings, budgets, and schedules, she founded and directed the school's Opera Institute, which staged works ranging from *Don Giovanni* to Michael Tippett's *Knot Garden* and Boston composer Andy Vores's *Freshwater,* all in English. The institute is for the student who has completed graduate school but is not ready for regional companies or the bigger companies' professional training programs. Although institute members get first crack at roles, other students may also audition to perform.

Unlike much of Silber's restive faculty, Curtin became a Silber booster— in good measure because Silber was a Curtin booster. When she arrived, she found the school's pianos in woeful condition, beat up from years of use. Silber asked her how many new ones she needed. She said about fifty. She got them all, including some concert grands.

Unlike Giamatti, Silber also attended her opera productions—all of them, beginning with the first, Dominick Argento's *Postcard from Morocco.* She would go to her office around 8:30 on the morning after an opening and find a hand-delivered letter from the president waiting on her desk. "For God's sake, why weren't there more people there?" she remembers a typical letter thundering. "That was a marvelous show."

During Christmastime, her students had prepared an English-language *Marriage of Figaro* for a performance at B.U. for public school pupils from Chelsea, a blue-collar Boston suburb whose run-down school system the university (under a state mandate) was running. Because the pupils could not be bused back to Chelsea in time for lunch, the performance was about to be canceled, to the disappointment of all. With Solomonic wisdom Silber decreed that the university would provide box lunches for the kids to eat on their buses back to school. Performance saved. Good time had by all.

Curtin retired as dean in 1991 but continued to teach full-time until 1997. The School for the Arts "was clearly stronger at the end of her tenure as dean than it was when she began," Silber said. He credited her with strengthening the vocal program through faculty recruitment and creating the Opera Institute. The success of graduates with opera companies in the United States and Europe offered proof of her success, he said. Among her other accomplishments he cited better auditorium facilities for opera productions and an effective collaboration between the opera and orchestra programs. She was also a dynamic fund-raiser, bringing in—among other gifts—an endowment for a series of annual career grants to new graduates.

In 1997, when she was well into her seventies, Curtin partially retired from teaching. From her country home in the Berkshires, she now goes into Boston two days a month to meet B.U. students. Silber provides a car and driver for the two-and-a-half-hour trip each way. She also continues to carry a full load at Tanglewood. But when students beat a path to her door, it is, more often than not, to the wing she built for herself onto the original country house, which is occupied by her daughter, Claudia, her husband, and their four children and menagerie of exotic birds, dogs, cats, chickens, sheep, and goats.

"The only objection I have to Phyllis is that she decided to retire," said Silber. She spurned all of his inducements to stay on.

It was a "sacred moment" for Sanford Sylvan: in 1974, the first of his four summers of study with Curtin at Tanglewood, he went before her to sing "L'indifférent," the last song in Ravel's cycle *Shéhérazade*. As the pianist was playing the introduction, Curtin whispered three sentences—Sylvan remembers that there were three and what they were—in his ear. Sylvan guards the message as a secret, so personal was it. All he'll say is that Curtin talked about the character of the song, with its strong whiff of homoeroticism, and how he could connect with it.

It wasn't only what she said but how she said it. Those three sentences, he recalled, "connected on a complete level the poet, the composer, and simply every level of my ability as a human being—physical, spiritual, mental, emotional." For a twenty-year-old with dreams of vocal splendor and a glamorous career, it was a revelation. "The world really did turn at that moment. I've been blessed to have great spiritual teachers in my life, and this was really as deep as anything any of those people have said to me."

Of the hundreds of Curtin alumni, possibly none embodies her teachings more than Sanford Sylvan. His nontraditional career has taken him from a storyteller's singing of Schubert's *Schöne Müllerin* to the role of

Chou En-lai in John Adams's opera *Nixon in China* and principal roles in Peter Sellars's hip-grunge-punk Mozart opera productions—but not to the Met or La Scala. A self-described conservatory brat, he was "in awe" of Curtin and thought she would lead him up the golden gangplank to the life he had imagined. When he stepped into her rustic studio along with two dozen fellow students, he suffered a rude awakening. Filled, like the others, with visions of glory, he "got to Tanglewood and here was this lady who really wasn't interested in any of that." All she was interested in was what the poet and composer were saying, "and most importantly, our own original response to those words and music." It was just the kick in the pants he needed.

"I think that the timing of Phyllis's arrival in my life was extraordinary," he said. "I went to Juilliard Prep [the preparatory division of the Juilliard School] in New York City, I went to the Manhattan School of Music, and when I met Phyllis, I was twenty and very overdeveloped in terms of kind of knowledge and repertoire and this and that. But I would say I was underdeveloped in the practicalities of what the life of a singer was, and young singers tend to live more in their fantasy of what things are rather than the reality of the practice, the work. I say without hesitation I am the singer that I am today because of Phyllis Curtin."

There was another big moment in that summer of 1974: Sylvan heard Curtin sing Tove in Schoenberg's *Gurrelieder*. Transfixed by her performance, he knew that was the kind of singer he wanted to be. His four years with her set him on that course, and the years since became a "reaping of that study."

It wasn't only Sylvan who changed. He pointed out that a whole generation of singers has emerged to whom baroque arias come as naturally as Schubert, Fauré as naturally as Rorem. For them singing in English means using their native tongue in ways that make audiences comfortable with it: no faux-British vowels or rolled *r*s. ("We shouldn't sound like Princess Margaret," he said. "We should sound like Americans.") Not all of these far-ranging Americans have come out of Curtin's classes. Sylvan lists Lorraine Hunt Lieberson, Ben Heppner, and Thomas Hampson as among the many singers who, wittingly or not, have followed in her path.

Clearly, other forces are also at work. Audiences today are less inclined to sit still for music in a foreign language, unless it is sung by a star of the Pavarotti or Andrea Bocelli magnitude—and then it is sung with a heavy admixture of pop. Opera thrives because it provides spectacle, sometimes of the Broadway variety, in addition to tunes. Opera supertitles, though Curtin detests them as a distraction from the stage action, guide the wary listener through the jungle of a strange language. With the rise of rock, rap, and pop and the decline of classical music in the school and home, the whole spirit of the age inclines away from—if it is not altogether hostile to—artistic expression of a serious nature. The change is visible in the casual attire younger listeners wear to the opera or concert hall, if they bother to attend at all. An old-fashioned song recital won't cut it anymore.

Still, Curtin forged the way for singers, and, as a result, for other musicians, too. To Sylvan her greatest teaching is that singers must develop their voices and sensibilities without worrying about the clamor of the outside world. He points out that he instantly recognizes his voice if he happens to come upon it on the radio. "And that is because of Phyllis saying to me, 'Your voice: I don't want some fantasy idea in your head. I want your voice, I want your sensibility, and I want your commitment to what is on the printed page'—saying it again and again and again."

And again and again she insisted on contemporary music. Sylvan had never sung a note of it when he arrived in her classes. Nor had most of his fellow students. The stuff was simply not taught in conservatories in the 1970s, he said. To him "it was as if contemporary music was for somebody else." Yet Curtin "would say, year in and year out, 'It behooves us as living, breathing musicians to be greatly concerned and involved with the music that is being written right in our own time.'" Seeing how she treated Mozart and Rorem as equals, Sylvan and his classmates learned to take it all in stride. "It's what one does," he realized.

The relationship came full circle in 2000 when Sylvan, at his own initiative, began teaching a yearlong opera workshop at B.U. and Curtin visited as a guest teacher. It was a thrill for him to present his own teacher and the former B.U. dean of arts to a new generation of students. Sylvan also gives master classes in conjunction with his concerts, passing along Curtin's teachings and the lessons of his own experience. He returns to Tanglewood at least once a summer to sit in on her classes and refresh himself. She taught him how to teach as well as sing, he said, "how to listen to a singer and how to focus on what can most help in the given time."

Curtin, on the other hand, never knows what to expect. Sylvan's destiny soon became clear, but her former student Dawn Upshaw was another matter. During Upshaw's only summer at Tanglewood, in 1983, Curtin felt that "nothing that I said or anybody said was really going to change or do anything to her. She was perhaps the most distant of the people that I worked with there." Upshaw tells a different story. When she got to Tanglewood, she had just finished graduate school and had spent three summers at Aspen, where she studied with Jan DeGaetani and Adele Addison. "By the time I got to Tanglewood, I think I knew myself a little better as an artist, as a performer. I knew what I needed to do to have the most productive summer that I could, and my memories are terrific memories. I remember feeling I got so much done and that I had improved a lot from the beginning of the summer to the end. . . . I think what Phyllis and Jan did for me, above anything else, was give me confidence in my own decisions and in my own opinions."[15]

Following the Curtin path, Upshaw ranges from the Mozart heroines Pamina, Susanna, and Cherubino to the role of the spoiled rich girl Daisy Buchanan that John Harbison created for her in his 1999 opera, *The Great Gatsby*. She readily sings programs of American music in concert and recordings. She is also at home singing Broadway tunes.

The ripples begun in Goldovsky's and Curtin's classes have spread to many places. Like Sylvan, Harbison names Upshaw, along with Lorraine Hunt Lieberson and Jerry Hadley, as members of a new generation of American singers for whom vocal and dramatic smarts come in a single package. They "think their way" into their roles, he said in the *New York Times Magazine,* describing how they took to the lead roles in *Gatsby*.[16] In the liner notes for the recording of his song cycle *Simple Daylight,* Harbison says he composed it for Upshaw because he had "complete confidence in sending her into uncharted waters."[17] On the same disc Sylvan sings *Words from Paterson,* which Harbison conceived for Sylvan's voice. Contemporary music, as Curtin showed, is "what one does."

Many singers teach, but usually it is as a visiting artist in a master class. The performer listens, gives advice to students, and then leaves. Or singers entering retirement will take up teaching as a way of easing the pain of what Regneas described to Curtin as the first death. At the age of sixty-four, for example, Marilyn Horne became chairman of the voice department at the Music Academy of the West in Santa Barbara, California. Five years earlier, in 1993, she set up her Marilyn Horne Foundation to sponsor young singers in recitals around the United States. Her protégés—there were eighty-one of them by the year 2000—are expected to speak and perform in schools in the communities they visit.

The master class can be a useful adjunct to regular study with a good teacher. Unlike a visiting artist who does a star turn in a classroom and is gone, Curtin struggles day in and day out with her students' vocal and emotional needs. She also gives master classes herself at various conservatories and universities, and she occasionally brings in guests to meet with her own students. She remembers a particularly rewarding three-year sequence of Boston University classes by tenor Carlo Bergonzi.

Perhaps the most celebrated master classes in recent times were those given by Maria Callas at the Juilliard School for twelve weeks in 1971 and 1972. In *Callas at Juilliard,* his book recapitulating the sessions, John Ardoin writes: "Callas labored to produce not a series of 'mini Callases,' but to bring out the individual personalities and gifts of each singer. In doing so, she gave not only her views but possible alternatives as well. She adamantly insisted, however, that her students remain faithful to the style of a given piece, and she carefully explained of what this style consisted. She did this by delving into the text and its emotions, usually correlating the drama to an aria's musical substance."[18]

The description could also fit Curtin's method, or lack of method. There is no fixed approach, no "this is how I did it." Though she deals with the fundamentals of vocal production, the emphasis, as Sylvan said, is on illumination of the text as filtered through the singer's life experience. She'll tell a student slathering hammy sobs onto an aria that he doesn't have to weep—the composer already did it. A crooner learns that relaxation is for going to sleep—singing is more like an athletic feat.[19]

Physical touch plays an important part. Curtin places a student's hands on her diaphragm to show how it moves as she produces a tone; she works her hand across a student's face to show where unnecessary tensions lie. She says the "whole business of text, of making Brahms sound different from Schumann or Schubert, and making Fauré different from Ravel," is central. She demands from students their "feeling of words, of emotion, of their particular understanding of that music," not "what I tell them to do, or the coach has told them to do, or I know they expect me to do." At Tanglewood members of the Boston Symphony and other musicians are often among the crowd of auditors sitting at the back of the studio. Like students themselves, they come for lessons in phrasing, breath control, and interpretation.

Even on summer's hottest days, Curtin shows up for her Tanglewood classes immaculately dressed in skirt and blouse (no uniform of jeans and T-shirt, like some faculty members) and with silvery hair immaculately coiffed. What's more, she looks just as composed at the end of a grueling three-hour session as she did at the beginning. Inwardly, though, she savors the triumphs and suffers the setbacks of her charges. She is exhausted, in fact. She has given her all, which is what she expects of them.

Back in the Maria Callas–Marilyn Horne heyday of the 1950s–1960s bel canto revival, Curtin said, every young soprano decided she had to sing the Rossini-Bellini-Donizetti repertory "when none of them had ever sung any of it before or ever heard any, and when no company was doing it except with those ladies." The worst of that is past, Curtin finds, and she's beginning to hear a more personal approach. Even so, gifted students still come to her with "very fixed ideas about what they must sound like, what they must do." It's so bad that in auditions she can often tell with whom a student has trained merely by the style and application of emotion. She's not hearing artists but "very well-trained people." But unless a trained body responds to "one's imagination, one's emotion, one's spirituality, one's anger, one's everything" in a song, the composer might as well have written a string quartet.

An even more unconventional route than Sylvan's was taken by Rinde Eckert, who studied with Curtin at Yale and Tanglewood in the mid-1970s. In her thrall, he hung around Yale for the next four years, sitting in on her seminars, living in her house, serving as a chauffeur and household factotum, and becoming godfather to one of her grandchildren. Like Sylvan, he heard a spiritual chord: attending her classes was for him like "sitting at the feet of a Zen master." Taking her teachings about individuality to heart, he turned himself into a musical jack-of-all-trades: singer, composer, librettist, playwright, dancer, and, for lack of a better term, performance artist.

Eckert remembers a watershed moment at Yale. He was driving Curtin home from a concert and complaining about all the things he had heard wrong in it. She listened for a while and then quietly asked if he had noticed a waltz tempo that had worked well. Eckert saw that "she was entirely awake during the whole thing," to the good and the bad, while he was fixated on the bad. "I realized that this was the kind of intelligence that I wanted to foster in myself. I wanted the ability to make critical distinctions and not just make blanket judgments of work."

Thinking about Curtin's emphasis on a performer's total immersion in his art, Eckert began working in the area of movement, often with dancers. At the Jacob's Pillow dance festival, in the Berkshires near Tanglewood, he performed his own *Dry Land Divine,* a twenty-five-minute piece combining vocal techniques, movement, and acting; Curtin was in the audience. During the same period, he began writing opera librettos, beginning with *Slow Fire*, with Paul Dresher as the composer. Perhaps his best-known piece is *Ravenshead,* a two-act, one-man opera for which he wrote the libretto and Steven Mackey composed the music.

The story is based on an actual incident. A blowhard English businessman sets out to sail around the world in a solo race, only to lose his way, go mad, and die at sea. In a virtuoso performance with the Paul Dresher Ensemble, Eckert sings and plays the part of the crazed sailor, sometimes swinging precariously—as if nailed to a cross—from his boat's wildly flailing jib boom. The production had a run of thirty premiere performances in 1998 at the Berkeley Repertory Theater in California and went on a national tour.

Singing and playing his *Idiot Variations,* Eckert blows on a tuba and wears what look like a surgical gown, a battered L. L. Bean shirt, and a skullcap. "I've fashioned this interdisciplinary role for myself," he said, "and Phyllis has always been in the back of my mind as a model of the kind of integrity that I've aspired to."

In a more conventional vein, Curtin nurtured the career of Haijing Fu. The strapping Chinese-born baritone went on to make the rounds of the United States' major opera companies, including the Met and the Los Angeles and Washington operas, in such roles as Verdi's Rigoletto, Germont in Verdi's *Traviata,* Count di Luna in Verdi's *Trovatore,* and Marcello in Puccini's *Bohème.*

Curtin first heard Fu in 1983 at a London vocal competition where she was a judge and he won second prize. He impressed her so strongly that she saved her notes about him, just in case, and took them home. It was against protocol, however, for them to speak. A year later, already well known as a singer in China, he came to Boston for a concert in a touring group of four "Young Soloists of the People's Republic." By then he already knew he wanted to study with Curtin. Although recordings and information about Western music were unavailable in China, he had heard about her from his teacher in Beijing, Ying Jiang, who had lived in the United States and taught Western arias and art songs.

Fu arranged through a Chinese piano student at B.U. to sit in on one of Curtin's classes. Remembering him from London, Curtin "felt like the spider that finally has the fly in the web." At her class he asked for a lesson of his own. Curtin agreed and he took it on the day of the concert. Since neither spoke the other's language, they communicated in sounds and gestures. At the concert that night, with Curtin in the audience, he tried out her suggestions. She was impressed anew, not only by his voice and intelligence but by his courage in trying new ways of singing without further rehearsal.

The story might have ended there, but while Fu was on the way back to China, an intermediary from the Chinese-American friendship association that had sponsored the Boston concert called Curtin from San Francisco. Was there any way she could take on the young baritone as a student?

It wouldn't be easy. Fu was clearly a major talent, but he had no money for foreign study. Nor was Chinese scholarship money available. But two years later, in 1986, Fu entered Boston University as a full-time opera student on a scholarship Curtin had arranged. He took voice lessons from her and lived on the top floor of the dean's university-provided mansion, later bringing over his wife and their three-year-old daughter to join him.

It was at B.U. that Fu sang his first complete opera. He headed the cast in *Don Giovanni,* which was done in English in Curtin's Opera Institute for the opening of the arts school's new theater, the Tsai Performance Center. In 1988 he was a winner in the Metropolitan Opera young artists competition. He spent a summer studying with Curtin at Tanglewood and graduated from B.U. in 1989 with an artist's diploma. He immediately acquired a manager in New York and began getting engagements—exactly the kind of opportunity that was lacking when Curtin was starting out.

Fu became a regular at the Met, often serving as a cover, or standby, singer but also taking major roles in his own right in much of the standard Italian repertory. He was also in demand on the regional opera circuit and sang with major orchestras in oratorios and sometimes in such other works as Carl Orff's *Carmina Burana.*

Curtin gave him just the kind of training and support he needed, he said. Like other Curtin alumni, he found that her emphasis was on self-discovery. The most important thing he learned from her was that "you have to think a lot. Every singer is different—different voices, different colors, different bodies. So you have to know yourself very well." When a serious illness forced him off the stage in the late 1990s, Curtin served as his counselor, giving him the confidence to return.

The international exchange worked the other way, as well. In 1987 Curtin went to China to give three weeks of master classes at the Central Conservatory in Beijing at the invitation of its director, Xugian Wu. Fu served as her host and sang for the class. Ying Jiang, his former teacher, served as translator. Impressed with the fourteen students she heard, Curtin nevertheless found that the men were handicapped by the same problem that she had encountered in Fu: use of the throat to produce a wide-open sound that is powerful up close but peters out quickly at a distance from the stage. Curtin went home a week early because of laryngitis, but not before Jiang had given her a pair of heirloom jade earrings as a memento. Jiang said she always knew Fu could sing like that but she couldn't find a way to bring it out.

Self-discovery can also come in a cornfield. That's how it was for Bejun Mehta, the son of musical parents and a distant cousin of conductor Zubin Mehta, who reached stardom as a countertenor in the late 1990s. After a prodigy's career as a boy soprano, the North Carolina–born Bejun suffered a mental breakdown when his voice changed at age fifteen. He took up the cello and conducting, achieving a degree of success in both. Dissatisfied, and still longing at some level to sing, he went to Curtin for lessons. In 1991, after what he describes as "seven years of vocal silence," he was able to return as a baritone. In Claude Kenneson's book *Musical Prodigies,* Mehta recounts the turning point:

"I was in a lesson with Phyllis Curtin, the renowned teacher who would carefully and lovingly steward my first sustained explorations with a changed, baritone instrument. I had been singing well that day, when she asked me a routine question about my earlier voice. Suddenly I was broadsided with such a wave of emotion that I had to leave the studio. We were working in her country house in Great Barrington, and I went out over the back hill into the lower cornfield, where I remained for quite a while, inconsolable."

As he wept, Mehta realized that grief "was what I had been avoiding all these years, that this would start filling up the hole in my chest." With that self-awareness he was able to reconnect with "the boy I once had been." "As I took his hand," he said, "I felt a resonance echo deep from the bottom of my soul and was warmed by the possibility of a partnership, of perhaps a turn in the road."[20]

Being a baritone never felt quite right, though, and in 1997, after another withdrawal from singing, Mehta decided to try turning himself into a countertenor. With Curtin's continuing nurture, he quickly obtained management and embarked on a successful career. Whatever Curtin said to him during that lesson in her country home had the same electrifying effect as her whispered words to Sanford Sylvan at Tanglewood.

*     *     *

At the end of *The American Opera Singer,* Peter G. Davis's survey of the vocal art over a span of nearly two centuries, he laments the "internationalization of American voices" as they take their place beside—and sometimes in preference to—once-dominant Europeans on the world's stages:

> What distinguishes American singers today is not their vocal individuality or creative fantasy but their craftsmanship and relentless industry. Inquiring singers like [Frederica] von Stade, [Lorraine] Hunt [Lieberson], [Dawn] Upshaw, and others continue to investigate a diversity of music in order to find their own special voices, and no doubt they will have successors. And yet it is more difficult than ever for such mavericks to make their way in a music world that prizes conformity above all and, as a result, becomes increasingly homogenized. It is also unrealistic to expect that the expensive and complex apparatus needed to support the continuing performance of classical music—at least as we have always understood it—will survive indefinitely as new social and economic realities alter our culture. After all, the royal European courts that sustained a glorious repertory of medieval music for centuries have long since vanished, and the world, while looking for new songs to sing, has spent little time in mourning the loss. Good things need not always last forever.[21]

If the complaint is true (and Curtin believes it is), it also has to do with a zeitgeist that has turned its back on tradition in its pursuit of the new and trendy. Operagoers may be a conservative lot who treasure their beloved arias and stage spectacles, but young singers face a bewildering array of choices, which only begin when they choose between a conservatory like Juilliard and a liberal arts school like Yale or Boston University. They may come in, like Sanford Sylvan, with dreams of glory and go out fired with idealism about their art. Or, with a taste of success, they may go where the celebrity and money are. The devil's snares are ever present and ever difficult to detect.

Meanwhile, compact discs, with their icy digital clarity, put a premium on technical perfection. They also make available one hundred years of great singers as models, daunting some would-be stars and tempting others to copy what has received history's stamp of approval. At another extreme popular culture holds out the ideal of the hip, the cool, the roar of the crowd. Pop music, with its instant—and instantly disposable—appeal, and spectacles like those of the Three Tenors (Pavarotti, Domingo, and Carreras) with their endlessly recyclable treacle of hit tunes and arias, are easy solutions to the difficulty of forging an artistic identity. Hollywood, television, the mall, the Internet—each offers further obstacles to reaching a distracted audience. Under the best of circumstances, only a few musicians will have the talent and drive necessary to overcome the obstacles and make their way as artists. The ability to reveal meaning and beauty from dots printed on a page is, as Curtin said, inexplicable. Is it any wonder that she drummed into Sylvan's head, over and over, that she wanted his sensibility and his commitment to the clues left by the composer?

Throughout history—and not just in music—progress has been made by those willing to swim against the tide. If there are mavericks like Sylvan and Upshaw abroad, seeking what is distinctive in music and themselves, it is partly because Curtin and others like her showed that it could be done. According to Carlisle Floyd, "she managed to escape that terrible ghetto that a lot of singers of contemporary music find themselves in, in which they're not approached to do anything except contemporary music." Her willingness to sing all the parts in *Susannah* when they were trying to get a New York premiere, he said, is "a testimonial to her marvelous graciousness as an artist and her attitude about the art of singing and also the art of opera."

To Renée Fleming, the Susannah in the opera's Met premiere, Curtin's performance was a "benchmark" for later singers. It was important to her that the original Susannah was in the audience on opening night of the Met's production.[22] A latecomer to the song recital, the wildly popular Fleming took up the cause of new music—specifically new American music—when she began recital work in midcareer. In that, too, Curtin was a benchmark.

Sanford Sylvan was "astonished" to find that everything Curtin said came true. Just as she promised, the years between thirty-five and fifty-five proved the prime of a career. "It'll come," she told him. "Just stick with it." Even her use of a fusty word like "behoove" in urging students to sing music of their own time, Sylvan said, demonstrated her willingness to go against fashion. B.U.'s John Silber, Yale's Philip Nelson, and singer-actor-librettist Rinde Eckert: Each heard the same prophetic voice, the same sensibility.

There is almost an air of unreality about these tributes, as if Curtin were too good to be true. The music world is a tight little island teeming with gossip, and whether because of jealousies or the peculiarities of an art form in which the body is the instrument, none of the gossip is more vicious than that about singers. Curtin seems to have escaped all of this. There is no dish about her—no tales of holding a high note longer than a partner, of succumbing to a manager's invitation to the sofa. Even when a fellow singer stabbed her in the back, as Beverly Sills did at City Opera, she accepted it without striking back.

Curtin's achievement lies not only in roles, concerts, and recitals sung, plentiful and successful as those were. Nor is it to be measured entirely in commissions and premieres. Just as important is an attitude toward music—what Floyd describes as "total selflessness and willingness"—and a legion of followers ensconced on stages and in music faculties across the land. Some of her alumni, such as Cheryl Studer and John Aler, are less conspicuously her disciples than others. But all, in one way or another, have carried her teachings out into the world.

Because Curtin was not a "star" in the ordinary sense, she did not leave a large recorded legacy. There is a Shostakovich Fourteenth Symphony, recorded with Eugene Ormandy and the Philadelphia Orchestra in conjunction with their American premiere performances. There is a Handel *Samson* (she is the Delilah to Jan Peerce's strongman) with the Utah Symphony under Maurice Abravanel. With the Boston Symphony she recorded Debussy's *Martyre de St. Sébastien* (with Charles Munch) and Berg's *Der Wein,* sung in French and retitled *Le vin,* and excerpts from Berg's *Wozzeck* (with Erich Leinsdorf). With Leonard Bernstein and the New York Philharmonic she did Sibelius's *Luonnotar.* There is a pirated *Don Giovanni* from Chicago (Curtin sings Elvira), but there are no commercially released complete operas on major labels.

Late in the 1990s, however, Ernest Gilbert, president of Video Artists International, heard that Curtin's husband had preserved tapes of many of her live performances. Long a Curtin admirer, Gilbert began mining the jumbled, largely uncataloged trove in her home. Compact-disc releases followed on his VAI label, which specializes in historic recordings, mostly from live performances, in both video and audio formats.

The debut disc offered a collection of ten arias by Mozart, Charpentier, Verdi, Giordano, Puccini, Floyd, and Strauss, recorded from 1960 to 1968. The mostly standard excerpts are taken from rehearsals and live performances, but the orchestras and conductors are unidentified. Either Curtin could not trust her memory of the tape's provenance or VAI could not get permission to identify the source. In the case of an aria from Umberto Giordano's *Andrea Chénier*, she could not even remember having performed the music.

A 1962 performance of *Susannah* with the New Orleans Opera provides the only recorded document of how she sang the role. Curtin felt the performance was marred by conductor Knud Anderson's slow tempos, but she agreed to the release out of admiration for the singing of her male partners, both friends and both dead, Richard Cassilly as Sam Polk and Norman Treigle as Olin Blitch.

In spite of her qualms, Anthony Tommasini, reviewing the initial releases in the *New York Times*, described them as "distinguished." Curtin's voice, he wrote, "eludes easy classification, because she so carefully and tastefully modified her sound and approach to the music in question. In 'Come scoglio,' from Mozart's *Così fan tutte*, her soprano is shimmering and focused. In the finale scene of Strauss's *Salome*, a remarkable performance from 1968, her sound is molten, rich, and gutsy." As for Susannah, Tommasini said Curtin made her "a figure of genuinely tragic dimension. The singer is faithful to the regionalisms of Mr. Floyd's libretto in phrases like 'lonesome fer the valley,' but she delivers them with such grace that the dialect never sounds mannered. And her cultured singing infuses this impulsive young character with an affecting maturity."[23]

Later releases in the series included two recitals, the first a mixed program, the second containing Fauré's *Chanson d'Eve*, followed by Fauré and Debussy settings of six poems by Paul Verlaine. The French program, recorded live in Boston in 1962, offers an imaginative Curtin variation on standard recital fare. The six Verlaine texts are the same for each composer. But instead of singing them as separate groups—one composer's set of six followed by the other's—Curtin alternates the settings, as she regularly did in recital. Spare and inward-looking, the late Fauré is set off against the extroverted, sensuous early Debussy. The rarely performed *Chanson d'Eve* proves a work of luminous beauty in the Curtin performance. Ryan Edwards is the pianist.

The next release, in 2001, paired live performances of Copland's *Twelve Poems of Emily Dickinson* with ten independent songs and the *Cycle of Holy Songs* by Rorem. In each performance the composer is at the piano, making the recording a historical document. Striking as each performance is, Copland's playing adds another dimension to the often-performed Dickinson set. Even more than usual, the poet's childlike wordplay becomes a mask for a face looking at mortality.

The Copland tape turned up in the studios of WHRB, a music-conscious radio station run by Harvard undergraduates. Unbeknownst to Curtin, the station had recorded the *Dickinson Songs* in a recital given at Harvard in 1971 to celebrate Copland's seventieth birthday. The Rorem songs were recorded at a Boston recital in 1969.

Apropos the *Dickinson Songs,* Howard Pollack writes in his Copland biography that "it is astonishing to observe how so many of Copland's characteristic gestures—the clangorous vitality, ironic humor, biting severity, heroic grandeur, and resigned sadness—can accommodate, with barely a nod to older musical styles, the verse of this mid-nineteenth-century poet."[24] Copland had recorded the cycle twice before, with mezzo-soprano Martha Lipton in 1957 and soprano Adele Addison in 1967. But Curtin regards this live recording with the composer as a landmark—so much so that she planned to use both it and the Rorem performances as object lessons for the six to eight pianists who study at Tanglewood each summer to become vocal accompanists and coaches. The performance of the *Dickinson Songs* was one of about ten that she gave over the years with Copland at the piano. In the recording's liner notes she recalls, "He let me set out on the work without any directive from him. Of course, with him at the piano, and with such a beautifully wrought score, there was little likelihood of straying into aberrant territory. However, we were very alive to each other and every performance was unique."

In an exchange of gallantries in the notes, Curtin writes that whenever she sang with Rorem, "we were really one mind full of HIS music, enhancing and poignantly bringing into the palpable present the reality of thought, emotion, wit, humor. With Ned Rorem I have always been richly alive in music, poetry—life." Striking a more mournful note, Rorem responds, "Has it really been thirty years since we gave this recital? Soon it will be forty years, then a hundred. The melancholy wonder of recording is that the past becomes the present. The dead walk again, though never with the same gait." He goes on to recall their two decades of happy collaboration in concerts, "sacred and profane."[25]

Also from the archives, the New York Philharmonic included Curtin's 1965 performance of four songs by Sibelius in its ten-disc set of previously unreleased live recordings made by Leonard Bernstein with the orchestra.

The dead walked again in an interview with Curtin in the liner notes. Wanting to perform Sibelius's *Luonnotar* in its original Finnish and the four songs, which were in Swedish, she needed help with pronunciation. So, she recalled, "darling old Gene Cook," her husband, "thought up just the right thing: he called the Finnish Embassy, and wondered if somebody could help me. Sure enough, they recommended a lovely lady, and I worked with her for two weeks on Finnish and Swedish, and it came out pretty well."[26]

"Time past and time future / What might have been and what has been / Point to one end, which is always present," T. S. Eliot writes in *Four Quartets*.

In 1986 Gene Cook suffered a ruptured aorta. Rushed to a Boston hospital, he was asked by the admitting office what his religion was. "I love music," he replied. He died forty-five minutes later. Curtin soldiered on eleven more years at Boston University until her retirement. Settled in her country home, with a view across the fields to the south, she has her miniature poodle, two cats, and daughter with her family and menagerie of beasts as company. Students still beat a path to her door, and she still travels into Boston two days a month, courtesy of John Silber, to teach. But like Mozart's Countess in *Figaro* and Strauss's Marschallin in *Rosenkavalier,* she looks back on the golden moments—*Dove sono?* the Countess asks in one of her great arias: "where are they, the happy moments of sweetness and of pleasure?"— with detachment mixed with nostalgia and ripe satisfaction. Arthritis limits her mobility but not her vigor of mind. She now prefers to catch up on a lifetime of reading—history, biography, politics, novels—instead of going to operas and concerts. Birdsong and rain on the roof replace the sound of practice.

Nothing stays the same, except perhaps human love and folly. In a 1997 purge of the Tanglewood school's leadership, Seiji Ozawa brought in a new director, Ellen Highstein, who dropped the designation Phyllis Curtin Seminars from Curtin's classes. At the same time Ozawa and Highstein lessened Curtin's role as an opera coach at just the time when a formal opera training program was being revived to supplement classroom work and occasional productions. They said they wanted new ideas and new faces. Yet Curtin— in part over Ozawa's opposition—had been a prime mover in the 1996 return of the opera program, which had lapsed in 1962 with the departure of Boris Goldovsky.

Curtin's world was changing around her. New singers were coming along, many of whom she had not heard of. New styles of composition were emerging. Yet the essential truths of her career remained. In her 1988 lecture at Boston University, she had recounted some of them.

Of Britten's *War Requiem,* which she had gone on to sing in thirty more performances after the American premiere at Tanglewood, she said its message about the barbarity and futility of war had been "by far the most important learning I have received about religion, war, the issue of war and Christianity, and the responsibility to living." Of Bach's *St. Matthew Passion,* "It seems unnecessary to be a Christian to find in this work an understanding of the human condition that transcends any kind of parochialism or locale or time. . . . I used to feel that a year was incomplete without singing this work, without simply being in the world of its performance. I miss it terribly. I miss the sense of participating in the communal sorrow and hope."

Commenting on Rorem's setting of the Robert Browning poem "Pippa's Song," with its evocation of spring, the lark, and the snail, Curtin told how she had approached the music through an understanding of nature, "though urban culture deprives many people of any knowledge of it." At one point Browning and Rorem picture a "dew-pearled" hillside. "Given the composer's two round half-notes, the last one lengthened a beat," Curtin said, "only an insensitive singer could resist the feel and shape of 'dew-pearled.' " And not miss its sound and feel when her time to sing has passed.

Summing up her career, she said: "Performing brought me every good thing of my adult life, and some of my youth—like the truth about myself that I found playing Emily in *Our Town* at age sixteen, or choreographing Bach's Little Fugue in G Minor for my modern dance class. Performing brought me my husband, took me and us to far parts of the world with all the attendant surprises. It livened up our parental skills as we tried to do our best by careers and family. It certainly added breadth and depth to my knowledge of people and their cultures. It made me know what a real republican, lower case, I am. It has kept me endlessly curious."

As dean, Curtin said, she looked for the same kind of "urgency and love and expertise" in her faculty and students. It seemed not only a fitting conclusion to a lecture but a fitting commentary on a career.

# GUNTHER *S*CHULLER

*Who cares what style it's in?*

Gunther Schuller conducts at one of his seventy-fifth
birthday concerts. (Kathy Chapman)

ON AN OVERCAST OCTOBER DAY IN 1999 TWO LARGE RYDER rental vans pulled into the circular gravel driveway at Gunther Schuller's house in Newton Centre, Massachusetts. Into their bowels went the scores and parts of more than 1,000 compositions—classical, jazz, and a mix of the two, by composers famous and obscure—published by Schuller over a twenty-four-year span. At the age of seventy-four he figured he had to cut back somewhere, so he sold his publishing business.

Did that stop him from working fourteen to eighteen hours a day, seven days a week? Hardly. This ex–horn player, Pulitzer Prize–winning composer, MacArthur Award–certified "genius," and Boston gray eminence kept right on going as a composer, conductor, record producer, educator, writer–jazz historian, professional scold, and champion of his fellow composers.

Like Wagner's Parsifal, Schuller is a knight of the Holy Grail. His grail is the purity of the art of music, Schubert's *holde Kunst*—the kindly art. But unlike Parsifal's holy spear, which healed the wound in the sinning Amfortas's side, Schuller's spear has been powerless against the equally grievous wound he perceives as inflicted on the body politic by commercialism and the process of dumbing down classical music, pop, jazz, radio and television programming, public discourse—the works. Not content like Candide to tend his garden, he put himself to work in the service of other composers. The money for his publishing and recording ventures came from his commissions as a composer and his earnings in his other chosen fields. As soon as the cash came in, out it went again. When he sold his two publishing companies, Margun Music and GunMar Music, to G. Schirmer, Inc., he estimated the value of their catalogs at $20 million. And that didn't include the costs of his own labors as director, editor, proofreader, and general factotum.

"I figured out a long time ago that I can't take it with me, and my philosophy has been that I should do good things with the money that I make that I don't myself need," he said in his living room, surrounded by the clutter of his trade. "I could have retired twenty years ago and been on a beach in Florida. But that's obviously not my life."

Obviously. Who else would have premiered Milton Babbitt's *Transfigured Notes*, a late twentieth-century composer's stormy take on the already stormy writing of Arnold Schoenberg's late nineteenth-century *Transfigured Night?* Forbiddingly complex in its technical and intellectual demands on conductor and players alike (to say nothing of audiences), *Transfigured Notes* is twenty-six minutes of hard labor for a string orchestra. It was commissioned in the late 1980s by the Philadelphia Orchestra, but when the Philadelphians went to premiere it, three conductors in a row got no further with it than rehearsal. Erich Leinsdorf looked at the score and sent his regrets. Dennis Russell Davies, a new-music specialist, gave up after forty-five minutes of one rehearsal. Hans Vonk lasted longer, but the orchestra management finally declared the piece unplayable.

Unplayable? Where composers like Babbitt are concerned, those are fighting words to Gunther Schuller. The Philadelphia players, he said, might have hated Babbitt's music, but they had worked hard and learned it. It was the management, hamstrung by the costs of adequately preparing a difficult new piece within the confines of a standard symphonic budget and season, that refused to stand behind the commission, Schuller said. Orchestra boards and managements are one of his bêtes noirs for just such reasons.

As a horn player and conductor, Schuller had been performing Babbitt's music since 1948. He decided that he was going to conduct *Transfigured Notes* as soon as he could get his hands on it. It took Babbitt two years to regain the performing rights. When he did, Schuller assembled a string orchestra of forty-three of Boston's best freelance players and, at his own expense, put them through twelve rehearsals—all he could afford—in preparation for two premiere performances. The concerts took place on consecutive days in February 1991 in Boston's venerable Jordan Hall. At each program Schuller surrounded the Babbitt with other twentieth-century works for string orchestra: *Transfigured Night* and Nikolai Miaskovsky's Sinfonietta on the first program, Arthur Honegger's Symphony no. 2 and Stravinsky's Concerto in D on the second.

Not content to show that the unplayable was playable, Schuller taped both programs. Then in 1998 he made a a composite of the two Babbitt performances and issued *Transfigured Notes* along with the Schoenberg and Stravinsky works on a compact disc on his GM Recordings label. At the concerts and in his liner notes, he cautioned that the Babbitt performance was not perfect, and in fact, as he put it in the notes, "it would be at least another fifteen years or so before a truly correct performance could be expected." Proud of the results nevertheless, he declared the finished product "at least, very 'representative' of the work, in mood and character, and in all its polyphonic, rhythmic/metric, and structural splendor."[1]

Each performance attracted an almost full house of about nine hundred listeners, but ticket sales weren't nearly enough to cover expenses. Schuller lost $42,000 on the project.

"I don't know of anybody else who would do things like that," Schuller said. "One can say you're a damned fool for doing these things. I don't see it that way."

Even before that heroic (or foolish) gesture, Babbitt was as much a fan of Schuller as Schuller was of Babbitt. In a foreword to *Musings*, Schuller's 1986 collection of his writings and lectures, Babbitt hailed "the singular capacities of a conductor who can achieve maximal results under minimal conditions, by knowing the score and knowing the performers, be they members of a celebrated 'major' orchestra or of a student orchestra." But that's not all, Babbitt said. Schuller's publishing and recording, though the least visible of his enterprises, "are among his most vital and influential advocacies." At a time when economic pressures were making music publishing "a disappearing act of faith," Babbitt went on, "the already extensive catalogues of Margun and GunMar embody the energy and discriminating catholicity that are the earmarks of Gunther's composing, conducting, teaching, and—of course—writing."[2]

One can say Schuller is a damned fool, as his critics in the music business do. One can say he is a Parsifal. But one can also say he is a Don Quixote, tilting in vain at the juggernauts of popular culture and the entertainment industry, as he does in *Musings* and other forums. He admits the folly of it all. Deep down, he said, he is the eternal optimist.

[But] intellectually I worry a great deal about where this society, where this country, where this culture is going. I mean, it's going down the tube real fast. And it's gotten a lot worse since the time I wrote that book [*Musings*], for example, and it's now just at an absolute nadir. It worries the hell out of me, not so much for myself— I mean, I'm not going to live that much longer, you know—but for my kids, for younger people, for the next generations. Where is all this going, this horrendous trash on television? But aside from the trash the very fact that no good music of any kind has been on network television in the last thirty-five years: not Ellington, not Beethoven, with the one exception of when Bernstein conducted the Brandenburg Gate performance of the Ninth Symphony [for the fall of the Berlin Wall in 1989]. That wasn't a musical occasion; that was a political one. Can you believe such a thing, that Beethoven, the greatest composer, along with Mozart and Bach, has never been on network television? Now of course we have public television. But that's watched by at most five percent of the American public. So the fact that the American population for almost the last forty years has been educated by television—and that means network television; even cable is a relatively recent phenomenon—means that there has been this total cultural illiteracy created, because what isn't on television nowadays simply does not exist. Either it doesn't exist intrinsically or it doesn't exist in people's minds.

It is no accident that Schuller mentions Ellington in the same breath as Beethoven. The champion of Beethoven and Babbitt ranks Duke Ellington as one of music's giants, has performed with such jazz artists as Miles Davis, Dizzy Gillespie, and John Lewis, wrote a two-volume history of jazz (a third volume is forthcoming), led the ragtime revival, resuscitated ragtime king Scott Joplin's opera *Treemonisha*, wrote a jazz opera, *The Visitation*, and pioneered the "Third Stream" movement—he also gave it the name—fusing classical, jazz, and ethnic styles. "All musics are created equal" is his motto and the motto of GM Recordings, Inc. Perhaps it is that damned fool in him that makes Schuller the closest thing to a Renaissance man of music that the fragmented new millennium can claim.

Schuller lives in a four-story, twenty-room house on a heavily wooded suburban street a half mile—but seemingly a couple of counties removed—from the bumper-to-bumper bustle on Route 9 in Newton Centre, a tony suburb of Boston. (That spelling, "centre," and the landscape tell you you're in rock-ribbed New England.) Gray stone and red-painted wood on the outside, strewn with books, scores, tapes, notes, and scribbled-over manuscripts inside, the mansion also serves as Schuller's offices. When those rental vans rolled out of the circular driveway, they carried the work of about 175 composers, often in multiple volumes. The trove was large in both bulk and range: It included "Silent Night, Holy Night" in its original orchestration by composer Franz Gruber; Monteverdi's 1607 opera *L'Orfeo* in its realization by Schuller, and little-known works by Tallis, Haydn, Mozart, and Beethoven, along with major compilations of the work of such twentieth-century figures as Alec Wilder, Nikos Skalkottas, William Russo, and Schuller himself.

Schuller didn't have to kiss the collection good-bye. At his insistence Schirmer retained him as a consultant. He wanted to be sure the Margun and GunMar catalogs "wouldn't just be swallowed up in the maw of Schirmer and never be seen or heard of again."

Like his house, which he bought in 1967 on moving to Boston to become president of the New England Conservatory, Schuller has an aura of weathered solidity and a face more settled than aged. As he turned seventy-five, even leg problems did not perceptibly slow his pace as he scurried across the United States and Europe to conduct, lecture, and advise. The house has music in its mortar. There he and his wife, Marjorie, an amateur pianist and singer, raised their two sons, percussionist George and bassist Edwin, both jazz players. There, too, he engages in his chief nonmusical pastime—gardening.

Marjorie Black and Gunther Schuller met while she was a student at the Cincinnati Conservatory and he was a horn player beginning his career in the Cincinnati Symphony. They were married in 1948. In a long life together, she became the Eurydice to his Orpheus.

In 1992 Marjorie died. A few weeks later death claimed Gunther's father, a violinist in the New York Philharmonic and notable musician in his own right. For ten months afterward, Schuller was unable to compose. Then the dam burst. The result was *Of Reminiscences and Reflections,* which he composed in five four-hour mornings. It won him the Pulitzer in 1994. Into the orchestral fabric he wove references—not all of them recognizable—to the music Marjorie and he had heard and loved together. Their names are entwined in the names Margun, GunMar, and GM (the record label), though she was not active in the business. (Under Margun, Schuller published music licensed to Broadcast Music, Inc., for the collection of royalties. GunMar was similarly affiliated with the American Society of Composers, Authors, and Publishers.)

Schuller had been collecting music since the age of twelve. What started him on a publishing career was a friendship with Alec Wilder, whom he had known for about twenty years in New York before moving to Boston. Both men were Third Stream composers. Wilder, in fact, was first known as a popular-music composer, and some of his songs were recorded by Frank Sinatra.

As Schuller tells the story, Wilder's songs were much too sophisticated for the average pop singer to navigate. In time he became disillusioned with Tin Pan Alley and Hollywood and returned to his love of classical music, writing it "by the yard," though with a jazz influence. Most of these were occasional pieces written for Wilder's friends. You want a wind quintet, horn duet, or tuba trio? Okay, Wilder would sit down and write you one. "Anything you can think of," Schuller said, "mainly for instrumentalists and particularly for brass players and wind players, who were or became his friends."

But Wilder was "a totally unrealistic, unbusinesslike free spirit who loved to travel around the country in trains and read books by the dozens." He was never commissioned to write these pieces, nor did he accept money for them. His serious music didn't get published. Finally Harvey Phillips, a well-known tuba player and Wilder's best friend, volunteered to serve as publisher. Phillips managed to collect and publish a few items. But Wilder had been careless, giving away his music right and left, and Phillips was busy with his tuba clinics and tuba Christmases (seventy-five tubists getting together and playing carols in places such as New York's Rockefeller Center). Requests for the music went mostly unanswered.

Enter Gunther Schuller. Many of the would-be performers, knowing that he and Phillips were friends—Phillips had been his vice president at the New England Conservatory—called Schuller. "Gee, Gunther," they would say, "can you help out? We've been trying to get this bassoon trio [or whatever] that Alec wrote and we can't get an answer out of Harvey."

It just so happened that Schuller could help out. For some time he had been thinking of founding a publishing house. So he did just what Phillips had done, founding Margun Music in 1975. Wilder's instrumental output of about three hundred pieces—all falling between the stools of classical and jazz—became his Opus 1 as a publisher.

Word got around. Soon Schuller was receiving inquiries from composers whose music he had conducted over the years in New York and Boston and at Tanglewood—dozens and dozens of composers, of all stripes, and all hungry for publication. "And when I found a good piece or a good composer," he said, "I decided to publish it because I figured that most big publishers—Boosey and Hawkes, Schirmer, all those—would not take these young composers. And they didn't. They didn't take [Charles] Wuorinen, they didn't take [Harvey] Sollberger, they didn't take [Donald] Martino, any of these people." Only after they became known, partly through Schuller's efforts, did the big houses wake up and show interest.

All of this was done at Schuller's own expense in the twenty-room house, where he set up offices on the top floors. And he did it "at the very highest quality of production," spending up to $25,000 to produce a single work. There were occasional problems of cash flow, but somehow he always got by. He never stopped to draw up a budget or figure out the total cost. He and a small staff, which at the height of the publishing and recording activity totaled seven persons, did most of the work, farming out the actual engraving and printing of the scores.

What kept him going? Schuller said he inherited his energy from his mother but mainly it "was the joy of doing all that and the feeling of accomplishment: I'm doing something for my fellow human beings that no one else is doing."

Each publication has a story. Many are transcriptions Schuller made early in his career for ensembles, both classical and jazz, that he worked with; others are editions that he made for other publishers but never got into print. One is a Mozart sextet, a "Grande Sestetto Concertante" for strings. Mozart never wrote a sextet. This is a transcription of the famous Sinfonia Concertante, K. 364, for violin, viola, and orchestra, by Anton Stadler, the clarinetist for whom Mozart wrote his Clarinet Concerto and Clarinet Quintet. Violinist Louis Krasner, a friend of Schuller's until Krasner's death in 1995, discovered the parts in an antiquarian store in Vienna in the early 1930s. Krasner was there to commission Alban Berg's Violin Concerto, a twentieth-century landmark. Schuller later paired archival performances by Krasner of the Berg and Schoenberg violin concertos, both of which he premiered, on a GM compact disc. And so it went.

Other scores and parts came to Schuller because he became known as a "composer's widow's publisher." Putting it in a more kindly way, widows came to him after their composer-husbands' deaths, beseeching publication. If Schuller thought the music was good enough, he took it on. Louis Gruenberg, Claus Adam, and Antal Dorati—the last better remembered as a conductor—made it into his catalog that way.

In another damned-fool story, Schuller discovered and championed Nikos Skalkottas. Working in obscurity until his death in 1949, this Greek, who sat on the last stand of second violins in the Athens Symphony, composed about three hundred pieces, including lengthy concertos and symphonies. Little of his music was performed during his lifetime—little is performed today—and he heard hardly any of it.

"People thought he was crazy, writing all this music," Schuller said. Yet he studied with Schoenberg and Kurt Weill, and Schoenberg declared him his best student.

Schuller first heard about the composer from Dimitri Mitropoulos, a Greek conductor who had performed Skalkottas's music and was an early champion of Schuller's own music. After Skalkottas's death his son began creating an archive. A few pieces were published and a few performances followed, but the project faltered. At that point John Papaioannou, a pianist-musicologist, asked Schuller to take over the archive in the interest of publication. Convinced of the music's worth, Schuller spent "hundreds of thousands of dollars" in publishing it. Schuller's catalog lists forty publications, some of them made up of numerous pieces. Schuller went on to publish and conduct *The Return of Ulysses,* a twenty-five-minute orchestral work that he considers Skalkottas's most important composition.

By 2000 Schuller was engaged in recording all thirty-two of Skalkottas's solo piano pieces for GM. The music requires "an enormous mind and intellect" to play it, he said, and a technique to match. Idith Meshulum, a young Israeli living in New York, met the requirements.

"I took her on even before I heard her," Schuller said. "I just believed in her. That's the way I am. I'm crazy. We talked on the phone many times and I believed in her enthusiasm, this burning desire, belief in this music. And then when I started recording her, I tell you I found an absolute treasure. The girl makes no note mistakes in an entire session. *No wrong notes.*" If Schuller suggested changes in interpretive details or in such matters as pedaling, rhythm, or tempo, "next time she just did it."

Like other composers, Schuller accepts publication (and recording too) where he can get it. Many of his large-scale works have been published by such major houses as Schirmer/Associated Music Publishers and Universal Edition. But his own Margun-GunMar catalog lists about fifty of his compositions, mostly early, previously unpublished ones in small forms or for small ensembles. Many of these works are jazz.

There are a few precedents for this labor by one composer on behalf of others. Coincidentally, the earliest instance took place only about ten blocks from Schuller's house, although he didn't learn about it until he was well into his own project. The composer Arthur Farwell ran the Wa-Wan Press in Newton Centre from 1901 to 1912, publishing the work of thirty-six contemporary composers, including nine women, in finely designed and printed volumes, which had to be purchased by subscription. The press took its name from an Omaha Indian ceremony for peace, fellowship, and song; Farwell published colleagues who used American folk materials. After a few years, subscriptions fell off and Farwell had to give up. Schirmer bought him out.

Most of Farwell's composers are forgotten today, as is Farwell. A composer-publisher with greater success in reading the future was Henry Cowell, who for nearly twenty-five years, beginning in 1927, published his contemporaries' music in his New Music series (later called New Music Edition). Cowell concentrated on fellow Americans who were shaking off the bonds of the European tradition. He began with Carl Ruggles's *Men and Mountains,* which is still not for the fainthearted today. He went on to other modernists from both North America and South America, including Charles Ives, Ruth Crawford Seeger, and Carlos Chávez, but also published important works by such Europeans as Arnold Schoenberg, Anton Webern, and Edgard Varèse. Though warned off Ives by friends, Cowell published many of the New Englander's works; Ives, a successful insurance executive, in turn provided Cowell with financial support. (Ives also ventured into publication of some of his own music.) In another anticipation of Schuller's activities, Cowell founded New Music Quarterly Recordings in 1934 to give American composers a further outlet.

In 1938, during a period of new-music ferment in the United States and Europe, composers Aaron Copland, Virgil Thomson, Marc Blitzstein, and Lehman Engel formed the Arrow Music Company. Leasing the catalog of the Cos-Cob Press, which had been founded in 1929 to publish American composers, they published Cowell, Elliott Carter, Walter Piston, Roy Harris, William Schuman, Roger Sessions, and other modernists, along with Copland and Thomson themselves. But Arrow, too, succumbed to financial and administrative difficulties, and after three years most of the catalog went to Boosey and Hawkes.

Publication, including self-publication, will get a composer only so far. Someone has to buy or rent the material and perform it. As Schuller put it in a 1998 interview in the *New York Times,* recordings today, for better or worse, represent "the real publishing of music." The reason: "For most composers paper publication is almost meaningless, except in terms of rentals of parts.

To publish a string quartet, for example, is the most ridiculous thing in the world. To the few players that will want to perform it, a composer winds up giving copies away. Recordings offer some way to disseminate this stuff."[3]

It was with that dilemma in mind that Schuller founded GM Recordings in 1981 as an adjunct to his publishing venture. Though he later obtained outside funding, for the first fifteen years he kept the business going with annual infusions of $15,000 to $30,000 of his own money, doing the planning and editing and choosing artists and repertoire himself. The 2000 catalog listed works by about 100 classical composers and 150 jazz composers. The classicists range from Bach and Beethoven, whose works are performed by soloists Schuller favored or in unusual arrangements, to Bartók, Stravinsky, and beyond. Many of the big names of jazz, such as Jelly Roll Morton, Miles Davis, Charlie Parker, and Ornette Coleman, are there. Schuller is represented by twelve releases; both of his sons appear as jazz composers.

GM is not alone in specializing in recordings of contemporary composers. Many other small labels, such as Composers Recordings, Inc., New World, Albany, and Bridge, working in the shadow of such giants as Sony and BMG, devote themselves to new music, primarily American. Like GM, they rely mainly on subsidies. But the only operation comparable to GM in being the labor of one man is Bridge. It is run by composer-classical guitarist David Starobin, who is also eclectic in his choice of material.

Like anyone who takes a stand, Schuller has come under attack at various times for the composers he has supported. One of the controversies that still rankles is a 1983 squabble at Tanglewood over his programming in the influential Festival of Contemporary Music, which he oversaw for twenty years.

The trouble began when Paul Fromm, a Chicago wine importer who was the festival's chief patron since its founding, demanded a voice in the programming. He contended that Schuller was ignoring the latest trends in composition, chiefly minimalism and other stripped-down, sometimes pop-oriented styles employed by such composers as Philip Glass, John Adams, and Steve Reich. These "downtown" composers were reacting against the more complex "uptown" music in the post-Schoenberg tradition that Schuller supposedly favored. The Tanglewood administration supported Schuller on grounds that as director, the artistic decisions should be his. Fromm left in a huff, taking his money with him. Schuller was saddened; he and Fromm had been colleagues and friends for more than twenty years.

Despite the administration's support, criticism in the press struck a tender nerve. Specifically, John Rockwell of the *New York Times* sided with Fromm, arguing that there were important new composers to whom Schuller was turning a deaf ear. Schuller scoffs at the charge. Although he has been accused of being narrow-minded and ideological, he said, "the truth is absolutely opposite," and he has performed such minimalists as Louis Andriessen, Adams, and Reich. Paradoxically, he said, he has also been criticized for being too eclectic.

"After all," he pointed out, "I do go all the way from the most primitive jazz to the most advanced twelve-tone or whatever other kind of music you want to talk about. So I've always been that way. I have always lived by this ancient bromide that there are only two kinds of music, good music and bad music, and who cares what category or style it's in? I happen to be a twelve-tone composer. That doesn't make me blind to the beauty of some of Samuel Barber's music or anybody else's."

The quarrel with Rockwell went beyond programming. In his 1983 book, *All American Music: Composition in the Late Twentieth Century,* Rockwell criticized Schuller on ideological grounds. He said the new-music programming at Tanglewood was timid and cerebral and ignored "not just jazz and serious rock but even much of the experimental tradition" exemplified in the past by Ives and Cowell and more recently by Glass, Adams, and Reich.[4] Lumping Schuller in with Babbitt and other composers working in the post-Schoenberg, twelve-tone tradition, Rockwell said that "for the mountain of unlistenable academic exercises they did so much to inspire, and for the now widespread belief among laymen that *all* new music is repellent pedantry, they have much to answer for."[5] Schuller and other jazz-loving composers such as Mel Powell even "made a mess of 'third stream' music because they were not really comfortable as classicists with the jazz tradition."[6] Despite their roots in popular music, they went astray by seeking "to express their 'serious' selves through serialism [a highly formalized kind of twelve-tone music] and idioms borrowed from abroad." Their "formal compositions reflect that love [of jazz] all too rarely."[7]

It's true that Schuller's music may appeal more to the intellect than to the nerves or viscera. Schuller points out, however, that he has programmed and conducted Ives, Cowell, and other early experimentalists. In any case, the essential point remains: who cares what category or style it's in? The good-bad dichotomy is one Schuller has returned to again and again in his battle against popular culture and the kind of simplified, pop-oriented music that Rockwell espoused. All musics may be created equal, but just as not everybody grows up to be president, the latest pop hit or Philip Glass is not the equal of Mozart or Stravinsky.

There was an unexpected sequel to the programming ruckus.

A year after Fromm left in anger, Schuller cut his ties with Tanglewood, resigning as director of the Tanglewood Music Center, the festival's school, which presents the contemporary festival. He accused the administration of undermining his autonomy, and his insistence on the purity of the art, through commercial compromises. Among his complaints was the choice of conductors, mostly from the parent Boston Symphony's guest-conducting roster, for the student orchestra. His protégé Oliver Knussen, a composer-conductor from England, replaced him as new-music czar. But hard feelings remained. Once a Tanglewood mainstay and BSO–commissioned composer, Schuller was rarely seen or heard either in Symphony Hall or at the summer festival after his unceremonious exit.

Schuller was born with music in his veins. His grandfather was a bandmaster in Germany, and both of his German-immigrant parents were musical. His father, Arthur, was the principal violist in the Mannheim Opera Orchestra under Wilhelm Furtwängler before leaving Germany because of the ruinous inflation of the 1920s. He became principal second violinist of the New York Philharmonic and kept that position for forty-two years. Schuller's mother, Elsie, was an amateur pianist. For good measure, Schuller was born in 1925 on November 22, the feast of Saint Cecilia, the patron saint of music. He recalls New York City, his birthplace, as a "cultural paradise" all during his growing-up and early professional years. Good music—both classical and jazz—was to be had with a turn of the dial on the radio.

With a start like that, it was natural that the boy would receive a musical upbringing. But because he was mischievous as well as precocious, his parents sent him at age six to a private school in Germany, where the children had to sing chorales every morning and learn a musical instrument. Already fluent in German from speaking it at home, he also learned French and Latin. Later in life he was able to translate his two operas, *The Visitation* and *The Fisherman and His Wife,* into both French and German. He also became an honored visitor to Germany as a conductor, lecturer, and Ford Foundation scholar. Back in the Nazi era, however, Germany was not a healthy place to be, although the family was not Jewish. Brought back by his parents to New York at age eleven, he entered the Saint Thomas Choir School in

Manhattan as a boy soprano. He took up the flute and French horn, eventually dropping the flute.

He also became acquaintanced with jazz—accidentally, but fatefully. It happened at home, where only serious music was approved for listening. Turning the radio dial in search of some proper music, the schoolboy stumbled upon a Duke Ellington performance. It struck him like a thunderbolt. He was hooked for life.

When Schuller's voice changed to baritone, he transferred to a public high school and also attended the Manhattan School of Music, where he studied horn and theory. But with his experience he was an overachiever, too far advanced for his studies. He dropped out at sixteen to become a professional horn player. The future conservatory president and recipient of eleven honorary doctorates never finished high school or went to college.

It was wartime when Schuller went out into the world, horn in hand. Perhaps destiny decreed that he should make his professional debut in an epochal musical event. He was an extra horn player in the NBC Symphony under Arturo Toscanini in 1942 when they gave the first performance in the West of Shostakovich's *Leningrad* Symphony (no. 7), composed amid the German siege of the city and reflecting its agonies. Because of wartime sympathy with the Soviet Union and the story of the symphony's composition, it caused a sensation.

The next year Schuller was playing horn in the American Ballet Theater Orchestra. Fired for laughing at the principal horn player's dirty jokes and almost missing entrances during performances, he joined the Cincinnati Symphony as first horn, a position he held from 1943 to 1945. There he enjoyed his first major performance as a composer, playing the solo part in his own Horn Concerto no. 1. In 1945 he joined the Metropolitan Opera Orchestra. In 1950 he moved up to principal horn, remaining in that position until 1959 and simultaneously teaching horn and chamber music at the Manhattan School of Music.

All this time compositions were pouring from him. Like Mozart, who could compose in carriages during his travels, Schuller would write down his ideas on the subway. The alternative was to waste five hours a day in the two round trips—one for the rehearsal, the other for the performance—between home and opera house. He later learned to compose in airplanes, taxis, and hotel lobbies. (He says one of the reasons he can get so much work done is that he can go from one activity to another without the break that many musicians require.) His determination to become a composer showed itself early. As a guest artist on a nationally broadcast performance of the Schubert Octet in 1947, when he was twenty-two, Schuller was asked by the radio announcer how he would like to be introduced. "Just say, Gunther Schuller—composer!" he replied.[8] Among his works from the Met years is the 1959 *Seven Studies on Themes of Paul Klee,* an orchestral piece that is the closest he has come to a hit.

During the fifties Schuller was also pursuing his interest in jazz as a composer, arranger, and man with a horn. He performed in the last of Miles Davis's celebrated *Birth of the Cool* recording sessions in 1950, and with Davis and Gil Evans in their 1958 recording of Gershwin's *Porgy and Bess.* For several years he taught at the Lenox (Massachusetts) School of Jazz, where young musicians such as Ornette Coleman and Don Cherry studied with such veterans as Bill Evans, Jimmy Giuffre, and Dizzy Gillespie. From 1962 to 1965 he collaborated with John Lewis as coleader of Orchestra USA, which mixed classical works with jazz. He and Lewis also teamed in many of the latter's premiere performances and recordings.

Today it's common for musicians to switch back and forth between classical and jazz. Not so in the forties and fifties, Schuller recalls. Yet he was, in his own words, "working consistently with the greatest musicians on both sides of the musical fence. You cannot name anybody else who in 1945 was working consistently with Toscanini and Miles Davis or Pierre Monteux and Dizzy Gillespie. And I don't just mean one gig but over a period of twenty or thirty years."

What could be better than playing Siegfried's horn call or the voluptuous horn part in *Rosenkavalier* for a living night after night? Yet by 1959 this one-man vanguard was ready to resign from the Met orchestra and strike out on his own as a composer. He was encouraged by such successes as the New York Philharmonic's performance of two of his works, the *Dramatic Overture* and Symphony for Brass and Percussion, in a single year, 1956—an unheard-of honor for an unknown composer, he recalls. Dimitri Mitropoulos, his early champion, led both performances. In 1960 Mitropoulos followed them with the still little-known *Spectra,* a one-movement, four-section work that Schuller ranks among his finest. James Levine later recorded it for Deutsche Grammophon with the Chicago Symphony.

The Symphony for Brass was a "breakthrough piece," Schuller said. Now performed with some frequency in conservatories and universities, it was a nightmare in the difficulties it posed for players in the fifties. It also called for brass instruments beyond an orchestra's normal complement—

an extra expense that still frightens major orchestras. Broadcast nationally on the New York Philharmonic's regular Sunday afternoon radio program, the symphony attracted congratulatory letters from Aaron Copland and William Schuman. It was also recorded in the same year for the Jazz and Classical Music Society, which Schuller and John Lewis had founded. Jazz was on the other side of the long-playing disc. Mitropoulos, Schuller said, put him "on the map."

Schuller in turn helped to give jazz intellectual legitimacy. One of his major contributions was the 1957 creation of the Third Stream concept, fusing classical and jazz, and later ethnic, styles. Though the concept only formalized what he was already doing, it opened the way for other composers to continue and broaden the experiment. It also generated considerable controversy among musicians and critics who were doubtful that there was a true common ground. The term Third Stream has dropped from use as the idea of stylistic fusion has become commonplace. Now the widespread matching (and mismatching) of styles extends to lucrative crossover ventures like The Three Tenors' arena and television concerts and their commercial offshoots.

Meanwhile, Schuller the writer and educator was also keeping busy. His first book, *Horn Technique,* was published in 1962 by Oxford University Press, which eventually published his later writings as well. In 1961 he concluded a three-year series of radio programs, *The Scope of Jazz,* with critic Nat Hentoff and simultaneously launched a series of 153 weekly radio programs titled *Contemporary Music in Evolution,* all without pay. In these broadcasts, Milton Babbitt wrote, "listeners heard many of our names for the first—and probably the last—time."[9] The three years' worth of programs were picked up by seventy-two educational stations across the country, some of which ran them three times, for a total of nine years. There is nothing like it on radio, much less television, today.

In 1963, at the invitation of Aaron Copland and Erich Leinsdorf, who were head of composition studies and music director, respectively, Schuller went to Tanglewood to teach composition. For twenty-one years, until his resignation in 1984, he was a bulwark of the Boston Symphony Orchestra's summer home in the Berkshires of western Massachusetts. He succeeded Copland as head of the composition program in 1964, and in 1965 became director of contemporary music activities as well. In 1969 he was named festival codirector with Seiji Ozawa and Leonard Bernstein. Upon Ozawa's appointment as Boston Symphony director in 1973, Schuller became director of the Berkshire (now Tanglewood) Music Center, the festival's internationally recognized school for advanced studies. Joining various audition teams, he went around the country listening to all auditions—a total of about 1,500 annually—for the coveted 150 fellowships the music center awards each year. He also founded and directed the Festival of Contemporary Music, the festival-within-a-festival that became the most important such event on the East Coast and one of the most important in the country.

In 1964, a year after going to Tanglewood, Schuller joined the Yale School of Music faculty as an associate professor. Three years later he left Yale to begin his ten-year presidency of the New England Conservatory in Boston. He spearheaded a near doubling of student enrollment, strengthened the faculty, rescued the institution from the brink of insolvency, taught composition, brought contemporary opera to the performance program, and conducted the conservatory orchestra in forty-one concerts.

Among the faculty members he recruited were two violinists who had been important figures in the new-music scene in pre–World War II Vienna: Louis Krasner, who had commissioned the Berg Violin Concerto, and Rudolf Kolisch, founder of the Kolisch String Quartet. Schuller summoned both men out of retirement to pass along their firsthand knowledge of the music of Schoenberg, Berg, Webern, and Bartók, gained from the composers themselves. Another notable recruit was pianist Russell Sherman, whose freshly imagined cycle of the Beethoven piano sonatas was released on the GM label in the 1990s. Schuller also gave the once-staid institution its first degree program in jazz, four jazz repertory orchestras (including one each for Ellington and Paul Whiteman), the New England Conservatory Ragtime Ensemble, and the Third Stream Department (now the Contemporary Improvisation Department). As an arranger, conductor, and cheerleader with the ensemble, Schuller sparked a worldwide ragtime revival.

In 1968 came *Early Jazz: Its Roots and Musical Development,* the first volume of Schuller's projected three-volume history of jazz. *The Swing Era: The Development of Jazz: 1930–1945* followed in 1989, and the essay collection *Musings* was published in between, in 1986. For *The Swing Era,* which runs to nearly one thousand pages, Schuller managed the herculean feat of listening to thirty thousand recordings. His next book, *The Compleat Conductor,* which appeared in 1997, was based on another listening marathon: more than four hundred recordings of eight works from the standard symphonic repertoire, each minutely analyzed for adherence—or in most cases, nonadherence—to the composer's score.

Schuller sets forth his educational goals in *Musings*. (The title, by the way, is misleading. Gunther Schuller does not muse. He scrutinizes, analyzes, and philosophizes. He has twice read the Bible from cover to cover.) In a chapter titled "The Compleat Musician in the Complete Conservatory," originally given as a lecture on the centennial of the New England Conservatory in 1967, he calls for the musician to dedicate himself wholly, like a modern Parsifal, to his sacred quest. Schuller laments that although we have Total cereal and total serialization (the extreme of twelve-tone composition—chuckle, chuckle), there are few total musicians. Later utterances make it clear that in his view, the situation has only worsened.

Instead of total musicians, Schuller says, "we have specialists—or worse than that: we have musicians who *think* they are specialists, who, though they are not particularly special in their chosen area, are at the same time totally oblivious of any other area." A conservatory must provide not just technical training but also a milieu in which students "try to absorb as much music across the board and in as much depth as possible, and try to integrate all of these ideas into a single personal conception."[10]

Schuller gives an example of the horrors of specialist training. He had recently come from several full days of instrumental auditions in which he heard more than fifty young musicians at the professional, postgraduate, and undergraduate levels. (Perhaps this was one of his rounds of Tanglewood auditions.)

"Of that number I am sorry to report no more than perhaps 5 percent seemed to have any idea of why they were playing music, what a musical phrase meant—indeed, what constituted a musical phrase—and what the expressive and intellectual range of music can really be. For 95 percent of them it was merely a matter of pushing down certain keys at certain times, moving arms or adjusting embouchures [placement of the lips] or whatever was involved in their instrument, to perform what appeared to be a purely mechanical operation. The whole sense of the joy of music, the beauty of music, of the ability to communicate through music, was absent."

If the computer takes over the world, Schuller says, it will not be because of any composer's intent—this at a time when more and more composers were turning to the computer for a wider sound palette—but "because the passivity and utter boredom of the player will have reached such a point that he might as well be replaced by the computer, for at least the computer is efficient."[11] Like his resignation from Tanglewood, this is vintage Schuller, a jeremiad against a world hijacked by barbarians, hucksters, and philistines. Nor is the demand for quality, whether in the classroom, the media, or the popular arts, a matter of elitism versus populism, as is commonly claimed, he says elsewhere in *Musings:*

"Indeed the elitism-versus-populism argument is completely mythical: a polemical sleight-of-words invented by clever ignoramuses to becloud the real issue: namely, that quality, creativity, and high craftsmanship can and do exist in all forms and categories of music. So can and do their opposites: mediocrity and absence of quality. *No* form of musical expression is either inherently blessed with quality or intrinsically devoid of it."[12]

After the conservatory and Tanglewood, Schuller held no major institutional affiliations. By then he had his conducting, publishing, and recording enterprises, jazz history, and a steady flow of commissions to occupy him during what for anyone else would have been retirement. He also served on endless committees, juries, and boards, including the National Endowment for the Arts Council and its panels. In addition, Schuller continued to reap the rewards of a lifetime of service to his art. He received the Alice M. Ditson Conducting Award for unselfish championship of fellow composers (1970), three Grammy Awards (1975, 1976, and 1985), the George Peabody Medal for contributions to American music (1982), the Sonneck Society's Irving Lowens Award for distinguished contributions to scholarship in American music (1985), Columbia University's William Schuman Award for lifetime achievement in American composition (1989), a MacArthur Foundation "genius" award (1991), *Down Beat* magazine's Lifetime Achievement Award (1993), a Pulitzer Prize and the Broadcast Music Industries Lifetime Achievement Award (1994), and the Gold Medal in Music from the American Academy of Arts and Letters (1997). In 1998 he was inducted into the American Classical Music Hall of Fame on the inaugural roster.

As his other activities took up more of his time, Schuller gave up the horn in 1963 and jazz composition shortly after. In the mid-1990s, however, he returned to jazz composition for the first time in thirty years to collaborate with tenor saxophonist Joe Lovano on a Blue Note recording, *Rush Hour on 23rd Street.* It is a typical Schuller project: jazz classics and pop standards rub shoulders with Lovano and Schuller originals. Schuller conducts, a string and wind ensemble features Lovano's sax, and the rhythm section has Schuller's sons Ed on bass and George on drums.

There have been countless tributes to Schuller as an educator, including those eleven honorary doctorates. But in a conversation with *Down Beat* magazine, Lovano and Schuller suggest that Schuller has been an educator in a broader sense, not just in the classroom but by opening the ears of other musicians—and thus of audiences—to new possibilities in music. Lovano told interviewer Bob Blumenthal, "I was inspired by Gunther's music to open up my horizons and concepts of using different timbres and sounds around me." He wanted to perform pieces by Duke Ellington, Ornette Coleman, Thelonious Monk, and Charles Mingus, for which—as in jazz generally—there is no written music. Because Schuller had known and worked with those composers, Lovano had him orchestrate the recorded originals.

"I didn't want to just do an album of some orchestrated songs," Lovano said. "I wanted to get deeper into the beauty of the music and where the tunes came from."

Schuller responded: "I wanted to not only challenge the musicians but also to raise the question of 'whither goest jazz?' in terms of extended form and new forms. After not doing something like this for thirty years, I wanted to break new ground for how an eleven-minute piece might be structured, including the entire range of possible expressions. Not in a way where you say, 'Here comes the jazz, here comes the classical.' Not as segmentation but where it all forms one unit, whether written or improvised, coming out of the germinal concept."[13]

In 1995 *Down Beat*'s critics voted *Rush Hour* the best jazz album of the year. Also in 1995 the *Musical America* classical yearbook crowned Schuller Composer of the Year and Germany awarded him its Commander's Cross of the Order of Merit for building bridges between the United States and Germany. Music, indeed, for Schuller knows no boundaries.

Every leader inspires followers. Timothy Geller and Richard Pittman are among the many who have hearkened to Schuller's call.

Geller grew up in Colorado and studied composition at the Cleveland Institute of Music and Southern Methodist University. He had a good teacher, Donald Erb, but no connection with the East Coast, where most of the country's music business—artists' management, concert bookings, publications, recordings, grants, awards—gets transacted. He was, as he put it, "not part of the party."

Then he applied to Tanglewood to study. Schuller examined his music and accepted him for the summer of 1984, Schuller's last at the festival and school. It is a testament to Schuller's openness and fairness, Geller said, that

"I could come from nowhere and he could accept me as a student at Tanglewood, just on the strength of my music. It was like a gift from heaven." Thanks to Schuller, he became part of the party.

The soft-spoken Geller is far from the best-known of the composers Schuller has helped, but his story is emblematic. He was broke when he arrived at Tanglewood. Though students were discouraged from working, it happened that Schuller, who has never driven a car, needed a driver. Geller got the job. Traveling to and from Schuller's house, he got to know the director, and vice versa.

Geller was "very wary" at first. He had an old, beat-up Datsun station wagon and didn't know how the esteemed conductor and educator would take to being chauffeured around in this wreck. If Schuller noticed, he didn't care. He invited Geller to come to GM Recordings in the fall and become its general manager and director of production and art. Putting in twenty to thirty hours a week on the job, Geller not only had a way of earning money, but soon was dealing regularly with music producers and well-known composers such as Babbitt and George Perle. Performances, publication, recording, commissions, prizes, and grants followed for the young composer. Schuller, he said, offered "the deepest and most powerful kind of influence, which really has to do with who you know and who knows you."

Schuller published and recorded Geller's *Where Silence Reigns,* a setting of part of Rainer Maria Rilke's *Duino Elegies,* for baritone and chamber ensemble. (On the GM release, Sanford Sylvan is the soloist and Schuller conducts the Griffin Music Ensemble of Boston.) Schuller also recommended his protégé for the National Endowment for the Arts grant that made the recording possible. With Schuller's support Geller also won a Guggenheim Fellowship and a Charles Ives Scholarhip from the American Academy and Institute of Arts and Letters. Associated Music Publishers took him on for publication.

The relationship also had a personal side. When Geller went to work in Boston, he was living rent-free as a house sitter in the home of a prominent arts patron. After he had been at GM for a year, the woman decided to sell her house. What to do? Geller could not afford to pay rent elsewhere. The landlord–arts patron took up her boarder's cause. At a dinner with her and Geller, Schuller and his wife agreed to take the young man in. He lived on the second floor, worked on the third floor, and ate lunch with the Schullers on the first floor.

Even earlier Geller got a taste of his boss's pliancy. After only four months at GM, Geller won a two-month residency at the MacDowell Colony, the artists' retreat in Peterborough, New Hampshire. Though he was terrified to ask for a leave so soon after starting the job, the opportunity was too big to turn down. According to Geller, Schuller "did not blink an eye" at the request. He merely needed to know when Geller would be gone and what kind of interim arrangements to make.

Geller left GM after three years to concentrate on his own work but returned twice on an interim basis to help out. He lasted only a year in the Schuller household. The arrangement "was too close for me really," he explained, "because it got so that I didn't have any other kind of life. But I also got a taste firsthand for what it was like to be someone who lived, ate, and breathed music twenty hours a day." Schuller was never actually Geller's teacher, but from him Geller says he learned a crucial lesson: "how an artist interacts in a professional way with what the profession should be."

Going the artistic rather than commercial route, Geller said, "puts you in a precarious place." But Schuller was somebody who had done it. "He's done it his whole life and succeeded in doing it. And every day he's alive and working in the world, he's saying, 'You see, you don't have to compromise your values and you can exist in this world.' What a huge lesson."

Richard Pittman, a conductor active today in the Boston area and in Europe, went to the New England Conservatory at Schuller's invitation in 1968, the second year of Schuller's presidency. He came from the Eastman School of Music to start a second school orchestra while Schuller led the existing group.

Wherever he had been before, at Eastman or in Washington or Hamburg, Pittman had founded and led performing ensembles—even an opera troupe in Hamburg, home of one of Germany's major opera companies. In his second year in Boston, he realized that the city had no professional new-music group. That led him to found the Boston Musica Viva, the ensemble with which he has been most closely associated. As director ever since, as well as director of community orchestras in and around Boston, he has maintained close ties with Schuller, regularly performing his music and the music of composers he has championed. But like Schuller, Pittman is no specialist. He and his freelance players perform all kinds of music, old and new, in all sorts of combinations, from chamber ensembles to symphony orchestras. You understand new music better if you have a feeling for Schubert, he said. And vice versa.

Pittman thinks Schuller learned his idealism and love of music from his father, Arthur, "a marvelous man and an ideal orchestra player" whom Pittman got to know at the conservatory. After fleeing Germany in the 1920s and settling in New York, Pittman recalled, Arthur Schuller chanced to meet a friend while he was walking along the street. The friend told him the New York Philharmonic was holding auditions for a principal second violinist. Arthur hurried over to Carnegie Hall and won the job. During the forty-two years he held it, he "never lost his enthusiasm for music," Pittman said. Even in retirement he continued to freelance, serving frequently as concertmaster of orchestras.

The first debt of gratitude the city and world owe the son—"the really lasting debt"—is for his compositions, Pittman believes. At times Schuller has had to rush commissions through to meet deadlines, Pittman said, but when he has had enough time to work carefully, the music is of the highest quality. Pittman believes that thanks also are due for "all these things he has got involved in that most people in the music world would say he's crazy to do, like his publishing company and his record company. But this comes out of his conscience about the state of music and what he thinks is important. He saw certain composers going unpublished that he thought really needed to be published. And since nobody else was doing it, typically of him, he threw himself into that and did it himself. I have a lot of friends in the music publishing business who shake their heads over his willingness to take on this enormous burden. But I think that's typical of his sense of responsibility and his capacity for work."

As a longtime observer of the Boston scene, Pittman also credits Schuller with raising standards at the New England Conservatory and thus in the city. He said that eminent faculty members such as Rudolf Kolisch and Louis Krasner, both pivotal figures in twentieth-century music, provided a "tremendous resource" for students and the community. (They also, Pittman thinks, reflected Schuller's appreciation of older men, arising out of admiration for his father.) Pittman remembers Arthur Schuller attending many of the conservatory concerts. At a program by the repertory orchestra, which Pittman conducted, Arthur was amazed by a performance of Stravinsky's *Petrushka*. In his days the New York Philharmonic couldn't perform it as well, even under the great Toscanini, the father said. Such were the standards the son inspired.

Pittman stayed on at the conservatory seven years after Schuller left but found the vitality drained, the school no longer offering "an idealistic approach to music, a really caring approach to music." But during Schuller's years, Pittman said, the conservatory turned out many musicians, such as conductor Craig Smith, who went on to enrich Boston's musical life And while Schuller never taught composition at the conservatory, Pittman credits him with being a "brilliant" composition teacher at Tanglewood. Likewise, in his service on many boards and panels, he was a "positive force."

When Schuller turned seventy-five in 2000, Pittman was a leader in the celebrations. Musica Viva gave two birthday salutes. The first, in April, offered three Schuller works from various periods: *Romantic Sonata* (1941/ 1983), *Sand Point Rag* (1986), and *Sonata Serenata* (1978). In a conversation with Pittman, Schuller reminisced about his career, recounting among other things his discovery of jazz and visits to New York's jazz clubs on his way home from playing at the Met. In November, five days before Schuller's birthday, Musica Viva repeated *Sonata Serenata* in a program dedicated to Schuller and entitled Improper Bostonians.

Four days after his birthday Schuller returned to the Pro Arte Chamber Orchestra, which he had conducted many times during their twenty-one-year relationship. He conducted three works, none of them his own. One, however, was the Concertino for Contrabass and Orchestra by Theodore Antoniou, a longtime associate, with Edwin Barker, the Boston Symphony's principal bassist, as soloist. The piece was composed as a birthday tribute for the occasion. Rather than stand to share in the audience's applause, the orchestra twice chose to remain seated and join in the accolades for the guest of honor.

There were other birthday celebrations—in Boston, Cologne, Switzerland, London, Syracuse, and Spokane, plus three in San Francisco's Bay Area. At each Schuller coached, rehearsed, and conducted his own music. "My entire life came to a standstill," he happily complained. In the midst of it all, he made his annual trek to Spokane, where he had a long-standing relationship with the Spokane Symphony, to lead a two-week Bach festival. That year's programming also included Beethoven's *Missa Solemnis*.

Back in Boston, the birthday celebrations culminated in a Third Stream–style marathon by the Pro Arte Chamber Orchestra on March 18, 2001, with guest artists from the worlds of classical and jazz. Recounting what the *New York Times* described as "his stubborn commitment to principles," Schuller told how it had taken him thirteen years to find four bassists to play his 1947 Quartet for Double Basses.[14] The tributes also included Russell Sherman playing a Brahms intermezzo, a favorite of Marjorie

Schuller's, and Schuller conducting his own *Lament for M,* a memorial in Third Stream style. Saxophonist Joe Lovano and Schuller's sons, Ed on bass and George on drums, joined in the performance. In the *Times* jazz critic Ben Ratliff described Schuller as "a model of catholic tastes" who "has championed a good deal of new music, much of which has an aggressiveness or intellectuality or overall tetchiness that ensures it a difficult reception."[15] In *The Boston Globe* Richard Dyer wrote that Schuller's music "brings many worlds together on the common ground of human feeling."[16] (Schuller's old friend and jazz colleague John Lewis was to have joined in the celebration, but canceled because he was seriously ill.)

In the summer of 2000 Tanglewood also toasted Schuller, its departed standard-bearer. He made one of his rare postresignation appearances for a student performance of his *Six Renaissance Lyrics,* one of nine works on a program in the Festival of Contemporary Music. But 2000 also marked the seventy-fifth birthdays of two Europeans, Luciano Berio and Pierre Boulez, and though they did not attend, each was honored with a program of his own. One was a marathon devoted to all fourteen of Berio's *Sequenzas* for single instruments; the other featured Boulez's recent *Sur Incises* for chamber ensemble. (The year was also the centennial of Aaron Copland's birth, an occasion duly noted in other music center events.) Schuller's position as one among nine on a program, despite his greater importance in his native country and his far larger role at Tanglewood than the two Europeans, confirmed his status as an outsider, both at Tanglewood and in the mainstream concert world. Proper in his dealings with musicians such as Geller and Pittman, he is indeed an improper Bostonian, if "improper" means an unwillingness to play the game by the market's rules.

Concert biographies say that Schuller has conducted many of the leading orchestras of the world. That's the kind of puffery that those biographies are supposed to say. It's true that he has conducted the Berlin Philharmonic, BBC Symphony, French Radio Orchestra, Boston Symphony Orchestra, and other name bands in the United States and Europe, often arriving with an American work in his suitcase. And clearly he has one of the best ears in the business. Milton Babbitt recalls a Schuller performance of Schoenberg's *Gurrelieder,* which calls for a gargantuan orchestra and chorus with numerous vocal soloists. "At a particularly dense point in the score," Babbitt writes, "with the full orchestra—including seven horns—loudly involved, Gunther stopped the music, looked up from his score, and asked, 'Where was that note in the third horn?' " Indeed, the third horn's chair was empty. The culprit was engaged elsewhere in an urgent performance of a more physical nature.[17]

Timothy Geller recalls another feat. While working at GM, he watched Schuller mixing takes of a jazz recording. Although each take was improvised separately from the others, Schuller, with almost imperceptible effort, spliced them to produce a seamless whole.

As with much else about Schuller, what the public sees and hears is only the tip of the iceberg. In the classical arena, Schuller conducts mainly new-music ensembles, orchestras interested in exploring byways as well as highways of the repertoire, and university and conservatory groups. On campuses he works in a meet-the-composer setting, lecturing and teaching the music as well as conducting it. In Boston he guest-conducts the new-music ensemble Collage, of which he is a former codirector (along with fellow composer John Harbison), and the Pro Arte Chamber Orchestra. He was often on the podium during his years at the conservatory and Tanglewood. At Tanglewood he rarely conducted the parent Boston Symphony, which generally draws its conductors from the international celebrity circuit. Instead, he conducted student ensembles, primarily in new music. The Tanglewood years are memorable for his performances of such landmark or exotic twentieth-century works as Karlheinz Stockhausen's partly electronic *Hymnen (the Third Region)*, Edgard Varèse's *Amériques*, Igor Markevich's *Le nouvel âge* (in its American premiere), Jean Barraqué's *Le temps restitué*, and Copland's *Connotations*. Such performances took place in the Festival of Contemporary Music. Many were world or American premieres.

For Schuller, in other words, conducting is just one facet of a many-sided approach to an art inexhaustible in its dimensions. In the contemporary festival's program book for what proved to be his last Tanglewood summer, 1984, he emphasized both the educational aspects of such performances and their broader implications:

"Although the contemporary music festival of necessity requires in its preparations an uncommon concentration of effort and involvement, it is experienced—by the weight and importance it is given—as an intrinsic, indispensable element of each summer's overall training. It is viewed and experienced not as something separate from ordinary professional musical life but as part of the ongoing continuum of musical history. New music at Tanglewood represents no more and no less than the latest manifestation of that historical continuity."

Schuller began conducting after he left the Met. Having seen for fifteen years how other conductors did the job, often not to his liking, he set out to see if he could do it better, or at least as well as these established figures. In one of his earliest ventures, he founded and led the Twentieth-Century Innovations concerts from 1962 to 1965 in New York's Carnegie Hall, premiering or performing hundreds of pieces from the United States and Europe. He says the series marked the return of new-music ensembles to New York for one of the few times—possibly the first time—since Aaron Copland and Roger Sessions gave the influential Copland-Sessions Concerts from 1928 to 1931. By the turn of the century, Schuller was able to count twelve such ensembles in Boston and at least seven in New York.

Again Babbitt describes the scene: "These concerts of chamber works (but often chamber works on the scale of Webern's Five Pieces for Orchestra and the Schoenberg First Chamber Symphony) were—as was to become characteristic of all of his musical activities where possible—all Gunther. He chose the works, the performers, and his administrators. And even then he arrived at the first rehearsal of a new work with the composition thoroughly in his ear and head, as well as a strategy for rehearsal determined by the composition's particular properties. Never did one hear Gunther say, 'Let's take it from the top,' and then proceed to allow the work to crawl its way to the bottom, whereupon the conductor would suggest helpfully, 'Let's try it again.' . . . Of course Gunther was demanding but no more so than the music he conducted."[18]

Schuller's greatest popular success was his almost accidental rediscovery of ragtime music. It began with an attempt to stage *Treemonisha*, the forgotten 1911 opera by Scott Joplin, in 1972 at the conservatory. Because the copyright was tied up in litigation, Schuller could not obtain performing rights. But upon learning of his interest in the black composer, Vera Brodsky Lawrence, who had published Joplin's collected works the year before, passed along the supposedly lost *Red Back Book* of Joplin-era rags. Schuller edited the orchestrations in the book, orchestrated dozens of other rags, and founded the New England Ragtime Ensemble at the conservatory to place the novel repertory before the public. The debut concert, with Schuller conducting, was such a hit that he repeated it at the Smithsonian Institution in Washington. He and his student band made the first of their two GM recordings two days later ("a delightful bevy of rags old and new rousingly led by maestro Gunther Schuller," the cover proclaimed).[19]

Word got around. Angel Records, a giant in the industry, asked Schuller to make a recording in New York with some of his big-name jazz friends. Schuller said he would make the recording at the conservatory with his student players or not at all. Angel gambled. The 1973 album sold thirty thousand copies in a week, became Angel's all-time best-seller, won a Grammy, and became the basis for the musical score for the Robert Redford–Paul Newman movie *The Sting*, which fed the flames of a worldwide ragtime revival. Schuller was asked to do the film score but was too busy. In a supreme example of lèse-majesté, Marvin Hamlisch, who did the score from Schuller's arrangements, never credited either Joplin or Schuller. Hamlisch won an Oscar.

*Treemonisha* tells the story of a black girl who teaches the lesson of understanding and forgiveness to her people on a plantation in post–Civil War Arkansas, the time and place of Joplin's childhood. Because in the early twentieth century nobody believed a black man could write a genuine opera, *Treemonisha*, with its earthy, dance-driven score, lay unpublished, unperformed, and unmourned. Eventually Joplin himself published a piano-vocal score, still without getting a professional performance. This failure probably contributed to his early death.

The appeal to Schuller was obvious: a neglected work from the earliest days of jazz, begging, like Babbitt's *Transfigured Notes,* for a knight on horseback to rescue it. *Treemonisha* had its world premiere in Schuller's orchestration in 1975. He conducted the Houston Grand Opera in a production that attracted a hundred thousand viewers, at first on an outdoor stage, where it was presented free of charge. For a week crowds of ten thousand and more cheered and danced in the aisles. From Houston, Schuller took the production to Washington's Kennedy Center and New York. It was to have had six weeks of performances on Broadway, but a strike shortened the run. Deutsche Grammophon, another industry giant, issued an original-cast recording with Schuller conducting.

After that major exhumation there were two others in 1989, one jazz, the other classical. Jazz bassist-composer Charles Mingus's concert-length *Epitaph* had never been performed while he was alive. Schuller edited the work and, with the help of Sue Mingus, the composer's widow, and the Ford Foundation, produced a full score and parts. He also formed an all-star jazz band, which included trumpeter Wynton Marsalis, to take the performance around the world.[20]

Also in 1989, Schuller conducted and recorded (on GM) John Knowles

Paine's 1872 oratorio, *Saint Peter,* a work never performed before, with Boston's Pro Arte Chamber Orchestra and Back Bay Chorale. The first chairman of music at Harvard University, Paine was a New Englander under the spell, like other American composers of the time, of the German Romantics—especially, in Paine's case, of Mendelssohn's *Elijah* and *Saint Paul.* In a commentary for the recording, Schuller declared, paraphrasing Alexander Pope, that the proper study of American music is the study of *all* American music:

"The neglect of our earlier American music has long been an unfortunate blemish on our musical life. Ignored by performers, orchestras, and conductors, the first century or so of American musical culture has for too many years been the private reserve of a few historians and musicologists (even far too few of them), leaving the impression that American music somehow began with Aaron Copland in the 1920s, and that anything created before was unworthy or irrelevant."[21] The message was sure to rile, or, more likely, be ignored by, an emerging generation of composers who believed that *any* music created before the Beatles was unworthy or irrelevant.

Back in the world of jazz, Schuller served from 1991 to 1997 as codirector (with David Baker of the Indiana University School of Music) of the Smithsonian Jazz Masterworks Orchestra. Congress created the offshoot of the Smithsonian Institution with a $220,000 line-item budget appropriation, engineered by the Black Caucus; it was the first such recognition of a musical venture, Schuller remembers. Again scholarship joined hands with performance. Working from performances preserved on records but never written down, Schuller transcribed classic or neglected jazz works to turn them into repertory items. The orchestra then toured them around the country. The conservatory-style codification of text and performance details did not always sit well with jazz fanciers, for whom jazz (unlike classical music) depends largely on improvisation. In a commentary in the *Wall Street Journal,* John McDonough said Schuller took his "mandate" for preservation "further than most in jazz would dare, bringing to Duke Ellington and Louis Armstrong something of the historical radicalism that Roger Norrington [the early-music conductor], in his sphere, has applied to Beethoven and Mozart."[22]

A summation of Schuller's forty-year involvement with jazz came with the 1996 release of *The Birth of the Third Stream,* a Sony/Columbia compact disc combining the classic albums *Music for Brass* (1956) and *Modern Jazz Concert* (1957). Schuller conducted; the composers and performers included

Miles Davis, John Lewis, George Russell, Charles Mingus, and Jimmy Giuf-fre, along with Schuller's colleague Milton Babbitt and Brandeis University's Harold Shapero.

But, critics like McDonough ask, isn't there an element of condescension—of the dust of the academy—in a white man's colonization and codification of what originated as black American music? It's one thing for Norrington to try to re-create the sounds of Beethoven with a period-instrument or-chestra and observance of the often-questioned metronome markings. Isn't it another thing entirely to reduce an art based on the impulse of the mo-ment to a written-out canon like Beethoven's?

Not so, says Schuller. Over the years he has maintained that he is ex-panding the opportunities for listening, composing, and performing in a so-ciety that for most of its existence has taken its cues from European culture. When talented musicians who are "lovingly and respectfully devoted to ear-lier jazz" play it in live performance, he says, they add a dimension that can't be heard on the recordings; the Masterworks Orchestra preserves great compositions that would die if not performed live as they were in the begin-ning. Schuller's enthusiasm is both visible and audible. To watch him con-duct Ellington, Joplin, or Mingus is to see a man jiving.

Schuller is no fan of his brethren of the symphonic baton. His 1997 book *The Compleat Conductor* casts a jaundiced eye at just about the whole lot, from the early twentieth century on. His complaint is willful violation of holy scripture—namely, the composer's score.

After a bar-by-bar scrutiny of more than four hundred recordings of eight standard symphonic works, Schuller comes to the "sad conclusion" that they add up to "hundreds (if not thousands) of recordings and perfor-mances whose main and common characteristic is that they ignore virtually all the basic information in the scores of the great composers." Faced with "incontrovertible, detailed evidence of how conductors mis-interpret, over-interpret, under-interpret, the great works of Beethoven, Brahms, Strauss, Tchaikovsky, Ravel, Schumann—and by extension the rest of the classical-romantic repertory"—Schuller confesses that he was originally tempted to entitle the book "Nobody Gives a Damn About the Composer." He now finds that title "rather mild. It hardly does justice to the situation and the ac-tual state of affairs."[23]

Few conductors escape the lash. Of the recent crop, Carlos Kleiber, Bernard Haitink, Stanislav Skrowaczewski, Otmar Suitner, John Eliot Gardner, and James Levine come off relatively unscathed, with Christoph von Dohnányi and Claudio Abbado squeaking through. From an earlier era, Arturo Toscanini, Fritz Reiner, Antal Dorati, Albert Coates, Felix Weingartner, and Erich Kleiber survive the test (although Schuller becomes a mite disillusioned with even his former god Wilhelm Furtwängler). To Schuller these figures "are the true keepers of the flame of musical, artistic integrity, without sacrificing one iota of the drama, excitement, and emotion that all great music contains and seeks to communicate."[24]

The rest, in Schuller's opinion, range from raging egotists to outright charlatans. (Understandably, Leonard Bernstein, the country's most celebrated baton-waver, score-twister, and podium acrobat, falls by the wayside. He often said that when he conducted, he *became* the composer. That gave him license to treat the score—anybody's score—however he chose.) Furthermore, Schuller says a conductor is unlikely to succeed unless he performs new music as part of his daily diet, for there the true test is to be found: the ability to penetrate to the heart of a score without falling back on performing tradition or other external guideposts to the composer's intent.

It all makes perfectly good sense: follow the composer's instructions and you can't go wrong. Why, then, did Paul Griffiths, writing in the *New York Times Book Review*, compare Schuller's logic to "using a fish net to capture sunbeams" and then being "surprised by the meagerness of his haul"?[25]

Primarily, Griffiths and other reviewers pointed out, because the printed score can be no more than a blueprint to such matters as tempo, dynamics, and phrasing. In actual performance, especially as opposed to a recording, countless details—from the state of the conductor's digestion or the lighting onstage to coughing in the audience or its warmth of applause—will give rise to countless fluctuations in tempo, dynamics, and shaping of the line. Indeed, the alternative is a metronomic, even mechanical performance, as Schuller clearly recognizes. It also happens often in new-music performance, as Schuller notes, that a composer will prefer and adopt a performer's ideas of how passages might go. Stravinsky is a famous case of a composer who disregarded his tempo markings when conducting his own works. What do these deviations say about how literally the conductor should take the printed page?

Discretion, Schuller argues, begins where the composer's instructions leave off. For this reason he prefers a "realization" (also, he points out, Ravel's and Sibelius's preferred term) of a score to an "interpretation"; interpretation implies an excess of discretion on the conductor's part. He quotes Susan Sontag: "To interpret is to impoverish, to deplete . . . in order to set up a shadow world of 'meanings.' "[26]

In *The Compleat Conductor* Schuller devotes 122 pages alone to ninety-one recordings of Beethoven's Fifth Symphony, declaring it, "alas, one of the least understood and most consistently misinterpreted" of symphonies.[27] Not content with reading offenders the riot act, he hired eighty-five of New York's best musicians for a freelance orchestra (much as he did for Babbitt's *Transfigured Notes*) to record Beethoven's Fifth and Brahms's First. They spent twelve hours, at his expense, at the task. In the liner notes for the GM compact disc, Schuller concedes that the performances are diamonds in the rough compared to the dozens of machine-tooled versions by glamorous conductors and orchestras available in stores. But, he says, this is how the job should be done:

"I consider it a profound privilege to have somehow had the opportunity to record these two great masterpieces, to present them in renderings whose prime interpretational purpose and *raison d'être* is to pay full, total, unswerving, loving respect to their creators' wonderfully precise and exact notations. If these are also inspired performances, it will be only because such inspiration came to us not from some previous performing tradition ('early' or 'late'), or from someone's previous interpretation or recording, but *from* and *through* the music itself."[28]

While the music comes through unfiltered by "interpretation," it is precisely the personal stamp that listeners might miss. Schuller argues, for instance, against slowing down for the triumphal return of the chorale in the brasses at the end of the Brahms First; Brahms, he says, indicates no change in tempo. Yet generations of conductors and listeners have felt a need for a slower tempo—not because it has become a tradition, but because it seems to express something intrinsic in the music. Indeed, fluctuation of tempo was common in the Romantic era. Brahms himself was known to indulge in it as a conductor and pianist, even in his own works.

For such reasons Griffiths and other reviewers poked holes in Schuller's argument. Griffiths pointed out, for instance, that Schuller by his own admission once found performances by Furtwängler and other fallen idols deeply satisfying and meaningful. "So are those satisfactions and meanings now to be discounted because of discrepancies from what is printed in the score?" On the contrary, Griffiths declared, the authority of the score "knows various levels, and there is a whole rainbow of shades between fidelity and alteration." But if Schuller's case won't hold up, Griffiths said, "the huge task of constructing it has led him into many valuable reflections. One may lament his use of the score as a weapon to belabor so many conductors and even kill off erstwhile heroes, but his knowledge of it—in the eight principal cases and more besides—is immense. He is astute in detecting performance problems and no conductor, whether hoping for compleatness or not, could read this book without learning a huge amount."

Is there an element of righteousness in Schuller's case, of showing that he has grasped the truth and everyone else has botched the job? No one else would go to the trouble of listening to four hundred recordings and writing a treatise showing how just about everything in them is wrong. It isn't only because Schuller lacks the charisma or showmanship of a Bernstein that he has never become a frequent flier to the famous podiums of the world. It's also because of the Parsifal-like purity of his quest. The very qualities that make him valuable as a conductor, composer, educator, polemicist, and thorn in the side put off the people and organizations that could benefit most from his teachings and preachings. That's what people in the music industry mean when they say Gunther Schuller is his own worst enemy.

Schuller is self-taught as a composer. Or rather, he says, the orchestra was his teacher. He grew up with the sound of the New York Philharmonic in his ear because of his father's work. During his own years of playing in various orchestras—especially the fifteen years at the Met—a feeling for instruments, harmony, and the subtle relationship between an orchestra and conductor seeped into his bones and brain. Compared to those experiences, he says, learning in a classroom is a secondhand affair.

Jazz was also a part of his musical education. When he discovered Ellington on the radio at age thirteen or fourteen, Ellington "knocked me out with his harmonic language and coloristic language, which was twenty years ahead of everybody else,"[29] Schuller recalls in a conversation with guitarist-producer David Starobin on a Bridge compact disc containing three Schuller pieces. Then and there, Schuller was transformed into a record collector, which has been an obsession ever since. To satisfy his curiosity, he began transcribing his jazz records—not just the solos, which many musicians transcribed, but the more complex orchestral mix, down to Ellington's subtle blendings of muted trumpets with saxophones. Later he was to do the same thing professionally.

"I had pretty good ears and I could hear it [the music]," he tells Starobin, "but as a sitting-down composer I also wanted to see: 'what does this look like?' "[30] During his two years with the Cincinnati Symphony alone, he must have transcribed fifteen to twenty Ellington pieces, he says.

Already influenced in his own writing by Scriabin, Debussy, and Ravel, Schuller also absorbed Ellington's advanced Debussy-Ravel language. It "brought these two worlds together for me and I was in love with it." The mixture became the basis of his style. That style has not changed fundamentally, he maintains, although he likes to think that it is "more matured, more refined, in some ways more challenging, and without the immediate influences of that time—let's say Scriabin or somebody like that—sticking out like a little bit of raw meat." But he's not ashamed of the raw flesh. We all learn by imitation, he says. "And then we digest those things that we love and eventually if we're good enough, we subsume them into our own personal style, if we're also lucky enough to develop one."

Schuller's classical or "serious" music, though also indebted to the twelve-tone expressionist style brought into the world by Schoenberg, Berg, and Webern, can't be categorized, much less located within a trend. That gives commentators a problem. To *The New Grove Dictionary of Music and Musicians* Schuller has "drawn discriminatingly and creatively on techniques developed by the great composers of the twentieth century: on Stravinky's metrics, Schoenberg's serialism, Webern's orchestration, Varèse's manipulations of planes and volumes, Babbitt's principles of combinatoriality."[31] (In other words, he's eclectic.) More simply, the Schirmer catalog of Schuller's works finds a "spontaneous, improvisatory quality" in them. (Perhaps the author was thinking of jazz.)

Neither description will do. Nor will John Rockwell's pigeonholing of Schuller as a hard-bitten twelve-tone operative. In fact, no description of more than 165 works in forms ranging from opera and symphony to band and chamber music—lots of chamber music—can encompass the letter or spirit of Schuller's work. Sometimes problematic or challenging, especially on first acquaintance, the music embraces the ambiguities and uncertainties of its times but remembers its debt to tradition. Schuller, the nondriver, is like the operator of a smoothly running car. A passenger/listener might not know where it is going or what is happening around him. But so sure is Schuller in his craft, so engaging are the incidents passing within view, that the listener can sit back and feel comfortable on the ride.

In 1996, taking advantage of his welcome in Germany and the lower recording costs there, Schuller recorded four of his orchestral works with the Radio Philharmonic of Hannover. Spanning fifty-one years, the selec-, tions on the GM disc give a bird's-eye view of his career as the composer of about sixty-five orchestral pieces. *Vertige d'Eros* (1945) and *Meditation* (1947) come from his earliest years. *Seven Studies on Themes of Paul Klee* (1959), Schuller's hit, is from midcareer. *An Arc Ascending* (1996) was his most recent orchestral work at the time of the sessions. Each piece bears the Schuller imprint in style, though each goes to a different place in expressive intent.

One other characteristic links the selections Schuller recorded with the Hannover orchestra, or at least three of them, and it holds a clue to the man within the composer. In all except *Meditation,* Schuller translates images from painting or photography into music. This is no accident, he comments in the liner notes, "since as a child and into my early teen years I showed considerable talent for drawing and painting, and thought of myself pri-marily as someone who would become a visual artist." Between the ages of seven and ten he made nearly a thousand drawings, mostly from nature. Trees particularly fascinated him "with their truly incredible 'no-two-alike' structural beauty and complexity."[32]

Schuller makes no apologies for the early works. Although they are somewhat "lumpy" or "lopsided" in form, he writes, posterity will judge them for what they are. And if they show a debt to Schoenberg, Berg, Scria-bin, and Stravinsky—his models when venturing forth—well, every com-poser has to learn by imitating and moving on. (He learned form "by vora-ciously studying all of Beethoven's string quartets, piano sonatas, and symphonies.")

*Meditation,* the only purely abstract work, shows the influence of Schoen-berg and Berg on the budding composer. *Vertige d'Eros* ("Delirium of Love"), Schuller's second complete orchestral work, following his Horn Concerto no. 1, is a tone-poem response to Chilean painter Echaurren Matta's surreal-ist painting of the same name. Schuller says that after first being captivated by the erotic promise of the title, he was swept away by "the extraordinarily free, to me almost *musical* composition and color spectacle of the paint-ing."[33]

*Seven Studies on Themes of Paul Klee* reflects a particular affinity with the Swiss painter, who, in a mirror image of Schuller's rite of passage, started out with musical inclinations but switched in his teenage years to the visual arts. The piece is a kind of twentieth-century *Pictures at an Exhibi-tion.* Each of the seven paintings, however abstract in design, has a musical theme, for which Schuller finds a counterpart in music. Klee's painting *An-*

*tique Harmonies* consists of 150 irregular blocks in subtle color variations. Schuller represents the progression through a "timbre-oriented" orchestration culminating in a "bright yellow" in the trumpets and high strings. *Abstract Trio,* depicting a trio of musicians, proceeds in a series of trios varying in instrumentation and color. Set to music, *Twittering Machine* not only twitters but also pokes fun at the "simpleminded" extremes of the serialist writing that dominated composition in the 1960s.

*An Arc Ascending* was inspired by three photographs by Alice Weston, a Cincinnati environmental artist. They show prehistoric Ohio earthworks pointing to the sun's arrival point at the turn of the seasons, much as the better-known standing stones do in Britain. Although there are ascending arcs in the orchestral writing, Schuller is more concerned with "musical reflections on the different seasonal aspects" brought about by the sun's course in the heavens. (There is an echo here of Beethoven's description of his *Pastoral* Symphony as "the expression of feelings rather than painting.")

Seated in his living room amid his scores and books, Schuller said he was proud of "an enormous consistency stylistically [and] linguistically" in his music, beginning with the Horn Concerto, which he wrote mostly when he was seventeen. All around him he saw composers trying desperately to be popular, to start or ride a trend, to woo the indifferent cadres of the young:

"After all, we do live in times where there are hundreds of composers who abandoned their former selves and have run after one trend or another. We're in this fragmented compositional and cultural scene where there are so many trends and schools and philosophies and ideologies, all vying with each other—battling it out, so to speak—and each of course thinks it has the claim to the future."

Such stylistical "detours" never happened before the twentieth century, Schuller said, perhaps because there weren't so many choices open to composers. Yet when Stravinsky, early in the century, switched styles almost as easily as clothes, from the primitivism of *The Rite of Spring* to his neoclassical and then twelve-tone idioms, the music remained high in quality. That, Schuller declared, can't be said of the recent descent into repetitive minimalism, the return of tonality, "and now—even worse—the pure catering to audience tastes" in works lacking in craft or substance. That kind of cheapening of the art is purely a product of the times and their surrender to the marketplace, he said.

Having a hit is not always the blessing it might seem. It gives performers an excuse to bypass the rest of a composer's music. In an essay in *The Or-*

*chestral Composer's Point of View,* a collection by various composers published in 1970, Schuller says that he has been fortunate in some of his orchestral performances. But "having also experienced on a number of occasions under-rehearsed, ill-prepared, misunderstood renditions of my works, I know all too well the feeling of helplessness and bitterness which the composer experiences as he hears his work massacred and senses the hostility of the audience rising about him." Yet, Schuller goes on, it is consistently his less adventurous orchestral compositions that reap the rewards of performance. "As a result, those works which I consider to be my most important orchestral works are rarely performed, largely because conductors are frightened off by the problems they present, and it is therefore easier to turn once again to the *Seven Studies on Themes of Paul Klee.*"[34] (A comparable situation arises with Copland; his *Appalachian Spring* and other ballets turn up on orchestral programs more often than his knottier symphonic works.)

Schuller contrasts the warm reception of *Seven Studies* with the difficulty of getting performances of his 1965 *Symphony.* In the symphony, he writes, he was "preoccupied with developing in my own way contemporary analogues to certain eighteenth- and nineteenth-century concepts which have been considered obsolete and unusable in serial writing by many of the present-day arbiters." (He is talking about the mandarins then dominant in universities—the same arbiters he satirized in *Twittering Machine.*) Yet these very novelties of style and form, which make the works interesting, at least to initiated performers and listeners, are precisely the qualities that put most musicians off. In an "ideal future," Schuller concludes, "a work like my *Symphony*—and hundreds of equally worthy works by the many gifted composers of our time—will be performed accurately, with ease, with conviction, and with a sense of beauty which unfortunately is now reserved by our symphony orchestras and their conductors only for the nineteenth- and late eighteenth-century classics."[35]

In the real world, conductors and orchestras usually take the path of least resistance, and an orchestra fed a constant diet of Beethoven and Brahms "gradually loses its mental, technical, and perceptual capacity to deal with anything but long-established musical ideas," Schuller says. Yet even here there is a paradox: "musicians are not intimidated by even the most extreme demands upon their instrumental virtuosity, but they are turned off by the slightest demands on their intellectual capacities."[36]

Works like *Seven Studies,* as Schuller says, are relatively easy to follow with their accessible language and visual equivalents. Other works, master-ly as they may be in concept and imagination, can have a cerebral air pre-cisely because of that intellectual scaffolding. Only with his wife's death did Schuller step out from behind the mask of objectivity. *Of Reminiscences and Reflections,* his Pulitzer Prize–winning 1993 work, is one of several he wrote as he came to grips with his loneliness and loss. He describes it as "in effect a symphony for large orchestra in five sections, which are played without in-terruption." But the references, some coded or hidden, to music the couple had enjoyed together give rise to a nostalgic feeling, somewhat like Ives's quotations of hymns, patriotic tunes, and snatches of Beethoven. The writ-ing has an intimacy and directness of expression not often found elsewhere in Schuller's work.

Critics noticed. In the *New York Times,* Anthony Tommasini spoke of a language that is "distinctive and deeply personal" and music that "evolves in fits and starts, though there are extended lyrical passages where instruments mingle wistfully."[37] In the *Boston Globe,* Richard Dyer compared the piece to Richard Strauss's tone poems but found it "simultaneously exhibiting origi-nality of form and expressing strength of mind and depth of feeling."[38]

Then there is the jesting Schuller, serious even when having fun. One of his GM releases bears the mock-serious title *Music for the Underdogs of the Orchestra.* The three works so labeled (or libeled) include two of his own making, the once-fearsome Quartet for Double Basses and the Concerto for Tuba and Orchestra, along with Vaughan Williams's Concerto for Bass Tuba and Orchestra. Schuller conducts the New England Conservatory Symphony with Harvey Phillips as the tuba soloist. The pieces show the vir-tuosic and expressive possibilities of instruments usually consigned to ac-companying or comic roles.

Like Paul Hindemith, the German émigré composer-teacher from ear-lier in the twentieth century, Schuller has written concertos—a total of twenty-eight—for virtually every instrument of the orchestra. One of his other underdogs is the contrabassoon, the bullfrog-voiced basement dweller of the wind section. In 1978, on a commission from Lewis Lipnick, contra-bassoonist of the National Symphony Orchestra of Washington, Schuller wrote what is apparently the first concerto ever composed for this unlikely solo instrument.

In the National Symphony's program notes, Schuller anticipated an imaginary listener's challenge: "What is a nice composer like you doing writing a contrabassoon concerto?" The nice composer replied that through the music that filled his house during his boyhood and through his own experience in American orchestras, he developed an awareness of the expressive capabilities of such stepchild instruments as the double bass, tuba, and contrabassoon. Then again, he said, his interest could "be related to my natural bent to defend or support the underdog." Wanting, like Lipnick, to show the contrabassoon's melodic powers, he had to find a "tactful" balance with the stronger-voiced, higher-pitched competition within the orchestra. Composer and soloist worked together in the preparation of the 1979 premiere.

Schuller's sympathy with underdogs extends beyond musical instruments. *The Visitation,* the first of his two operas, is based on Kafka's novel *The Trial,* but the hero subjected to the nightmare of arrest and murder is a black man in the United States (Kafka's *Amerika*). Commissioned as a "jazz opera" by Rolf Liebermann for the Hamburg State Opera, the 1966 work emerged in Schuller's then-new Third Stream style.

In his book *Musings,* Schuller says that after a three-year search for a text, he decided to "transpose" the novel from Kafka's murky European city to America, even though he conceived the opera for a German company. "From the outset the idea was not to write a Kafka-opera as such, but to articulate the Kafkaesque elements in the American 'Negro problem.'" The protagonist, Carter Jones, is not the stereotypical downtrodden black, though. He is in some ways an even greater outsider: an educated liberal who can fit into neither black nor white society. Somewhat like Schuller in his refusal to fit into either an academic or a populist composers' slot, "he is caught midway between two worlds, and is not a true—or accepted—member of either."

The musical style is also caught between worlds. Schuller describes the opera, with its black cast and jazz group, as less a jazz opera than an attempt "to fuse jazz elements with a contemporary (in my case) atonal, dodecaphonic [twelve-tone] language." The true jazz opera, he says, is yet to be written, because it will require true jazz singers and an orchestra capable of jazz improvisation. *Porgy and Bess,* also a hybrid, fails that particular test but remains a "masterpiece" in Schuller's mind.[39]

Above all, Schuller concludes, "I want to say that it was not at all my intention in *The Visitation* to produce some consciously 'radical' or 'avant-garde' work, as the European opera houses have witnessed so often in recent years, but something much more difficult: a singable repertory opera. For that is still the mostly unresolved challenge of late twentieth-century opera: to provide a singable operatic repertory that does not compromise stylistically"[40]

The challenge has remained unresolved for Schuller as well. Because of the mix of styles, *The Visitation* was a cause célèbre at the time of its performances in Hamburg, New York, and San Francisco in the 1960s. It has had only occasional revivals since then in Europe, and none in the United States.

Schuller's other opera, premiered in 1970 by Sarah Caldwell's Opera Company of Boston, is *The Fisherman and His Wife*, a work for children with a libretto by John Updike. Thirty-two years after *The Visitation*, Schuller returned to the theme of the black man's struggles in *Black Warrior*, a work for narrator, chorus, and orchestra based on excerpts from Martin Luther King Jr.'s *Letter from the Birmingham City Jail*. Schuller conducted the premiere in 1998 in Birmingham, the scene of many of King's civil rights struggles, on the thirtieth anniversary of his death.

The Third Stream tag can provide a handle for critics who find no other easy way of getting hold of Schuller's music. He said only a small fraction of his work is in that fusion style, but that hasn't stopped critics from writing "thousands" of reviews sticking the label where it doesn't belong. The Symphony for Brass and Percussion is one of the works so mislabeled. The error only mildly amuses him.

As he passed his seventy-fifth birthday, Schuller was at work on his autobiography. Even during a twelve-day vacation in Greenland and Iceland, his first vacation in seven years and, in the case of Greenland, the realization of a boyhood dream, he was writing several hours a day. He was only up to his nineteenth year but had already written 250 pages—clearly too much.

Schuller had begun work on the book a few years before, when he planned to start on the third volume of his jazz history. He decided, "I had better make a little detour because I've had this incredibly varied and rich life," particularly in working with some of the greatest musicians on both the classical and jazz sides of the musical aisle. There were his gigs with Toscanini and Monteux, Miles Davis and Dizzy Gillespie, and others like them during the first thirty years. And then there were the composers and orchestras, the publishing and recording, the schools and committees, the friends and colleagues, all part of a rich period in musical history, waiting to be documented.

The book, then, would be the story not just of Gunther Schuller's life but "a grand chronicle or commentary on what it was like to be a musician in the last three-quarters of the century in social, political, and professional terms."

In his living room, reflecting on a life spent in music, Schuller longed for some time off: "Do you realize how hard I have worked? Like eighteen hours every day of my life for the last sixty-five years. It's not that I want to retire, but I just want to find some leisure and take some vacations. I want to read a book. I want to do something besides being chained to the table answering a thousand letters a year. I want to do more things that I want to do instead of what the whole world wants me to do."

It was not easy to say no when he had said yes to everybody for sixty years. Even occasional problems with his health had not kept him from going on to the next gig with orchestra or university. But this musician with a mission was going to have to learn the magic two-letter word.

When Schuller got to age fifty-four in his story, he would have to deal with perhaps the most controversial hour of his career: his 1979 welcoming address to students at Tanglewood. In the bosom of the Boston Symphony Orchestra he denounced a "corporate mentality" among orchestra managements and players and "absentee music directors" jetting from podium to podium around the globe. He intended the talk as a warning to students about what to expect in the job world outside, and he cushioned the criticism with a plea that everyone work together toward common goals rather than pursue adversarial relationships.

For those reasons, and because he did not mention the Boston Symphony or director Seiji Ozawa by name, Schuller apparently did not anticipate the shock waves that cascaded across his employer's campus and out into the world beyond. (Did you hear what he said? We're just another corporation! He attacked Seiji!) The uproar was probably a prelude in some way to his Tanglewood resignation five years later, although frictions, if there were any, remained discreetly hidden from view. But relations with Ozawa apparently never recovered, and Schuller left in anger. In a parting shot, he said Ozawa had turned down his request to restore the autonomy he had formerly enjoyed at the school, as in such decisions as the choice of guest conductors for the student orchestra. Now explicitly linking Ozawa and the orchestra administration to the center of classical-musical commerce in the United States, he termed his resignation "an artistic and philosophic statement against the heavy hand of Fifty-seventh Street [New York] on management decisions."[41] The orchestra, which had commissioned and performed his music in the past, even his *Deai,* a commissioned work for three orchestras and eight voices, returned the favor by quietly dropping Schuller from its repertoire.

Unrepentant, Schuller went on to elaborate on his charges in a series of talks around the country. He picked up the theme in a magazine article reprinted in *Musings:*

> One of the most serious problems facing the modern symphony is that of the absentee music director. Jet travel has afforded the possibility of simultaneous directorships, and conductors have shamelessly indulged themselves, taking on as many as three or four orchestras and, in one case some years ago, even five. Since boards have generally not been wise or strong enough to resist such temptations, many orchestras have become directionless, amorphous aggregations with no personality, style, or point of view. Their season is often a mere stringing together of programs—usually of the classical hit-parade variety—that permits no artistic growth of either the orchestra or the conductor, much less of the two *together.*

Schuller held up Maurice Abravanel, for thirty-two years (until 1979) director of the Utah Symphony, as a model of what the conductor should be. Abravanel devoted himself week in and week out to his orchestra, nurturing it, giving it a distinct personality, and growing in stature with it, Schuller wrote. More than that, "fully realizing his role as an 'educator' of the orchestra, the audience, and the greater community, he developed excellent relationships with the state legislature and with city officials, seeking their support—and getting it." Salt Lake City's other arts and cultural organizations also prospered as a result.

"What Abravanel achieved should be a lesson to us all," Schuller concludes. "But such things take time to achieve; and time is precisely what few people are willing to give to anything anymore. Artists and conductors want instant fame, instant careers, instant success, without putting in the time and effort that such results require."[42]

After Tanglewood Schuller accepted the only permanent conducting position he ever held. Far from the musical power centers of the East and West Coasts, he became principal conductor and artistic adviser of the

Spokane Symphony in 1984-85. Through that connection he went to the year-old Festival at Sandpoint, an Idaho mountain resort ninety minutes' drive from Spokane, where he served as director until 1999. The two-week summer music series offered concerts by the Spokane Symphony, chamber-music and conductors' training programs, and a music camp along with blues, country, pop, rock, and jazz. The festival and school were small and remote by comparison with Tanglewood's. But they were his.

At the heart of Schuller's quarrel with the world is a quarrel with the pap peddled by network television and popular culture generally. When he was growing up in New York, he said, he was surrounded by great music and art, and there was no reason why anyone had to be culturally illiterate, as much of the public is today. Radio, which at least in New York regularly broadcast classical music and jazz, was his great teacher. Since the 1960s network television has been the great American teacher. Money, Schuller said, is the only value it knows. The music it promotes is music that makes money, and the music of that marketplace is the only music that most people get to know—a vicious circle. Saying that people can find good music on public television is no answer, Schuller added. It only allows the networks to shirk their responsibility for the situation. Unless, say, a Picasso painting sells for millions of dollars, the networks happily go their way, ignoring the fine arts. Yet "if some idiot guitarist can play three chords, he's on television right away."

This view of pre-television America, at least outside New York, may be too rosy. But the gulf between high and popular culture that opened up in the 1960s did not exist at that time. Trivial as Tin Pan Alley music was, it shared the essentially life-affirming values of most art music. With the advent of rock and rap (whose easy salable values were picked up by television and film), popular culture adopted a nihilistic, in-your-face stance. Classical music and the high arts generally were no longer a nurturing part of the life well-lived. They were the province of an elite: the enemy. Never mind that this premise was based on the same ignorance that had spawned much of the pop music in the first place. The point was the willed ignorance. Ignorance became the ideal that Bach and Mozart and Beethoven had stood for in the past.

Schuller's anger rises as he points out that for two generations, 95 percent of Americans have grown up without exposure to quality in music. It was that determination to put good music—good music of all kinds—

before the public that led him into publishing in the first place. As he once put it in the *Boston Globe Magazine:*

"My philosophy is to publish every good thing I hear, if possible, to get it down in visual form for the professional or amateur who wants to ponder it and play it. I see myself as filling in the gaps left by the music publishing establishment, because I embrace it all—fourteenth-century *ars nova* music, twentieth-century experimental music, American Indian and Third World music, Yugoslavian mountaineer brass band music, Eskimo music, aboriginal music from Borneo—you name it."

In Africa alone, Schuller said, there are about three thousand kinds of musical dialects. "Most Westerners consider the microtonal music of the East and the musics of Asia and Africa primitive. What they don't know is that by comparison to their music, *ours* is primitive."[43]

And so this great explorer of many musics, this bloodied Parsifal, this Quixote at the head of a small but fearless army of knights, is at once a classical music insider and outsider. He can win the Pulitzer (though belatedly) and help a young composer to get a recording grant and Guggenheim fellowship, yet he can't win the respect of the Fifty-seventh Street music-management establishment, which he stands against and which gladly stands against him. He can't even get a major-label recording. It bothers him that except on his own label, he is the country's "most unrecorded" composer of any consequence. Even after he won his Pulitzer, he failed to receive a recording by a major label, as other Pulitzer winners routinely do. It fell to the new-music label New World to put out the prizewinning *Of Reminiscences and Reflections,* with Schuller conducting the Radio Philharmonic of Hannover. The last piece of his committed to disc by a major conductor and orchestra was *American Triptych,* recorded in 1967 by Leonard Bernstein and the New York Philharmonic.

"I'm a twelve-tone composer," Schuller told the audience at a New York concert of his music in 1998. "But don't let that scare you. There's been so much twelve-tone trashing these days, I feel I have to apologize. But not *all* of my music is ugly and difficult."[44] He was joking, but only partly. By 1998 twelve-tone music was in full retreat, overtaken by the simpler, often atavistic styles of composers brought up on rock and pop. To even a fairly sophisticated audience, twelve-tone was a dirty word, as it had been for most of the century since Schoenberg sprang the idea on an uncomprehending public.

The New York program opened with the Borromeo String Quartet of

Boston playing Schuller's Quartet no. 3 and the first quartet by his fellow Bostonian and twelve-tone composer Leon Kirchner. Both works, wrote Anthony Tommasini in the *New York Times*, were reminders of the new-music wars of the 1950s and 1960s, when twelve-toners seemed to dominate university music departments and create an impregnable orthodoxy. But both also, Tommasini added, "were reminders that, despite the polemics, a lot of gripping, twelve-tone music could energize and linger in the repertory if given a chance."[45] After intermission Schuller led an ensemble of classical and jazz musicians, including Joe Lovano, in three of his Third Stream pieces.

If twelve-tone music required an apology, Third Stream in a way had done its job too well. Today it is not just classical and jazz streams that have mingled and merged; a flood of rock, rap, pop, and ethnic styles has swept away orthodoxies of all kinds. Classical music, often as foreign to American ears as Yugoslavian mountaineer music and aboriginal music from Borneo, is just one of many genres competing in the marketplace. As classical composers have tried to be heard amid the din, they have resorted to "the pure catering to audience tastes" that Schuller decries as a diminution of the art. Third Stream didn't break down the walls all by itself. It had plenty of help from campus and sexual revolutions, disc jockeys, dumb-and-dumber sitcoms, "crossover" artists, the elimination of arts programs in the schools, and boundless technological gimmickry. No longer does a division between high and low culture prevail. High and low have been leveled, and a giddy near-anarchy prevails.

Schuller knows the talk in musical circles: He's tetchy. He's crazy. He's a damned fool. He's his own worst enemy. On the contrary, he says, he feels "quite heroic." In these days when the barriers between not only classical and pop but also good and bad have come crashing down, when bad taste is cultivated and rewarded if it sells, "heroic" is putting it mildly.

# ROBERT SPANO

## Turning Babel into buzz

Robert Spano asks for a little quiet, please. (Walter H. Scott)

*Stand up, tall masts of Mannahatta!*
*—stand up, beautiful hills of Brooklyn!*

*Throb, baffled and curious brain!*
*throw out questions and answers!*

—WALT WHITMAN, "Crossing Brooklyn Ferry"

ROBERT SPANO WAS TWENTY-NINE WHEN HE FIRST CON-
ducted a professional symphony orchestra. There's nothing unusual about
that. If a conductor hasn't started his career by twenty-nine, chances are he
never is going to start it. The unusual thing about Spano's debut was that he
started at the top. He conducted the Boston Symphony Orchestra.

A conductor of student orchestras until that momentous day, Spano
reached the pinnacle not by working his way up through the ranks, making
his name elsewhere, or filling in during an emergency, the usual routes for a
newcomer. He was the scheduled conductor for a series of subscription
concerts in the hallowed spaces of Boston's Symphony Hall. He was nervous for a month in advance—"nauseous and terrified," he said. The 1991
program consisted of George Crumb's *Haunted Landscape,* the Grieg Piano
Concerto (Garrick Ohlsson was the soloist), and Sibelius's First Symphony.

"It was terrifying but wonderful," Spano recalls. What made it wonderful was the orchestra's flexibility and cooperation. "They were very good to
me—very supportive, really good."

Spano was an assistant conductor with the Boston Symphony when he
got the call. The assistant's job is usually to do routine chores for the music
director and be on standby to step in if the scheduled conductor is, in the
parlance of the trade, indisposed. But the Boston Symphony has an admirable practice of giving its assistant conductors, of whom there are usually a pair, a shot at concerts of their own. Some of these promising young
men—no woman has made it so far—go on to jobs with lesser orchestras
and never again reach the heights of a Boston Symphony debut. Within five
years of Spano's debut, he had conducted most of the country's principal
orchestras and become director of the Brooklyn Philharmonic. There he attracted attention for yet another reason: his programming. Five years later,
in 2001, he became director of the Atlanta Symphony Orchestra as well,
drawing further attention as a young man on the rise. Some critics said he
should have gotten the New York Philharmonic or Boston Symphony.

Founded in 1954, the Brooklyn exists in the shadow of that better-known philharmonic on the other side of the Brooklyn Bridge. For twenty-five years before Spano's arrival, the Brooklyn Philharmonic had championed new music along with the classics under his predecessors, Lukas Foss and Dennis Russell Davies. Taking over in 1996, Spano continued the tradition. But in 1999 he gave it a new twist: each season would be built around a theme. In 1999–2000 the theme was The Century, looking back at some aspects of twentieth-century music and culture; in 2000–01 it was Liebestod, music of love and death; in 2001–02 it would be Songs of the Earth.

Balding and bespectacled, of medium height, and slightly built, the Ohio-born Spano belongs to the nice-guy school of American conductors. Nervous energy crackles not far below the surface as he puffs on a cigarette and his foot rocks restlessly during conversation. There is nothing of the maestro about him. He makes jokes about his faintly owlish appearance. He says he is not by nature a glad-hander or party goer, two requirements of a modern music director. Meeting him on the street, a stranger would sooner take him for a high school band director. Yet when he springs into action on the podium, the coiled energy translates into vigor and clarity, qualities that also make him a valued teacher.

Spano says he doesn't think much about why the so-called Big Five American orchestras—New York, Boston, Philadelphia, Cleveland, and Chicago—have nearly always chosen foreigners as music directors. Pointing out that such native sons as Leonard Bernstein, Michael Tilson Thomas, Leonard Slatkin, David Zinman, and James Levine have held major American podiums, he says he doesn't feel discriminated against and doesn't believe there is a general prejudice against Americans waving batons. Orchestras such as those in Houston, Pittsburgh, San Francisco, and Atlanta are now comparable in quality to the Big Five, he says. So why so much talk about a Big Five?

Nor does he worry much about titans of the podium who have gone before him. If he spent a lot of time thinking about those footsteps, he "could never," for example, "step onto the stage of Symphony Hall in Boston."

Thematic programming in itself is nothing new. In its most familiar guise, it consists of a concert or series of concerts devoted to one composer or school of composers. Its more recent variant explores a cultural concept such as a historical period or music with a literary association. The American Symphony Orchestra, under Leon Botstein, is a leading practitioner of this brand of programming. Its six-concert 1999–2000 New York season offered such programs as Tales of Edgar Allen Poe (works by Florent Schmitt, André Caplet, Einojuhani Rautavaara, and Sergei Rachmaninoff), Creative Differences: Bruckner's Divided Vienna (works by Ignaz Brüll, Karl Goldmark, and Anton Bruckner), and Beyond Good and Evil: Nietzsche and Music (Nietzsche's *Hymnus an der Leben,* works by Wolfgang Rihm and Frederick Delius, and Richard Strauss's *Also Sprach Zarathustra).*

The Brooklyn Philharmonic had engaged in concert-by-concert thematic programming before Spano. He took the idea a step further. Under the rubric The Century, his five 1999–2000 programs went from Strings of War (war-influenced works by Bartók, Richard Strauss, and Shostakovich), *Nixon in China* (the John Adams opera recalling one of the century's political landmarks), and Culture of the Cabaret (works by Conlon Nancarrow, Kurt Weill, Toru Takemitsu, and Astor Piazzolla showing popular influences) to Northern Lights (works by Magnus Lindberg, Rautavaara, Aulis Sallinen, and Jean Sibelius). The northern program had a dual theme: the growing importance of Finns in music and, as shown by the role of nature in their work, environmental awareness. The season ended with three tableaux from Olivier Messiaen's opera, *Saint Francis of Assisi,* reflecting a late-century revival of interest in mysticism and religion.

Major orchestras tend to shy away from such programming. Subscribers, the backbone of an audience, are mostly a conservative lot who want a familiar symphony and a celebrity soloist, and no music composed after 1910, please. Conductors like Botstein and Spano are freer to experiment because they can appeal to a niche audience. This is especially advantageous in a city like New York, where concertgoers can choose from as many as half a dozen major events in an evening. It may even have helped to keep the financially precarious Brooklyn Philharmonic from tumbling into the grave.

"It's been good for the institution," Spano said of his programming. "Given this musical marketplace we're in, it is important for us to have some distinguishing features." But he also has a personal reason: "I love the experience of doing these programs and finding the links between things or the unusual placement of familiar things in an unfamiliar musical environment."

It's been good for the players too, according to the two philharmonic veterans who auditioned Spano for the job, principal oboist Henry Schuman and double bassist Louis Bruno. They admire in him the qualities that musicians everywhere look for in a conductor: he comes to rehearsal well prepared, he gets results quickly, he makes the orchestra sound good, his programming is stimulating, subscribers are increasing. "I think he's about as near to a genius as you can be without being certified," said Schuman.[1]

"I haven't seen him yet get on the podium for a rehearsal and not know the score cold," said Bruno. "It's just amazing. You feel like he's been somehow connected with that music for a long time, even though you know he couldn't be."

Spano, at forty, might not be the conductor for every city. He never studied with Bernstein or received his blessing, as Tilson Thomas and a legion of other acolytes did, often getting a jump start in their careers. Though he has won the Seaver/National Endowment of Arts award for rising young conductors, he has never served an apprenticeship with a provincial orchestra, as many of his contemporaries have. He moves easily between symphony and opera, new music and old, but fits into no particular slot and makes no visible attempt to differentiate himself from the pack, except through his programming. But in Brooklyn, like Tilson Thomas in San Francisco, he seems to have found the right match with a city and orchestra. Or, to put it another way, the city and orchestra have found the right conductor in their climb up the artistic ladder.

Robert Spano—the family name is Italian—was born in Conneaut, Ohio, and brought up in Elkhart, Indiana, the self-styled "band instrument capital of the world." He grew up amid music. His mother is a pianist, his father a clarinetist and flute maker who is fond of Debussy, Ravel, Stravinsky, Bartók, and their contemporaries—music that the son imbibed early and never lost his taste for. As a boy Robert studied flute, violin, piano, and composition, taking as many as nine lessons a week. By the age of ten, he had composed two flute concertos. At fourteen he won a prize for a piano composition, and the conductor of the Elkhart Symphony asked him to orchestrate and conduct it. That became his conducting debut.

In a 2000 talk to a group of Tanglewood patrons, Spano recalled that he used to go to rehearsals and concerts with his father and go out for drinks afterward with him and his friends. So when the fourteen-year-old got up on the podium, he wasn't afraid. "I knew the players in the orchestra," he said, "and I felt very comfortable with them. And I wasn't at all nervous. I didn't know what I was doing, so of course I wasn't nervous. And it was the most wonderful experience, to hear my music played by this wonderful orchestra, and I'm standing there beating time relatively correctly, at some rudimentary level. I had gone to my violin teacher, who was the high school orchestra director, and asked her to give me the beat patterns, so I would at least know what I was doing. And I finished the first time through the piece at the rehearsal and thought, 'Well, that's terrific,' and the music director said, 'Wouldn't you like to rehearse?' And I said, '*Why?*' "

The reasons for rehearsal weren't the only thing he learned as he went along. He discovered that the podium is the best place to hear an orchestra. "It's sense-surround," he told his Tanglewood audience. "It's fabulous. I don't know a better way to make a living, so I do this." It was a thrill then and it's a thrill now, he said.

At the Oberlin Conservatory in Ohio, Spano tried for a couple of years to turn himself into a composer. He found he had nothing to say. He turned to conducting instead, and continued working on piano and violin, knowing they would someday be useful to him. Before his senior year his conducting teacher, Robert Baustian, retired. Because the vacancy went unfilled for a while, Spano sometimes took the orchestra podium, conducting works the other substitutes didn't care for. He put his compositions away. He says there are only two or three he would think of letting anyone perform now.

Spano's versatility and questioning turn of mind caught the attention of Marilyn McDonald, who teaches violin at Oberlin. As a pianist accompanying her students, he was "phenomenal," she recalled in an online interview on the Oberlin Web site. "He asked me at the end of his first year if I would take him on as a secondary [nonmajor] violin student. I was curious to hear how he would play and encouraged him to audition. I remember he came onstage with an old, musty violin case and a beat-up old violin and played the Sibelius Violin Concerto for me. Of course I took him on as a student. He actually performed a recital of violin music when he was here and his program included the first Bartók sonata. As he progressed, we talked more about bowing and issues more related to his conducting."[2]

Although Spano no longer plays the violin in public, he is a fine pianist, occasionally joining colleagues such as McDonald in recitals and chamber concerts. He gave seven recitals with her in the sixteen years following his graduation in 1983. In a 1999 program, the teacher and her former student played Bartók's first sonata along with Mozart's Sonata in G, K. 301, and Karol Szymanowski's *Three Myths*. McDonald described the exchange of ideas during rehearsals as "fantastic. Nothing is too far out to be tried by Bob. . . . It is rare to find talent like that in the world."

While at Oberlin a month earlier to conduct Jules Massenet's *Manon*—it was his first go at the opera—Spano played a program of all three of Brahms's violin-piano sonatas with another faculty violinist, Gregory Fulkerson. In another online interview Fulkerson praised the "intense musical collaboration between instrumental artist and conductor."[3]

On graduation from Oberlin, Spano went to the Curtis Institute in Philadelphia to continue his conducting studies under the noted Max Rudolf. He supported himself by playing the piano in chamber music performances and as a vocal accompanist, but also in a French restaurant where he performed sonatas. He likes to quote Rudolf's advice for aspiring conductors: "The best way to learn to conduct is to conduct. The second best way is to observe. The third best way is to get a teacher." A conductor learns best, in other words, by getting up in front of an orchestra and hearing the sounds and expression (or lack of expression) his actions produce. The orchestra must contribute to the creative process, Spano also learned. "It's not a game of the conductor fascistically producing a certain sound but rather of facilitating a kind of giant chamber music."

From Curtis, Spano went to his first full-time job, at Bowling Green State University in Ohio. He spent three years there as conductor of the student orchestra and head of the new-music program. The experience he gained took him back to Oberlin in 1989 as opera conductor and assistant professor of conducting, a part-time position that he retained as he moved to Boston, Brooklyn, and Atlanta in succession.

Spano had been on the Oberlin faculty a year when the assistant conductor's job in Boston opened up. Already rejected once by the Boston Symphony as an applicant for a conducting fellowship at Tanglewood (he now heads the student conducting program for which he was turned down), he was rejected for the assistant's job without so much as an audition. (He was in good company as a reject for a conducting fellowship. Simon Rattle, who later became an important Boston guest conductor and director of the Berlin Philharmonic, and Keith Lockhart, later the conductor of the Boston Pops, shared the same fate.)

Then lightning struck. One of the auditioners for the assistant's vacancy canceled. Spano was next on the list. He won the audition, went to Boston in 1990, and made his debut in 1991. Sibelius, whose First Symphony was the principal work on the program, became his calling card as he began to ply the podiums of the world.

"And the wonderful thing about that job is those concerts that they give the assistant conductors," Spano said. "Living around the orchestra is wonderful in itself. But then the opportunity to really have important repertoire, a real concert: it's fantastic."

Fantastic indeed. Even before his three years in Boston were up, Spano began getting what he describes as "911 calls": a scheduled conductor had canceled and a substitute was needed—fast. Thus he began making the rounds of the Chicago, Cleveland, Philadelphia, Los Angeles, San Francisco, Saint Louis, Montreal, Toronto, and other major North American orchestras, sometimes as a substitute but sometimes as a guest conductor in his own right. Opera engagements also followed at the Houston, Santa Fe, and Chicago opera companies, London's Royal Opera, the Welsh National Opera, and other companies. Abroad, he also conducted principal orchestras in Milan, Frankfurt, The Hague, Helsinki, Zurich, and Tokyo.

Not all those experiences were good ones. Spano doesn't like to talk about it, but while most orchestras, such as the Boston, were supportive, a few let him know that a young unknown wasn't welcome. Or as the young unknown put it, "You know when you're not getting cooperation. You know when your work is not appreciated. It's made clear in any number of ways." Inattentiveness in rehearsal can be one way. Unresponsiveness, even in concert, can be another.

Spano is neither a larger-than-life, fire-and-brimstone conductor like Bernstein nor an athlete-choreographer like Ozawa, who hired him to be assistant conductor in Boston and installed him in 1998 as head of Tanglewood's student conducting program. Though some players have complained of a certain rigidity in his approach, others respond, as his Brooklyn players said, to his down-to-earth attitude, knowledge of a score, and ability to get results in rehearsal.

It was that professionalism that made him one of three finalists to succeed the American-born Dennis Russell Davies in Brooklyn when Davies announced his resignation in 1994 in order to expand his guest-conducting activities in the United States and Europe. One of the other finalists was Neeme Järvi, conductor of the Detroit Symphony Orchestra and the Gothenburg Orchestra in Sweden, and one of the most recorded conductors of the day. (The third candidate was never identified.)

"We were faced with the choice between a very well-known conductor in his fifties who had two other orchestras and a younger American conductor with no other orchestras," Joseph Horowitz, then the Brooklyn's executive director, told *Newsday*.[4] "It had to be someone for whom this position was absolutely crucial careerwise," board chairman Robert Rosenberg told the *New York Times*. The right person would "make a full commitment to the orchestra and that included doing auditions, fund-raising, and community concerts. We couldn't be an 'also.' That was the problem, I felt, with Dennis." Rosenberg also wanted a relatively young American who could attract younger audiences.[5]

Horowitz, Henry Schuman, and Louis Bruno, representing a five-member search committee, traveled to Tanglewood in 1994 to hear Spano conduct a rehearsal of the student orchestra and a class on *Carmen* for student singers. The visit was in effect an audition, and Schuman and Bruno went home thinking they had found their man. An itinerant up till then because the right job had not come along, Spano was interested enough this time to talk. Over the next few weeks he met with the Brooklyn Philharmonic's players and board members. His willingness to play the piano in chamber concerts, speak to audiences, and appear at fund-raising functions only enhanced his appeal. He was offered a three-year contract in December.

Spano stepped into a difficult situation. Subscriptions had dropped precipitously when Davies took charge of the orchestra in 1991 and started the audience on a strong course of new music. Although marketing may have been a problem, the season had been cut from ten pairs of concerts to five because of the loss of ticket revenues. Davies, moreover, served as principal conductor rather than music director. Despite his musical skills he was—in Rosenberg's term—an "also," often unavailable for everyday needs like fund-raising and community appearances. Meanwhile, debt accumulated and staff turnover created a revolving door, through which four executive directors, including Horowitz, and five development directors passed between 1990 and 1998. By 1999 the situation had temporarily stabilized and the budget was balanced for the first time in five years. Subscriptions doubled and Spano began building toward what he hoped would again be a ten-program season.

Spano inherited thematic programming—but not thematic seasons—from the Davies-Horowitz regime. Lectures, discussions, and chamber concerts were part of a weekend package built around the philharmonic's concerts. In 1996 Spano's first philharmonic program, titled Orientalism, combined the familiar with the unfamiliar: Rimsky-Korsakoff's *Scheherazade* and

"Empress of the Pagodas" from Ravel's *Mother Goose* Suite with the Second Symphony by Colin McPhee, an American influenced by Balinese gamelan music. The other weekend activities included an Interplay concert of traditional gamelan music, performances by minimalist Steve Reich, and piano duets played by Spano and former director Lukas Foss.

Subsequent programs jumped around on the musical map. There was an A to Z evening (John Adams to Frank Zappa) showing connections between contemporary classical and popular styles. Parables of Death, including the Foss work by that name, brought in former rock diva Marianne Faithfull to sing Kurt Weill. A flamenco evening featured traditional numbers, sung and danced by the veterans Carmen Linares and Pilar Roja, along with symphonic works by the Hispanic composers Joaquin Turina, Carlos Surinach, Roberto Gerhard, and Manuel de Falla. The season ended on a springtime note—Britten's rarely heard *Spring* Symphony and Ravel's complete *Daphnis and Chloé* ballet, with its lush evocations of nature.

In a look back over the season in the *Wall Street Journal,* Greg Sandow found more to admire in Spano's work than in the programming itself, which at that time was largely of Horowitz's creation. Sandow termed Spano "a real find, an unforced and powerful conductor who lets music unfold naturally, a man who makes you think the works are speaking for themselves, even though he's in command of every detail." Sandow quibbled over some of the repertoire and performers, but his principal complaint suggested the inherent difficulty in thematic programming: its intellectual scaffolding can serve as a prop for artistic flimsiness. In the flamenco program, for instance, Sandow questioned whether the demonstration of links between classical and popular styles broke down the barriers that seem to set classical music apart from everyday life:

"To people who don't care about flamenco already, won't its influence on de Falla seem no less academic than Haydn's influence on Beethoven? And what about the people who *do* come, who pack the house for Marianne Faithfull? Do they learn to care about the Brooklyn Philharmonic? I doubt it. At the last subscription weekend—a purely classical event, featuring Mr. Spano's vivid and sensuous performance of Ravel's *Daphnis and Chloé* ballet—the hall appeared to be half-empty."

Naturally, Sandow said (though without proposing a solution). Whatever the music, there sat an orchestra in conventional black-and-white concert dress, looking like penguins. The philharmonic was sending out mixed signals: "Its programs shout 'we're new and different'; its appearance mutters 'same old story.' What a missed opportunity! Here we have an orchestra that has done what the classical music business dreams of—it has found new listeners. But it hasn't learned how to keep them."[6]

Other critics, other opinions. In the *New Yorker*, Alex Ross praised the philharmonic's "brazen" programming, which "more or less went off the grid of American orchestral culture."

At a 1997 After Mahler weekend, Ross was especially impressed by Spano's performance of Sofia Gubaidulina's *Stimmen . . . verstummen (Voices . . . Silenced)*, a twelve-movement symphony with overtones of apocalypse. (Also on the death-haunted orchestral program were Claude Vivier's *Zipangu*, a tortured work by a murdered Canadian, and the Adagio from Mahler's Tenth Symphony, a work he left unfinished at his death.) Spano, Ross wrote, had obviously rehearsed the Gubaidulina piece "with an eye not only to the musical argument but also to the theatrical effect." Rather than Sandow's missed opportunity, Ross heard craftsmanship, showmanship, and intelligence that reminded him of "Leonard Bernstein's pathbreaking concerts with the New York Symphony in the nineteen-forties, before he took on the more glamorous challenge of the New York Philharmonic." Yet for Spano, Ross added, the Brooklyn "need not be a stepping stone to something greater. It could become something great in itself."[7]

In the *Times* Paul Griffiths hailed the same program, hearing in the Mahler performance a climactic moment so "glorious" that it was "as if a skylight had been opened on new possibilities."[8] Critics were sitting up and paying attention, which meant that others were watching and listening. Among them was David Letterman, on whose *Late Show* Spano and the philharmonic appeared in 1998 and again on New Year's Eve in 1999.

At the dawn of the twenty-first century classical music, like the universe, was flying apart in all directions. On the supply side there were more musicians and audiences than ever. The American Symphony Orchestra League counted 1,800 professional and amateur orchestras in the country in 2000. They filled an estimated thirty-two million seats, almost five million more than in 1990–91, and reported total revenues of $1.267 billion, an increase of 9.8 percent over the 1997–98 season. On the demand side the customers ranged from devotees who had grown up with classical music in their homes and schools to younger listeners who, if they attended concerts at all, brought with them the expectations bred by the jittery world of rock, television, and the Internet.

The new media and the new values they spawned had done their work. Standard concerts offering an overture, a concerto, and a symphony seemed a relic of the past, not just to younger listeners, but also to younger composers and performers. To stake out an identity and reach new audiences, concert presenters were experimenting with many formats and strategies. Some adapted the trappings of rock concerts, with lighting effects, video screens, casual dress, or talks from the stage. Some freely mixed pop, jazz, or ethnic music with the classics. Others served a steady diet of new music. Some bet on thematic programming. All became dependent on marketing— more dependent than concert organizations had been in the less competitive past. The alternative was to lose, or risk losing, what even in musical circles was being called market share. Only the major orchestras, such as those of New York and Boston, could afford to retain the concert repertoire, format, and airs handed down from the nineteenth century, even when those orchestras placed new or unfamiliar music before audiences.

Conservatism did not stop some orchestras from plunging heavily into new music. The Cleveland Orchestra under the German Christoph von Dohnányi, the Los Angeles Philharmonic under the Finn Esa-Pekka Salonen, and the Chicago Symphony Orchestra under the Argentinian-Israeli Daniel Barenboim regularly mixed contemporary works with the classics. The composers ranged from young, pop-influenced figures such as Steven Mackey, whose *Eating Greens* included delivery of a pizza onstage, to such established figures in the cerebral tradition as Elliott Carter. Even before those foreign-born music directors arrived on the scene in the late 1980s and early 1990s, the Saint Louis Symphony under the American Leonard Slatkin was swimming in similar waters. In 1995 another American, Michael Tilson Thomas, went to the San Francisco Symphony with a new-music agenda reinforced by a series of postseason festivals devoted to specialized repertoire.

These were risky ventures. They virtually guaranteed that some old-line subscribers would leave in a huff. The hope—apparently realized in San Francisco—was that younger listeners would take their place and show old-timers they'd be smart to stick around. Underneath lay a conviction that music required constant renewal: that both the repertoire and musicians themselves had to be reinvigorated by infusions of the new. If some of it turned out to be ephemeral, well, that was the chance you took. The only way to know was to play the stuff and find out. And there was no guarantee that the first, or even fifth or tenth, hearing would yield a final verdict. That was the way it had been for Mozart, Beethoven, Brahms, and the others. The cream found its way to the top. The rest sank to the bottom and disappeared. But without Dohnányis, Salonens, Barenboims, and Tilson Thomases, symphony orchestras would become, in the often-used analogy, museums stuffed with artifacts from the past. Spano arrived on this scene just when an older generation of conductors was taking leave of it.

Bernstein, who had a lifelong association (not always amicable) with the Boston Symphony, died in October 1990, just as Spano was taking up his duties there. Over the next decade the directors of all the marquee orchestras—all foreign born—either left or declared their intention to leave: Georg Solti in Chicago, Riccardo Muti and then Wolfgang Sawallisch in Philadelphia, Kurt Masur in New York, von Dohnányi in Cleveland, Seiji Ozawa in Boston. An echelon below, other veteran maestros moved on to emeritus status as laureate or guest conductors. These included, along with the Russian Mstislav Rostropovich in Washington, four with American roots: Herbert Blomstedt in San Francisco, André Previn in Los Angeles, Lorin Maazel in Pittsburgh, and David Zinman in Baltimore.

There was a time, back in the era of Arturo Toscanini, Serge Koussevitzky, Leopold Stokowski, and Eugene Ormandy, when a music director spent all or most of his time with his orchestra and, together, they grew in stature. In the jet age music directors became part-timers, flying from podium to podium. Careers speeded up and conductors burned out. The job requires a large commitment of time and energy not just in study and the concert hall but also in such housekeeping and public-relations chores as auditions, care and feeding of patrons, and meetings with players, managers, and board members. At some point the director feels the drain and wants to concentrate on music. Or routine sets in. Or internecine warfare takes a toll, as it apparently did at the New York Philharmonic, where Masur reportedly had been in conflict with former executive director Deborah Borda (who was in turn reported to have been in conflict with the board).

There was no shortage of Americans coming up behind the departing veterans. Except for James Levine and Tilson Thomas, however, none had the experience, authority, and staying power of a Bernstein. After thirty years at the Metropolitan Opera, the highly respected Levine in 2001 took on the additional directorship of the Boston Symphony, effective in 2004. He would then be sixty-one. Tilson Thomas, unlike his mentor, Bernstein, whose star was already streaking across the heavens when he was in his twenties, was fifty when he arrived at the San Francisco Symphony in 1995 from the London Symphony Orchestra. Among other Americans of their generation, James Conlon was more or less out of sight, making his career in Europe, and Slatkin, after a notable career in Saint Louis, moved laterally to the National Symphony Orchestra in Washington to succeed Rostropovich. Maazel, who had made his career in both the United States and Europe, was chosen to succeed Masur in New York. Fifteen or more years younger than these veterans, Spano was canny about his career. He knew he had little chance of landing one of the big-name podiums—or if he did land one, he might not be ready for it. Instead of Boston or New York, for which critics touted him, he went to Atlanta when it was time to make a career move. There, as in Brooklyn, he could experiment and mature.

Legend has it that the seventeenth-century French composer Jean-Baptiste Lully was the first conductor. In 1687, in the heat of conducting his own *Te Deum* to celebrate Louis XIV's recovery from an operation, Lully accidentally banged his toe with the staff he was using to beat time. He died of gangrene. For most of the next two centuries, the conductor remained a relatively minor figure, though not because of occupational hazards. He was usually the concertmaster, who beat time and gave cues from the first violinist's chair. The modern conductor is a product of the Romantic period, with its larger symphonic structures and heroic conception of the leader. From such titans as Mahler and Hans von Bülow sprang the tradition that culminated in Bernstein and Herbert von Karajan.

The general level of conducting and playing in the United States today is higher than ever, and probably as good as or better than that in the sanctified European tradition. Many a medium-sized American city boasts an orchestra comparable in quality to those of big cities in the past. These orchestras provide employment, experience, and exposure for the conductors (and of course players) pouring out of conservatories and universities. Yet in today's democratic society the hero-tyrant model will no longer work. Even if custom allowed it, the musicians' union would not. Contracts and regulations shield union members from a conductor's authoritarian instincts.

Whether the conductor is hero or nice guy, some indefinable chemistry of personality and vision, emotion and intellect, is needed, with the balance between these elements shifting from orchestra to orchestra and from period to period. In his book *Findings,* Bernstein defines the conductor as "automatically a narcissist, like any other performing artist; he is an exhibitionist by profession—why else would he be a performer at all? He has a built-in suction pump attached to his ego, and no torrent of praise is big enough to slake his thirst." A few sentences later Bernstein draws a distinction between "the conductor who is vain on his own behalf and the conductor whose ego glories in the reflected radiance of musical creativity."[9] Bernstein is probably talking more about himself than anyone else. But the point remains: it takes a certain amount of presumption and ego to stand up before one hundred highly skilled musicians and say, do it my way.

Watch Spano conduct, or talk to him or his players, and you get a sense of a new breed of musician: solidly grounded, rich in gifts, democratic in spirit, aware of his limitations. No mania for control, no outrageous interpretations, no Promethean fire snatched from the heavens: just good, honest workmanship.

Is this the spirit of the times, when to play the hero is to make yourself ridiculous, unless you are a rock musician? Or are the times merely waiting for a new kind of hero to be born?

No one knows. No one will know until the hero strides onto the scene, trailing whatever clouds of glory.

If Spano isn't that hero, he came close enough for Schuman and Bruno, the Brooklyn players who scouted him at Tanglewood. They and their fellow players, they said, soon learned to admire him for his ability to make the orchestra sound good, and to do it quickly.

Spano has to get results quickly. The Brooklyn Philharmonic is made up of freelancers who play under him, on average, one week a month. They get only four rehearsals (five if the program is unusually demanding) to put together eighty or more minutes of music, which they often have not played or even heard before. It helps that turnover is low and many of the players perform together in such other New York freelance assemblages as the Orchestra of Saint Luke's and the New York City Opera orchestra. But the key, according to Schuman and Bruno, is Spano's rehearsal skills.

"It's not just a process of getting to rehearsal and reading the music through twenty times," Bruno said. Spano knows how to "make the thing work musically, how the piece works structurally." Schuman said, "Rather than staring at the same thirty or forty bars forever and wondering what's on the next page, the orchestra really learns the piece."

There was Magnus Lindberg's *Arena,* a one-movement piece dependent on a shimmer of colors and textures, which Spano gave its New York premiere in the Northern Lights program in 2000. Bruno recalled taking the Finnish composer's 1994–95 work home and practicing it. But because it was new to him, he had no way of knowing how his part fitted into the whole. At the first rehearsal Spano, following his usual practice, went through the piece once without stopping for corrections. He then started over, working on trouble spots, until he obtained a gleaming concert performance that suggested sunlight on arctic waters.

Schuman, whose orchestral experience went back to playing in the Symphony of the Air in the 1950s under Leopold Stokowski, also valued Spano's ability (he compared it to Stokowski's) to get a distinctive sound from the orchestra. Within twenty minutes of a rehearsal, Spano, like a fine violinist with his instrument, gives the orchestra its own voice, Schuman said. Trust in the leader allows the players to blend and put a glow on the sound. Both musicians also described Spano as open to questions and suggestions from his players.

Bruno said the orchestra was playing so well that it should be attracting a wider audience, particularly from Manhattan. He would like to see it playing two or three times the number of programs, touring (particularly to Manhattan), and making more than occasional recordings. Getting Manhattanites to cross the Brooklyn Bridge, Bruno said, is like getting them to travel to a foreign country.

Ah, but there's always a snake in Eden: The players worried that because of Spano's success in Brooklyn, he would be a target for headhunters from more active or glamorous orchestras. That was, in fact, the only concern that Schuman and Bruno confessed, for either themselves or their colleagues, about their leader.

It was almost foreordained, as the Brooklyn players suspected, that higher-profile orchestras would cast an envious eye at their conductor. On February 8, 2000, Spano made the jump, becoming director-designate of the Atlanta Symphony Orchestra. But he held onto the Brooklyn job, which permitted him to do things he could not—at least not immediately—do in Atlanta. Requiring his presence only six weeks a year, Brooklyn allowed time for another orchestra. If not quite a jet-age conductor, Spano became, like most of his colleagues, a maestro with two masters. Rather than cause alarm, the Atlanta appointment seemed to make Spano an even better catch. It allowed him to hone his skills in a different kind of programming and environment and brought him wider recognition, all of which would come home as better concerts and more recognition for Brooklyn.

Though Spano was working just across the river and New York critics, weary of the standard repertoire, furnished him with a cheering section, he was apparently never a contender for the New York Philharmonic, where Kurt Masur was on the way out and Lorin Maazel on the way in. In the *New York Times,* Anthony Tommasini lamented that Spano's admirers, "including many critics, may wish that a major American orchestra, especially the New York Philharmonic, had had the courage to give him a chance."[10] Boston critics raised the same cry about their orchestra, from which Ozawa had recently resigned. Europeans continued to dominate this trans-Atlantic checkerboard.

Spano flew from Cardiff, Wales, where he had been conducting the Welsh National Opera in Mozart's *Cosí fan tutte,* to Atlanta for the coronation. Amid the hoopla and hype customary for such occasions, he stood before giant posters of himself at a champagne reception in the Four Seasons Hotel. Gesturing toward the larger-than-life Spano visage, he joked that his mother had warned him not to get a big head.

In two crowded days he met hundreds of people—not just symphony musicians, staff and board members, and volunteers, but also government officials, arts council members, and other prominent Atlantans. For someone who loves his time alone or with small groups of friends, "it was the whirlwind aspect that was overwhelming," and promised to remain so. Yet he welcomed the challenge of meeting people and becoming involved in the community. Someone, he recalled, once asked him, "Do you miss the days when all a conductor had to do was conduct?" He replied, "I'm not so sure that that isn't just a myth."

Spano had been a guest conductor four times in the past. Now, under a four-year contract, he would conduct the Atlanta Symphony for five weeks in 2000–01 as director-designate and up to fourteen weeks during each of the next three years under the full mantle of director. Donald Runnicles, music director of the San Francisco Opera, would join him as the Atlanta's principal guest conductor.

Spano had turned down previous offers of directorships. He won't identify the orchestras beyond saying that they were smaller than Atlanta. He accepted Atlanta because it presented a greater opportunity, not just to lead an outstanding orchestra, but also to make that orchestra a vital part of the community.

For a long time, he said, he had wanted the longer working periods that go with a bigger post, and Atlanta offered a full season. Another part of the appeal, he said, was that "the orchestra is so damn good. They're a wonderful orchestra, they're very cultivated. And the other thing is, I like the city. I have friends who live there, so I started visiting about five years ago, socially, not to work with the orchestra. And it's very exciting, what's happening, because the city is growing so fast. It's booming and very vital for that reason. But it's a very different kind of vitality from New York. It doesn't have that manic level."

Founded in 1944, the Atlanta Symphony Orchestra in 2000 was ranked thirteenth in the country by budget size—$21 million—by the American Symphony Orchestra League. Unlike Brooklyn, with a $1.8 million budget, it performs full-time and year-round, with regular pops, family, casual, and holiday concerts. Under Robert Shaw, the well-known choral conductor who served as director from 1967 to 1988, the orchestra achieved a high degree of quality and, using its own chorus, made a series of acclaimed recordings of major choral works. The concert programming was standard: a sprinkling of twentieth-century works in a season dominated by classical and Romantic favorites.

In Atlanta as in Brooklyn, Spano walked into a situation with both problems and opportunities. He succeeded Yoel Levi, who for five years had been at the center of a running battle between factions in the orchestra, administration, and board disputing whether he should be kept on as director. The orchestra had recovered from a ten-week strike at the beginning of the 1996–97 season, but was still struggling with an accumulated deficit, which stood at $900,000. Concerts took place in a hall with difficult acoustics. And at many concerts, as Spano found when he was a guest conductor, the hall was only half full. On the brighter side, the players had signed a four-year contract, effective in 2000–01, and as a gesture of reconciliation, Levi had been engaged as conductor emeritus for five years (though he had no concerts in 2000–01). Planning for a new hall was in progress. Whatever the problems with Levi, Spano said he wanted to distance himself from them and concentrate on his work with the fine orchestra his predecessor had bequeathed him.

In his season as director-designate, Spano led an opening-night gala with soprano Sylvia McNair, a Brahms–Witold Lutoslawski program with pianist Emanuel Ax, an all-Rachmaninoff program with pianist Horacio Gutierrez, and, as the finale, the Verdi Requiem. He planned no programming changes in the transitional year; indeed, he inherited a season already in place before his appointment. But he declared himself committed to taking the orchestra on tour and getting a new hall built.

Atlanta is not New York City, and if he did the same kind of program-ming in Atlanta as in Brooklyn, Spano said, he wouldn't have an audience. And rightly so. The Atlanta Symphony, he said, is "the New York Philhar-monic of Atlanta," conservative in outlook and repertoire. But Atlanta was in for a gradual dose of new music.

First Spano planned to change the public's perception of new music by introducing accessible works by lesser-known living composers. A new gen-eration, he said, had broken with the cerebral exercises favored by older composers working in post-Schoenberg styles. Two colorfully titled exam-ples would provide a start in 2001–02: *Rainbow Body* by Christopher Theo-fanidis (from whom Spano had commissioned a work for Brooklyn) and *Blue Cathedral* by Jennifer Higdon. When he did *Rainbow Body* as the open-ing piece in concerts with the Houston Symphony, "the audience was on their feet at the end of every performance," he said. *Blue Cathedral* proved a "gorgeous piece" when he premiered it as a seventy-fifth anniversary com-mission at the Curtis Institute in Philadelphia, where Higdon teaches.

At the outset Spano would not subject Atlanta to music by the Second Viennese School of composers, Schoenberg, Berg, and Webern. Schoen-berg, he recognized, "is a name that strikes terror in the hearts of many lis-teners." But he would work his way up to the fearful trinity and other tougher music year by year, as he scattered new works through the season. Among the five other living composers' works included in the 2001–02 sea-son were Joseph Schwantner's Percussion Concerto, Richard Danielpour's Violin Concerto, and John Adams's *Harmonielehre,* all in fairly accessible styles. Other new ventures included a showing of video interviews with the living composers before performances of their works. A new ASO to Go se-ries would take the orchestra to five family-style concerts in the Atlanta sub-urbs. Four Interactive Fridays would engage Spano and guest conductors in conversations with the audiences about works to be played, and Spano would conduct such diverse repertory as a cycle of Bach's six *Brandenburg* Concertos and Ralph Vaughan Williams's *Sea Symphony*.

All the music, Spano said, would be "candy" to audiences, helping to fill those empty seats. "I don't think of it in terms of programming things that they have to listen to and things that they're going to want to listen to. I'd rather think everything we're doing people are going to want to hear."

Every conductor has strong spots, weak spots, and blind spots in his repertoire. The talk about Spano as a prospective music director in New

York or Boston overlooked one point: he was not as consistent in the standard repertoire as in the new and unusual music that endeared him to the critics who talked him up.

Spano conceded that there was some music—the Schubert and Bruckner symphonies, for example—that he loved as a listener but didn't yet feel able to conduct well. The transitions in Bruckner still gave him trouble (as they do many another conductor) and he found the early Schubert symphonies (but not the big C Major) lacking in the depth of Schubert's songs, which he loves to listen to and perform as a pianist. He says he is fanatical in his passion for Schumann. But when he conducted some of Schumann's orchestral works a few years before, he thought his performances were "really lackluster." The thick orchestration was a problem, but the deeper issue was his own connection to the music: "I feel so close to it I'm always just disappointed in myself." Out of such dissatisfaction comes growth. In Atlanta he planned to go back to Schumann and see if he could do better.

Spano would provide Atlanta with a measure of stability it had lacked in the preceding years under Levi. Assistant concertmaster Jun-Ching Lin, one of five musicians who served on the eleven-member search committee, told the New York Times, "Very early on in the process it became apparent that we wanted more collaboration among the orchestra, the music director, the board, and management. It was obvious to us that the days of the music director simply lording over his domain needed to change."[11] Atlanta in turn would give Spano a platform on which to develop his repertoire outside the glare of New York publicity. Brooklyn would let him demonstrate and refine his new programming ideas in the full blaze of that scrutiny. It was an ideal situation for a conductor on the way up. Perhaps in five or ten years he would be ready for New York or Boston, if they were ready for him.

As director of the student conducting program at Tanglewood, Spano runs an annual weeklong seminar introducing his charges—there are usually five to eight of them, between the ages of eighteen and thirty—to the unglamorous, nuts-and-bolts aspects of their trade. The classes, which take place over lunch in a former mansion comfortably distant from the main campus, focus on the needs of small-city orchestras. That is where the beginner, if he is lucky enough to land a job at all, is likely to find himself.

From Spano and a series of guest speakers, who come from both the artistic and management sides of orchestra life, the students learn that there is a lot more to being a budding music director than studying your scores and conducting your orchestra. In the symphonic minor leagues, the conductor will spend more time on such matters as negotiating contracts with players, meeting the public, and shaking the money tree than on making music. One of the class exercises consists of making up sample concert programs. After the maestros-in-the-making have drawn up their plans, Spano and the guest speaker of the day offer critiques. The flaws they find may be practical (too many extra players needed, and hence a budget-busting expense) or artistic (the chosen works clash instead of complementing one another). Or a speaker may describe a ticklish problem such as forcing the retirement of a beloved older musician who no longer plays well. The students are invariably surprised, and sometimes dismayed, to discover that so much of their lives will be devoted to practicalities rather than art.

Spano's canniness about career building makes him an ideal leader for these classes. He also is not so much older than his students that he seems a father figure, as did his highly regarded predecessor, Gustav Meier. As the classes make clear, politics is part of the music director's job. He must cultivate friends in business and government if the orchestra and he are to be accepted in the community. The problems with Yoel Levi in Atlanta suggest what can happen when the director loses a broad base of support.

Spano understands the rules of the game. He knew he would not be moving up to the director's job in Boston, no matter how much the critics huffed and puffed in his favor. As he told the *Boston Globe,* "I knew I wouldn't be right for the Boston Symphony job, and that it wouldn't be right for me. I'm too close to the situation. The new music director ought to come from the outside, and should bring his own priorities and fresh perceptions to the situation."[12] For that reason, and because of his wider experience, the orchestra chose James Levine.

Atlanta, on the other hand, greeted Spano like a conquering hero when he returned in September 2001 to begin his reign as music director. His face appeared on billboards, the sides of buses, and giant video screens at Braves baseball games (he wore a Braves uniform to conduct the Atlanta Symphony). Reviews were ecstatic. With the country in shock over that month's terrorist attacks on the World Trade Center and the Pentagon, a television station used his performance of "The Star-Spangled Banner" with the Atlanta Symphony to close its newscasts. He and the orchestra made their first recording, Rimsky-Korsakov's *Scheherazade;* it was done for Telarc, the company that had helped to bring the orchestra to national prominence under Robert Shaw. Spano was already planning further recordings, including a collection of American music, Vaughan Williams's *Sea Symphony*, Tchaikovsky's Fourth Symphony, and Bernstein's Mass.

As Spano promised, Atlanta was in for a dose of new ideas and music. In a preview of his first full season, the *Los Angeles Times* recounted how Spano, principal guest conductor Runnicles, executive director Allison Vulgamore, and other orchestra administrators had planned the year's programming. At one point during the brainstorming session, which took place in what they call their "war room," Vulgamore pointed out that they had put together a season without including a single symphony. "It was exciting to see how far out there we had gone," she observed. Climbing in off that limb, they brought the season back closer to listeners' expectations.[13] It was as if Spano had been subjected to the kind of critique he inflicts on his Tanglewood students.

For the *Sea Symphony*, in which Vaughan Williams sets verses by Walt Whitman, Spano planned a computerized show of lights and images as an accompaniment. The idea is not new, Justin Davidson wrote in the *Los Angeles Times,* "but Spano comes to Atlanta with a longer track record of such experiments than most conductors, and far more powerful convictions." Davidson noted, for example, a staged version of Schubert's song cycle *Die Winterreise* in which Spano, as the pianist, teamed with a baritone soloist. To dramatize the Romantic tale of a rejected lover who fades from life, the set featured ranks of backward-facing chairs and "dim black-and-white films [that] flickered like fading memories."[14]

For Spano's videotaped talks with composers to introduce their works, Davidson wrote, a large screen unfurls behind the orchestra after it has tuned and the concertmaster has taken his place. But instead of walking out to the podium, Spano makes his first appearance on the screen, interviewing the composer. "It's not a groundbreaking idea," Davidson said, "but it is a small act of sedition, an unsettling of the concert's comfortable rituals. It's also an acknowledgement that in our visually oriented world, sounds don't necessarily speak for themselves. Music must be seen to be heard."

The willingness to try new ideas brought Spano to the attention of venturesome opera companies. The Santa Fe Opera engaged him to conduct the American premiere of the Finnish composer Kaija Saariaho's dreamlike, avant-garde *L'amour de loin* during the summer of 2002. The assignment would require him to miss Tanglewood that year. The Seattle Opera chose him to lead a cycle of Wagner's four *Ring* operas, tentatively scheduled for

2005. In the *Los Angeles Times,* Spano recounted his reaction when Speight Jenkins, the Seattle Opera's general manager, called:

"Speight said, 'I want you to do the *Ring,*' and I said, 'You're out of your mind. I'm a Wagner hater!' He said, 'I knew you'd say that, which is why I asked you.' So I thought about it. I've always had violent reactions to Wagner. I find him too musically manipulative. On the other hand, I'm a sucker for that. I've never doubted his genius and never questioned the brilliance. But his politics are revolting, and I think that they're evident in the sound. Anyway, I'm very excited about doing this now. I really want to. It's a life-changing decision: I have to carve out the time to learn the damn thing."[15]

He was also carving out time during the 2001–02 season to make his debut with the New York Philharmonic and conduct Tchaikovsky's *Eugene Onegin* at the Houston Opera and Leoš Janáček's *Jenůfa* at the Welsh National Opera. On another front, he was becoming the voice of classical music for Atlanta-based Delta Airlines. Passengers will hear his programming and announcements of it on two classical music channels on Delta's planes. One channel will feature recordings by the Atlanta Symphony. "The other," Spano told the *Boston Globe,* "will be things I just happen to like. I'm starting off with Vladimir Horowitz playing his own transcription of 'The Stars and Stripes Forever.' "[16]

Also in the fall of 2001, Spano stepped into the kind of political entanglement that sometimes trips up classical music. For a guest-conducting stint with the Boston Symphony, he planned to lead three choruses from John Adams's opera *The Death of Klinghoffer* on a program with Sibelius's symphonic poem *Kullervo.* The opera tells the true story of a wheelchair-bound Jewish passenger who was pushed overboard to his death in 1985 by Palestinian terrorists on the cruise ship *Achille Lauro.* The terrorists are portrayed as human beings, not stereotypical villains. With the shock of the New York and Washington terrorist attacks still fresh in the public's mind, the Boston Symphony said it decided "to err on the side of being sensitive." With Spano's consent, it replaced Adams's music with Aaron Copland's challenging but uncontroversial Symphony no. 1. Adams and his librettist, Alice Goodman, were outraged. They accused the orchestra of evading serious issues and offering audiences escapist fare instead. Adams refused to allow a performance of one of his other works in the place of *Klinghoffer.*

Spano demonstrated that, however advanced his views on programming might be, his political instincts could be conservative. He told the *New*

*York Times,* "John is angry, and I feel terrible that this has hurt him. I'm a big supporter of his music. I perform it all the time, and I will continue to, and I'm sorry he took offense. But I don't agree with him that we did the wrong thing. I, as a person, am deeply wounded [by the terrorists' acts], as so many people are, and I think we're being sensitive to that."[17]

The tension between politics and music has a long history. As composition of the *Eroica* Symphony progressed, Beethoven first hailed Napoleon as liberator but later scorned him as emperor. Mahler was driven out of the directorship of the Vienna Opera by anti-Semitic intrigues; Hitler banned Jewish and other so-called "decadent" composers. But the year 2001 marked a new era, one in which it was possible to use jetliners to promote your symphony orchestra, but also to destroy skyscrapers. Spano, shaking up expectations right and left, seemed a musical paradigm for the times.

Before taking a loft in Atlanta, Spano shared a comfortable but modest fourth-floor walk-up in the upscale Brooklyn Heights neighborhood with his concertmaster, Laura Park, a former assistant concertmaster of the Boston Symphony who followed him to Brooklyn and later joined the Philadelphia Orchestra. Many of his neighbors were his age; many worked across the river in law offices or on Wall Street. On weekends they filled the restaurants and cafés along the tree-shaded main streets.

In his living room Spano walked to a bookshelf and pulled down a volume titled *Walt Whitman's New York.* His face wrinkling with pleasure, he opened it to the page where the bard of Brooklyn boasts of "our magnificent *Academy of Music,* so beautiful outside and in, and on a scale commensurate with similar buildings, even in some of the largest and most polished capitals of Europe."[18] More recently *BBC Music* magazine presented an up-to-date English view of the magnificent academy, where the Brooklyn Philharmonic performs:

> BAM is one of the certified miracles of the past ten years. There's a reason why on most nights limousines are lined up outside Brooklyn's least salubrious addresses and it rests in the quality and variety of the avant-garde experimental performances on offer here. BAM presents concerts, contemporary and classical dance, performance art, theater for young people, repertory and first-run films, and reaches out to artists and audiences throughout the city as well as being home to the Brooklyn Philharmonic (a first-rate orchestra

with more adventurous programming than the NY Philharmonic) and the Next Wave Festival. BAM is also blessed with the Harvey Theater—a peeling, elegant wreck of a playhouse with faultless sight lines.[19]

The present academy is not the "temple of Italian song" whose praises Whitman sang. It is not even on the same Brooklyn Heights site. The original building, which according to Whitman stood on grounds previously hallowed by "big baggage-wagons and iron-grated cages of animals belonging to some perambulating 'show,' "[20] burned down in 1903. The new beaux arts edifice, located in the once-fashionable Fort Greene section, opened in 1908. The festivities culminated in a gala evening starring Geraldine Farrar and Enrico Caruso in a Metropolitan Opera production of Gounod's *Faust*. Over the succeeding years, the stage also hosted such luminaries as Isadora Duncan, Arturo Toscanini, Paul Robeson, and Lily Pons.

The neighborhood and audiences went into decline with the middle-class flight to the suburbs that followed World War II, and language and martial arts classes succeeded Farrar and Caruso in the performing spaces. As financial troubles mounted, the city took over the building in 1951. A revitalization began in 1967 under a new director, Harvey Lichtenstein, who served in that capacity for thirty-two years. Among his innovations was the Next Wave Festival, which has attracted adventurous audiences to the less than "salubrious" environs with an eclectic mix of Shakespeare and Rameau, performance art and African dance, the Royal Shakespeare Company and Les Arts Florissants, Merce Cunningham and Mark Morris, and the operas of John Adams and Philip Glass. The stately temple now boasts, in addition to its gilt-and-cream, box-encircled opera house, a four-screen art cinema, the highly touted BAMcafé, and series of events for young adults. Thanks to all that culture, the neighborhood is gradually going up-scale.

The Brooklyn Philharmonic was founded in 1954 by Siegfried Landau. He was succeeded in 1971 by Lukas Foss, who left in 1990 and was in turn followed by Dennis Russell Davies. During Davies's tenure the philharmonic became the academy's resident orchestra, performing in many of the musical and dance programs. Foss's Meet the Moderns series presented recent works alongside the classical and Romantic masters, earning the philharmonic annual awards from the American Society of Composers, Authors, and Publishers for adventurous programming. Davies stepped up the new-music quotient and in 1996 the orchestra received the American Symphony Orchestra League's Morton Gould Award, conferred each year on a single group for innovative programming.

It was also during the Davies reign that the philharmonic's subscribers began heading for the exits. From an all-time high of 2,800 in 1990–91, Davies's first year, subscriptions dropped to 1,800 in 1991–92 and 1,000 in 1992–93, finally hitting bottom at 428 in 1998–99. A rebound then began, reaching 929 in 1999–2000.

Although Schuman and Bruno blamed new music for the decline, Christopher Stager, the orchestra's former director of marketing and communications, said a different approach to marketing was at least as much at fault. The Brooklyn Academy, which was doing the marketing in the early 1990s, sold everything on a single-ticket basis rather than by subscription. The approach didn't work as well for the philharmonic as for dance and theater, Stager said. He put more emphasis on subscriptions, but said Spano was the key to the rebound.

"Clearly Spano has been connecting with this community and with our key audience. He creates programs, even if they're contemporary, that are extremely easy to communicate to the potential audience. It's an easy season to sell because the links are there." For instance, Stager said, he would have had trouble selling Messiaen's opera, *Saint Francis of Assisi*, the 1999–2000 season's final program, if it had been dropped into a season of Beethoven symphonies and Tchaikovsky concertos. But "in a season like this, it relates to the concert before—and in fact four before it."

For 1999–2000 the philharmonic had a balanced budget of $1.8 million (approximately 4 percent of that of a top-ranked orchestra), though $350,000 in accumulated debt was outstanding. Ticket prices were kept low; they ranged from eight to forty dollars in the 1999–2000 season. The minimum price was in fact the lowest for any professionally presented classical concert in New York, Stager said. But because of the pay arrangement with the orchestra, he figured that even if he sold every ticket in the 2,100-seat opera house at full price, he could bring earned income to only 25 percent of the budget.

The orchestra's most recent marketing survey, taken in 1999, showed 60 percent of the audience was from Brooklyn, 15 percent from Manhattan, and the rest from elsewhere. The average age of subscribers was fifty-six, the same as it was in 1983 and about the same as for other orchestras. The big difference in Brooklyn, Stager said, was that single-ticket buyers were almost ten years younger than the industry average, though the actual number varied according to program. Younger listeners attracted by Marianne Faithfull or a flamenco evening won't generally come back for Strings of War or Northern Lights. While it would be wonderful to have a younger audience, Stager said, the young are less likely than older concertgoers to become subscribers. These older concertgoers typically have high incomes, low debt, and more leisure time because they are well along in their careers and their children are grown up. It would take Brooklyn's younger followers ten years to catch up.

The Brooklyn Philharmonic has only sporadically made recordings. The most recent was a Musicmasters release of music by Lou Harrison, made in 1996 under Davies but not issued until 2000. With the record industry in financial disarray, the orchestra is more likely to turn to the Internet in the future, rather than make recordings to get its wares before a wider public, Stager said. Community outreach includes school and neighborhood concerts, presented free of charge. Spano also does a season preview for subscribers and potential subscribers, talking about the music, playing the piano, and playing recordings.

For Spano's first three years in Brooklyn, he continued the eclectic programming mix begun by Foss and expanded by Davies and Horowitz. Though themeless, the 1998–99 season had a twentieth-century perspective, with glances back at earlier traditions. It opened with an "A B & C" program, which revived Luciano Berio's *Sinfonia* for voices and orchestra (with the New York Virtuoso Singers) and culminated in John Adams's *Harmonielehre*. These two principal works cast widely divergent backward looks— Berio through a mélange of quotations from many sources, Adams through allusions to Wagner and Mahler—to make up-to-the-minute statements. The evening's "C" was Elliott Carter's still-new *Allegro scorrevole,* given its New York premiere in honor of his ninetieth birthday.

The second program, something of a coup, offered the New York premiere of Thomas Adès's opera *Powder Her Face* in a partial staging. The hot young English composer, then twenty-eight, uses a grab bag of popular and classical styles to tell the story of a deceased "Duchess of Argyll," who sums up her unsavory sex life with the motto "go to bed early and often." In a program commentary Spano said that when he first saw the opera, he knew instantly that "it must be heard at BAM." Both the "A B & C" program and *Powder Her Face* were part of the academy's Next Wave Festival.

Shostakovich's Symphony no. 7, a commemoration of the World War II siege of Leningrad, which the composer lived through, made up the entire third program. Then came a Music and Religion program combining Stravinsky's Mass, Bach's cantata *Christ lag in Todesbanden,* and Steve Reich's *Tehillim,* a setting of four Psalms in Hebrew (again sung by the New York Virtuoso Singers). Mahler's *Resurrection* Symphony, a concert-length testament of faith and optimism (with the Dessoff Choirs), closed the regular season. A family concert followed, featuring Beethoven's Symphony no. 5. It was to be the first of a family series Spano and the philharmonic would give.

The year 2000 clearly called for a millennial touch. Spano knew he couldn't be encyclopedic about an entire century in the five programs of his subscription season. At the same time, he said, he and his fellow program makers wanted to touch on some of the century's historical as well as musical landmarks. Budget constraints were also a consideration in planning.

Certainly a distinguishing characteristic of the century was war. So the opening program, Strings of War, offered three works that were shadowed by Europe's two world conflagrations: Bartók's Divertimento for string orchestra, Richard Strauss's *Metamorphosen* for twenty-three strings, and Shostakovich's Chamber Symphony (an arrangement of his String Quartet no. 8). The program was given twice in the academy's Harvey Theater, the "peeling, elegant wreck of a playhouse" whose décor suggested the aftermath of a war. The use of the smaller venue and a chamber orchestra of strings reduced costs.

"Another salient extramusical feature of the century," Spano said, "was East meets West." Hence, John Adams's opera *Nixon in China,* with its political and historical implications, was the second program, presented as part of the Next Wave Festival.

"The notion of pop culture and popular music's interaction with serious or art music was the idea behind the third program," Spano said. It was called Afterhours. Also given in the Harvey Theater, and enhanced with visual effects such as streamers, it offered an eclectic mix: six player-piano studies by Conlon Nancarrow in orchestral dress, *The New Orpheus,* a populist cantata by Kurt Weill, three lush film scores by Toru Takemitsu, and Astor Piazzolla's Double Concerto for guitar and bandoneon.

Spano then visited Finland as "the locus of a great deal of musical creativity and activity" in the late twentieth century, a period in which "nature and the notion of environmental awareness" also became important concerns. Northern Lights explored these ideas in three works by living composers; Magnus Lindberg's *Arena*, shimmering with arctic light; Einojuhani Rautavaara's *Cantus Articus*, a concerto for taped birdsong and orchestra, and Aulis Sallinen's mock-serious *Some Aspects of Peltoniemi Hintrik's Funeral March*. The evening's finale was the forest and fjord-flecked Fifth Symphony by these composers' spiritual forebear, Sibelius.

For the final program Spano memorialized "a general sense of spirituality" that pervaded the late decades of the century, performing the fourth, fifth, and eighth tableaux of Messiaen's only opera, the specifically Roman Catholic *Saint Francis of Assisi*. (Perhaps coincidentally, the opera, filled with birdsong, which occupied Messiaen throughout his career, provided a connection with Rautavaara's avian rhapsody on the previous program.) The opera was given only once because of the high costs of soloists, a chorus, and an enlarged orchestra.

The reviews were rapturous. In the *New York Times* Paul Griffiths described the performance as "a triumph for all concerned: the enormous orchestra spread out on a large stage, the chorus (the Westchester Oratorio Society) that brought celestial glory and strength to the close, the magnificent central soloists (David Wilson-Johnson as the Saint and Heidi Grant Murphy as the Angel), and the conductor, Robert Spano, encouraging them all to shocks of brilliance, strangeness, and warmth."[21]

To Murphy, who had previously sung Pamina in Mozart's *Magic Flute* under Spano at the Santa Fe Opera Festival, he was "Superman." Singing the Messiaen, with its difficult but superbly prepared orchestral part, under him "was just an extraordinary experience," she said.

Spano had stumbled on a plan. "The whole Century thing worked for us so well," he said, "that we realized this was a good idea." He and his fellow planners decided that they should furnish all their seasons with themes. After the initial success, however, thematic designs proved more difficult to pull off.

Spano was themeless when he began laying out the 2001–02 season. He knew he wanted to program Philip Glass's Fifth Symphony, Frank Martin's *Lay of the Love and Death of Cornet Christopher Rilke*, and Berlioz's *Romeo and Juliet*. They made up nearly half a season—the first half, as it turned out. At that point he realized that he was dealing with the idea of love and death. Taking its cue from Wagner's *Tristan und Isolde*, the season became *Liebestod* (love-death). Spano went on to fill out the schedule with Bach's *Art of the Fugue* (unfinished before his death), Luciano Berio's *Requies*, the Prelude and Love Death from *Tristan*, Scriabin's *Poem of Ecstasy*, Stravinsky's *Oedipus*

*Rex*, and Schoenberg's *Transfigured Night* (paired with the Martin). In addition, he commissioned works by two younger composers, Michael Hersh and Christopher Theofanidis. The Theofanidis work would be based on Greek choruses to complement *Oedipus Rex*.

There would be six programs, the first step in Spano's plan to build back up to a ten-program season. Future thematic seasons would culminate in commissions and revivals of major premieres to celebrate the orchestra's fiftieth anniversary in 2003–04.

Midway through the 2000–01 season, however, the Brooklyn Philharmonic underwent another of its periodic financial and management upheavals. Catherine M. Cahill, former executive director of the Toronto Symphony and general manager of the New York Philharmonic, was brought in as chief executive officer, with an eight-member staff of managers, advisors, and consultants to work under her. Christopher Stager, who had planned the new marketing strategy with Spano's strengths in mind, was among the staff members sent to the exits. Whether because of management concerns, artistic needs, or some combination of them, three of Spano's six programs had to be revised. The *Liebestod* theme was preserved, but two of the new programs seemed calculated to reduce personnel and expense.

Berlioz's *Romeo and Juliet*, which would have required a chorus and three vocal soloists, was dropped in favor of a purely orchestral program consisting of Arvo Pärt's *Cantus in Memory of Benjamin Britten*, Rachmaninoff's *Isle of the Dead*, and Shostakovich's Tenth Symphony. *Art of the Fugue* (which would have been performed in Spano's own transcription for small string orchestra) gave way to a program of French songs featuring soprano Dawn Upshaw, principal players of the philharmonic, and Spano at the piano. Mahler's Third Symphony, with mezzo-soprano Michelle DeYoung and a chorus, replaced the *Oedipus* program, which, like *Romeo and Juliet*, would have required several vocal soloists in addition to a chorus, and possibly some staging besides. The Hersh premiere, *Umbra*, for strings, woodwinds, and percussion, took place as planned, but the Theofanidis premiere was postponed for a year.

Reviews of the concerts remained favorable. Allan Kozinn of the *New York Times* wrote that the Pärt-Rachmaninoff-Shostakovich program "looked at the dark corners of the Eastern European musical soul, yet it was anything but monochromatic."[22] If there was any danger that the orchestra would lose Spano, as the players feared, it seemed more likely to come from front-office turmoil than dissatisfaction in the musicians' ranks.

Moving on to Songs of the Earth in 2001–02, Spano planned such heaven-and-earth choices as Stravinsky's *Rite of Spring,* orchestral excerpts from Wagner's *Ring* cycle, and Mahler's *Song of the Earth.* Milhaud's jazz ballet *La création du monde* was paired with Copland's raucous *El salón México* in a program on the vernacular side. Newer composers in the lineup included Ramon Zupko, Ross Edwards, and Bright Sheng, who would be represented by two works, one a Brooklyn commission in its premiere. Both Sheng pieces, mixing Chinese and Western traditions, were paired with Mahler's world-weary *Song of the Earth,* with its setting (in German translation) of Chinese poems and its Chinese tints in the orchestration. The Theofanidis commission emerged as *The Cows of Apollo,* a modern interpretation of an old satyr play using song, theater, and dance to tell a tale of the invention of music.

Spano puts the programs together in consultation with players, board and staff members, and such colleagues as Joseph Horowitz, the orchestra's program annotator (and former executive director), and Anthony Fogg, artistic administrator of the Boston Symphony. Although many orchestras are making a conscious effort to corral the young, Spano said that is not Brooklyn's primary aim. The new programming is simply a matter of performing music of substance. New music or not, thematic or not, "we take the old-fashioned attitude that the quality will sell itself, that we're doing something that's intrinsically valuable," Spano said. Nevertheless, he and the management began to notice more young faces in the audience. Subscriptions doubled in the first thematic year, and the programming continues to attract composers, publishers, and other musicians as well as critics and knowledgeable laypeople.

Spano confesses to a lot of "scrounging around" among compact discs to come up with ideas. Sometimes he will have done a work with another orchestra before bringing it to Brooklyn (or Atlanta). Sometimes a colleague's recommendation sparks his interest in a piece. That was the case with the Frank Martin work to be performed in 2001–02. Spano heard about the Swiss composer's virtually unknown *Lay of the Love and Death of Cornet Christopher Rilke,* with its text by Rainer Maria Rilke, from Reinbert de Leeuw, the new-music specialist from Amsterdam. They discussed repertoire while working together during Tanglewood's new-music week.

Once in a while Spano will program a work that is not to his taste. This was the case with Glass's Fifth Symphony, which is based on texts from the Bible, the Koran, the Tibetan Book of the Dead, and other religious writings from around the world. Davies was brought back to conduct the choral symphony in its United States premiere to open the 2000–01 season. Spano wanted to include this work because of the orchestra's long association with Glass under Davies and the Brooklyn Academy's history of performing Glass's operas. Yet because of the long spans of repetitive minimalist music in Glass's work, Spano "couldn't commit to it in the right way," and invited Davies to conduct.

So the programming was inventive and the critics came. Spano also acquired a disciple. His name was Federico Cortese.

The two men first met when Cortese was a conducting student at Tanglewood in 1995 and Spano was a conducting teacher. When Spano went to Brooklyn in 1996, he invited Cortese to join him. Cortese left Italy to become an artistic and management assistant—unpaid at first—at the philharmonic. "I learned a lot," he recalled with an acolyte's wide-eyed admiration. "He [Spano] knows everything, he has heard everything, he has conducted everything, he has played everything."

Several times during planning sessions, Cortese said, he questioned Spano's decisions about repertoire. Cortese feared, for instance, that Berlioz's *Damnation of Faust* would be too ambitious an undertaking because of the need for a chorus. He also pointed out that rehearsals would have to take place during Easter-Passover week, when some musicians might not be available, and that James Levine had led a performance of the same work the previous year in Carnegie Hall.

"So there were a lot of concerns," Cortese said. "It's not that Bob disregarded them, not at all. And then the performance was a great success." In fact, Spano's decisions always turned out for the best, Cortese said.

Following in his mentor's tracks, Cortese became an assistant conductor at the Boston Symphony in September 1998. Six days later he made his Boston Symphony debut in an even more spectacular fashion than Spano had done. Seiji Ozawa was scheduled to conduct a free public performance of Beethoven's Ninth Symphony on the Boston Common in celebration of his twenty-fifth anniversary as the orchestra's director. Ozawa came down with one of his periodic bouts of bronchitis, and in his place, before a crowd of eighty thousand, Cortese went on without rehearsal. Though running a fever, Ozawa was able to take the last two movements—it was his celebration, after all. Two months later Ozawa's bronchitis returned. As the standby conductor, Cortese had to take the last two of three staged performances of Puccini's *Madama Butterfly* in Symphony Hall. It was his first time conducting either work, though he had served as a vocal coach and standby conductor for *Butterfly* in Italy.

"It could have been worse," Cortese said of the double ordeal. Like Spano, he credited the orchestra with helping to pull him through. Once he got up on the podium and went to work, in fact, he had a good time.

"He's so immensely gifted, musically, intellectually," Spano remembers thinking about Cortese from the start. "His affinity for certain repertoire—Verdi, Mendelssohn—is special." Cortese went on to his scheduled Boston Symphony debut, and then debuts with the Boston Lyric Opera and Saint Louis Opera, and a *Trovatore* in Parma, Italy—Verdi country—in celebration of the Verdi centennial in 2001. Spano signed him up as an Atlanta guest conductor for 2002.

As globalization and multiculturalism increasingly shape both commerce and the arts—many of the music students pouring out of American conservatories, for example, are Asian or Asian-American—Spano finds himself riding the crest of a wave. It's not merely a matter of trendiness, always a temptation in style-setting, trend-conscious New York. Brooklyn's programming reflects broader cultural tendencies. Spano says that such Chinese-American composers as Bright Sheng, Tan Dan, and Chen Yi, for instance, form a school that blends Chinese and Western styles to achieve a musical synthesis. Glass uses Jewish, Christian, Muslim, Mayan, Hawaiian, African, and Asian texts in his Fifth Symphony. The examples are countless.

Nor is this process new. Bach, as Spano points out, learned from Couperin, Vivaldi, and other composers and walked three hundred miles to meet Dietrich Buxtehude. Mozart borrowed in turn from Bach after he was introduced to Bach's music by the great Viennese patron Baron Gottfried von Swieten. But in the last half of the twentieth century the process of assimilation speeded up, bringing into question what Spano describes as "a nineteenth-century notion that a composer works in a vacuum and comes up with 'the truth,' the artistic truth, much like Moses coming down from the mountain." Instead, composers "are constantly learning from each other—stealing, if you will."

In an introduction to the 1999–2000 season in the program book, Spano pointed out the implications for programming:

> Some people talk about the fragmentation of music in our time. That is not my perspective. In this century it became common to hear music that was being made on the other side of the globe. De-

bussy already heard a Javanese gamelan in Paris in 1889 and it greatly influenced him. Closer to our time, the composer Colin McPhee actually lived in Bali and Steve Reich studied African drumming. Music has never been a universal language. In different cultures it has pursued different paths but the picture is now coalescing rather than fragmenting. We are witnessing a fusion—an aesthetic mirror of the global village. Almost every composer we are performing this season manifests that in some way: Messiaen, Adams, Takemitsu, Nancarrow, Piazzolla.

Some critics and listeners felt that this fusion of interests was producing not a global village but a Tower of Babel. But in Brooklyn, Whitman's "beautiful hills of Brooklyn," Spano's "baffled and curious" brain, like Whitman's, could "throw out questions and answers!"

"The great thing about Brooklyn," Spano went on in the program book, "is that what is considered far out elsewhere is normal fare in Brooklyn. I feel a great rapport with the orchestra and with the Brooklyn audience, which is clearly sophisticated, intelligent, and savvy." So great was the rapport that, on at least one occasion, he gave part of his salary back to the orchestra to help keep it afloat. Not the least of his achievements was to throw the focus onto the music instead of star performers, who had come to dominate many orchestras' programming in their pursuit of audiences and money. But the pesky problem remained: how to get the children of rock, television, and the Internet into the concert hall and persuade them to come back for more than a taste?

On the West Coast, Michael Tilson Thomas made a calculated play for a younger, hipper audience. He caught a bigger fish in his net: a receptive audience of all ages and many predilections.

Although his subscription season at the San Francisco Symphony was peppered with new music, it did not look radically different from other orchestras' mixtures of old and new—or, for that matter, from the season Spano envisioned for the Atlanta Symphony of the future. The 2000–01 calendar ranged from old standbys such as Dvořák's *New World* Symphony and Handel's *Messiah* to Mahler's gargantuan Eighth Symphony, the world premiere of David Del Tredici's *Gay Life,* and the United States premiere of the Nativity oratorio *El Niño* by John Adams, a San Franciscan. (Kent Nagano, another San Franciscan, conducted *El Niño.*) Of the nearly one hundred programmed compositions, twenty-five were new to the orchestra, forty-nine were from the twentieth century, five were by Americans, and twelve were by living composers. But with generous portions of the classics (including twentieth-century classics) to balance the moderns, the season appealed to many tastes in an area noted for its diversity of lifestyles and tastes.

The Del Tredici and Adams works, both San Francisco Symphony commissions, offer a clue to Tilson Thomas's reorientation of the symphonic repertory away from the nineteenth century and toward the present. These aren't just major new works in the standard symphony-oratorio tradition. Both draw on the pop-hip icons and artifacts of contemporary life and celebrate alternative lifestyles. Del Tredici's orchestral song cycle employs poems by Allen Ginsberg, Thomas Gunn, Paul Monette, and others in a frank embrace of out-of-the-closet sexuality. Adams relocates the Nativity to the freeways and malls of southern California, with Hispanic teenagers as Joseph and Mary.

Tilson Thomas's other departure from traditional programming was a series of postseason festivals of new or thematically chosen music, with the conductor as master of ceremonies. The emphasis was on the American maverick strain going back to Charles Ives (from the East Coast) and Henry Cowell (from the West Coast). The first of these orgies, An American Festival, in June 1996, actually ranged over two centuries of mavericks, from William Billings, Charles Ives, George Gershwin, and Aaron Copland onward to John Cage and Meredith Monk. It also had pop appeal: the first appearance by the four surviving members of the Grateful Dead since the death of Jerry Garcia the year before. They joined Tilson Thomas, who played the piano, in *"Space" for Henry Cowell*, an improvisation on melodies by the early experimentalist. Deadheads mobbed the hall and imbibed three hours of other artistic iconoclasm before getting to see and hear their idols in action. As David Littlejohn put it in the *Wall Street Journal*, the influx "helped ensure not only sold-out houses but also an exuberant mix of costumes, characters, and aromas inside and out of Davies Hall."[23]

In the *New York Times*, Alex Ross described the two weeks of concerts as "astonishing, perplexing, often thrilling." He added: "The festival will be remembered longest for the spectacle of a concert hall populated by fans of the Grateful Dead. Michael Tilson Thomas scored a coup not only for publicity but also for education when he lured young Deadheads to the symphony and gave them a whirlwind tour of an American experimental tradition. Whether or not he takes over for Jerry Garcia (his dissonant jam with the surviving members of the Grateful Dead reportedly may not be the last), Mr. Thomas managed the deft feat of a tasteful big sell." Given the overall result, Ross concluded, "no one can come to know American musical history without listening to California."[24]

Other reports told of ungrateful Deadheads, bewailing the long wait for a taste of the holy nectar and complaining they had been conned. In the *Wall Street Journal* Littlejohn praised the wildly eclectic mix of pop and classical (or "vernacular" and "cultivated") but voiced doubts over the kitschy and faux-populist slumming of some selections. Like many another observer, he also commented on the recently arrived Tilson Thomas's resemblance to Leonard Bernstein, "whose platform style and spirit 'M.T.T.' reincarnates with admirable flair."[25]

Walking into the opening concert of Tilson Thomas's 1999 Stravinsky festival, Anthony Tommasini of the *New York Times* had a New York moment. He thought he had been "zapped to a Manhattan movie theater on a weekend night. Among those who filled the 2,700-seat concert hall were the middle-aged and elderly culture buffs who traditionally have been the mainstays of American orchestras. But there were young people everywhere, arrayed in jeans, sports shirts, sneakers, and other casual wear, as well as many snazzily dressed young couples (mixed and same-sex) clearly enjoying a special night out. It was enough to make the heart soar with hope for the future of classical music."[26]

A three-week American Mavericks festival in June 2000 went from A to Z with music by (among others) John Adams, George Antheil, Aaron Copland, Duke Ellington, Lukas Foss, Lou Harrison, Steven Mackey, Meredith Monk, Steve Reich, Carl Ruggles, Ruth Crawford Seeger, and Frank Zappa. The performers were also an eclectic lot, including Meredith Monk and her ensemble and Steve Reich and his musicians, who were playing the West Coast premiere of his video piece *Hindenburg*. Tilson Thomas played up the iconoclastic character of the ten concerts. In the publicity for the series he said the composers "were free-spirited. They kept irregular hours, many of them. Most of them were politically radical. They were interested in sound for sound's sake. They were not writing music for a concert society. Many of them never expected their pieces to be performed. And this is the group of people who, in retrospect, contributed the majority of the original musical ideas of the twentieth century."

In the festival program book Tilson Thomas went out of his way to tweak the noses of musicologists and polite society, two pillars of culture and uplift:

"What the mavericks *did not* do was make nice little pieces to fit comfortably into the nice little holes of traditional concert life. The maverick composers were people who had the confidence to work without any system. Like a lot of the great American visual artists, they just rolled up their sleeves and made these things. They didn't create intellectual systems to define aesthetics and then churn out cookie-cutter pieces that would conform to some idea of academic respectability. These pieces were all made with equal parts of the sweat of their brows, the heft of their hands, and the seat of their pants."

Tilson Thomas also rattled the academics' cages by slighting the works of the difficult Elliott Carter, whom he described as part of the establishment and too intellectual besides. The orchestra's publicity brought the mavericks' message down to the level of the great American consumer, promising that "it's for you if you're tired of being told where to eat, how much you should earn, and how you can look like everyone else. You're not like everyone else. Neither are the American Mavericks."

The concerts reached an apex—or, to some, a nadir—when Tilson Thomas invited listeners to bring instruments of their own choosing to the opening program for a play-along in San Francisco composer Terry Riley's *In C*. The minimalist work, a landmark of the 1960s, consists of fifty-three melodic fragments that can be played by any number of instruments any number of times to a recurring pulse. In effect, a giant canon arises from the cacophony. Tilson Thomas started the work by conducting a stage ensemble from a piano. He then waded into the crowd like an afternoon talk-show host, orchestrating performances by one group of listeners and then another. Riley devotees called the stunt a betrayal of the democratic simplicity and sonic shimmer of the piece: sixties anarchy yielded to a conductor's control. The composer, forewarned, spent the evening elsewhere.

There were other ironies. In a lengthy postmortem in the *New York Times*, Richard Taruskin pointed out some of them: " 'A.T.&T. is the main corporate sponsor of *American Mavericks*,' was the sign that hit your eye as you entered Davies Symphony Hall last month. Then you picked up your program and read an essay by Alan Rich, 'No Brands, No Labels, No Boundaries,' which did little but tack a brand label on the favored elite and reinforce an implicit boundary that enraged advocates of the unfavored many. Their postings clogged classical cyberspace in the weeks leading up to the San Francisco Symphony's *American Mavericks* festival and all through it. Everybody, it seemed, wanted in to the vaunted pack of loners, the in-group of outsiders, the icons of iconoclasm."[27]

Yet even Taruskin wound up enchanted by the ten programs. "Never in my concertgoing life," he marveled, "had I encountered such a catholic barrage of not-to-be-missed programming." He was also in awe of Tilson Thomas's technique and musicianship, which he compared to Bernstein's. And the audiences, he said, "lapped it all up." In the *San Francisco Chronicle*, Joshua Kosman was equally amazed "not only at the music itself—from the boisterous, two-fisted outbursts of Charles Ives, George Antheil, and Edgard Varèse to the gentler blandishments of Morton Feldman, Lou Harrison, and Steve Reich—but also at the sense of electricity and enthusiasm that was evident throughout the hall." And these enthusiasts, he pointed out, "weren't all new-music buffs either."[28]

Among the concertgoers—a total of 22,517 tickets was sold—the orchestra tallied 40 percent who were symphony subscribers and another 33 percent who had bought single tickets for concerts during the regular season. The remaining 27 percent had never before heard the San Francisco Symphony live. That was impressive. But in the *Chronicle* Kosman saw a more significant flip side of the statistics: Tilson Thomas had sold San Francisco on the idea that new music could be exciting and fun. "What San Francisco now has in Michael Tilson Thomas," wrote Kosman, "is a music director so musically forceful and so personally persuasive that he got an entire city to go along with his individual vision of the most exciting and innovative strains in American music over the past one hundred years—and like it too."[29]

Having established his maverick bona fides, Tilson Thomas proceeded to a postseason Mozart festival for 2001, with Sir Neville Marriner as conductor. In the publicity, Tilson Thomas said that after five years of postseason mavericks, as well as Mahler and Stravinsky, it was time to step back and "turn our attention to Mozart, whose very familiarity can lull us into overlooking his genius." He balanced the backward look with a 2001–02 subscription season that included four world premieres (one of them his own *Songs on Texts of Emily Dickinson*), a minifestival of pan-American and Italian mavericks, and a three-week summer festival of Russian music.

M.T.T. (the name he bears in the Bay Area, thanks in part to the orchestra's publicity) comes from a milieu very different from Spano's Midwestern background. He was born in 1944 in Los Angeles. His parents, Ted and Roberta Thomas, worked in New York and Hollywood in theater, television, and film; his grandparents were Boris and Bessie Thomashefsky, founders of the Yiddish Theater in New York. Though Tilson Thomas, as he chose to call himself, is twenty-six years Bernstein's junior (and eighteen years Spano's senior), in many ways his career parallels the master's. To put it another way: while Spano had to make his own way in the world, Tilson Thomas had Bernstein as a mentor and model. In effect, they took different routes to the same destination, renewal of the repertoire.

Bernstein made his breakthrough debut when, as assistant conductor of the New York Philharmonic, he stepped in at the last minute in 1943 for the ailing Bruno Walter. Tilson Thomas got the same break when, as the Boston Symphony's assistant conductor, he substituted at the last minute in 1969 for William Steinberg in a New York concert. (It's interesting that these high-achiever assistants keep turning up in Boston.) Like Bernstein, Tilson Thomas is a gifted pianist, a champion of American music, and a composer. Like the mentor's music, the protégé's sometimes carries a Jewish or pacifist message. Two of his best-known works are *From the Diary of Anne Frank,* for narrator and orchestra, and *Shówa/Shoáh,* an orchestral work commemorating the fiftieth anniversary of the Hiroshima bombing and at the same time reflecting Jerusalem's travails amid war.

Tilson Thomas became one of the tribe of Bernstein protégés as a student at Tanglewood in 1968 and 1969, years when Bernstein was a fixture there. Like Bernstein, he became a globe-trotting teacher and model for the young. From 1971 to 1977 he succeeded Bernstein as leader of the New York Philharmonic's televised Young People's Concerts. In 1982 he joined Bernstein in founding the Los Angeles Philharmonic's training institute for conductors. In 1990 they founded the Pacific Music Festival, a teaching and performance institute in Sapporo, Japan, at which Tilson Thomas remains artistic director. Both projects were modeled on the Tanglewood Music Center, where both men blossomed as musicians. In 1987 Tilson Thomas founded the New World Symphony, a Miami-based training orchestra that he later brought to the American Mavericks festival for two concerts. One further thing master and protégé have in common: a gift of gab about music and any topic, however remote, it calls to mind.

Until his 1995 arrival in San Francisco, Tilson Thomas had never basked in the celebrity that Bernstein wore like a robe and halo. As a young man, Tilson Thomas had held important assistantships and become principal guest conductor of the Boston Symphony and Los Angeles Philharmonic at different times. But he had held only one leadership position—as director of the third-tier Buffalo Philharmonic from 1971 until 1979—before succeeding Claudio Abbado as principal conductor of the London Symphony Orchestra in 1988. In London his interest in new music and new approaches to music found a congenial outlet. He led a series of Discovery concerts in which he spoke about the music, Richard Strauss's *Also Sprach Zarathustra,* for example, in the first half and then performed it in the second half. In 1990–91, picking up on the thematic idea in the air, he devoted a Childhood series to music inspired by a child's life. Other festival-type programming examined the legacy of Saint Petersburg, and Beethoven and his time.

In San Francisco Tilson Thomas succeeded Herbert Blomstedt, a solid, middle-of-the-road conductor in the European tradition. He immediately sent out shock waves with his programming and the brilliance of his performances. He programmed local musicians and composers. He also got the orchestra a recording contract and made recordings that sold—this at a time when most American orchestras' recording activity had come to a standstill because of the economics of recording and the glut of compact discs on the market.

Tilson Thomas seemed a perfect fit, not just with the orchestra but with the community. In a city with a large gay contingent he made no secret of his preference, sharing a house with his male companion. He could also be seen walking his dog in the park and hiking in the Marin County mountains. For a conductor who in his early years had seemed fussy and self-conscious, this newly acquired openness paid rich dividends. It drew attention to him and the orchestra and nicely suited Americans' love for heroes who could both stand on a pedestal and act like just folks. If the San Francisco Symphony, orchestrally speaking, was the biggest show in the orchestra-rich Bay Area before M.T.T. arrived, it was that even more so after he put his initials on it.

San Francisco is a continent away from Brooklyn in more than geography. While Spano was struggling to put on six concerts a year in the shadow of Manhattan's musical colossi, Tilson Thomas enjoyed the luxury of a full season with widespread community support. The goal, however, was the same. Tilson Thomas said that over time, if the performances are committed and a sense of partnership develops with concertgoers, they will find "something vivid and interesting enough about the music that makes it worth their while to pay attention to it. That's not to say they will necessarily like everything. But there will be something about the music which will be thought-provoking, which will be spirit-provoking, which will cause them, in the best sense—as when we all go to the theater, the opera, the ballet, or the symphony—to experience something which will be worth talking about and thinking about afterward, as opposed to something which will just be comfortable, status quo, or, even worse, boring." To that extent, he said, the San Francisco model can be adapted in any city, with allowances for its history and personality.

Tilson Thomas said he had always done this kind of programming, beginning with the Spectrum concerts that he led as assistant conductor and then principal guest conductor of the Boston Symphony in the early 1970s. To illustrate a theme, he would both talk about and conduct a mix of old and new music. First as a separate series, then as part of the subscription season, these programs explored such topics as music in Venice, the American avant-garde, and the influence of ballet impresario Sergei Diaghilev, who commissioned Stravinsky's Paris ballets and others. It was "an enormous thing" for the Boston Symphony to give him such an opportunity at age twenty-five, Tilson Thomas said, noting that the Spectrum concerts became a prototype for other orchestras' new-music series. Among those in the future, though not necessarily influenced by the Boston experiment, were Pierre Boulez's celebrated "rug concerts" with the New York Philharmonic in the 1970s. Spano's programs, and Leon Botstein's with the American Symphony Orchestra, seem clear descendants of the M.T.T. model. That model, in turn, seems descended from Leonard Bernstein's palaver-and-play Young People's Concerts in the 1950s and 1960s with the New York Philharmonic.

Spano's career followed a more or less direct route from the Midwest to Brooklyn to Atlanta. Tilson Thomas, on the other hand, had to go away to find his place at home. Gifted as he clearly was, something in him did not quite click during his *Wanderjahre* in Boston, Los Angeles, Buffalo, and places between. It seemed more a personal than a musical thing. He couldn't, in the parlance of the sixties, of which he was in many ways a child, get it all together. He was always the assistant or groundbreaker, never the master architect or builder. The seven years in London seem to have brought him a newfound assurance as a man and a musician.

Tilson Thomas attributed his maturation to his role as principal conductor of the London Symphony Orchestra, which is run by its members and employs no music director. (He remained the London's principal guest conductor as well as director of the New World Symphony after leaving for San Francisco in 1995.) The principal conductor relationship is not one favored by American orchestras for reasons that emerged when Davies occupied the podium in Brooklyn: the principal conductor takes little or no part in planning and day-by-day responsibilities. Not only did London free Tilson Thomas of the administrative chores, he said, but "the musical-social contract is writ differently in such a situation. It's much more collaborative, and you [and the musicians] are collectively perceiving things that are very strong to build and grow the orchestra. And particularly in London you're up against the real pressure, the very direct experience, of the marketplace, because there's so much competition from other ensembles and London is a town which is craving new directions, new concepts in music. If you are presenting the same-old same-old, you will very quickly be upbraided for that by the press and others."

Like Spano, Tilson Thomas is conscious of the symphony orchestra as a hand-me-down from the nineteenth century. Having been conceived on the European model, with European directors and repertoire, American orchestras would naturally have set out to preserve the values and traditions of an older society, he said. Yet for orchestras today, being "in a strategy of growth rather than of maintenance is obviously the strongest guarantee of a real future. And an essential part of this, I believe, for us as Americans, is to get past the Eurocentricity of all of this. It's really important for us to understand that we are in a position to lead the direction in which taste and practice in the performing arts will develop, and thus in the sort of repertoire and the kind of musical future we're going to have."

That doesn't mean abandoning the past. Tilson Thomas likens the symphony orchestra to a repertory company in the theater; on any given night it can give a brilliant performance of a work by Aeschylus, Anton Chekhov, Neil Simon, Stephen Sondheim, or Samuel Beckett. (Similarly, he likens himself to a director in the theater or a sports coach instead of a "hierarchical" boss.) Each playwright will attract a different audience but each has a place, and in time the fans of one may become fans of the others. And indeed, Tilson Thomas says, "we are seeing a larger and younger audience as a trend in San Francisco. I think part of that is that the older and younger and the more conservative and more radical parts of the audience actually enjoy one another. They enjoy the experience of the way that they are expanding one another's boundaries. On the one hand, there are conservative parts of the traditional audience that we are trying to make more au courant and more interested in what is happening in twentieth- and twenty-first-century music. And also we want very much to interest audience members who might be coming exclusively to hear a new piece by John Adams or Steve Mackey or Charles Wuorinen, that they would come and be impressed and take to heart a piece by Schubert or Tchaikovsky or whoever. They realize that this music of the past has something very important to offer to them."

Music becomes not just an artistic experience but also a testing ground for values, for the old and the young. The "buzz," Tilson Thomas said, "has made the whole experience of the concert a more exciting one for all concerned."

At Bard College, where he is president, Leon Botstein leads an annual music festival exploring, through two weekends of discussions and performances, the work of a single composer and his milieu. Anticipating his 2000 Beethoven festival, Botstein told the *New York Times:* "I think we struck a nerve generally in the classical music world with the Bard festival and with the American Symphony concerts by curating concerts, by treating the public seriously in a way that is not forbidding, and by making music not a dead object behind glass, but a subject of living controversy and reinterpretation on the part of the audience as well as the performers. People walk out of the concert hall arguing. We actually have influenced the way programming is thought about, and the relationship between our role as museum keepers and the current culture."[30]

Spano is more modest in his claims. He makes no pretense that thematic—or, to use a more inclusive term, conceptual—programming is the way to go as classical music heads into a cloudy future. All he can say is that as both a performer and a former composer, his own interests lead him in that direction. And it's not just a matter of rooting around in new music. He also loves "a lot of old music and a lot of world musics": flamenco, for instance, which introduced him to a "fantastic" sound world when he did his flamenco program in Brooklyn. "So my own interests are eclectic," he explains, "and it's natural for me to keep exploring and finding things that I think go together and inform each other."

On the other hand, he says, changes in concert formats in response to the new times and new media can help to bring the public along. But concert presenters must get over their "phobia" about losing audiences and drop their resulting obsession with "sex symbols" when choosing conductors and soloists.

The idea of music as something more than courtly privilege or ecclesiastical accoutrement is only two centuries old. The concert format in general use today—overture, concerto, symphony for orchestra—evolved from the rise of the middle classes and their aspirations to culture. In nineteenth-century Germany and Austria, and as recently as mid-twentieth-century America, classical music was a reigning art form, generating "buzz" in public forums, whether the coffeehouse or the radio station. Now classical concerts are just one—and by no means the preferred one—of a whole panoply of entertainment options ranging from television, film, and pop to compact disc, videocassette, and the Internet. Everywhere the emphasis is on star power and youth culture, leaving potential audiences with little patience for the time and reflection required for classical music's more complex structures and pleasures. Concert givers have had to find creative ways to adapt, even if, as Spano says, Liszt was the equivalent of a rock star in his day.

Meanwhile, recorded music has changed habits of listening, Spano points out. The technical perfection possible with editing on tape creates the expectation that live performances should be note-perfect—an impossibility in the first place, and, if a performer tries for it, a sure way to kill the spirit of the music. The fact that music can happen anywhere, at any time, also creates a new environment, Spano says. In the past you either made music yourself or had to make an effort to hear it. Today it's often necessary to make an effort *not* to hear music anywhere outside a cork-lined room like the one to which Proust retreated. Try to escape music—typically the lowest grade of music—in any supermarket or dentist's office.

In the middle of the twentieth century composer-critic Virgil Thomson, probably the wisest musical sage of the day, fulminated against the music "business" and the music-appreciation "racket." Both are still with us, trying with ever greater slickness to sell classical music as if it were an irresistible luxury item, like a Rolex or Jaguar. ("You're not like everyone else. Neither are the American Mavericks," cooed the San Francisco Symphony's siren song.) But, now that music education has been eliminated from many schools or fallen on rock-deafened ears, partisans like Spano, Tilson Thomas, and Botstein have taken it on. Programming by concept becomes a platform.

In an age when Elvis, film, and comic books are treated as academic disciplines, this conceptual approach makes a certain degree of sense. So these kids coming out of college know nothing and care less about the crowning musical achievements of Western civilization? Okay, we'll show them it's worthy of their lifestyle, just like the latest rock hit. Do talk shows on radio and television generate buzz? Good, we'll talk people into acquiescence. This, of course, is multiculturalism's trap: all cultures are equal, so pop music, no matter how cheap or trivial, is as good as Mozart. Gold or garbage, it's all the same thing.

Handled well—and Spano and Tilson Thomas are masters of the game—the conceptual approach can illuminate historical movements and rope in new listeners. But there is something sad about the concert hall as lecture hall. Music can no longer speak for itself; it must be part of an intellectual construct. The scaffolding becomes as important as the cathedral.

Perhaps there is a connection between the rise of conceptual programming and the decline of the godlike conductor. Bernstein—and before him Toscanini, Koussevitzky, and Stokowski—could perform what he liked, and audiences would come because of the force of his personality and because music itself was a vital force in public life. But the genius-autocrat's days are over: unions, democratic standards, the new media, and fund-raising niceties saw to that. The new breed of conductor lays music-appreciation traps like lectures and conceptual programming for audiences. Or, where traditional programming prevails, frequent-flier conductors become caretakers in thrall to marketing departments and the need to please moneyed patrons. The standard concert format and repertoire become the same-old same-old: a yawn for the young, critics, and musicians (some of them) alike.

In an essay in the American Mavericks program book, Alan Rich underscored the maverick strain in American life, beginning with Moses Maverick, who married a fellow passenger on the *Mayflower,* and going on to such cultural icons as Thomas Paine, Henry David Thoreau, and Walt Whitman. It was Moses' nineteenth-century descendant Samuel Augustus Maverick, Rich wrote, who won a herd of cattle in a poker game and let them roam free, unbranded, on the range. That, Rich says, is the point: "to lend your name to the free-roaming creative spirit, resistant to labeling and to confinement in corrals, the dissenter who refuses to go along with the majority views and actions."

Beethoven was a maverick. So was Brahms, in his backward-looking way. Now they're mainstream and domesticated, confined in our concert-giving corrals. Focusing on mavericks or on a period, to the exclusion of all else, is a way of closing people's eyes as well as opening them. Americaniza-tion is an old battle cry—at least as old as Dvořák, who at the turn of the last century urged American composers to turn away from European models and look to such native traditions as African American and Indian music. Nearly a century later, in 1993, the American Symphony Orchestra League issued a report, *Americanizing the American Orchestra,* warning its members to adapt to multicultural realities or face a painful death. Neither the league's alarm bells nor Tilson Thomas's "strategy of growth" seems to have stopped American audiences from demanding the European masters, or conductors like Tilson Thomas from playing them.

Rather than the bogeyman that strikes fear into traditional listeners' hearts or the messiah that Tilson Thomas's audiences cheer, new music is actually part of a continuum going back to the medieval cathedral and Re-naissance palace. The true distinction, as Gunther Schuller pointed out, is not between old and new but between good and bad, however they may be defined. And posterity, not musicians, has a way of defining them pretty clearly, though musicians can give posterity a push.

Spano still has his work cut out for him. The Brooklyn Philharmonic performs impressively but stands on shaky financial ground. In Atlanta the situation is reversed. The financial crises are past, but quality remains an is-sue, at least by New York standards. Two weeks after the 2001 festivities that marked Spano's investiture, Bernard Holland of the *New York Times* attend-ed a regular-season concert and found it wanting.

Christopher Theofanidis's *Rainbow Body,* proudly programmed by Spano as an example of attractive new music, is actually "a user-friendly, feel-good piece bearing the imprimatur of modernity and beckoning to lis-teners skittish of the new," Holland wrote. As the piano soloist in Richard Strauss's *Burleske,* Jean-Yves Thibaudet offered "icy perfection" rather than "stabs of wit." And Spano's performance of Brahms's Symphony no. 4 re-minded Holland of the "layer of multicolored smog" that his plane had passed through en route to a landing at the Atlanta airport. "These are evi-dently good musicians, and they play the right notes at just about the right time," he declared. "But there is little unanimity of thought."[31]

Spano is still experimenting and learning, as a musician must. With his two orchestras in two environments, he seems to have the advantage of two worlds. Yet he describes performing Mozart and Steve Reich as two aspects of the same discipline. In an interview in the *Oberlin Conservatory News,* from the scene of his beginnings as a musician, he said:

The challenge of doing new music is primarily the capacity to constantly expand one's vocabulary. The approach is essentially the same as with old music, which is to understand the composer's voice, circumstances, environment, aesthetic. When approaching Mozart, we try to be in touch with the musical sources that created his voice: his study of J. S. Bach, his friendship with the Baron Gottfried von Swieten, his involvement with freemasonry, and Viennese culture in the eighteenth century.

When approaching Steve Reich, we need to understand what had happened to music in America post–World War II, understand his need to find his voice apart from the academically entrenched twelve-tone music, his study of African drumming and Hebrew chant. So it's a similar process but it's always a new study when approaching any given composer. In music today there's such tremendous variety, whereas the disparity between Mozart and Dittersdorf is more one of quality than one of language.[32]

That, rather than roaming free of the corral, is the point: in music there *is* such a tremendous variety. Conceptual programming is one way—if not the best or only way—of turning the present Babel into buzz. In music as in much else, the Brooklyn Bridge has become the span that *The Bridge,* Hart Crane's ode to it, envisions, linking America's present to the past.

# THE JUILLIARD
# STRING QUARTET

*Long live the revolution*

The Juilliard String Quartet digs into the music. (Walter H. Scott)

THE OVERFLOW AUDIENCE WAS WHOOPING AND CLAPPING as soon as Robert Mann walked onto the stage at Tanglewood on the evening of July 2, 1997. But that was just a prelude to the torrents of emotion that swept through teak-splendored Seiji Ozawa Hall at the concert's end.

Amid a standing ovation and repeated curtain calls, Mann flung an arm around the shoulders of first one and then others of his fellow Juilliard String Quartet members. His wife, Lucy Rowan, came down the aisle to kiss him at the edge of the stage, and he dedicated an encore to her. And still there was more tumult, more clamor. Before the shouting was over, violist Samuel Rhodes, the group's unofficial historian, presented Mann with a log of the concerts he and the Juilliard had played in the last eleven years, with a promise of the other thirty-nine years' worth to come. In the grand finale to the Juilliard's fiftieth-anniversary celebrations, Mann, its first violinist for all fifty years and its only remaining founding member, retired.

The program was Mann's, chosen as his farewell. Characteristically for the Juilliard, it was not a tear-dabbing wallow in self-congratulation, encore-type bonbons, and auld lang syne but a tough, weighty grappling with two monuments of the quartet literature, Beethoven's Op. 132 followed by his Op. 130. At every turn expectations were rewarded, mysteries revealed, divine madness glimpsed. In the gentle descent from the heights at the end of Op. 132's hymn of thanksgiving, in the timeless arch of Op. 130's cavatina, in the furies of the succeeding Great Fugue, in the constantly revealing inner lines, conviction burned in every note. When the Juilliard finishes a performance, whether of Beethoven or of Elliott Carter, the listener has the feeling that he is surfacing after an immersion in an ocean many fathoms deep. Even the encore offered no concession to frivolity. Also chosen by Mann, it was the grave lento movement from Beethoven's last quartet, Op. 135.

The Juilliard's return to Tanglewood was a sentimental one. It was where, in 1947, the quartet had played its first concert as a trial run before its formal New York debut later that year. In 1948 at Tanglewood the Juilliard played the first American cycle of Bartók's six quartets, then considered revolutionary in style and little known even by chamber music aficionados. It was at Tanglewood in 1986 that second violinist Joel Smirnoff, who became first violinist Joel Smirnoff on Mann's retirement, made his debut with the ensemble. And five weeks after Mann departed, it was at Tanglewood that the reconstituted Juilliard gave its maiden concert, with Ronald Copes taking his seat as second violinist alongside Joel Smirnoff, Samuel Rhodes, and cellist Joel Krosnick.

Retirement, however, was no retirement for the irrepressible seventy-six-year-old Mann, whose playing had taken on an edgy quality in recent seasons but lost none of its spirit. He simply stepped up his solo playing, conducting, and composing. He also planned to write a memoir about twentieth-century American musical life and his role in it.[1]

"You've heard of the seven-year itch," Mann told the *New York Times*. "Well, I've got the seventy-six-year itch. I feel terrific. This isn't anything to do with health. And the quartet gets along fabulously. But at a certain point intimations of mortality set in, and my feeling is that while I'm still at the height of my powers, I want to do other things in a more concentrated way than I've been able to do until now."[2] Among first violinists only Arnold Rosé, the Austrian who led the Rosé Quartet from its founding in 1882 until 1945 (he moved from Vienna to London in 1938, when Hitler joined Austria to the Third Reich), had a longer tenure in a major string quartet.

For all of its fifty-plus years, the made-in-America Juilliard has been in the forefront of quartet playing, once the province of European-born musicians, in the United States. By the jubilee year the Juilliard had premiered more than sixty works (of five hundred performed over the course of half a century) by American composers, served as quartet in residence at the Library of Congress, amassed a discography of more than one hundred releases, won three Grammy Awards and numerous other honors, and fathered such other quartets as the LaSalle, Tokyo, Emerson, American, Concord, Mendelssohn, Brentano, Shanghai, and Saint Lawrence. Elliott Carter, the severe modernist composer, found a champion in the Juilliard. But before Carter there were Bartók and the Second Viennese School—Schoenberg, Berg, and Webern. The Juilliard played them all when almost nobody else in the United States was playing them, and kept on playing them right into the twenty-first century.

Before settling in at Tanglewood for the transition to the post-Mann era, the Juilliard celebrated its fiftieth birthday with a three-continent marathon.

It played the Beethoven cycle (sixteen quartets) in Bonn, New York, and Tokyo, the Bartók cycle (six quartets) in New York, the Hindemith cycle (seven quartets) in Venice, and two twentieth-century legacy concerts, consisting of works by Elliott Carter, Henri Dutilleux, William Schuman, Roger Sessions, Ralph Shapey, and Richard Wernick, at the Juilliard School. The ensemble also premiered a concerto for string quartet and orchestra by David Diamond and a quintet for clarinet and string quartet by Milton Babbitt. Both were anniversary commissions, as was the Wernick quartet premiered at the legacy concert. Amid all this there was the Library of Congress residency, teaching at Juilliard, and a schedule of other concerts.

Goethe's famous dictum that chamber music is a conversation among intelligent people doesn't wholly apply to the Juilliard. What these intelligent souls engage in is also something of a friendly argument. Quartets like the Emerson and Tokyo deliver a smooth homogeneity of sound. The Juilliard has cultivated a more blended sound in recent years, but it is noted for emphasizing the differences among the four voices. It's no accident that Smirnoff, Copes, Rhodes, and Krosnick, and Mann in his day, are leading exponents of Carter, the nonagenarian American who makes it a point of honor to have his players go at one another like cowboys and Indians. Composer and quartet are kindred spirits.

The Juilliard's first recording of the Bartók quartets, made in 1949, was full of jagged edges, biting rhythms, savage attacks. Two later recorded cycles, while retaining the original's intensity, took a more considered view of the mysteries. When the Emerson recorded the cycle in the 1990s, it made the music seem a natural extension of Beethoven's late quartets in sound and thought. The evolution isn't an Oedipal matter of sons getting ahead by slaying their fathers; the music is of such depth that it is amenable to any number of approaches. But without the Juilliard to show the way, other ensembles—audiences, too—would have been slower to come to an understanding of Bartók's twentieth-century landmarks. Without the Juilliard, much of American music would not be what it is today. No American string quartet—perhaps no American ensemble of any kind—has amassed a greater record of service to the art.

"We're flexible," Joel Smirnoff said in the Juilliard Quartet's music-strewn studio overlooking New York's Lincoln Center on the fifth floor of the Juilliard School. If a concert presenter wants a meat-and-potatoes program—none of this modern stuff—the Juilliard will accommodate him. On the other hand, Smirnoff made it clear, the quartet will also try to slip in a challenging piece, doing it in a way that will make the music attractive, or at any rate nonthreatening, for an audience.

Whether by the front or back door, the performance of challenging, that is, modern, music was the ensemble's charge from William Schuman, president of the Juilliard School and a composer himself, when he formed it in 1946. But unlike such latecomers as the Kronos Quartet—which plays nothing written before 1900 and much that owes its origins to rock, folk, or pop—the Juilliard has always mixed the classics with the moderns, treating them as equals. A typical Juilliard program will open with a Haydn or Mozart quartet, move on to something from the twentieth century, and end with Beethoven, Schubert, or Brahms. It's no accident that this is a standard program today for string quartets. The Juilliard helped to make it that way.

Playing new music isn't necessarily the way to an audience's heart. Raphael Hillyer, the founding violist, remembers meeting resistance at nearly every turn in the early years. Buffalo, New York, had an important chamber series with the nationally reigning Budapest Quartet as its mainstay. But when the Juilliard was negotiating to get on the schedule, the Buffalo sponsor wanted no part of Bartók and insisted that the upstarts audition like students. The upstarts refused. A reluctant compromise was struck. The Juilliard could play its Bartók at the beginning of a program. That way, anyone so disposed could arrive late and thereby avoid the ordeal. In due course the Juilliard became a regular Buffalo attraction, playing even a Beethoven cycle, formerly the province of the Budapest.

On another occasion Hillyer approached Community Concerts, which used to send musicians out as circuit riders to venues large and small across the country, about possible engagements for the Juilliard. Looking at the Juilliard repertory list that Hillyer proffered, the manager delivered a verdict that ran something like this: "We can't have all that modern stuff. We'll lose our audience. You have to play things that people really like."

"That's not the way we want to make music," Hillyer replied. The Juilliard went onto the Community Concerts circuit anyway. But the concerts' management "forced the quartet down the throats of their audience," which had to take the upstarts if it wanted to get stars like Jascha Heifetz and Artur Rubinstein, recalled Robert Koff, the original second violinist. Even so, concert venues for string quartets in the early years were few, mostly at colleges and universities.

"We were a wild bunch and we depended on riding the crest of the wave for our ability to play well," Koff said. The group played the Beethoven quartets according to Beethoven's tempo markings. Faster than the tempos generally in use, the pacing upset audiences then and can still upset them today. "But that suited our temperaments," Koff explained. "In order to keep the edge of performance, rather than take one program and play it for five weeks six times a week, we tried to take a different program for every concert. That meant a lot of music. It also meant that sometimes we would not have played the scheduled piece for a couple of months. And therefore there was an edge which we liked and made us play the way we played."

The Juilliard wound up with a large repertoire of contemporary works that it could play only once or twice in a season. "You couldn't sell it," Koff said. "You couldn't play it on tour, because it was incomprehensible to an audience and it would destroy us. We always flirted with destruction anyway with promoting contemporary music."

Koff left in 1958, eleven years before Hillyer did. In his twenty-three years with the quartet, Hillyer saw tastes change. With repeated hearings, he said, audiences and presenters learned to like and ask for Bartók. Audiences also came to enjoy Berg's *Lyric Suite,* a Juilliard signature piece. (Not so Webern, though. Hillyer recalls walking through the vestibule after a concert that included Webern and overhearing a mother threaten her child, "And if you don't practice, that's the way you're going to sound!" That reaction never changed, Hillyer said.)

The Juilliard acquired its passion for Bartók from Eugene Lehner, who had been the violist of the celebrated Kolisch Quartet in pre–World War II Vienna. Though he refused to become the Juilliard's founding violist— he recommended Hillyer, a fellow member of the Boston Symphony Orchestra—Lehner offered to coach the new group in the quartets of Bartók, Schoenberg, Berg, and Webern. He had known and worked with all these composers in the Kolisch Quartet, which championed their music and premiered the Schoenberg Third and Fourth Quartets. Under his tutelage, the Juilliard learned all six Bartók quartets, beginning with the third. Lehner warned that the Fourth Quartet might be hardest of all for the audience and the players. Hillyer remembers the group thinking, " 'People are not going to like this.' And it turned out that they didn't, very much. But we had such faith in him [Lehner] and the music itself, after we'd played it a lot, that we just didn't care about the reaction. 'We did it and it's good for you, listen to it,' we thought. And people began to see what's in it."

Carter's music, which replaces traditional melody, harmony, rhythm, and tonality with intricate relationships of pitch, meter, and motive, was, if anything, an even tougher nut to crack. Yet it too became a Juilliard trademark.

The Juilliard gave the world premiere of Carter's Second Quartet in 1960 after the Stanley String Quartet of the University of Michigan, which had commissioned it, found it unplayable. Rhodes, who replaced Hillyer in 1969 and is now the quartet's senior member, first heard the work before joining the Juilliard. He was awestruck. It was so visionary, he said, that he "couldn't conceive how anyone could play it." On entering the Juilliard, he played it repeatedly and became passionate about it. He also played in the Juilliard's 1973 premiere of the Carter third, which the group had commissioned. It is perhaps the most difficult of Carter's five quartets, turning the four instruments into duos that oppose each other through ten overlapping movements. Other players learned it by using earphones and a click track to follow the meters, Rhodes recalls. Not the Juilliard.

The Second Quartet was hard enough, Rhodes said, but it took the Juilliard two hours just to get through the first bar of the third. Yet the premiere of the third "was one of the most tremendous musical events ever" for him. It was overwhelming "in all the good ways. It was the beginning of a monumental work. It created a tremendous amount of interest. People from all over the country and abroad came to Juilliard to hear the dress rehearsal and the first performance. It was really a momentous event for all of us." In a preface to the score of the five Carter quartets, Mann recalled the same difficulties with the opening measure of the third. After the breakthrough, he wrote, "the sensation is similar to catapulting over a roaring waterfall at the start of a white-water journey."[3]

With experience, Rhodes said, the Carter second has come to seem almost like a repertory work by Mozart or Brahms. "You go through the birth pangs of learning a piece, familiarizing yourself with a language that's revolutionary, that carries everything just a little farther than you are prepared [to deal with] as a musician through all your training with rhythm, with ensemble. And here's a man who has the imagination to think of all these things in a different way. He has accelerandos that are not intuitive [for the players to work out on their own] but they are precisely notated, and you have to figure out how to do that. You have to figure out relationships that you never thought could be made to coherently exist in music. And yet what you figure out expands your ability to deal with these things. It finds techniques and ways of doing that." Carter, like Bartók before him, opened the quartet's eyes to new possibilities in performance of music both old and new.

Chamber music in the United States in the 1930s and 1940s was largely the province of European émigrés, many of them refugees from Hitler's Reich. The Budapest String Quartet reigned as the ne plus ultra of quartet playing, the crème de la crème. Although it had well-known predecessors and contemporaries—the Flonzaley, Kneisel, and Busch among them—the Budapest was the quartet most programmed, most highly esteemed, and most recorded. It also stood as an emblem of the genteel, Old World values embodied in chamber music.

The Budapest Quartet was founded in 1917 by four Hungarians from the Budapest Opera Orchestra. By 1946 it was made up of Russian-born men who had become naturalized Americans. (Women in quartets were a thing of the future.) The group played, sparingly, new music of its day, including some of the quartets of their fellow Hungarian Bartók, and endured the frictions inevitable when four people spend endless hours together in pursuit of an elusive goal. Sometimes the arguments were such that players wound up not talking to one another. Yet in public their image was gentlemanly, cultivated, benign. Until its final years, in the 1960s, when the members were showing the effects of age, the Budapest was celebrated, as Joseph Wechsberg wrote, "for its beautiful tone, its perfect integration, its impeccable taste, its careful phrasing, character, and style, and, above all, its depth of interpretation, power, and sweep."[4]

These, of course, were the very qualities that a relatively small band of devotees prized and promulgated in chamber music before the Juilliard and other newcomers democratized the genre for a larger American audience. Wechsberg, an amateur violinist and chamber player himself, as well as a refugee from Nazi Vienna, caught the spirit:

"The performing of chamber music—'the music of friends,' it has been called—engenders an atmosphere of warmth and a degree of psychological rapport that are unknown to most virtuosos, prima donnas, or members of large orchestras. For them, music is ordinarily a competitive business, a race that goes to the fastest or loudest. Not so with chamber music. It is based on give-and-take; it is civilized and egalitarian; it is a garden of musical fellowship from which the law of the jungle has been banished and in which ego-tism simply cannot thrive."[5]

Into this Eden, this utopia, burst a bunch of bomb-wielding revolution-aries.

When William Schuman went to the Juilliard School as its president in 1945, a resident string quartet was the first item in his memo book. He made a list of the best quartets of the day. Then he rejected all of them.

"What did I want?" he recalled in Harriet Gay's book, *The Juilliard String Quartet*. "It seemed terribly simple in my mind; we needed a quartet that would play the standard repertoire with the sense of excitement and discov-ery of a new work . . . and would play the new works with a sense of rever-ence usually reserved for the classics."[6] And it had to be a quartet both authentically American and international in stature.

Terribly simple? Resident quartets are on campuses everywhere today— they're a badge of prestige as well as a teaching asset—but in those days the only group comparable to the Juilliard was the Fine Arts Quartet. Also founded in 1946, it was engaged as a radio quartet in Chicago.

On Fisher's Island, off New London, Connecticut, while Schuman was rejecting the best quartets of the day in search of perfection, Robert Mann was talking with an Army buddy, cellist Arthur Winograd, about playing chamber music once the war was over. They were stationed at Fort Wright in the coast artillery, defending the mainland against an attack that never came. To pass the time of day—or night, rather, since the day was spent in drilling—they began playing jazz with a classically trained jazz pianist, Bernie Leighton. Though "pop music was never my thing, or Bobby's for that matter," Winograd said, the trio wound up playing for dances at the of-ficers' and enlisted men's clubs on the base.

With Winograd signed up, Mann chose Robert Koff for second violin. He and Mann had been graduate students together before the war at the Juilliard School, where Mann gained a reputation for hostility to *Wun-derkinder* of the kind that populate conservatories. Both at Juilliard and dur-ing two summers in Albuquerque, New Mexico, Koff and Mann had often played quartets together. There was also a connection between Winograd and Hillyer. They had known each other as students in the early 1940s at Tanglewood, where Hillyer's roommate was Leonard Bernstein. The three-quarters of a quartet received an important assist from Edgar Schenck-man, the conductor of the Juilliard School orchestra. When Schuman asked him who might create the dream quartet, Schenckman recommended his former conducting student Mann.

Newly discharged from the Army early in 1946, Mann went to see Schuman about a job—a resident quartet's job, with Koff and Winograd as partners. Each had what the other wanted. Schuman found Mann "extraordinary" as a musician and person, Helen Epstein recounts in *Music Talks*. Mann "was always—and I will not apologize for my purple prose—a moral force," Schuman said.[7] But the quartet-to-be had no violist.

At Schuman's suggestion the players approached Eugene Lehner. While in the Kolisch Quartet, Lehner had not only played the Viennese masters, both classical and modern, but also performed the quartet repertoire from memory and thus with enhanced freedom. Now forty years old, married, and wanting the security of his Boston Symphony job, Lehner suggested that the young men of the quartet-to-be find an American closer to their own ages. He proposed his colleague Hillyer, who was then in his fourth year as a Boston Symphony violinist. Leonard Bernstein and Hillyer's Boston Symphony colleagues urged him not to do it, but after agonizing consideration Hillyer decided the quartet's offer was attractive enough for him to quit the orchestra and switch to the viola. He became the quartet member and Lehner became the quartet's mentor.

The group spent the summer of 1946 in Cambridge, Massachusetts, frequently rehearsing in the soft-spoken, courtly Lehner's home in nearby Newton. After only three weeks, the budding ensemble played a trial concert at Dartmouth College in Hanover, New Hampshire, where Hillyer had grown up and taken an undergraduate degree (his father taught mathematics there). The group was so green that, lacking Schuman's final imprimatur, it couldn't yet call itself the Juilliard Quartet. During that summer, Hillyer recalls, Lehner coached the group in both the classical and modern repertoire. The Bartók Sixth Quartet was still so new that it was unpublished, and the players had to learn it from parts copied by hand from the manuscript.

For Lehner, Hillyer said, "music was like a spoken language, a way of breathing, a way of pacing. As he used to say, 'Have the courage to take time.' Most people are afraid to do that. They think there's a tempo and you just start." Lehner also encouraged the quartet to follow Beethoven's metronome markings, just as the Kolisch Quartet had. But his greatest teaching, Hillyer said, was to introduce the Juilliard-to-be to the new Viennese trinity of composers, Schoenberg, Berg, and Webern. Then as now, they were an object of fear and loathing to the uninitiated because of their twelve-tone rigors, which did away with traditional key relationships and replaced themes with rigidly pitched (but manipulable) tone rows.

In Koff's sharpest recollection from that summer, Lehner comes in to listen to the group play the scherzo of the Schoenberg Third Quartet. The players have learned the notes but have not gotten the sense, the musical line. Lehner kneels before the quartet, pleading. He hums the tone row as if it were a melting, lilting waltz. He says the music should be Romantic, Viennese. He entreats. He corrects. He shapes. The notes become music.

"It just overwhelmed me that Schoenberg was writing real music, not this mathematical formula," Koff said. Fifty-five years later Hillyer could still hear Lehner, who lived until 1997, singing passages from Schoenberg to bring the neophytes safely through the thickets. Lehner believed the Schoenberg quartets were the successors to Beethoven's, Hillyer said.

Viennese tunes or no, Lehner was swept along on the Juilliard tide. The group arrived, he later told the *New York Times,* "with this youthful enthusiasm, this reckless daring, not weighted down by tradition; they bewildered the old amateurs but it was irresistible—the fire, the courage."[8]

In the fall the quartet took up its residency as faculty at the Juilliard School and Lehner continued coaching them when the Boston Symphony came to New York for concerts. On October 11 the group played its debut concert at the school—to show that "we were good enough to use the Juilliard's name," as Hillyer put it. The ambitious program was attended by violinist Yehudi Menuhin, who brought along Bartók's fellow Hungarian composer Zoltán Kodály. It consisted of Walter Piston's First Quartet (Hillyer had taken postgraduate studies with Piston at Harvard), the Bartók third, and Beethoven's Op. 127. Because this was a faculty concert, there were no reviews, but the reception was mixed, to say the least. Schuman told Helen Epstein:

"The chamber music authorities of the day as well as the board deplored the fact that I could have permitted this to happen. There were choreographic excesses similar to Leonard Bernstein's podium behavior. They played like angels and looked like pigs. They did not shine their shoes. Sometimes they wore colored socks. And the Beethoven! They played Beethoven *differently* from the way Beethoven had been played before! They had none of the subdued mannerisms that people associated with chamber music. They dug into the strings. They cared about total honesty of approach. They didn't think everything had to be beautiful. And they were such purists that they didn't even play quintets!"[9]

Schuman was ecstatic. To Harriet Gay he said, "And I'll never forget it if I live to be a thousand [he died in 1992]. It was greater than anything I'd ever dreamed of, because here were four men absolutely on fire with what they were doing . . . just on *fire* with it."[10]

The word spread. Serge Koussevitzky, who was the Boston Symphony's director and a new-music champion, learned from Hillyer about the new adherents to the cause. (Koussevitzky had, in fact, tried to talk Hillyer out of leaving the orchestra to go to the quartet.) At Koussevitzky's invitation the Juilliard spent the summer of 1947 at Tanglewood, playing a program of young Americans. The residency also provided an opportunity for further study with Lehner, who was in residence with the orchestra. At summer's end Lehner pronounced the quartet ready to go out into the world, though he continued to listen to it from time to time and pass along suggestions through Mann. Isaac Stern, always a friend of the new and talented, and a friend of Mann's, also pronounced his blessing. After the group had played for him in his home, he began talking it up among other friends on the concert circuit.

The formal New York debut took place in Town Hall on December 23, 1947. The program, a model of those to come, offered Haydn's Op. 77, no. 1, Berg's *Lyric Suite,* and Beethoven's Op. 130, including the taxing Great Fugue. The next day in the *New York Times,* Carter Harman declared it "a debut of unusual distinction." The Juilliard's reputation "as a responsible interpreter of contemporary music," he added, "was attested by the large percentage of New York's creative musicians in the well-filled auditorium, and its formidable performance of the *Lyric Suite* by enthusiastic applause." Questioning some details of the Beethoven performance, however, Harman suspected "that the players have a better natural understanding for the music of their contemporaries."[11]

The Juilliard's reputation as a path breaker grew the following summer with the quartet's Bartók cycle at Tanglewood. Curiously, the *Times* did not see fit to review the two concerts, spaced a week apart. The influential magazine *Musical America* noted the occasion in a single paragraph buried within a roundup of Tanglewood events. Quaintance Eaton wrote of the music, somewhat cryptically, "For all their ranging technical expertness, these quartets exude ozone rather than the scents of the salon or the academy." Of the performances she said, "The Juilliard players consistently kept these works on the small side dynamically but imparted to them a fine intensity."[12]

It remained for Virgil Thomson to catch the full significance of the event when the Juilliard repeated the cycle in two concerts in New York's Times Hall in March and April 1949. Thomson concluded his lengthy *Herald Tribune* commentary on the first program by declaring that Bartók's music, as it matured, "rendered more and more truly and convincingly the state of European men in his time. His six string quartets are the cream of Bartók's repertory, the essence of his deepest thought and feeling, his most powerful and humane communication. They are also, in a century that has produced richly in that medium, a handful of chamber music nuggets that are pure gold by any standards."[13] Hillyer remembers that Shostakovich, then in New York as a Soviet delegate to a world peace conference, attended at least one of the concerts.

By 1950 the *Times* was characterizing the Juilliard as "one of the most stimulating young ensembles hereabouts." Reviewing the first of four New York concerts pairing a Schoenberg quartet with a quartet by Schubert, Carter Harman described the performance of Schoenberg's Third Quartet as "often of the turbulent intensity that characterizes this quartet, with the artists bending far forward and seeming to play to each other." Schubert's *Quartet Movement* and *Death and the Maiden*, Harman wrote, "were played with devotion to the word and spirit of the music, with occasional forcing of tone that had less place in the classical style than the modern."[14]

Three decades before the early-music movement claimed the moral high ground of allegiance to Beethoven's metronome markings, the Juilliard, following Lehner's precepts, was horrifying chamber music authorities with its open-throttle approach to the master and his tempos. In a 1997 interview in the *Chicago Tribune* on the eve of his retirement, Mann was unrepentant: "With our youthful enthusiasm we trod paths we knew were imperfect for the time, but we were so convinced that was the way to do it. We were still convinced, and still are convinced, that Beethoven's metronome marks were important. It didn't matter that we broke our necks and sometimes didn't play them so well. The important thing was that we got those tempi into our systems. In a funny way it worked to our advantage later on, because we never would have learned to handle faster tempi if we hadn't gone through those birthing pains 'way back when."[15]

Necks were broken in other ways. Rehearsals were tempestuous, with

Winograd evidently the best scrapper, outtalking even the voluble Mann. In one interview Mann recalled a rehearsal argument so fierce that he and Winograd wound up throwing music stands at each other. Hillyer also remembers throwing a music stand at Winograd, who usually won the battles. "I was pretty successful at getting what I wanted," Winograd modestly recalled. A Juilliard faculty colleague was so incensed by Beethoven played at breakneck tempos that he burst into the rehearsal room and knocked over all four of the offending music stands. Other stories tell of Mann stamping his feet and throwing himself around so hard during a concert on a shaky stage platform that his partners couldn't read their music. A critic suggested nailing Mann's shoes to the floor.

Arguments over musical nuts and bolts are everyday occurrences in ensembles of all sizes and shapes; even the gentlemanly Budapest players could wind up not talking to one another. The Juilliard's disputes took on a more civil tone as the quartet underwent personnel changes over the years. In the 1980s Earl Carlyss, then the second violinist, recounted a dispute over tempo in which Mann wanted "a fast speed which sounded to me like Doberman pinschers barking." Carlyss, on the other hand, wanted a slow speed that sounded to Mann "like we were dragging our feet in the mud." Since they were playing the same Mozart work two nights in a row, they decided to try it one way one night, the other way the next. To their surprise each combatant found he liked the other's tempo.[16]

The Juilliard was not alone in breaking down doors in an America buoyed by a victorious end to the war. Amid the optimism and release of energies—and the fears loosed by Soviet expansionism—the old ways of thinking and doing were facing challenges in all the arts. In music such figures as Leonard Bernstein, Maria Callas, and Glenn Gould were reinterpreting the masters. Composers such as John Cage and Milton Babbitt, as Mark Swed wrote, "were turning to everything from Zen and chance operations to higher mathematics and electronic technology to make American music modern."[17] In the academy the disciples of Schoenberg were soon to exercise an iron grip that created a twenty-year orthodoxy for twelve-tone music. But more than other performers—more by far than any other string quartet—the Juilliard plunged into the new music being written in this new America.

In part the legacy was William Schuman's. The composer of five string quartets himself, the new Juilliard School president changed the character of the school dramatically, making it "probably the most aggressive force for contemporary music in the country and perhaps in the world," Koff said. He added:

> Schuman was a superb administrator and a very aggressive and suc-
> cessful diplomat outside of the school. Then all the excellent com-
> posers within the school became well known and the Juilliard Quar-
> tet was one of the reasons. The composers in residence were faculty
> members, and what was unusual was the fact that they were the
> teaching faculty. They taught literature and materials, they taught
> theory, they taught counterpoint, but they taught it from their ex-
> pertise point of view, as leading composers rather than academi-
> cians. The role of the quartet at that time was to be the primary
> chamber music faculty, and then be a touring quartet that was na-
> tional and international. But what was most important was that the
> quartet was a servant to the resident faculty and the president in
> terms of playing the quartets that they wrote.

Another impetus for new music came from the recording industry. Columbia Records, whose classical division was then under the tutelage of the
farsighted Goddard Lieberson, quickly signed the Juilliard to a contract.
But since Columbia (later taken over by Sony Classical) was also the Budapest Quartet's label, the Juilliard clearly wasn't going to be recording
Beethoven and Company any time soon. (In due course the Juilliard recorded a Beethoven cycle, still a landmark, on Sony.) Instead, Columbia issued
the country's first recorded Bartók quartet cycle, in 1949, performed by the
Juilliard. Characteristically, the group did it the hard way. Because magnetic
tape was still new and deemed untrustworthy, the whole job was done without the editing and splicing that make most recordings composites from
many takes. The set of three long-playing records, appearing only four years
after Bartók's death, helped to bring the composer into the mainstream.

Recording music by living composers—the Juilliard later did it for other
labels as well—had its hazards, however. Hillyer recalls a time when Virgil
Thomson insisted on being present for the recording of one of his quartets.
He kept interrupting the session to give the players instructions, often con-
tradictory. It became impossible to satisfy him. The exasperated players finally told him to conduct the piece so they could figure out what he wanted. That was how the recording was made.

A partial list of the twentieth-century Americans performed during the first twenty-five years includes such Juilliard faculty members as Peter Mennin (Schuman's successor as the Juilliard School's president), William Bergsma, Fred Jacoby, Alexei Haieff, Vincent Persichetti, Claus Adam (Winograd's successor as cellist), Roger Sessions, and Schuman. Other Americans on the list are Charles Ives, Aaron Copland, Lukas Foss, Irving Fine, Harold Shapero, Elliott Carter, Wallingford Riegger, Walter Piston, Samuel Barber, George Gershwin, Ralph Shapey, Henry Cowell, John Cage, Quincy Porter, Morton Feldman, Virgil Thomson, Andrew Imbrie, Jacob Druckman, and Roy Harris. Their works represented a staggering array of styles. Many of the performances were premieres. The best-known of the foreign-born composers played by the Juilliard are Stravinsky, Hindemith, Milhaud, Shostakovich, and Ginastera, as well as Bartók and the Viennese trinity. The latter four were by far the most often performed of the group from abroad.

Two composers better known as pianists sought out the Juilliard as an exponent. Artur Schnabel, the German celebrated for his playing of Beethoven and Schubert, heard the debut concert, invited Mann to his apartment, and offered the scores of his five string quartets. Hillyer recalls that when the musicians finally got around to playing one, they were surprised to find it sounded like Schoenberg. Glenn Gould, the eccentric Canadian who eventually refused to play in public at all, doing everything in the recording studio instead, offered a quartet from his pen. On a trial reading it sounded like César Franck. The Juilliard never played it in public. (Gould and the quartet did collaborate, however, in performances of Schoenberg's *Ode to Napoleon* and Robert Schumann's Piano Quintet.)

Now that an ensemble was actually playing twentieth-century quartets, "suddenly quartets began to get written and sent to us, and people came our way in droves," Koff said. Similarly, Hillyer remembers a cabinet of unsolicited scores, "full from floor to ceiling." Because of the volume, many never got read, much less played in public. This remains the situation for today's Juilliard; scores pile up and up and up.

Although some critics and serious listeners recognized the significance of the Juilliard's missionary work, others were baffled or downright hostile. In Europe, where the group first toured in 1950 under State Department auspices (to show that an American string quartet could do what Europeans did), critics complained of butchery in the traditional repertoire, especially in the tempos. The French refused to book the quartet at all. In Rome rude noises greeted the moderns. In Milan the players forgot to bring the music for Schubert's *Death and the Maiden*, the evening's scheduled finale. As a substitution they offered to repeat the Bartók third from the first half of the program. "The entire two thousand people screamed 'no!' " Hillyer said. Instead, the audience waited an hour while an emissary went to the hotel and retrieved the missing music. The concert ended after midnight but earned the players what Hillyer recalls as a "hysterically enthusiastic" ovation.

Eventually, broader European acceptance came. "Little by little as we went back," Koff said, "we began to get a core of an audience, primarily in Scandinavia and Germany." In Budapest, Hillyer said, an audience screamed, " 'You belong to us!' Never before or never after did we hear anything like that."

There were some pleasant surprises at home. Progressive colleges such as Antioch and Earlham welcomed the moderns. On the quartet's first southern tour, around 1950, it played Bartók and Mozart for an audience of schoolchildren. After the concert Koff asked the students how they had liked the music. They hated the Mozart—it had no melody or rhythm, they said—but loved the Bartók. (Stan Kenton's jazz band was popular then, and its arrangers knew their Bartók and Schoenberg.)

Like daredevils, the Juilliard seemed willing to try anything. It played for modern dance troupes and once performed at the Eighth Street Club, a New York watering hole frequented by Abstract Expressionist painters (whose work bears a certain resemblance to the music of Carter, just as Picasso's paintings are reminiscent of Stravinsky). The artists were too poor to pay for the evening's entertainment. Money wasn't the point for the musicians; though earning a meager $2,500 apiece at the school, they played gratis just for the chance to try things out. The program was Webern and Bartók. As the players headed for the door after their gig, two painters hailed them and presented tokens of appreciation. Each musician received two paintings scrolled up like diplomas. Under a street light outside the players opened their gifts. Their reaction, Hillyer said, was, "We were happy to play for nothing. They didn't have to give us this awful stuff. Should we tear it up now or wait till we get home?"

One of the group's benefactors is forgotten. The other was Willem de Kooning. Each musician owned an abstract black enamel painting that would later be worth a good bit more than his $2,500 a year at the school.

Bartók died in 1945, too early for the Juilliard to have known him. But in 1950 the quartet visited Schoenberg in California to play his music for him and learn what lessons the master might impart. Recollections of the meeting differ, but what appears to have happened is this:

Still young and short of money, the quartet had traveled across the country in a Jeep to play at the Ojai Festival, near Los Angeles. A friend of Schoenberg's arranged for the group to see the aging, ailing composer. A refugee from Hitler's Europe, Schoenberg received the players in his home in Brentwood, outside Los Angeles, where he had settled because of the warm climate and an offer of a professorship at the University of Southern California. Mann remembers the composer asking to hear his First Quartet. After listening in ominous silence, he chuckled and said that though he would have preferred a more *gemütlich* Viennese approach, he liked the players' style and they should continue doing the piece their way.[18]

The First Quartet, however, was apparently the last of the Schoenberg four to be played at that session. Hillyer remembers sitting down with the four quartets on the four music stands and asking Schoenberg what he would like to hear first. "Play Dvořák!" the composer called out.

*Dvořák!* The Juilliard didn't even play Dvořák at that time. The only Dvořák quartet it liked was the *American,* and the Budapest held a virtual patent on that. After that inauspicious start, according to Winograd, Hillyer, and Koff, the Juilliard began the Schoenberg third. After the first movement, Hillyer remembers, the astonished Schoenberg interrupted. He wanted to know whether the group had studied in Vienna. No, he was told, it hadn't. He couldn't believe it. Only players who had studied his music and music like it in Vienna could play it so well.

With that compliment under its belt, the Juilliard proceeded to play the rest of the Third Quartet, all of the fourth, and the two movements of the second that do not require a soprano soloist. "And each time we finished a quartet," Winograd recalls, "he said, 'When are you going to play the First Quartet for me?' " Koff also remembers Schoenberg's lack of interest in the late quartets and a desire to hear the first. Schoenberg wouldn't even answer Koff's question about the form of the fourth's last movement—a question Koff posed as much to draw Schoenberg out as for the information itself. The visitors obliged with the first but as before, Schoenberg offered little in the way of criticisms or suggestions. The disappointed players had expected practical pointers, if not wisdom, from the font.

In retrospect Hillyer found the composer's interest in Dvořák unsurprising, since an early Schoenberg quartet, then unpublished and seldom played, sounds much like Dvořák. (It is sometimes known as Op. $^1/_2$ to distinguish it from the four mature quartets in a twelve-tone style.) Winograd and Koff felt the same pull in the aging composer toward the music of his youth. Mann later told friends that he took the composer's lack of substantive comment as a sign of approval. Although the performances were not what Schoenberg was used to and would have expected, he apparently liked hearing them with a fresh slant and didn't want to discourage the newcomers. Approval was also suggested in his reply to questions Hillyer raised about tempos and strictness of observance of tone rows. Schoenberg answered that the players shouldn't think of them as tone rows. "Just play the music the way you feel it," he said.

Hillyer and Koff think Schoenberg was also impressed by the young Americans' playing technique and energy levels, both of which would have been superior to what he had been used to in Vienna. It was Lehner, Hillyer said, who gave the group an understanding of the Schoenberg works that was deep enough to impress the master. In the role of teachers the Juilliard members would pass that knowledge along to later generations of quartet players.

Although the string quartet has its roots in earlier forms, it was Haydn who in his eighty-three mature quartets perfected the four-movement classical form that treats the four voices as equals. In both technical and emotional range, Mozart carried the process further in his twenty-seven quartets, retaining the four-movement form but touching on depths of pathos unknown in Haydn's music.Beethoven's sixteen quartets begin within the conventional framework but, with the three *Rasumovsky* quartets of Op. 59, enter new, richer worlds of form and expression. With his five late quartets, which run to as many as seven movements, he looks yet more deeply toward both the cosmos and what it means to be human. Such time-honored devices as polyphony, fugue, and variations take on new dimensions in both time and effect.

In fifteen extant quartets, Schubert stretched the form in other ways, lengthening the movements and moving further into the realms of personal expression characteristic of the Romantics. His successors, however, walked in the shadow of Beethoven, and the quartet generally played a less central role in their work. Though Dvořák wrote fourteen quartets, Mendelssohn wrote six, and Brahms, Schumann, and Tchaikovsky three apiece. These works reverted to the four-movement classical form, so daunting was the example of Beethoven's experiments. But always the tendency was toward greater autobiographical, even confessional content.

In the twentieth century, the quartet experienced a rebirth. Although

Schoenberg, Berg, Webern, and others wrote important works, the twin cornerstones of the repertoire are the six quartets of Bartók and the fifteen of Shostakovich. Both composers found powerfully individual ways of going beyond Beethoven. Bartók, often drawing on the folk music of his native Hungary, altered the sequence of movements, sometimes as palindromes, and extended the instrumental palette to include biting dissonances and eerie or ironic pizzicatos, glissandos, harmonics, quarter tones, and other idiosyncratic effects. Shostakovich's experiments in form extended in his last quartet to six slow movements, all of an elegiac cast. In much of his music his initials, D S C H (as the pitches are designated in German notation), appear and reappear as a signature motto, like an old-fashioned seal on a letter.

What these two composers have in common is an introspective, often sorrowful response to personal loss and the political dislocations of twentieth-century Europe. Bartók fled to New York in 1940 and died five years later, recognized and assisted by fellow musicians but longing for Hungary and largely ignored by the public. His first five quartets descend into brooding and mystery, but they are also marked by gaiety, humor, and grotesquerie. The last quartet, written amid the Nazi menace and his mother's final illness, descends into unrelieved tragedy.

Shostakovich, who remained in the Soviet Union until his death in 1975, spent his entire career under the threat of disapproval—and possible death—by Stalin and his cultural commissars. Shostakovich's quartets often have an ironic or angry edge, but what primarily distinguishes them is an abiding grief.

The Bartók, Schoenberg, and Shostakovich quartets evolved out of the European tradition of Haydn, Mozart, Beethoven, and Brahms. In their works, as in those of the earlier composers, the listener can sense an underlying unity of purpose and means, however much the voices of the four instruments may diverge. The traditional resources of melody, harmony, and rhythm, of development and transformation, remain the basis, however much those devices are themselves transformed. Like their predecessors, Bartók and Shostakovich confide their inmost thoughts to the quartet, as if it were a diary. Beethoven's last symphony, the ninth, is a shout that embraces the world; his last quartets take him on an introspective journey far from that world. Similarly, Shostakovich's symphonies—there are fifteen of them, like the quartets—reflect the conditions of life and death under an iron dictatorship. His quartets, which would not have come to the attention of the commissars, speak of the turmoil those conditions caused within him.

The five quartets of Elliott Carter, the most prominent American composer of quartets—and much else—at the end of the twentieth century, represent a break with tradition, a complete rethinking of the resources of counterpoint, harmony, and texture. David Schiff begins his book *The Music of Elliott Carter* with a description of the Third Quartet, which stands for the whole of Carter's output:

> A string quartet sits on stage—oddly. To the left, a violin and cello; to the right, a violin and viola. Between the two pairs a small, but unexpected space, perhaps six feet wide. The players eye each other nervously across this divide. The left-hand violinist gives a beat with his head; the right-hand violinist gives a beat with his head—a different beat. Suddenly all four begin scraping at their instruments furiously. After a few seconds you begin to notice that they are not following the same path—and that their toes are tapping at different speeds. One pair becomes more spasmodic, their sounds come out in erratic bursts; the other proceeds dogmatically in even notes—and then fades away, exposing the ornate filigree of the other duo to the harsh, judgmental glare of silence. For the next twenty minutes this strange game of parallel play proceeds. . . . With the same screech that launched it, the music ends. It has been a wild ride for the players and for you. Some listeners are baffled, others elated. After one such performance Aaron Copland walked out on stage and told the audience, "If that's music, then I don't know what music is anymore."[19]

Schiff likens Carter to Henry James and Wallace Stevens in their attempt to create "an art of ideas and perception." "Far from the willed simplicity of Copland or the idealized nostalgia of Ives," Carter's mature work, Schiff says, mirrors "the energy, violence, and instability of contemporary American life, sometimes finding pathos in this situation, sometimes elation, and at other times tragedy."[20] But what the listener is most likely to notice—certainly on first acquaintance—is the adversarial relationship of the instruments, the furious scraping, the willed violence. Deciphering this music is not much easier for the players. It was in the Third Quartet that the

Juilliard, which commissioned it, needed two hours just to get through the first bar.

Carter, who was born in 1908, is the American composer most closely identified with the Juilliard String Quartet. Indeed, the Juilliard today is as well known for its Carter as for its Bartók. It premiered Carter's Second and Third Quartets, in 1960 and 1973. Both won Pulitzer Prizes; the second also won the New York Music Critics Circle Award and was chosen the year's most important work by the International Rostrum of Composers. For its forty-fifth anniversary, in 1991, the Juilliard played all four Carter quartets in a New York marathon. (A fifth quartet followed in 1995 and was taken up by the Juilliard in 1998.) The audience of cognoscenti rewarded the composer and performers with a big ovation. In his review in the *New York Times*, senior music critic Edward Rothstein ranked the Carter cycle with those by Bartók and Shostakovich. "And the Juilliard Quartet has already established a corresponding place for itself in the history of quartet performance," he continued. "This turned out to be one of those rare musical events in which it was unclear which deserved more celebration: the players or what they played." [21]

A recording of the four quartets, prepared under Carter's supervision, was released in conjunction with the anniversary concert. In a dedicatory note, the composer praised the Juilliard for its service to new music, including taking it out of the ghetto of new-music concerts: "The Juilliard Quartet has provided a model not only of high artistry and outstanding musical interpretation but of professional responsibility toward renewing the musical repertory. Unique among first-rate performers, it has stressed this aim throughout its forty-five years, carrying out the vision of William Schuman, who with Robert Mann brought this quartet into existence. The aim has been to bring the best of new music out from the proving ground of specialized concerts and present it to the general music public with the same care and commitment devoted to past classics, thus making what seemed inaccessible, accessible."

Whatever one thinks of Carter's music—and some musicians and knowledgeable listeners think it unintelligible—the Juilliard-Carter association wasn't always so friendly. Raphael Hillyer recalls that when the not-yet-famous composer offered the score of his First Quartet, the players tried it and rejected it. Whatever was there, it wasn't for them.

Hillyer was chosen to call the composer and break the news. He didn't relish the task. "I called up and had to say, 'We tried the piece and I'm awfully sad to say that we didn't agree on playing it,' which was a terribly painful thing to have to say." Later the group went back and tried the work again. Upon further study it seemed to speak "in epic terms," Hillyer said.

Koff recalls great difficulty in selling Carter to concert presenters, who found the music "incomprehensible." During the 1950s, in a typical six-week tour of about thirty concerts, he said, the group would play Bartók as the modern work on a program perhaps fifteen times, Berg's *Lyric Suite* eight times, William Schuman a couple of times, and, he added, "maybe Sessions, maybe Carter, but probably not." But Hillyer remembers good receptions for both the Carter first and second as time went on. "We really became very strong advocates of that music, and we must have played it with conviction. It did strike people as being something very worthwhile—very different, but I think the feeling was that when people heard the Carter music, they knew that it was an important work and an important experience. There was just something about it that gripped people."

When the Second Quartet was new, some commentators even discerned in the Juilliard players the different personality that Carter assigns to each instrument. Thus the first violin (Mann) was "fantastic, ornate, and mercurial"; the second violin (Isidore Cohen) "laconic, orderly," and "sometimes humorous"; the violist (Hillyer) "expressive"; the cellist (Claus Adam) "impetuous." These adversaries get one movement each to be in charge and lord it over their brethren. Whether accurate in terms of the individual players, the characterizations of the instruments suggest why the Juilliard and Carter share sympathies. His emphasis on four distinct voices is also the players'.

Hillyer is impressed that the complexities of a Carter performance fail to daunt younger ensembles today. He remembers hearing the Arditti Quartet (which commissioned the Carter fifth) read through the Piano Quintet with pianist Ursula Oppens one day and then play it through for the composer the next day. *"The next day!"* Hillyer gasps. "It was just astonishing. And they play whole programs like that!"

Musicians are also identified by the music they don't play, and the Juilliard of today doesn't play the repetitive, trancelike music of Philip Glass or other so-called minimalists. Nor does it find interest in a loose assortment of younger composers influenced by rock or pop styles and championed by such quartets as the Kronos.

"We like sensuality, we like intelligence, we like music which is powerfully, spiritually cathartic, wonderful, sophisticated," said Joel Smirnoff, the current first violinist. They like, added violist Samuel Rhodes, "something that carries forward the tradition of what the quartet has stood for through the centuries."

Cellist Joel Krosnick said the Juilliard has a different mission from, say, the Arditti Quartet, which plays programs of all new works. "We're trying to carry a balance of repertoire, and at this point if we're the old statesmen at it, we still are intending to play a lot of new works."

As for the Kronos, Krosnick said it plays the kind of music it believes in, just as the Juilliard does with its chosen repertoire. Consumer surveys show that the eclectic, pop-edged programming favored by the Kronos is more salable than the Juilliard's—a bottom-line reality that the Juilliard's record companies keep trying to impress on it, Krosnick said. But "the passions of the Juilliard Quartet for Beethoven metronome marks, for Bartók quartets, for the Vienna school when it wasn't being played, for the five quartets of Elliott Carter, for Milton Babbitt, for Sessions, for all of these things, were never a matter of market surveys. Our passion for Ralph Shapey, that's not market survey. That's our belief that this is remarkable stuff."

The first of the founding members to resign was Arthur Winograd. He left in 1955 to begin a conducting career, first in Birmingham, Alabama, then with the Hartford Symphony in Connecticut, where he remained from 1964 to 1985. With his departure, Robert Koff said, the quartet lost much of its wildness and improvisatory edge in concerts. The new cellist, Claus Adam, insisted on planning and rehearsing each piece down to the last detail.

The remaining members considered Adam the logical choice to succeed Winograd. A member of the New Music Quartet—the idea of a new-music quartet was itself new at the time—he was the only cellist who already knew the Juilliard repertoire. Even so, he had to be persuaded to trade one quartet for another. It helped that both Adam and Mann were composers; indeed, the Juilliard had premiered Adam's quartet in 1947. Adam's refined playing style brought a measure of stability and helped to win the group further acceptance, Koff said. "We had to do it his way. That made it much more polished. [But] it ruined the joie-de-vivre, devil-may-care Winograd style, because he [Winograd] was the ringleader. He played in the quartet as if he were a conductor and if we didn't go along with him, there was conflict." With his rhythmic drive and strong leadership, Koff said, Winograd "even overwhelmed Bobby Mann, who is a pretty aggressive leader himself."

Mann later described himself and Adam as "tremendous positive but confronting forces." The real peacemaker, he said in the *New York Times Magazine,* was Earl Carlyss, the second violinist from 1966 to 1986, "an almost beatifically rational person" who could stop fights almost before they started. But Mann, while always the founder-leader and in due course the father figure, said he tried not to impose his will on the younger players who came to surround him. "Being the older and more experienced player, it would be very easy to say, 'Why not do it this way?' But I realized that it would be the end of me and the quartet. I recognized that it would have to be a whole new ball game. I would just have to go through the whole learning process again—would have to become more youthful. It was a little hard on the ego but I think I've succeeded pretty well."[22]

In 1958 Koff left to go to Brandeis University and become a teacher and member of the Brandeis Quartet, in which he was reunited with Lehner, its violist. He was replaced by Isidore Cohen, who moved on to the Beaux Arts Trio in 1966 and was in turn replaced by Carlyss. When Hillyer left in 1969 to begin a teaching career that led ultimately to Yale and Boston Universities, Rhodes came on board. In 1974 Adam, in ill health, retired as cellist and Krosnick replaced him. Smirnoff joined as second violinist in 1986, succeeding Carlyss, who went to the Peabody Institute in Baltimore to head its chamber music program. The present lineup came into being when Smirnoff succeeded Mann as first violinist in 1997 and Copes assumed the second violinist's chair.

Since the Juilliard treats even a newcomer as an equal partner with full voting privileges, each change altered the character of the playing to some degree. With so few personnel changes over half a century, the record is one of remarkable continuity. But behind the scenes there was turmoil. Frictions with Cohen became so intense in 1966 that Carlyss, just one year out of the Juilliard School, had to replace him in the middle of the season. Hired only three weeks before, Carlyss barely had time to learn the repertoire. In *Music Talks* he told the author, Helen Epstein:

I don't know how I did it. I remember one of the Chicago critics wrote that I must know how it feels to be in an airplane, given a parachute, and pushed out the door. Not only did I come in in the middle of the season but I was in the strange and rather awkward position of playing with three men, all twenty years older than me, who had been my teachers. They made it very clear to me that it was no longer a teacher-student relationship, that I had a twenty-five percent share in the organization, and that I was supposed to contribute my ideas. That they wouldn't have picked me unless they thought I had ideas. But we didn't have time for long, leisurely discussions about music and I didn't have time to think about *anything*. We were to do most of Bartók, all of Beethoven, and several Schubert quartets. I had to cram for sixty concerts in less than five months.[23]

The pivotal appointment appears to have been Rhodes's, in 1969. For nine years before that, he had studied and performed at the Marlboro Music Festival with two members of the Budapest Quartet, violinist Alexander Schneider and his brother, cellist Mischa Schneider. He had also performed with the Galimir String Quartet, another noted Viennese ensemble driven out by the Nazis, and with the Budapest's violist, Boris Kroyt. Although Lehner had coached the Juilliard in the European tradition, Rhodes was the first member who was steeped in that tradition. He believes his appointment brought together the strains of New World vitality and Old World expressiveness, broadening and deepening the Juilliard's playing and helping to give it the maturity it enjoys today.

A player doesn't apply to a group like the Juilliard for a job; the job goes looking for him. Rhodes didn't know any of the Juilliard members when he unexpectedly received a call from Adam in the spring of 1968, inviting him over to play some chamber music. It sounded like a musician's idea of fun, and Rhodes went.

When he arrived, he joined Adam, Carlyss, and a violinist from the New York Philharmonic in reading through quartets by such lesser lights from the eighteenth and nineteenth centuries as Louis Spohr, Friedrich Kuhlau, and Franz Krommer. The unfamiliarity of the music, which came from Adam's large collection of such esoterica, guaranteed that everybody except the host would be sight-reading. Rhodes enjoyed himself, went home, and thought nothing more about it, not realizing that he had undergone a test.

A few weeks later he got a call from Itzhak Perlman inviting him to another reading. He knew Perlman from having gone to high school with his wife, Toby. Again it sounded like fun; again Rhodes accepted. Perlman mentioned that Bobby Mann would be coming. Rhodes remembers the following conversation ensuing:

Rhodes (casually): "Oh, that's wonderful, that's great."

Perlman: "Don't you know him?"

Rhodes: "No, I don't know him."

Perlman: "That's funny. He especially asked for you."

Rhodes: "I can't imagine why he did that. I never met him."

The group read through some late Beethoven, including the Great Fugue. Again Rhodes had a good time, and that seemed to be that.

A couple of weeks later another invitation came. This time it was from Daniel Saidenberg, a conductor and cellist. Again Mann was there. The group read through a Mozart quintet and the Debussy Quartet. At the end Mann came up to Rhodes and said, "If there's ever an opening in the Juilliard Quartet, I hope you'll consider it." But the comment was "very hypothetical and cryptic," Rhodes recalls, and he more or less dismissed it.

That summer Rhodes went to Marlboro as usual. About two-thirds of the way through the season he received a long letter from Mann asking him to join the Juilliard. Rhodes was "stunned." Joining would mean a drastic change in his life. But how could he refuse? He couldn't. He played his first concert as a Juilliard member in a tryout of the new Juilliard Theater at Lincoln Center in the spring of 1969. He still marvels at the intensity of his feelings at being asked to play in such exalted company.

The audition-initiation process was similar for Krosnick five years later. He had studied privately with Adam but it was still a shock when Mann called up out of the blue and asked him to audition for Adam's job. Incredulous as Krosnick was then, he was even more surprised when, after two auditions ten months apart, the three members offered him the position. Krosnick accepted in a daze, hardly knowing what he was saying.

Looking back in 1986, Mann could see a maturation over the first forty years. "In the early days," he said "we were quite fanatical about certain things, and also very tempestuous and one-dimensional in our thrust. As we've grown and changed, we've enlarged our emotional expressivity and we're willing to allow the sound of the quartet to speak more eloquently, in many directions rather than one. There's more color and sonority in our sound and more variety and character in the moods that we sustain."[24]

Highlights of the middle and later years included the world premieres of Copland's Quartet for Piano and Strings in 1954 and Stefan Wolpe's String Quartet in 1969, and the American premieres of Shostakovich's final quartet in 1976 and Henri Dutilleux's *Ainsi la Nuit* in 1977. On first reading through the Shostakovich, with its six unrelieved adagio movements, Mann told Leighton Kerner in the *Village Voice,* "We were horrified. It seemed like a Russian Orthodox service. But after working on it, we wound up not being able to play it without crying. I suppose the lesson of that goes back to Arnold Schoenberg telling musicians like the Kolisch Quartet who were struggling against various new twelve-tone scores: 'Your responsibility is not to judge music but to play it.' "[25]

The Wolpe quartet, the composer's last work, was a Juilliard commission; the group considers it a neglected masterpiece. On the other hand, the Dutilleux work, which the Juilliard studied with the French composer, has won recognition in chamber music circles as a masterpiece of its kind. In 2000 the players were still waiting, after seven years, for the elderly Dutilleux to complete what they hoped would be a work of comparable or greater quality. It was a fiftieth-anniversary commission, to have been premiered in the legacy concerts. The Juilliard returned to *Ainsi la Nuit* instead.

Other commissions went to composers ranging from Elliott Carter, Roger Sessions, and Milton Babbitt—the grand old men of the cerebral school of writing—to Alberto Ginastera, Donald Martino, Richard Wernick, and John Harbison. The Martino work, which the Juilliard struggled with over two seasons, also falls into the players' buried-treasure category. Rhodes compares it to the Carter third in stature. The Juilliard also played a jazz piece, *Homage,* written for it by Billy Taylor. Each of the three movements is in the style of a different jazz composer; Smirnoff describes the work as "a kind of postbebop piece where he uses the quartet pretty much like a sax section." Another landmark was the 1986 premiere of the quartet's performance of Bach's *Art of the Fugue,* a monumental work in four parts with no designation of the instruments to be used. Instead of altering the notes to fit the ranges of their instruments, the players altered their instruments to fit the notes. For Rhodes this meant having a special viola built.

In 1961 the Juilliard became the first American string quartet to visit what was then the Soviet Union. A thunderous ovation at the opening concert, given in the Tchaikovsky Conservatory in Moscow, ended only when the quartet returned to the stage to play a fourth encore forty minutes after the end of the regular program. The next year, in an event symbolic of the passing of an era, the Juilliard replaced the Budapest as quartet in residence at the Library of Congress. In that prestigious position the Juilliard, like the Budapest before it, plays four pairs of concerts a year on a set of Stradivari instruments owned by the library and used only in those programs.

Ever since the founding, the quartet was also carrying out the other half of its mission: coaching chamber music at the Juilliard School. For many years each player coached six student quartets a year, for a total of twenty-four. But in the early 1990s Joseph Polisi, president of the school, asked Mann, Rhodes, and Krosnick to head the violin, viola, and cello departments and, along with Smirnoff, to teach their instruments in addition to chamber music. Krosnick was so inundated with cello students that he had no time left for quartets. Copes, well known as a teacher, had the same experience when he joined the group in 1997. With reinforcement by Mann, Carlyss, and other noted chamber players on the faculty and an adjustment of teaching loads, the Juilliard now coaches about fifteen student groups a year. It also organizes and teaches a quartet seminar.

Krosnick thinks the quartet's move into instrumental teaching, with support from colleagues such as Mann and Carlyss, was "a good thing in terms of a nuts-and-bolts, realistic approach to teaching, to music-making, to being useful in the musical community." Koff, on the other hand, remembers going into his first class as a faculty member at the ripe age of twenty-six and facing a roomful of string players in their early twenties. All were students of the celebrated pedagogue Ivan Galamian and "could play fifty times faster and better than I could."

Because the Juilliard is on tour as much as two months a year, it has a professional-level graduate string quartet to take its classes during the five or so weeks of the school year—never more than two weeks at a time—that it is away. The assistants in turn receive two coachings a week from the Juilliard and get to do two concerts a year at the school. Out of the program have come a number of leading quartets from a younger generation, including the Saint Lawrence, Shanghai, Cassatt, Lark, and Colorado.

Most of the student ensembles are ad hoc groupings that do not survive the practice room. Those with professional intentions may be already formed when they arrive at the Juilliard's door, or they may be put together by the Juilliard, with the hope that four players will someday meld into a unit. The now-defunct LaSalle String Quartet (named by Mann for the New York street where he was living when he formed the group) was the first student ensemble to go on to a professional career. Of the many that have emerged since, the two that have won greatest recognition, ranking in a class at or near the top with the Juilliard itself, are the Tokyo and Emerson. The former was embryonic when it came to the Juilliard; the latter was an entity.

The Juilliard's first encounter with the Tokyo—or what was to become the Tokyo—took place at a chamber music workshop the Juilliard gave in Nikko, Japan, during the summer of 1965. Knowing of the Juilliard by reputation, three Japanese men in their early twenties who were studying chamber music at the Toho Gakuen School in Tokyo signed up for the workshops: violinists Kazuhide Isomura and Koichiro Harada and cellist Sadao Harada. For two weeks teachers and students lived in the same hotel, eating, rehearsing, and performing in close communion.

"The Juilliard String Quartet inspired us so much. We watched how they rehearsed, how they played, how they taught, and we made our decision that someday in the very near future we should really form a string quartet and play quartets the rest of our lives," said Isomura, the only member of the original trio who in 2000 still played in the quartet that emerged.

Still, money was short, and jobs and school called. It was not until 1967 that the Juilliard connection could be renewed. That summer Isomura and cellist Harada followed their mentors to the Aspen Music Festival in Colorado, where the Juilliard regularly taught. Wanting to remain in the United States afterward and continue their studies at the Juilliard School, the pair took jobs as assistant concertmaster and principal cellist of the Nashville Symphony in Tennessee to earn money.

By the fall of 1968 Isomura and Harada had saved up enough to go to Juilliard with the help of scholarship money. They were joined at the school by a Toho Gakuen friend, Yoshiko Nakura, whom they had invited to be second violinist. First violinist Harada came over the next fall, and Isomura switched to viola. After a year's study the Tokyo Quartet made its New York debut in October 1970 as a winner of the Young Concert Artists International Auditions.

Isomura said Robert Mann and Raphael Hillyer, in particular, had gone beyond the call of duty as teachers. At Aspen Mann gave extra lessons and encouragement, spending time with the young players and talking passionately about the quartet literature and other musical issues whenever they had time to get together. At Juilliard Mann gave extra lessons in his apartment, never charging the fee that is customary for private study. The influence was "profound," Isomura said. (When the players finally decided to force Mann to accept a fee, Isomura's check bounced. He described the incident as one of his most embarrassing experiences. Mann thought it was a fine joke.)

Hillyer had already taken a personal interest in the players in Japan. Now he was to help to launch the Tokyo on an international career. Before graduation in 1970, having already won the Coleman Competition in California, the Tokyo decided it wanted to enter the Munich International Music Competition that September as preparation for its October debut, and perhaps for a prize to enhance it. Hillyer arranged for the group to spend the summer on scholarships at Kneisel Hall, the chamber music festival and school in Blue Hill, Maine, where he taught. He didn't think a relatively untested quartet stood a chance in a competition that would attract more experienced ensembles from around the world. But, impressed with the Tokyo's determination and talent, he coached the group every day for all eight weeks of the summer session. Determined to make a good showing, the Tokyo practiced as much as fifteen hours a day.

In September Hillyer received an excited call from his protégés in Germany: the Tokyo had won first prize. It was "a big step foward," leading to European management and the start of a European career, Isomura said. Two years later a Grand Prix du Disque for a recording of works by Haydn and Brahms confirmed the obvious: the Tokyo was on its way. Though not a believer in competitions, Isomura makes an exception for the 1970 Munich.

The Emerson, born in America, followed a different route. Violinists Eugene Drucker and Philip Setzer, the only original members still in the group in 2000, and violist Guillermo Figueroa had studied at the Juilliard School with violinist Oscar Shumsky. To round out the ensemble, they enlisted Eric Wilson as cellist. When they went on to study as a quartet, Mann became their principal coach. They spent almost their entire first year working on Bartók's Second Quartet, moving on afterward to the other Bartóks and serving, meanwhile, as a graduate assistant quartet to the Juilliard. The players were aware that they were learning their Bartók at the knees of the masters who had launched Bartók in America. Drucker recalled:

"At that point, in the early to midseventies, Bartók still seemed pretty contemporary in many respects. And, of course, we knew that the Juilliard was doing a lot of American music, like Elliott Carter, though we didn't study that music with them. But I think that some of the sense of cutting-edge familiarity with the new style of playing that had characterized the Juilliard Quartet's performances practically of the whole repertoire, including the Beethoven quartets—some of that intensity came across to us in the coachings that we got, particularly from Bobby Mann."

Taking its name from Ralph Waldo Emerson, the quartet made its debut in the American bicentennial year, 1976. Despite Mann's misgivings, Drucker and Setzer decided from the start on the democratic, though then unorthodox, idea of dividing the first and second violin duties fifty-fifty.

"We're credited for having two violinists who can play first violin, but we're not credited enough that there are two of us who can play *second* violin—who know when and how to get out of the way," Setzer said in the *New York Times Magazine.*[26]

In other ways, too, the group embarked on the trail blazed by the Juilliard, playing and recording works by contemporary composers as well as the classics and the Bartók quartets. Drucker said the Emerson was following in the Juilliard's footsteps "without thinking about it that much. It was the natural thing for us to do."

The new group didn't immediately follow the old in observing Beethoven's metronome markings. But when the Emerson went to make its 1997 recording of the Beethoven cycle, it examined the tempos more closely and adapted them to the extent it found possible in the recording studio, which allows less freedom to experiment than a live performance. The goal in all cases, Drucker said, is to come as close as possible to the composer's intentions. For the Emerson and Juilliard, as for other performers, that skill is sharpened by working with living composers, who can tell you what they intended in their scores. From them "you get a sense of prioritizing what is the most important thing to this composer in his or her score," whether in Beethoven or a new piece, Drucker said.

While cultivating a more blended tone and more Olympian playing style than the Juilliard, the Emerson followed its teachers in performing and recording the major quartet cycles of Beethoven, Bartók, and Shostakovich, along with the late Schubert quartets. In the eight concerts of its 1996–97 Beethoven cycle in New York, the group inserted a twentieth-century work between two Beethovens on each program. The newer work always had some relevance to Beethoven: the Ravel Quartet, for instance, which is rooted in sonata form, or a Shostakovich quartet, which enters into deeply personal states akin to Beethoven's. Other composers in the series were Berg, Webern, Bartók, and Wolfgang Rihm. The sandwich format recalls the Juilliard's standard program, which places a twentieth-century work between two classics.

Venturing beyond the Juilliard, the Emerson has also done a highly compressed Beethoven cycle within eight days, the sixteen works falling in chronological order. In 2000 it took part in a five-program Shostakovich project at New York's Lincoln Center, with director Simon McBurney fashioning a multimedia framework for the death-haunted last quartet. In the final program, titled *The Noise of Time,* the performance of that quartet was preceded by a staged recapitulation of Shostakovich's troubled life using actors, old radio broadcasts, and video clips. *The Noise of Time* was later toured in the United States and abroad, and the Emerson's 1999 recording of the fifteen Shostakovich quartets won two 2001 Grammy awards. Another collaboration was with physicist Brian Greene, author of *The Elegant Universe*. The program illustrated his string theory, which melds quantum mechanics with Einstein's theory of general relativity. The Emerson played music that either reflected Greene's concepts or suggested parallels between the development of music and of physics. Mozart transcriptions of Bach fugues suggested a well-ordered Newtonian universe. Webern's post-Romantic *Slow Movement* (1905) and pointillistic *Five Movements* for String Quartet (1909) were matched with Einstein's 1905 theory of special relativity, which broke with Newtonian physics.

If Mann and the Juilliard taught the Emerson its Bartók, violinist Felix Galimir of the Galimir Quartet schooled it in Schoenberg. (Like the Kolisch Quartet, the Galimir Quartet had known Schoenberg and played his quartets in prewar Vienna.) In effect, Mann and Galimir were the Emerson's Lehner. The Guarneri Quartet, with which the Emerson studied privately, was another important influence. But, Drucker said, the Guarneri was a different kind of model, which had less to do with contemporary music. Rather, the Emerson admired the Guarneri "for the lushness of their tone and their technical expertise and the warmth of their music-making."

The Emerson, like the Tokyo, has cultivated its own sound and personality, distinct from either the Juilliard's or the Guarneri's. Said cellist David Finckel, who joined the Emerson in 1979 and is responsible for its programming: "I don't think it's possible for any group to have worked as many years, as hard as we have on as much repertory, and not sound different from other people. It's easier when you're young and you're copying teachers to sound more like other groups, but after this much work I think anybody would develop something that's uniquely their own." Like the Juilliard, the Emerson went on to teach, bringing along younger groups at the Hartt School of Music in West Hartford, Connecticut.

Bartók is no longer basic training for a Juilliard-coached quartet. Today the studies begin with the standard repertoire, usually Haydn, "the trough from which all other composers drink," as Smirnoff puts it. Then come a middle or late Beethoven quartet and possibly a twentieth-century work. There's no problem in teaching Bartók when the time comes, Smirnoff said. Bartók is so universal that most students know the music by the time they get to Juilliard. The Bartók and Berg violin concertos are taught at the school, and so is some of Bartók's chamber music for smaller ensembles. In the broader picture, the school orchestra plays his Concerto for Orchestra and there is a Focus Festival featuring a variety of twentieth-century music.

The Juilliard insists, however, on what Smirnoff describes as "a board game named quartet." It is designed to prevent what he remembers from his own Juilliard studies: a quartet that self-destructed because of personality conflicts. "You have to inform them of the fact that it's a democracy," he says, "that they have to try any suggestion that anybody [in the quartet] makes. You have to inform them of the intonation basics, which have to go from the ground up in the cello. All these things are basically the rules of the game at the world-class level of quartet playing. And then either it takes or it doesn't, and either they're mature enough to work together or they're not. That's a big if with young people."

Hardest of all to teach, said Smirnoff, is an understanding of a work written by a composer near the end of his life. The youthful energy appropriate to the Bartók first and second or the Schoenberg first comes naturally to students. But much as they might want to tackle a valedictory work like Beethoven's Op. 132, the Bartók sixth, or the Schoenberg fourth, those works require a fund of experience that the young simply don't have. It's the same as with Mahler, Smirnoff said: they can play one of the early symphonies but not the ninth, with its titanic struggles against and eventual acceptance of death.

Yet times have changed, and new music comes more naturally now to students and audiences. "Classical music students are not squares anymore, exactly," Smirnoff said. "Everybody seems to live in the same world, and they warm to new things very often."

Joel Krosnick watched Joel Smirnoff squirm, wiggle, bob, and weave as he dug into the music in the back rows of the Boston Symphony Orchestra's violin section. I don't know if he belongs in the Juilliard Quartet, Krosnick reported afterward to his colleagues, but you can sure see he's into the music in the Boston Symphony. The choreography came naturally. Smirnoff had been a dancer in his youth.

Krosnick took on the job of scout at a 1985 Tanglewood concert. Smirnoff didn't know he was being considered for a job. An old Juilliard friend, Eugene Lehner, who had recommended his Boston Symphony colleague Raphael Hillyer thirty-nine years before, was playing matchmaker again. Though retired from the orchestra, he was still teaching at Tanglewood, where Krosnick and Smirnoff also taught. Take a look, Lehner had said. Smirnoff might be the violinist you're looking for. And so it happened that in 1986 the thirty-six-year-old Smirnoff, joining Mann, Rhodes, and Krosnick, became the Juilliard's second violinist and only the sixth new member in its forty-year history.

Smirnoff went through the initiation process that Rhodes and Krosnick had gone through. Once the remaining players got over the shock of Earl Carlyss's unexpected resignation, they drew up a list of candidates with the help of friends like Lehner. The candidates could be, and were, soloists, orchestra members, or chamber players. Over the next few weeks Mann, Rhodes, and Krosnick approached the nominees, sounding them out. Some knew the purpose of the talks, others didn't. Three were eventually asked to perform with the three remaining members of the Juilliard in a series of readings in their homes. Each candidate had to play four quartets of the Juilliard's choice: a late Beethoven, a Bartók, a Mozart, and a Romantic work.

Smirnoff had other recommendations besides Lehner's word. The son of Zelly Smirnoff, who had played violin in the NBC Symphony, and jazz singer Judy Marshall, he had graduated from the Juilliard School in 1977. Mann and Rhodes had coached him in chamber music during his three years of study and more or less kept an eye on him ever since. Although they had been impressed with his playing, it was also his personal qualities that caught their attention. Mann saw in him a person with wide-ranging gifts. Rhodes remembered the student's intellectual curiosity.

Smirnoff did himself no harm in his future colleagues' eyes by going on after graduation to become a member of composer Ralph Shapey's Contemporary Chamber Players in Chicago. A second prize in the 1983 International American Music Competition in Carnegie Hall, at which Smirnoff performed Roger Sessions's difficult solo sonata, also made a favorable impression. His work with the BSO, which he had joined in 1980, was noticed, as was his new-music activity in Boston and his teaching at Tanglewood. Fellow musicians said good things about him.

Still, none of the Juilliard players knew Smirnoff well. So as part of the scouting operation, Krosnick tried to set up some chamber music readings at Tanglewood with the unwitting candidate. Schedules didn't mesh. In September Krosnick took the frontal approach. He called Smirnoff and asked if he would like to try out for the quartet. The call came just as Smirnoff, planning to stay in Boston, had moved into a new apartment in the suburbs and was about to leave on a vacation.

"Well," he replied, "I was going to Italy but I guess I'll have to change my mind."

Smirnoff had three reading sessions with the group over three days. Krosnick recalled that "from the moment he walked into Bobby Mann's apartment, there was no question." Not only did Smirnoff play "seriously and well," but he was clearly capable of the "commitment to a long-term emotional and musical seeking" that the Juilliard demands in its rehearsals and performances.

For Smirnoff, a fan of the three men since his student days, playing music with them was like being caught in a hurricane. "When I sat down to play with them, they were going for blood and it was a thrill—it was the thrill of a lifetime. I had to catch my breath at the end of every damned movement and say, 'Can you hold on a second?' " Just remembering it, he had to catch his breath again.

Smirnoff made his Juilliard debut at Tanglewood during the quartet's fortieth-anniversary celebrations. Invited by the Tanglewood administration to rehearse and reemerge at the place where it had scored its earliest successes, the Juilliard played two programs: first a standard Mozart-Debussy-Schubert evening and then, a week later, works by Irving Fine, Sessions, and Bartók in Tanglewood's Festival of Contemporary Music. The residency also reunited the Juilliard with Lehner—still a member in "inner spirit," as Krosnick put it.

Mann saw the induction of the new member as a sign of continuity amid change. "In a funny way," he said, "we're kind of self-perpetuating in style because never more than one player has left at a time, which means that the three players who remained would go for a particular kind of person who lives in the same world."[27]

The move from orchestral to quartet playing was not as radical for Smirnoff as it might have seemed. He had grown up with the quartet literature, partly through his father and partly through his own studies, and was moving more and more into the solo repertoire. A successful solo debut, the prize in the Carnegie Hall competition, and a series of recordings he had made suggested to him that it was only a matter of time before he branched out into solo or chamber work. Ten years later, at the Juilliard's fiftieth-anniversary celebration and his own ascension to the first chair,

Smirnoff was able to say that, yes, he missed the orchestral repertoire but he was still catching his breath at being in the Juilliard.

Also ten years later, the breaking-in process was repeated with Ronald Copes. He had even less quartet experience than Smirnoff when the Juilliard discovered him in California. For sixteen years he had been the violist of the Los Angeles Piano Quartet and then the violinist of the Dunsmuir Piano Quartet, meanwhile serving on the faculty at the University of California at Santa Barbara.

There was no audition for first violin. Smirnoff was his partners' choice to succeed Mann when Mann decided to retire. Six violinists whom the players knew, or knew of, were invited to try out for the second chair. Five bulwarks of the repertoire were chosen to test the auditioners: Beethoven's Op. 131, Bartók's Fourth Quartet, the Debussy Quartet, Mozart's K. 387, and Schubert's A Minor.

The testers also tested themselves. "We felt an enormous responsibility, the three of us, to play really full tilt as the Juilliard Quartet in a combination in which we were not normally playing," Krosnick said. "We felt, and I think played, in a very, very serious, virtuosic sort of way in these auditions because we wanted to present our style to the person who might be joining." The quartet was concerned, Rhodes said, with "how individual a voice the person has. And not only that: how does that individual voice fit with the voices that are already there, and how does it complement and complete the group? Does it conflict or does it add?"

A willingness to rehearse endlessly, play contemporary music, and teach was also a requisite. What the job came down to, Krosnick said, in what could be a Juilliard credo, was an "obsession" with music: "needing and wanting to do this thing passionately, seduced by it, driven by it, can't live with it and can't live without." It was like a lover's obsession, maddening in its intensity.

As one of the invited six, Copes had come to the Juilliard's attention via Rhodes's wife, violinist Hiroko Yajima, who met him at the Marlboro Festival, and Rhodes's daughter Harumi, who had studied violin with him at Kneisel Hall. Krosnick had heard him at the Friedheim Competition in Washington and been impressed.

"Ron walked in somewhere about the middle of the auditions," Krosnick said, "and there was something special about the voice and his sound—a real complex, inner, deeply felt spirit in the sound and the way he approaches the music." Soon Krosnick began to get goosebumps and think, "Thank God, here's the one." After hearing Copes play Beethoven's Op. 131, a work he would not have played in a piano quartet, Rhodes told him, "Well, if that's the one you haven't played, I don't know whether I have the nerve to play the ones you have played." When Copes returned for a make-sure audition three months later—both sessions took place in Rhodes's Englewood, New Jersey, home—a bottle of Champagne was waiting in the refrigerator.

Copes, it turned out, had had a month without any concerts before the auditions and spent the time learning Op. 131. He figured, "If nothing else comes of this, I'll have the opportunity to play this magnificent work of music with these guys. And I'm going to come away from this process enriched regardless of what actually happens."

For Smirnoff, moving up to the leader's position meant succeeding someone whom he and many other musicians had grown up idolizing. Mann, Smirnoff said, had been properly recognized for "the energy, the intensity, the headstrong musical personality" that he brought to quartet playing, but those qualities had overshadowed his lyrical gift in such music as the cavatina of Beethoven's Op. 130. On top of that, Smirnoff said, Mann is a composer himself, and his ability to understand and interpret how other composers think was "one of the things that have distinguished the quartet." His contributions would remain a polestar, a reference point. The only concession the group made toward having a new member onboard was a slight reduction in the number of pieces it would learn and play in the coming season.

The Juilliard members, at the turn of the twenty-first century, appear to be less dysfunctional as a family than their forebears, but their personalities and backgrounds are no less diverse. All are in their fifties or early sixties, and all are articulate. Smirnoff is still in almost constant motion onstage, recalling Mann, whose shoes a critic once wanted to nail to the floor; offstage, Smirnoff has a quick sense of humor that belies his faintly cherubic face. Lanky, bewhiskered, and thoughtful, Copes looks Lincolnesque. The soft-spoken Rhodes, with his whiskers and kindly gaze, could be mistaken for an old-fashioned family physician. Krosnick has a coiled intensity, with hair to match, that makes him look wound on a spring. Like pianist Emanuel Ax, the group has clowned with Garrison Keillor on his *Prairie Home Companion* radio show, first playing two movements of Debussy's Quartet and then taking part in a send-up of concert life. Never have so many been initiated into Debussy.

The quartet plays about eighty concerts a year, or about four times as many as it played in the early years. In a typical year there are two two-week tours of Europe, a national tour during the winter, another tour—sometimes to the Far East—in the spring, recording dates, and the four pairs of Library of Congress concerts spread through the season. While the Emerson ventures into multimedia and scientific experiments, the Juilliard collaborates with such other musical adventurers as pianists Martha Argerich and Maurizio Pollini. The emphasis on individual voices remains, although the brashness of the early years is gone. The reason for the four-voice emphasis, Smirnoff once said in the school paper, the *Juilliard Journal*, is that each voice should "truly suggest the possibility of a living, breathing being spontaneously uttering its own, unique musical phrases." This "is the basis for real counterpoint, after all, which is not only a counterpoint of melodic line but counterpoint of gesture and personality as expressed through individual nuance and quality of sound."[28]

Rhodes, the senior member, thinks the sound has become more blended and attractive than the public realizes. Because of their reputation for having a "wired sound," he said, "everybody thinks it's impossible for the Juilliard to play with a beautiful sound and have that same vitality. I think we've been doing it for a while. At least that's what we strive for and that's what I think I'm hearing when I play."

That hasn't stopped some critics from hearing a sound more like the New York subway. Reviewing a Library of Congress concert in 2000, Philip Kennicott of the *Washington Post* complained that "the violin tone established by quartet leader Joel Smirnoff was thin and abrasive; tempos were supercharged to an aggressive extreme; dynamic levels were reached and exceeded in interpretations that consequently lost the larger architecture." All in all, Kennicott declared, the playing "had all the charm of the exposed pipes and girders of bad postmodern architecture."[29]

A collection of seven compact discs, mostly reissues, released by Sony Classical for the quartet's fiftieth anniversary suggests the range of the Juilliard's vast discography (which in turn suggests the range of its repertoire). From Bach, Haydn, Mozart, Beethoven, and Schubert, the set ranges through Verdi, Debussy, and Bartók. Two discs offer collaborations with other leading artists, such as Leonard Bernstein, Rudolf Firkušný, Jorge Bolet, and Dietrich Fischer-Dieskau. Another disc explores, in the words of its title, *The Scherzo Through Time*. Outside the anniversary edition, the Juilliard has recorded the Beethoven, Schoenberg, Bartók, and Hindemith cycles and a trove of other material, including Haydn's *The Seven Last Words of Christ*,

Sibelius, Janáček, and Hindemith. The Beethoven and Schoenberg cycles and a pairing of the Debussy and Ravel quartets won Grammy awards.

A legacy project of a different order is a recent compact disc devoted to three twentieth-century works for string quartet and soprano soloist, all commissioned for the Juilliard: Alberto Ginastera's Third Quartet, Richard Wernick's Fifth Quartet, and John Harbison's *The Rewaking*. All are performed with Benita Valente, who premiered them with the Juilliard. The Ginastera, with texts by various poets, dates from 1973; the Harbison, with texts by William Carlos Williams, from 1991. The Wernick is in an unusual sequence of two scherzo movements followed by two settings of poems by Hannah Senesch, a Jewish activist assassinated by the Nazis in Yugoslavia. It was a fiftieth-anniversary commission, given by the school and premiered in the legacy concerts. When Sony Classical, the Juilliard's primary label, rejected the project on grounds that it wouldn't sell, the smaller Arabesque company accepted it. The recording memorializes the Juilliard's long association with Valente.

In any given season the Juilliard carries about eighteen pieces (of the lifetime total of more than five hundred) in its active repertoire. Only a few of them are repeats from the previous season. About a third will be from the twentieth century, and only one of them is likely to be new to the repertoire. The year's eighteen pieces are offered to concert presenters in four prepackaged programs, though only two at a time. The players will drop the modern work if so requested. Or they will add a second modern work. As Joel Smirnoff said, they're flexible. In an age when marketers often have the last word, they have to be.

The percentage of new music in the schedule hasn't changed appreciably over the years, the quartet says. But the context is different. The blizzard of new-music activity at the quartet's start, Joel Krosnick said, was a statement that "needed to be made at that point," and it was made "with a vengeance" because, with the Budapest Quartet still on the scene, nobody was about to hire the Juilliard to play the Beethoven cycle. Now that the Juilliard plays the Beethoven cycle, it likes to restudy all sixteen quartets in the years that the cycle is on the programs. That limits the time for new-music activity in those years. Other major projects, such as the anniversary commissions, consume the time available for preparation of other new works. The players also spend time reading through scores, including some by a younger crop of composers, in search of additions to the repertoire. These may never show up in the programming. There is a funnel effect: the relatively few new pieces performed from year to year belie the amount of new-music activity that actually takes place.

The point, Krosnick said, is that "we'll learn anything. Playing it for people in a concert is another matter. We have to be sure we really believe in it."

There is no consistent pattern in audience response to new music. The Juilliard finds Amsterdam and Boston receptive to it, but other big cities turn a chilly ear. Ronald Copes thinks it is often concert presenters who are the obstacle. "I don't know how many times we'll play in a small town and the presenter says, 'No, no, nothing new.' We somehow get something new in there anyway and we go in to play, and the audience comes back and says how much they like it." Speaking to an audience about a new piece helps, the quartet has found. Elliott Carter, Donald Martino, and Ruth Crawford Seeger are among the composers who have benefited from a word from the sponsor. Of course, there are always complainers too, and they're usually the people who get the presenter's ear.

On the other hand, Smirnoff said, there are presenters in smaller places, such as Modesto, California, "who have cultivated a rather chic, forward-looking attitude in their listeners." These are usually venues where the presenters take their educational responsibilities seriously, attracting a younger audience.

Surprises still happen. Copes remembers playing the Schoenberg fourth and Bartók fifth for schoolchildren in Port Arthur, Texas. "They loved it," he said. The Bartók fourth was the audience favorite during a tour of China. Since Western classical music was forbidden in China during the Cultural Revolution of the 1960s and 1970s, "it's the young people who think it's revolutionary and are open-minded," Copes said. They'll be a "huge market" in the future, he believes.

Then there was the curious case of Beethoven versus Verdi in Europe. One of the Juilliard's two tour programs offered Beethoven's Op. 131 as the finale; the other offered the Verdi quartet. The Germans wanted the Italian Verdi, and the Italians wanted the German Beethoven. "This was really weird," Smirnoff said. "It was so consistent that it was very suspicious."

Unlike the Juilliard in its earlier years and quartets such as the Guarneri, whose members try to keep their distance when not rehearsing or performing, today's Juilliard members usually travel in the same planes and stay in the same hotels while on tour. Outside the quartet each player pursues a career as a soloist, chamber player, teacher, or all three. Smirnoff spends summers at Tanglewood, where he performs, teaches, and conducts the student orchestra, a counterpart to the Juilliard School orchestra he conducts in the winter. Rhodes is a regular at the Marlboro Festival in Vermont, Krosnick and Copes at Kneisel Hall in Maine.

Among leading American quartets, the one with the next-greatest record of longevity is the Guarneri. From its founding in 1964 until cellist David Soyer resigned in 2001, the Guarneri consisted of its original members: violinists Arnold Steinhardt and John Dalley, violist Michael Tree, and Soyer. The Guarneri comes out of the Budapest stream of musical thought, with homogeneity of sound and interpretation. In the book *The Art of Quartet Playing*, Soyer told author David Blum: "Our style of playing has evolved towards greater continuity of rhythm and tempo. We try, nowadays, to avoid impositions and exaggerations. If one player takes a little musical liberty, the quartet goes along with him. We allow each other freedom—but there's a natural give and take."[30]

The Budapest, the Juilliard, the Guarneri, the Tokyo, and the Emerson have all contributed to and benefited in turn from the post–World War II boom in chamber music. While in 1945 the Budapest was virtually the only show in town, today dozens of quartets make the rounds of cities and towns, playing in schools, churches, museums, and libraries as well as concert halls. Other chamber ensembles, from duos to small orchestras, abound. Chamber music has its own umbrella organization, Chamber Music America, which publishes a magazine about activities in the field. In the summer every village with aspirations to culture and tourism seems to have its own chamber music festival, drawing audiences from both the local environs and the weary cities.

The Juilliard put new music on the map, and new music put the Juilliard on the map. Audiences may like the stuff no better than before, but now it is expected at concerts that a quartet—and other musicians too—will voyage outside the solar system bounded by Haydn at one end and Ravel at the other. William Schuman saw his rowdy creation mature into a part of the establishment. As the quartet turned twenty-five, he told Harriet Gay:

> It's so established that when another quartet comes along, like the Guarneri, another marvelous quartet, it gets compared to the Juilliards. They occupy the position the Budapest once occupied. The price of success is to become the establishment; but to me that's not a dirty word, because there are establishments and establishments.

There are forward-looking ones and progressive ones and live ones, and others that are quite dead. To the public at large, the Juilliard String Quartet stands for a certain excellence that goes unchallenged. The quartet has built up a chamber music audience that wasn't there in such numbers before. And the way they play the Beethoven, Haydn, and Mozart repertoire is just astonishing, considering they were supposedly modern music specialists at first.[31]

The Juilliard spent the summer of 1997 at Tanglewood, teaching, rehearsing, and preparing for its rebirth with Joel Smirnoff as the new first violinist. Five weeks after Robert Mann's farewell, the reconstituted quartet made its debut in Seiji Ozawa Hall. The outpouring of emotion on the stage and in the audience equaled the demonstration for Mann in the same place. Amid the audience's whoops and whistles after the final chord, the four men at the center of the tumult leapt out of their chairs. In their summer tuxedos, they turned from bows to the house to bear hugs for one another, and then bowed and hugged some more. Bouquets arrived at the stage, and in the continuing uproar, the musicians seemed dazed by their own feats.

The Juilliard remained the Juilliard. The same all-out intensity was there, and the same focus on underlying meanings and resonances rather than beauty of sound and execution. But in myriad lesser matters, this was a different quartet. Smirnoff played with a smaller, sweeter tone than Mann did, and in adapting to the change, the Juilliard became more like a high-performance compact car than a powerful but sometimes balky V-8. But within that smaller compass, the range of effects in dynamics, articulation, phrasing—all the particulars that make up a whole—was a revelation.

The debut program was a typical Juilliard sandwich, but each piece had significance. The twentieth-century meat in the middle was Copland's relatively unknown Three Pieces for String Quartet, recalling the American icon's twenty-five years as a Tanglewood leader and the Juilliard's own championing of his music. The bread on either side was Mendelssohn's Quartet no. 1, which the Juilliard was learning for a recording, and Schubert's *Death and the Maiden,* performed for the bicentennial of his birth.

Of the many remarkable things during the evening, none was more impressive than the slow movement of *Death and the Maiden*. Consisting of variations on Schubert's song of the same name, the movement is drenched in pathos. Here pathos became tragedy. The playing began sotto voce, without vibrato, like a dirge. As the variations moved inescapably toward the denouement, the mood could shift from stillness to fury without breaking stride. The quiet ending was utterly bereft, the grief that lies beyond grief.

The whole Schubert quartet, like the Juilliard itself, was a work born anew. It had clearly benefited from a rethinking during the quartet's five-week retreat. Nothing was taken for granted. Everything was turned over like a stone, looked under, made fresh. The patches of wayward fingers and pitch counted for nothing. When the music ended amid anger that bordered on savagery, the audience could find release only in shouting and exultation.

Nothing was different but everything was different. The struggles, the premieres, the cheering, the protégés, the rejections, the honors had come to this: the Juilliard remained the Juilliard, raised to establishment status but unchanged in its can't-live-with-it, can't-live-without-it commitment to vital music, regardless of its age.

# MIDORI
## *Growing flowers in the desert*

Midori enthralls New York City schoolchildren. (Courtesy Midori & Friends)

THE GUTTING OF MUSIC EDUCATION IN SCHOOLS DURING
the budget-cutting frenzies of the 1970s and 1980s was like a car stalled in
traffic. Everybody saw the danger but steered around it. Then in the 1990s,
as prosperity returned to the private sector but not the schools, it seemed
everybody wanted to give the troubled vehicle a push. Symphony orchestras got involved, sending their players into the schools to perform, counsel,
and teach their future audiences. Chamber ensembles and concert presenters created residencies, with players settling in for days or weeks at a time
as performer-teachers. Community organizations created enrichment programs. Foundations and corporations funneled in money. Some schools
even rehired music teachers.

One of the least likely rescuers was Midori. Twenty years old and busy
making a career as a child-prodigy violinist, she was hardly beyond school
age herself. But the example of Leonard Bernstein had stuck in her mind
ever since she was thirteen, when he took her to Hiroshima to be a soloist in
two 1985 concerts commemorating the fortieth anniversary of the atomic
bombing. She played a Mozart concerto with the European Community
Youth Orchestra under Eiji Oue, a conductor born in Hiroshima. On the
same program Bernstein conducted his own *Kaddish* Symphony, offering a
Jewish prayer for the Japanese dead, and Oue led a new *Hiroshima Requiem*
by Tomiko Kojiba, a woman born in the ravaged city.

Humphrey Burton sets the scene in his Bernstein biography:

> By sunrise on the anniversary day, August 6, Hiroshima's Peace Park
> was crowded and the air was pungent with the smell of incense
> burning at the monuments and shrines dotted about the area. At
> one of the shrines Leonard Bernstein joined a delegation of musi-
> cians led by Seiji Ozawa and his brother Mikio, who laid wreaths of
> flowers and sang a newly composed Requiem chorus as well as Japa-
> nese and German folk songs. . . . The memorial ceremony, attended

by fifty-five thousand people, began at eight-fifteen, the precise moment of the bomb's explosion, with the ringing of the Peace Bell. Its sound was echoed by more than three hundred temple bells across the city of Hiroshima, where sixty thousand citizens had instantly perished and three times as many had since died as a direct result of the bomb. The mayor of Hiroshima and the Japanese Prime Minister both made speeches calling for the abolition of nuclear arms.[1]

It was a classic Bernstein event, using music and theater for the greater glory of peace and reconciliation. It was also enough to plant an idea in the mind of the teenager who had left Japan just three years before to study and make a career in New York. In her first encounter with the charismatic Bernstein, she felt the energy radiating from him like a force from the cosmos. She recalls that just being in the presence of a person she admired greatly was compelling enough. "But this was a person that was very hands-on. He was taking action and doing something about a cause that he strongly believed in. For me it was learning by experiencing what was really going on, rather than being told or reading in a book, 'This is what you're supposed to do.' "

Then there was the example of Linda Chang, Midori's best friend. A violinist whom Midori had met at age ten when they were at New York's Juilliard School together, Chang went on to become a corporate lawyer. But as a teenager she was involved in community work, and she also showed Midori the importance of working for a cause.

Midori does not look the part of a crusader. Still girlish in stature, gesture, and chatter, she looks as if she would be happier cycling in Central Park (risky for a violinist) or having coffee with friends in a Starbucks. But when she was in her late teens, she found her cause. As a musician and someone who enjoyed children, she would do something about the disappearance of arts programs in the schools. With Bernstein and Chang as exemplars, she began offering to perform in schools when she traveled around the country as an already famous soloist. She met with what she describes as a "lukewarm response." The organizations she dealt with were more interested in putting on concerts.

As she pondered the idea further, she decided her scattershot approach wasn't enough. "I realized that I wanted to have an opportunity to develop a program that was organized, that was to grow and meet the needs of different communities. To be able to do something to have coherence within the program. To have a philosophy. I realized more and more that I needed my own organization."

In 1991 she set about approaching well-placed men and women she knew—lawyers, educators, and people in business—to solicit their help and advice. At their suggestion she decided to create a foundation. Volunteering their services, her advisers took her through the steps of incorporation and in 1992 set her up as Midori & Friends. (In the logo the ampersand appears as a musical G clef.) Once she was incorporated, other doors opened. When she asked people to help, she said, "they knew that it wasn't just a twenty-year-old with an interest on the side, that I was very, very serious.

"I really lucked out," she said, looking back. "Being twenty and trying to establish a foundation—if I hadn't had the help from these people, I couldn't have done it. I didn't know anything about law. I'm not a law student. I didn't know anything about a nonprofit, I didn't know anything about accounting. I can balance my checkbook, but that's not enough."

In the beginning the foundation operated out of the apartment in Manhattan where Midori lived with her mother, Setsu Goto, who had brought her to New York for further violin studies, and her stepfather, half brother, and two dogs. Midori typed the letters on the computer and was the only teacher-administrator. She started with schools whose children had written her letters.[2] Midori would go anywhere to play in schools then: Washington, Boston, Jonestown, Pennsylvania—big city, small town, wherever she was wanted and could arrange a visit. Having to bear all the costs herself, she tried to coordinate school appearances with her concerts to save on travel expenses, but, as she explained, not for long.

> That stopped very quickly because I wanted to have a coherent program, I wanted to build a program, and I didn't want a random, one-time-only exposure for the kids. In the beginning you have to start somewhere. It's like *Alice in Wonderland* when Alice is told by the mock turtle to be quiet and not to interrupt. So she stops interrupting and nobody speaks. Alice wonders, "How's he ever going to finish the story if he never starts?" It's the same thing. You have to start somewhere. We started to concentrate just in New York City. I learned very quickly that building partnerships and cultivating relationships with the districts and the district [arts] coordinators, also becoming partners with individual schools, are all very important to

make the programs work. We began asking other musicians to play for the kids as well.

The program has been a catalyst for restoring music education in the New York City schools, not a substitute for city-run programs. With about 565,000 pupils in 675 elementary schools, it's unlikely that any outside organization could shoulder a burden like that alone. But neither can the school system, with its limited funding, aging buildings, and large proportion of children from impoverished, broken homes, do the job without help.

From its Alice-in-Wonderland start with Midori as the whole show, the program gradually expanded to become a three-tier operation serving grades one through five. By 2001 it was sending fourteen artist-teachers and assorted ensembles—strings, winds, brasses, saxophones, jazz, Latino, African drumming—into eleven New York schools at an annual cost of $800,000. Businesses, foundations, other benefactors at many of the schools, and the schools themselves were putting up money. Midori played annual concerts, and such celebrity friends as Yo-Yo Ma and pianists Emanuel Ax and Yefim Bronfman donated their services from time to time. The programs have reached more than a hundred thousand students, many of whom went on to participate in middle and high school orchestras and bands.

The classes occur regularly throughout the school year, rather than on a now-and-again basis, which is the rule in many imported school programs. The three levels of instruction are arranged sequentially to lead from informed listening to active participation, whether through written responses to concerts or by learning an instrument.

Explorations in Music (tier one) provides first- and second-graders with instruction in the basics: listening, rhythm, singing, movement with music, and rudimentary composition. The Adventure Concerts Series (tier two) consists of three in-school concerts a year by professional musicians for third-graders, followed by a family concert based on a theme that dovetails with the overall curriculum. With materials provided by Midori & Friends, teachers prepare students for what they will hear, and the children keep a journal of their responses. Midori performs in every school at least once every two years. Making Music (tier three) provides instrumental instruction in the fourth and fifth grades, with twice-weekly group lessons. Through partnerships with other organizations, students are supplied with an instrument, free of charge, that they can take home after school for practice—

indeed, it is a requirement of the program that they be allowed to take instruments home. Each child performs in a student recital at the family concert, which is open to the community. Other activities include choruses (which are sometimes intergenerational and include parents and community members) and an Adopt-a-School campaign, which solicits support from individuals and corporations to help in schools with a high proportion of disadvantaged children.

A large percentage of the children in New York City's public schools are African American, Asian American, and Hispanic, and many are from families who immigrated recently. The difficulty of accommodating an influx from many cultures aggravated the problem of insufficient resources. In the 1990s, however, the city made a brave start on bringing the arts back into the schools, allocating fifty-three dollars per pupil per year under a Project Arts incentive program. The money provides instruments and other support for the teaching artists whom Midori & Friends and other arts organizations send into partner schools. Though Midori & Friends planned to expand further, even thirteen schools, the immediate target, was only a shout into a well in terms of need.

Those needs sometimes crop up in unexpected ways. Midori tells of a time when a television station wanted to do a program on the foundation's activities in one of its schools. The school couldn't allow it. Too many of the children were in foster homes, and who knew what might happen if a biological parent bearing a grudge recognized a child's face on the television screen?

"It's heartbreaking to know that this is going on," Midori said. It's also heartbreaking for her to hear children say their instruments and music are the only things they can take with them when they are shunted from home to home. But it's a consolation, she said, "to be able to provide that consistency in that child's life."

Cards, letters, drawings, and other tributes from children show that they are benefiting. In a *Newsday* article children from Queens described their experiences. Kayla Duffy, a third-grader at Public School 229, said: "Everybody in the third grade takes this program. There are twenty-eight kids in my class. I like how we get to do things at home over the weekend, like make drums and shakers. . . . We used the drums and shakers for our storm piece. We drew up all the rainbows and snows and made up sounds for each one. We also hit paper to make other storm sounds. For the rainbow we would use our voice to go, 'Do, do, do.' We recorded our storm piece and listened to Beethoven's song [from the *Pastoral* Symphony] on the recorder [record player]. Our recording sounded nice. It started quiet and then it got noisy. We also did singing parts and made clicking sounds with our tongues."

Kiearra Reynolds, a fifth-grader at P.S. 160, said she was inspired to take up the flute after hearing Midori play in her school: "Playing the flute has made me become more settled and not so quick to do things. You have to keep on going. If you fall, you have to get up. That is part of the discipline I learned. I don't necessarily want to play an instrument professionally but I want to be a rhythm and blues singer, and I want to take singing lessons too. I sing all around the house. Everything that comes on the radio or TV, I sing. If someone puts a piece in front of me, I want to be able to play it. I kind of want to learn to play other instruments but I want to get better at the flute first."[3]

There is an echo here of the experience Midori had in her own education. At the Professional Children's School, a private New York school for children headed for careers in the arts and other fields, she remembers classes in singing (mostly current hits) and performances at assemblies and fund-raising events. Later, as a psychology student at New York University, she learned that "whatever we learn or whatever we teach has to be something that goes beyond that classroom." When she acquired some new knowledge or understanding, she said, "I was always encouraged to take that into the rest of my world." She wanted a program like that for her foundation—one that taught music for its own sake and as part of an overall curriculum.

It is rare, if not unique, for a superstar musician—especially one so young—to devote her talent, time, and resources to so unglamorous a project as taking music into the public schools. Midori's own performances are only a small part of the foundation program. Regardless of who is onstage, she prefers to stay in the background and put the focus on the program, children, and music. Writers as well as television crews are discouraged from attending her performances. But in 1997 it was Midori the *New York Times* homed in on when it went to a school to cover an Adventure Concert in Queens. She is, after all, the founder and guiding spirit. On this occasion she was also the star attraction.

About 350 students had assembled in P.S. 114's auditorium, which—because an influx of immigrant children had pushed enrollments beyond capacity—doubled as a music classroom and extra cafeteria space. Teachers had coached the students on the music and on proper concert decorum:

dresses for the girls, shirts and ties for the boys, and silence for all. They would have to write journal responses to what they heard.

Anthony Tommasini of the *Times* reported:

Midori's program, a "musical journey," as she called it, took the children through Russia, Austria, Italy, Germany, Spain, England, and the United States. Just what the bees in Rimsky-Korsakov's "Flight of the Bumblebee" had to do with Russia Midori did not indicate. But she did helpfully explain that the phrase "making a beeline" was inaccurate, since bees fly in zigzag patterns that the music's buzzing violin line captures perfectly. And the students were struck silent by her playing.

Before she performed a movement from the "Winter" Concerto of Vivaldi's *Four Seasons,* a boy whose first language was Italian read the short poem that is inscribed in the score at the beginning of the piece. And before performing an Elgar work, Midori and her pianist, Thomas Sauer, played the first phrases out of sync to show what can happen when musicians do not learn to cooperate. There were whoops and cheers when four female teachers bravely demonstrated a square dance during a performance of "Hoe Down" from [Aaron] Copland's *Rodeo.*[4]

During a question-and-answer period afterward a boy asked Midori if she ever "messed up" during a performance. She confessed that yes, she sometimes did. A girl asked if Sauer, her male pianist, toured with her. That too sometimes happened, Midori replied.

The school's enrollment, reflecting its multiethnic neighborhood, was 8 percent African American, 15 percent Hispanic, 39 percent white, and 38 percent Asian American or other. Students spoke about thirty languages. Midori told Tommasini it made a difference to children that she was an Asian American. The questions she was asked as she traveled from school to school dealt often with issues the students were struggling with in their own lives, such as when she came to the United States and how she learned English. Principal Sydell Kane said that for such students Midori—foreign born, young, and famous—was invaluable as a role model. The schools bear the primary responsibility for bringing the arts back into the curriculum, Kane said, "but what she has done you couldn't begin to pay for."[5]

Playing the same program at P.S. 165 on Manhattan's Upper West Side,

Midori began by talking about how and when she had learned some of the music she would play. "I would imagine that I was traveling to the country where it was written," she said, according to an account in the strings magazine *The Strad*.

When she came to the "Winter" excerpt from Vivaldi's *Seasons*, she asked, "How many of you like pizza?" As a roomful of hands shot up, she announced, "We're going next to the country where pizza was invented. Can anyone guess where we're going?" Two students read the prefatory poem, one in the original Italian, one in English translation. "Let's imagine that we are cozy in front of a fire and listening to the sound of rain," Midori said, setting the mood for her performance. Tumultuous applause greeted the teachers' square dance in Copland's "Hoe Down." A few questions—"mostly of the 'how old are you?' and 'why did you come to New York?' variety," according to the *Strad*—followed. And though attention was wandering, the end of the show was met with disappointed moans.[6]

Bernstein, who was a master at this sort of thing, remains an inspiration for Midori. When he died in 1990, she said in a 2000 talk at a Grammy Foundation screening of some of his *Omnibus* telecasts, "I remember writing down my thoughts that to me he represented a garden of flowers, where there were a number of blossoms waiting to bloom. Every time I am with schoolchildren, I feel that a new flower blossoms in that garden."[7] Consciously or not, she was echoing the final chorus from his *Candide*, "Make Our Garden Grow." But unlike Voltaire's and Bernstein's naïve young adventurer, she knew this was not the best of all possible worlds—not as long as there was no music in some schools and children were growing up deprived.

Was there something odd about the fact that a society so affluent could so impoverish its children that a young woman barely past childhood herself had to show what was missing? Midori didn't stop to fret about that. She and her foundation had a job to do.

"We believe strongly that music is a gateway to different cultures and to learning about your own self, your own culture, your background—everything," she said. Even if nothing concrete comes out of the lessons, just having a child say, "Oh, I had a great time in that class" makes a difference for that child and society.

Yehudi Menuhin went through a double crisis in his late twenties: the breakup of his first marriage and breakdown of his violin playing. "There was nothing in my past to teach me how to cope with failure," he says apropos the divorce in his autobiography, *Unfinished Journey*. The problem was the same in his playing. He never had to think things through. "Considering that I played without thinking, without analysis, without, as it were, taking the machine apart for overhaul, just keeping it running at any cost, my performance stood up remarkably well; but there were times when I knew I wouldn't be able to go on until I understood technique and could recapture that ease I had once possessed without thinking and which was now deserting me."[8] He had, in fact, to rebuild his technique and start again without the child's instinctive ease.

The lore of musical prodigies—Menuhin was one of the twentieth century's most famous examples—abounds in such stories. Ruth Slenczynska, an American pianist who created a worldwide sensation in the 1930s, only to suffer a breakdown and withdraw from concert life by the age of fifteen, is another celebrated case. At age thirty-two she published a memoir, *Forbidden Childhood*, recounting her violinist-father's abuse, physical as well as emotional, in his determination to force her into a career. She said he woke her at six in the morning to begin practicing (in a nightgown), kept her at it eight to nine hours a day, and slapped her or deprived her of meals if she made a mistake. Among the other indignities visited upon her, she had to submit to a doctor's examination in Copenhagen to determine whether she was a child or a midget. In a sense her breakdown was the opposite of Menuhin's. His parents and teachers furnished love and support at every step of the way. Menuhin was able to pick up the pieces and go on; she wasn't.

Mozart was a prodigy, shown off in the courts of Europe like a trained monkey by his ambitious father, Leopold. All the major composers have shown their talent early, as have most major performers. The issues are different for performers, though, since they must function in the public eye. And in any case, the only composers the public now clutches to its bosom listen to the beat of Elvis and the Beatles, not Mozart.

Cellist Jacqueline du Pré underwent a period of doubt and depression in her midteens after winning numerous honors as a prodigy. Only by taking up painting, fencing, and other activities was she able to regain the confidence that had buoyed her as a child. Among violinists Itzhak Perlman's talent showed early, but he does not consider himself a prodigy, he said, if by prodigy you mean "somebody [who] can step up to the stage of Carnegie Hall and play with an orchestra one of the standard violin concertos with aplomb," as du Pré was able to do. Though one of the twentieth century's great violinists, Perlman said in a *New York Times* interview that it was not until he graduated from the Juilliard School and won the Leventritt Prize at eighteen that he began to play professionally—and then mainly at benefits for Jewish organizations.[9]

Bejun Mehta, the singer whom Phyllis Curtin rescued when his professional fortune was at a low ebb, enjoyed the parental freedom and support in his prodigy years that Menuhin had enjoyed. In his case the price of being unusually gifted was loneliness. In Claude Kenneson's book *Musical Prodigies* Mehta recalls:

> I didn't consider why I sang all the time, why a tune bubbled up in my throat twenty-four hours a day. Something just made it so. I was a joyful child, but I also sensed that somehow I was substantially different from everybody else, and that made me quite lonely at times. What I thought made me different was not that I could sing, but that I seemed to feel everything very deeply. My inner world was so active, and the power of my imagination accelerated to such a degree, that I could make emotional connections far beyond the scope of my years. I realize now that my singing stemmed from this combination of joy and gifted loneliness.[10]

Not all prodigies experience this sense of loneliness—Midori, for one, seems to have escaped it—but the sense of separateness is common. Yo-Yo Ma felt it when he drank and skipped rehearsals to prove himself "one of the guys" at Harvard. Dorothy DeLay, the Juilliard teacher of Midori, Perlman, and such other notable talents (many of them prodigies) as Pinchas Zukerman, Gil Shaham, and Sarah Chang, says parental or other adult support during childhood years is a key to a successful transition to an adult career. In *Teaching Genius,* Barbara Lourie Sand's study of DeLay's life and work, the noted pedagogue says that adult guidance is necessary to steer the child into healthy practice and work habits. If such a routine is established and followed, DeLay says, the child will be prepared to cope with the inevitable "crisis period" between the ages of seventeen and thirty. That, according to DeLay, is "when, having been put on a track by someone older, we then have to decide whether we want to continue on that track."[11] Ma's history, with his father as a steadying force, would seem to prove the point.

Elaborating on DeLay's views, Sand says there is no way that a child can have a "normal life" when he or she is truly gifted and obsessed with the violin, piano, or—more rarely—cello the way other children are obsessed with basketball or video games. (Winds and brasses, Sand points out, require too much lung power to develop prodigies.) Sand describes the pitfalls:

A childhood that includes all the familiar pleasures of regular school, friends, sports, movies, and so on may be possible until the child begins to be known in the outside world—that is, to perform in public—but once that happens the universe shifts on its axis. You miss school because you have a special concert coming up. You miss more school because you are away on tour. Your classmates start seeing your picture in newspapers and magazines, and while your best friends may feel the same about you, your relationships with others are inevitably altered—maybe some of them start to feel jealous. You are already leading a very different life. You are practicing four, five, or six hours a day while your classmates are hanging out at the mall or the movies. Of necessity, school work becomes secondary.[12]

The pressure to perform early and often, Sand writes, comes more from overeager parents than money-hungry managers. Parents, like Mozart's and Slenczynska's fathers, can try to turn their little geniuses into vehicles for the success they themselves never had. Managers recognize that they have a long-term investment to protect.

For these reasons Sand commends the Professional Children's School, which Midori and a number of DeLay's other students, along with Yo-Yo Ma and Emanuel Ax, attended. It provides a normal education—more or less normal, Midori says skeptically—while making allowances for young musicians, actors, and athletes to perform on the outside. (Midori remembers having more actors, actresses, and models than musicians around her during her years.)

Midori was born in 1971 in Osaka. She never lived in Tokyo or attended its Toho Gakuen School, which produced many of the leading Japanese string players of the post–World War II years. Nor, like Ma, did she ever win a major competition. Except for her violin studies, she doesn't like to talk about her growing-up years in Japan. Still legally named Midori Goto, she assumed the stage name Midori at eleven, shortly after coming to the United States. Her father, an engineer divorced from her mother, remains in Japan.

Midori received her first violin as a gift—she had requested it—at the age of three. Lessons began at age four with Setsu Goto, her mother, who was a strong force on her during the early years. Though Midori says, "I never, ever had a time when I didn't listen to music," she believes she was more interested in what her mother was doing than in the violin itself. As a child, she recalls, "I saw my mother practicing and I wanted to do that too." But she also remembers her mother emphasizing the joy of music rather than pure technique, the usual bane of childhood music lessons.

When she was about eight, a violinist friend of her mother's heard Midori practicing. The friend, who came from New York, took a Midori tape back with her and gave it to a neighbor who was an assistant to DeLay. The neighbor in turn took the tape to DeLay. It won Midori a scholarship to study with DeLay at the Aspen Festival in Colorado in the summer of 1981. In 1982 mother and daughter moved permanently to New York so Midori could study with DeLay in the Juilliard's precollege program.

Setsu Goto continued to coach Midori at home when she was studying with DeLay. Midori said the two mentors exerted complementary influences. Her lessons with DeLay were like performances and she went into them with the same preparation and attitude as for a public performance. Her mother would practice with her, she said, "in order to prepare me for these 'performances.' "

Over the next few years recitals and engagements followed with the Philadelphia, Cleveland, Montreal, Detroit, Osaka, and other orchestras. Television cameras, always hungry for new sensations, discovered the wonder child. Midori's appearances included *The MacNeil-Lehrer Report,* a CBS special, "Juilliard and Beyond: a Life in Music," and, in 1983, a performance before President and Mrs. Reagan in an NBC special, "Christmas in Washington." She also went on Bernstein's 1985 Hiroshima anniversary peace tour to Japan, Greece, Vienna, and Hungary and played recitals in the inaugural Schleswig-Holstein Festival in northern Germany, to which Bernstein lent his influence and talents.

The musical press worried a lot about Midori in those days. Was she really a musician or just a wind-up doll with a knack for the violin? Was Setsu Goto a stage mother, pushing her daughter into a premature career? Would her early celebrity stunt Midori's growth? Conversely, would the next batch of prodigies send her into a tailspin from which she could not recover? A cancellation of five months of concerts for medical reasons in 1995 added fuel to the fire. Was Midori anorexic? Was she going through what Menuhin had gone through? Did prodigies have to fail?

Looking back in 1996, Tim Page of the *Washington Post* suspected that Midori had gone through a crisis in her early twenties:

> Long after it was appropriate, she still dressed in little-girl Popsicle colors and came across as an eternal moppet. She talked incessantly about Snoopy, and her body language—when she wasn't playing the violin—was that of a child, one well aware of her Lilliputian charm. At age twenty-two, she took a season off for an unspecified "digestive disorder." Fortunately, when she returned to performing the following year, she came back with a new and pronounced maturity, dressed in a dark green evening gown, greeting the audience with a dignified bow and then playing magnificently. Further appearances (Midori is now twenty-five) have confirmed the impression of a fully grown artist who has finally put the sideshow behind her.[13]

Whatever happened offstage, it seems evident that Midori, like Menuhin, underwent a crisis necessary for rebirth as a mature artist.

The media gaze began when Zubin Mehta turned his attentions to the eleven-year-old Midori. Introduced to her by DeLay, the conductor featured her as a surprise soloist in the New York Philharmonic's traditional New Year's Eve concert in 1982. Full celebrity was conferred when, in a sequel to the 1985 Hiroshima concerts, Bernstein featured the child star as his soloist on a summer evening at Tanglewood in 1986.

It was in her Boston Symphony Orchestra debut, and while playing a slightly less than full-size violin, Midori broke a string during Bernstein's *Serenade* for solo violin, strings, and percussion. Hardly missing a beat, she stepped over and swapped violins with the concertmaster—standard practice in such emergencies. He, of course, handed over a full-sized instrument. The whole drama was reenacted barely a minute later when she popped a string on the concertmaster's violin and had to take from his hands the instrument he had borrowed from a neighbor.

The freak occurrence was about as likely—and significant—as lightning striking twice in the same place. It nevertheless ignited a sensation in both the audience and the press. "Girl, 14, Conquers Tanglewood with 3 Violins," the *New York Times* headlined its front-page story the next day, nicely missing the point. The point was that Midori's coolness under fire was of a piece with the suavity of her performance. Midori seemed the only sane person in the subsequent media frenzy, explaining in interviews that she couldn't stop the performance, could she? But the musical issue was lost in the sound and fury about three violins with Bernstein on a starry night.

Midori was in the vanguard of a crop of seemingly ever-younger violinists paraded before the public in the 1980s and 1990s. Among the other newly minted stars—the women frequently of Asian ancestry—were Gil Shaham, Joshua Bell, Hilary Hahn, Sarah Chang, Anne Akiko Myers, and Yura Lee. All are formidable talents. The musicianship and technical mastery instilled by teachers like DeLay were a factor in their emergence, but so was the music industry's need to whet the appetites of a media-jaded public through sensations of one kind or another. What better than an eight-year-old (Sarah Chang first played with the New York Philharmonic under Mehta at that advanced age) to pump life into a staid concert routine or old warhorses like the Mendelssohn concerto? "I was fourteen until I was eighteen," Joshua Bell once said apropos the need to tickle the audience's fancy.[14] The wry comment could stand as a motto for the whole young-and-younger movement. Nor were marketers above exploiting the sexual angle. Ads and compact disc covers featured the nubile Vannessa-Mae, who aimed her wares at the teenage market with a mix of classical and pop, in varying stages of undress.

Short and spindly in her shiny green dress, Midori looked like a doll on her big night at Tanglewood. As a grown woman she has much the same aspect, even when, in bare feet and a T-shirt, she pads around her crowded, college-girl-style New York apartment, which she shares with her two dogs and a female roommate. But she speaks with adult vehemence about the difficulties of growing up famous. She calls the words *child prodigy* "a label that people put on somebody."

When you're a child of twelve, thirteen, or fourteen, she said, "you're trying to form an identity and discover yourself. If you're constantly being told who you are, you're denied that opportunity, whether you're a prodigy or not. So you have to think hard: are you really what people say you are?" On top of that curse is the "constant negativity"—the certainty that you won't succeed—that surrounds a prodigy. At first the child finds the attention positive and exciting.

But, she went on: "It always comes with the baggage that says, 'Well, a prodigy always fails at the end.' Imagine being a child that is trying to develop, that is trying to grow, that is trying to do something with his life or her life, trying to do the best he or she can—and is constantly being told, 'You're going to fail.' That's a lot of negativity. But having said all that, my mind right now is very neutral. I have no one feeling or another. I see it as something I went through. Am I glad that I went through it? Yes, I am glad because without having had those experiences, I would be a very different person. I wouldn't say a better person but I would be different. And I like being who I am right now."

It's like being royalty in a restaurant, Midori says. If you're just plain Susie Smith and break a dinner plate, nobody cares. But if you're Princess Susannah, you'll be on the eleven o'clock news and the front page tomorrow.

"You get very self-conscious," she adds, "not because you are a prodigy. At thirteen you become very self-conscious—that's just normal. To have that extra feeling of being scrutinized for every little action you take—that's a challenge. But the thing is, you see, if you're not making mistakes in public, the mistakes won't have that capacity to destroy you as much" when you do make them. Meanwhile, she says, a prodigy has to mature as a musician. "You don't do it just because you're pressured to do it. You do it because that's what you're trying to do. That was my musical growth."

Midori attended the Juilliard precollege division until she was fifteen, meanwhile continuing her academic studies at the Professional Children's School. At Juilliard she spent all day Saturday in class—on theory, solfège, orchestra, and piano—and took one or two violin lessons with DeLay or occasionally her assistant during the week. She prepared a different concerto for each lesson, but at first played only a few in public—the Mendelssohn and Paganini in her first year of concertizing. The choice reflected orchestras' preference for trying out new soloists, particularly teenaged novices, on the lower levels of Parnassus before allowing them onto the Beethoven-Brahms summit. When she left Juilliard, Midori began learning the sonata literature and playing recitals. She received occasional coaching from her regular pianist, Robert McDonald, and went to Isaac Stern for a lesson about once a year. She never had stage nerves, she claims, but she admits her playing was less spontaneous when she was still finding her way.

In effect, she says, she became her own teacher. Looking back in a 1995 interview in *Strings* magazine, she said she had no time during the Juilliard years to develop her own thoughts about the compositions she was learning and playing in rapid succession:

I mean, it's not that anyone stopped me from doing it, but there isn't enough time to think and feel through a piece of music when you prepare a new concerto every week. In addition, I was going to school full-time and doing at least three or four hours of homework every night. But it was good for me to go through this kind of training, because it made me very relaxed in my later years, when I had to perform and study different concertos at the same time. It taught me to learn pretty fast.

I feel I really started to learn about music when I was about fourteen or fifteen, going to operas and concerts, listening to recordings, applying what I knew to my music. I wasn't just playing the violin and then having a life; it sort of became connected. To a certain extent it probably always was, because I used music as a form of expression. But now it all started to come together, the knowledge of history and culture and theory, the experience of playing in concerts, as well as personal experiences. And when I left Juilliard, it opened up so much free time, and it made me really think for myself; that's what was so good about it. I had to be my own teacher, to develop my ears, to be very critical. It was a very positive experience.[15]

If Midori had to be her own teacher, she never stopped being a student. In 1995, at twenty-four, she cut back on her concerts to begin studying at New York University. At its Gallatin School, a liberal-arts division, she entered a degree program in psychology and gender studies. In an independent study program she immersed herself in the relationship between society and culture in the Expressionist world of Arnold Schoenberg, Gustav Klimt, Oskar Kokoschka, and Edvard Munch at the turn of the twentieth century. Meanwhile, she restricted her playing during the summers, first to participate in the Marlboro Music Festival in Vermont and then to give herself "unstructured time" to learn about music or any other subject that caught her interest. She took a five-month sabbatical to complete her bachelor's degree, graduated magna cum laude in 2000, and immediately plunged into a master's degree program in psychology, education, and writing for children. Her thesis focused on pain, both physical and emotional. Expecting to finish that program in 2002, she set up a temporary schedule of schoolwork on Monday, Tuesday, and Wednesday and performance Thursday through Sunday.

"So this free student life is finished and I have to go back to the work-force full-time!" she squealed delightedly, like the schoolgirl she was, as she anticipated life after May 2002. More seriously, she said she was especially interested in studying language development and the issues posed by nature versus nurture. And the study of pain showed her, in the light of her own experience, that "it's actually abnormal not to have pain."

The study of psychology had nothing to do with either self-analysis or child psychology for Midori & Friends, she said. Rather, she just loves going to school. She also enjoys spending time with her half brother, Ryu, a violinist nicknamed J.R. who is sixteen years her junior. He and her mother, who have always lived nearby, have an apartment one floor above hers; also taught by their mother, he embarked on a concert career at age eleven. Midori's other interests include reading and going to museums and the theater. She cooks for herself because she doesn't like to eat out. One of her two dogs is a West Highland terrier named Willa, after Willa Cather, one of her favorite authors; the other is a dachshund named Franzie, after Franz Joseph Haydn. In her spare time she interviews musicians like Yo-Yo Ma and Gunther Schuller—not for publication, but for her own education.

"I like to ask questions," she said, and she takes advantage of the opportunities that come her way to query those in her field. "I ask them questions that I would absolutely stumble on if I were asked." She won't tell what those questions are but allows that they have to do with the nature of music.

"Mis-sis-sip-pi hot dog," chanted Mark Gunderman. "Mis-sis-*sip*-pi hot dog, Mis-sis-*sip*-pi hot dog, Mis-sis-*sip*-pi hot dog," he repeated as he went around the room, helping the ten beginners in his Making Music class at Public School 229 to tune their violins to the rhythm. Finger here, finger there. Four D's and two A's: Mis-sis-*sip*-pi (D-D-D-D) hot dog (A-A). Long-short, long-short, long-long. Finger here, finger there. Mis-sis-*sip*-pi hot dog. Mis-sis-*sip*-pi hot dog. Mis-sis-*sip*-pi hot dog. The rhythm became hypnotic.

"Very nice!" Gunderman declared when everybody was playing D-D-D-D A-A more or less in tune and in rhythm. "Are we ready for 'Twinkle, Twinkle, Little Star'?"

We were. We played "Twinkle, Twinkle" in unison, each note twinkling in the long-short rhythm.

"Fantastic!" Gunderman proclaimed. "Everybody's practicing really well"—so well that he had them play "Twinkle, Twinkle" as a round.

In Gwen Appel's beginner class, three flutists, three clarinetists, and a saxophonist were learning about pitches and rhythms. As they played a quarter-note pattern on a repeated note, one boy miscounted. Stopping the exercise, Appel asked him if he knew what he had done wrong. He wasn't sure. She said he had played during a rest.

"You don't do anything in the rest," she gently reminded him. "You count."

In a band room Robert Susman was taking an ensemble of seven trumpets and four trombones through "Twinkle, Twinkle, Little Star." The lessons here were on getting the notes right and playing as an ensemble. P.S. 229 was starting its first band.

Susman was trying to get his team-in-the-making to keep an eye on him over the top of the page instead of looking directly at him. The split-level viewing is what the professionals do, he said. "You guys are looking at me," he complained when "Twinkle, Twinkle" lost its twinkle. "You should be looking at the book."

Down the hallway during the next period, Jennifer Raine was leading an Explorations in Music class for younger children. They were creating a poem about a volcano. They had an opening line: "Calm, peaceful Pompeii mountain." Now they had to describe the molten magma about to erupt. Raine explained what a simile is and called on the class to give her a suitable one. After a round of suggestions such as "a comet on fire," the class voted. The magma became "as hot as the sun." When the poem was finished, Raine would lead the class in composing a song to the words. That was one of the goals of the class.

The Explorations in Music poets were taking part in the first tier in the three-tier Midori & Friends program. The instrumentalists were practicing in Making Music classes, tier three. The Adventure Concerts Series, tier two, would begin a few days later with the preparatory classes for the first of four performances to take place between February and May 2001. The season's Adventure artists were the Whitman String Quartet, the Vanguard Chamber Players (a wind quintet), the Sean Lyons Quintet (jazz), and Un Mundo (a Latin folk ensemble).

From the outside P.S. 229, in a working-class section of detached houses and low-rises in Queens, New York, looks like a factory: institutional yellow brick, barred windows, chain-link fence. Inside, despite the security guard at the door, the stereotype of the troubled urban school turns into something much friendlier. The corridors are bright and cheerful, the classrooms festooned with children's drawings and lessons in block letters. Happy, noisy children queue up behind teachers to move from class to class; the teachers are smiling, courteous, and helpful. It is a multicultural neighborhood. In 2001 the student population of about 1,350 stood at 38 percent Hispanic, 33 percent white, 2 percent black, and 27 percent Asian and other. Despite some fidgeting among the young poets and some horseplay among the mostly male brasses, everybody was intent on the Midori & Friends lessons.

P.S. 229 is well-off compared with some schools in the Midori & Friends fold. P.S. 96 in East Harlem, for example, is in an impoverished neighborhood with an enrollment that is about 36 percent African American, 63 percent Hispanic, 1 percent Asian and other, and less than 1 percent white. With the help of Midori & Friends, donated instruments, and other institutional support, principal Victor Lopez initiated programs in music, theater, dance, and painting. Test scores rose. President Clinton visited the school to show his support for music education. The *Today Show* was there to catch the action.

One hundred and five languages have been tallied in the neighborhood around P.S. 91 in Queens. It is a recent addition to the Midori & Friends fold, with programs in tiers one and two. At P.S. 7 in Brooklyn, Midori & Friends joins the American Ballet Theater, Metropolitan Opera, and other institutions in bringing the arts to a neighborhood that is 1 percent white. After three years of Adventure Concerts, Midori & Friends added a third-grade chorus as a pilot program. The other partner schools are also multiracial, with whites a minority.

Like other school systems, New York City's once offered music lessons to children who wanted them. And like other systems, New York scuttled those programs when the financial troubles of the 1970s and 1980s arrived. The crisis year for the city was 1975. Its tax base drained by white flight to the suburbs and union demands, the city went to the brink of default before a reorganization of services and finances led to recovery.

In 1996, as the economic boom of the 1990s roared ahead and the financial picture grew rosier, the city began budgeting for a Project Arts program to restore arts education to the curriculum. The annual budget allotment of fifty-three dollars per child was not enough to do the job by itself. The idea was that the city's contribution would be seed money to enlist outside support from organizations like Midori & Friends and the Met. Several schools, including P.S. 229, also obtained grants for the purchase of instruments from cable television network VH1's Save the Music program, a private initiative created for that purpose.

Formerly, Midori & Friends would enter a school with an Adventure Concerts series for grade three or grades three and four. The program would then expand to include the activities for the lower and higher grades. Now the usual scenario is to start with the first-tier listening classes and progress to Adventure Concerts and then instrumental instruction. The goal is to lead children step by step from listening to active participation, if only to become better listeners when they grow up. Listening also leads to curiosity and learning about other subjects and cultures, as in the composition of a song about volcanoes.

"That's the way I was taught," Midori said. "I learned about one thing and I was always encouraged to take that into the rest of my world." Learning about Bartók, for example, led her to the history of the Austro-Hungarian Empire, its literature, and its folk music. That in turn led to United States–Soviet relations and Russian music. From there she progressed to Shostakovich, opera, literature, the visual arts, and dance—Mikhail Baryshnikov, in particular.

In 2000–01, P.S. 229, which includes grades one through five, was running Midori & Friends' largest program, with all three tiers of instruction. It was one of the first schools to join, entering in 1994. Peter McNally, the principal until 2001, said he first learned of the organization from a newspaper article. Impressed, he wrote a letter saying, in effect, if you're ever expanding to other schools, please think of us. P.S. 229 wanted in, McNally said, because "we identified a tremendous void in our arts education program. At that time there was no funding for the arts and we saw that this foundation was trying to fill that desperate need." A two-year grant from Midori & Friends enabled the school to present the Adventure Concerts Series. By the next year the city's Project Arts money became available. The school was able to provide matching funds, and the Midori & Friends program grew to cover all five grades.

In P.S. 229, as in other schools, classes in tiers one and two are part of the regular day, attended by all children in those grades. Students have to sign up, with a consent from home, for the instrumental lessons in tier three. The school, using city and VH1 funds, provides the instruments, and Midori & Friends provides the instructors. In 2000 P.S. 229 bought forty violins in preparation for string classes. In 2001 it added some brass instruments and ten more violins. Some parents buy their own instruments if they see their children seriously committed to the lessons; other parents, of course, can't afford them. Out of the enrollment of about 1,350 in 2001, the school had fifty pupils studying violin, forty studying winds, thirty studying brasses, nine Explorations in Music classes (tier one), and the entire fourth grade (225 children) participating in the Adventure Concerts. After school hours there were also a band and a third-grade chorus.

For McNally P.S. 229's December 2000 concert was "goosebump time." He saw the first crop of forty violinists "stand up on the stage on risers and actually perform with the violins—something we have never had in this school. To see something go from a seed to that was absolutely heart-warming, and those boys and girls truly enjoyed performing—something that they never would have had the opportunity to do if it wasn't for Midori." Winds and brasses, just getting started, would debut in concert the next year.

Parents (or guardians) and their children in the instrumental program must sign an agreement promising that the children will practice in the home and the instruments will receive good care. Since the instrumental lessons take place during regular school hours, classroom work missed during those lessons must be made up—McNally was emphatic about that. But he said that when it was sign-up time for the second year of violin classes, so many hands shot up that he had to start a waiting list. The Midori & Friends teachers "definitely have an understanding of how to work with and teach children," he said. The program enables children from the multicultural community to learn about and play music in different forms, and when Midori herself plays music from many lands in the Adventure Concerts, pupils "see the commonality of the language of music."

McNally could draw no direct correlation between musical activity and overall classroom performance. But, he said, "the children of Public School 229 have a great deal of respect for the arts because the school has communicated that in both the visual arts and the music." When the children perform, carry their instruments to class and home after school, and make up classroom work they missed during music lessons, "they get the utmost respect and attention."

Many studies have suggested a correlation between music education, heightened intelligence, and improved classroom performance. Perhaps the best-known of these findings is the "Mozart effect," popularized by Don Campbell as a way to improve health, education, and well-being through the teaching of music. A variety of follow-up studies has failed to confirm anything beyond a short-term effect on limited areas of reasoning.

The National Commission on Music Education has, however, documented considerable research showing benefits of music education for learning. One study found music training far excelled computer lessons in raising children's abstract reasoning skills, the basis for learning mathematics and science. A Rhode Island study showed marked improvement in reading and math skills among students who took an enriched, sequential, skill-building program in music. In another study children who took piano lessons showed more significant gains in spatial-temporal skills, which play an important role in some types of mathematical reasoning, than children who took computer lessons, casual lessons in singing, or no lessons.[16]

In a lengthy 1991 report, *Growing Up Complete,* the music education commission cited, among many other sources, research by Howard Gardner suggesting that music study can be an aid to teaching in all subjects. Midori & Friends' approach draws on work by both Gardner and Rudolf Steiner in attempting to develop the "whole child" by sharpening cognitive skills and emphasizing creative expression through music making.

Gardner, according to the commission's report, is a leader in research showing that there is no single "intelligence" but many intelligences, "any or all of which can be developed." Gardner identifies seven basic intelligences: linguistic, musical, logical-mathematical, spatial, bodily-kinesthetic (athletic-sensory), intrapersonal ("intelligence about one's own feeling life"), and interpersonal ("intelligence about human interactions, temperaments, and motivations"). The commission says: "Everyone has some capabilities in each of these; some intelligences are more dominant in some individuals than in others. . . . Gardner's ideas are significant for the relationship of music education to general education. Since music is, for some learners, a powerful way of *knowing,* it can become, for teachers, *a way of teaching.* When important ideas, information, and ways of thinking can be approached through the strategies and structures provided by music, learning can be reinforced." Gardner and his colleagues, the report contends, "may have come up with a powerful new argument for placing and keeping music at the core of the curriculum." At best, the commission found, the American educational system "works diligently and systematically at developing only two of the seven intelligences," the linguistic and the logical-mathematical.[17]

The subject is controversial and the findings do not always agree. A comprehensive review of research on the value of the arts in schools was published under the auspices of the Harvard Graduate School of Education in 2000. Titled *The Arts and Academic Improvement: What the Evidence Shows,* the report casts doubt on many of the National Commission on Music Education's claims. But after studying all available research on the subject between 1950 and 1999, the Harvard investigators were able to pinpoint two specific ways in which music study does improve reasoning.

Learning to play music, it was found, has a "large" positive effect on spatial-temporal reasoning in such courses as mathematics and geography. Among three- to twelve-year-olds, the effect worked for 69 percent of students, whether normal or at risk. Listening to music has a "medium-sized" positive effect on spatial-temporal reasoning, sometimes only temporary, according to the researchers. Correlations between music and improvement in other learning skills, such as verbal and mathematical scores, were dismissed as unproven. The authors also issued a caveat, terming instrumental instruction a double-edged sword: "If the arts are given a role in our schools because people believe the arts cause academic improvement, then the arts will quickly lose their position if academic improvement does not result, or if the arts are shown to be less effective than the three R's in promoting literacy and numeracy. . . . Arts educators should never allow the arts to be justified wholly or even primarily in terms of what the arts can do for mathematics or reading. The arts must be justified in terms of what the arts can teach that no other subject can teach."[18]

Although Midori & Friends draws on Howard Gardner's educational principles, it steers clear of the theoretical wars. Neither Midori herself nor the foundation wants to get caught up in the contentious issues of achievement and music's correlation to brain power, according to Judi Linden, Midori & Friends' executive director. The goals are simpler: pleasure in music, self-expression, and stimulation to look beyond the classroom. Regular classroom teachers in Midori & Friends schools report, however, that music increases attention spans, especially in children with learning disabilities, Linden said.

"We know it assists attention span. We know it makes children feel good about themselves and therefore become more successful." That's "the No. 1 comment we get," Linden said: that "Joey or Susie or Jimmy, who has no regular attention span in the classroom, absolutely loves music, is thriving with it, looks forward to it, goes on stage—whatever—with excitement, on and on."

A long-time fund-raiser and administrator of arts and other not-for-profit organizations, Linden knows of only one case—and that early in Midori & Friends' history—where a partnership with a school did not work out. In the beginning, she said, the foundation did mostly Adventure Concerts, shipping them around to schools in a standardized format. As the organization grew and gained experience, it began tailoring its programs to the particular needs of a smaller number of schools.

"We really are very careful now in how we choose the partners," Linden said. "We make sure that we are on the same page as the principal and the district [arts] coordinator and that our goals are complementary. We go in first and find out what they need, what we can support, what the pitfalls are, and then we really work with them. And that has worked beautifully for us."

At first it was necessary to solicit partner schools. As word spread, schools came to the foundation and it had to start a waiting list. Linden said, however, that if she heard of a disadvantaged school that wanted to start a music program, she would offer support. The greatest challenge, she said, will be getting the schools to hire their own teachers and keep the programs going after Midori & Friends leaves. But since few schools have left the three-tier program so far, it is too soon to know to what extent schools will provide follow-up.

There have been few disciplinary problems, Linden said, because discipline is primarily the responsibility of the schools' own teachers. Midori & Friends' instructors have been trained to deal with such situations, but the premise of the program is to make it enjoyable. "This is meant to be enriching," Linden said. "We very much emphasize that. We really want our program to be looked at as pleasurable. There is a philosophy behind this, which is that music gives children an outlet for expression that they don't otherwise have."

Enrichment was what P.S. 160 in Queens, with a 90 percent African-American enrollment, was looking for in the early 1990s. Gifted-students specialist Judy Eisman and principal Ann Irrera wanted a music teacher on staff. But P.S. 160, like many other New York elementary schools, had no money for one. Instead, Eisman and Irrera applied to Midori & Friends, which began a program of instrumental instruction in 1994. In support of the project, the VH1 Save the Music fund gave the school $10,000 to buy seventy instruments. In a 1999 report in the educational newsletter of Chamber Music America, a national coordinating organization, Eisman and Irrera said:

"Our school is in a very economically deprived community that holds many challenges from day to day. When P.S. 160 sought to collaborate with Midori & Friends almost five years ago, we wanted to provide children in grades 4–6 with an opportunity of a lifetime—to study a musical instrument. Teaching artists provided by Midori & Friends have arrived each Friday morning to instruct group lessons as well as form a large band, string orchestra, and many small ensembles. They established an atmosphere where each child was sure of his own worth and could therefore learn and fulfill his/her potential. This is quite a feat and they made it look easy."[19]

Eisman and Irrera told the story of Nadine Harris, a violist who went from P.S. 160 to the Juilliard School's Music Advancement Program, which offers supplementary music instruction for minority-group students from the city's schools. The girl would come back to P.S. 160 and describe her studies of Bach and Handel, her private lessons, and her classes in theory and chamber ensemble. "Just a few years ago Nadine Harris had never even heard of a viola!" Eisman and Irrera exulted. And she was only one of several who went on to further musical studies.[20]

Instruments can also turn up in unexpected places. As classes were beginning in the fall of 2000, Nina Liebman, Midori & Friends' director of programs, learned from a district arts coordinator that a school in Brooklyn had forty-two violins stashed away, unused, in a closet. Liebman and violin teacher Mark Gunderman went to the school the next day to investigate. Indeed, there were forty-two violins in a closet, though many needed repair; there were also some brass and wind instruments. The collection was left over from the days when the schools routinely offered music lessons. Liebman arranged violin lessons for thirty fourth-graders in the Brooklyn school and began discussions for the addition of other programs. Instruments left over from better days have been found in other partner schools as well.

Midori joins the foundation staff in choosing the teachers, sometimes with the assistance of professional educators who observe as the candidates present a lesson. Recruitment is not a problem, according to Liebman. Most teachers who come to the foundation are recommended by fellow teachers or other musicians. All are freelancers who perform professionally themselves. The same teacher will stay with a class throughout the school year. At P.S. 229, for example, four teachers return twice a week for thirty weeks to give instrumental lessons. "We look for teachers who are good musicians, who have had experience teaching, and who are creative and have a good manner with children," Liebman said.

All those qualities, Linden said, are personified in Midori herself. She is "a very open person and nonjudgmental, and very easy for the children to relate to. She does not set herself on a pedestal."

By 2000 the variety of music education programs being brought to the schools by outsiders was almost as endless as music itself. The reasons were many, and self-preservation was one of them. Government, foundation, and corporate grants were easier to come by for education programs, or for performing programs with an educational component, than for performance alone. Education took some of the sting out of the elitist image that clung to the fine arts. And, of course, without music education there might not be a music audience—or at least an audience for classical music—in another generation or two. Flag-bedecked politicians weren't the only ones to embrace child, family, and schoolhouse as part of a brighter tomorrow.

Behind all the educational effects there has been a genuine will to do good. Just before dying in 1990, Midori's hero, Leonard Bernstein, founded the Bernstein Education Through the Arts Fund to give grants for school music programs, provide curricula, supplies, and other resources, and sponsor professional development conferences. The nationwide project describes itself as putting into practice Bernstein's belief that "education [should] be concerned not merely with imparting received knowledge, but in cultivating a lifelong appetite for new discovery." In practical terms that means "the processes of the arts both draw upon and illuminate learning in a variety of academic disciplines"—ideas that sound similar to Gardner's. Among the fund's projects are a nationwide network of schools that follow the Bernstein precepts of innovation and improvement.[21] The Bernstein fund took its place alongside such institutions as Young Audiences, a nationwide network of teaching organizations. Founded in 1952, Young Audiences reached 7.8 million young people in 2000 through programs in schools and other educational activities, including programs to help musicians and educators to improve their skills.

In the world of performance no self-respecting symphony orchestra or opera company would be caught without a public education program as a jewel in its crown. At the head of the class in New York, the New York Philharmonic and the Metropolitan Opera offer traditional listening and learning opportunities such as youth concerts, classroom visits, attendance at rehearsals, backstage tours, and partnerships with schools. But activity is also taking place at the grass-roots level, where the glamour quotient is low.

Like the settlement houses of old, community organizations—some of them long established—offer programs in and after school to bring the arts to children who wouldn't ordinarily encounter them. In 2000 the Orion String Quartet hit upon a way to celebrate Beethoven, reach new audiences, and help six of these not-for-profit New York City organizations at the same time. It played the cycle of sixteen Beethoven quartets in six free concerts, each honoring and benefiting one of the six friends of the arts: the Brooklyn Children's Museum, the Harlem School of the Arts, the Jamaica Center for Arts and Learning, the Mind-Builders Creative Arts Center, the Opus 118 Music Center, and the Songs of Love Foundation.

All these groups have an inspirational story to tell. The Opus 118 Music Center, which sponsors a violin program in the East Harlem schools, was recently featured in the movie *Music of the Heart*. Meryl Streep played the role of Roberta Guaspari-Tzavaras, the real-life violin teacher who saved the program when budget cuts threatened to shut it down. Members of the Songs of Love Foundation, a collaborative of songwriters and performers, compose and record songs personally addressed to acutely ill children and young adults.

Each of the Orion's programs included a film clip showing the honored organization at work, and each provided the group with two hundred tickets to use for fund-raising purposes. But why Beethoven? Wouldn't contemporary pieces, especially with some reference to life on the streets, have been more fitting for organizations that dealt with kids coming from street life? "Beethoven reaches to express the struggle between man and the universe, between man and his own soul," Orion violist Steven Tenenbom explained in the *New York Times*. "He's universal, and he's visceral. That's a good choice for this kind of project. The organizations we're celebrating are changing lives out there, saving lives."[22]

Celebrity artists also pitch in. In 2000 Leontyne Price went before three hundred elementary and middle school students in Harlem to read to them from *Aida,* her recently published book. The reading, in a Police Athletic League building, was one of a series the retired African American diva gave at urban schools around the country. Her book tells a children's version of the opera in which she became most famous, Verdi's *Aida*. The story of a black heroine and hero—an enslaved Ethiopian princess falls in love with the military hero of her Egyptian captors—had special resonance for Price's Harlem audience. Ill at ease in the beginning, the children crowded around the singer at the end, begging for autographs and exchanging hugs and kisses. Opera would seem a little less unreal to three hundred youngsters after that day.

Itzhak Perlman teaches and conducts at the Perlman Music Program, a summer camp founded by his wife, Toby, in East Hampton, Long Island, where the Perlmans have a home. Instead of ghetto schoolchildren, though, these students are budding soloists aged ten to eighteen. Isaac Stern, meanwhile, went around the world in his retirement giving what he described as "encounters"—not master classes—for conservatory-age players seeking careers. The initial sessions took place in New York, Amsterdam, Jerusalem, Tokyo, and, in Stern's first postwar visit to Germany, Cologne. For about ten days Stern and a few colleagues, such as members of the Emerson String Quartet, hammered away at the nuts and bolts of performance. Stern rejected the master class label on grounds that he was teaching not technique but how to understand the music more deeply. He told the *Los Angeles Times*:

"What I can do best and what I think is most worthwhile is teaching the players how to think. I teach them how to listen to themselves and be honest, so they can become independent and go as far as their talent can take them, which is usually farther than they've gone at the time that they come to me. The main direction is teaching them not how you play but why. Why do you want to be a musician?"[23]

Most professional musicians at this level—Yo-Yo Ma is another example—do some teaching, but it is usually in master classes for the older, career-oriented student. Or if they go deeply into teaching, as Phyllis Curtin did at Yale and Boston Universities, they take a conservatory or university position where, again, they work with preprofessional students, including those at a postgraduate level.

Rarer is the established artist who will roll up sleeves for music education in the public schools. In 1999 Frederica von Stade took up the challenge. Wanting to bring music to the schools in Alameda, the San Francisco Bay Area island where she lives, the beloved mezzo-soprano struck up a relationship with the Oakland East Bay Symphony. She cajoled friends from the San Francisco Conservatory to join her and some young players in a program of chamber music as a benefit to bring the Oakland orchestra over to Alameda for a concert series. In the old theater where the gala was to be held, she did much of the dirty work herself—vacuuming, dusting, washing windows, putting up letters on the marquee.

That fall the symphony came over to play a series of four concerts and begin teaching in the schools. Von Stade told *Opera News* that students had to become accustomed to recitals and music study. "It's a difficult task, I know, because teachers have a fierce curriculum they have to enforce, and they're under a lot of pressure—as are the students. But if we don't do this, we're going to be in even more trouble in our society. After all, you rarely see a gang member carrying a violin case!"[24]

The remark echoes one sometimes made by Michael Morgan, the orchestra's director, who had spent a decade getting music instruction back into the Oakland schools before crossing the bay to Alameda. Looking back on his Oakland victory, he said: "At 3:30 in the afternoon when you're driving around and you see kids walking home with musical instruments, that's something you didn't see ten years ago. That is your most important impact on that city and the most rewarding thing, to see that happening in all sorts of neighborhoods where you know they couldn't possibly afford to have instruments at all, except in the public schools. You don't see many violin-playing gang members."

Morgan said it was because von Stade wanted music lessons for her grandchildren, who attend the Alameda schools, that she got involved. "She is such a regular person. She jumps in and does whatever needs doing, basically. I've seen her before one of our concerts in an Alameda school over at the side, dusting the piano. She'll have events in her home to raise money. She'll have receptions before or after our concerts. She's great." In his second season in Alameda, Morgan added the Oakland Youth Orchestra, which he also directs, and the Sonos handbell choir, which grew out of his Oakland Symphony Chorus, as attractions.

Morgan's missionary work on the West Coast mirrors Midori's on the East Coast. But it is a world apart from the missionary work that Michael Tilson Thomas is doing across the bay from Oakland with the San Francisco Symphony. With a more cohesive, established constituency for classical music, Tilson Thomas can concentrate on programming and being out front musically. Morgan is concerned, as he puts it on the Oakland orchestra's Web site, with "setting an example for other arts organizations by demonstrating the convergence of artistic excellence and community service," and with making classical music "accessible to the diverse population of Oakland, particularly to those individuals in the community who might otherwise never hear live symphonic music."[25]

Morgan describes Oakland as a multicultural community with "a very great disparity between the very rich and the very poor." The differences in wealth, ethnic backgrounds, and interests require "a wide variety of content" at concerts and make it difficult to "corral" audiences for them. The job becomes "developing a new audience not just for us but for all the other orchestras in the Bay Area," which number about a dozen.

Founded in 1989 amid the rubble of the disbanded Oakland Symphony—the first orchestra in the United States to go bankrupt, Morgan notes—the Oakland East Bay Symphony devotes 40 percent of its budget to education and outreach. This is high by most orchestras' standards. Morgan, an effervescent African American, regularly brings in other community groups to perform with his orchestra. Reflecting the city's diversity (and Morgan's own preferences), these include a frequently programmed gospel choir, jazz ensembles, an Afro-Cuban dance and drumming group, the Sonos bell ringers, and the Purple Bamboo Orchestra (an ensemble of elementary school children who play traditional Chinese instruments). The parent orchestra also performs with the Oakland Ballet and in such community settings as senior centers and recovery programs.

Morgan programs a good deal of new music, much of it by local composers, along with the standard symphonic repertoire. Ticket prices are kept low. He said he gets a younger, more diverse crowd than traditional symphony orchestras do, with many first-time listeners. The concerts have an informal feeling, "even though we wear the same tails every other orchestra does. There's more of a feeling of community and more of a feeling of ownership of the orchestra because of the variety of the music on the stage and the variety of people in the house."

Soon after becoming director of the Oakland East Bay Symphony in 1990, Morgan began lobbying for music instruction in the city's schools, which, like schools elsewhere, were victims of the 1980s cutbacks. He cultivated City Hall. It's crucial to have that relationship in good times and bad, he said, so "you can go to the city government, and the city government feels that the orchestra is a very important part of the community," even when other priorities beckon. He attended City Council meetings, especially when votes were to be taken. "It's hard for them to vote against you if you're sitting in the room, because you are seen as an asset to the community, and so the City Council wants to do everything they can to keep you happy." He also pounded on the doors of individuals and corporations, pitching his appeal toward their specific areas of interest, such as education, public outreach, or concerts. By his tenth year he had orchestra-sponsored music programs going in most of the city's schools and was working on getting them into the rest. The multipronged approach consists of school visits, young people's concerts, side-by-side performances, a young artist competition, and Music for Excellence, an in-school program of instrumental instruction.

In the school visits, Morgan and ensembles from the orchestra give demonstrations and workshops in about fifty elementary and middle schools. The young people's concerts consist of four matinees a year featuring young soloists from the area. The biennial side-by-side performances seat musicians from the schools with Oakland East Bay players in one of the orchestra's regular subscription concerts. Winners of the young artist competition appear both in the young people's concerts and on an Oakland East Bay program. In Music for Excellence, Oakland East Bay players go into schools to give lessons throughout the school year. In a typical year, twelve players visit seven schools, reaching about a thousand students. Open rehearsals and preconcert lectures provide additional community outreach.

As is the case in the Midori & Friends program, the Oakland schools provide the instruments and the orchestra provides the instruction. The orchestra has, however, occasionally dipped into its own educational funds to buy instruments when there weren't enough to go around for all the children who wanted to play them. Despite the limited number of schools reached and precariousness of the funding, the instrumental lessons are the orchestra's biggest educational venture in terms of financial commitment and continuous work with children.

"That is not something the symphony orchestra necessarily has to do," Morgan said. "It only affects a few of the musicians who teach in that program, and so it's not as though the orchestra wouldn't go on without it. But it's very important to those kids that are in it, and that's who you really are making the pitch for."

The orchestra can only supplement, not substitute for, a program of instruction offered by the schools themselves, Morgan said. "But if there's not a public school music program, it's the job of the symphony orchestra, and particularly the music director, to say to everyone, 'Well, listen, the program is not there and it needs to be there in order for the children to have a basic, decent education.' "

Advocacy is the key, Morgan said. It's also what he enjoys doing, along with making music. He and the orchestra kept beating the drums for a schools program, he said, until the school board, "because of what programs we had started and what advocacy we had been doing, and the outcry that parents and other students also made about having music," restored instrumental instruction as core curriculum.

"The schools actually do the heavy lifting," Morgan said, "and we help them. The orchestra's being advocates for instrumental music is what keeps the adult population interested in making sure that it stays there. A lot of adults think school music programs are just as they were when they were in school and had a band and orchestra and all those things available. And they don't realize that it's really gone, probably from most places now. So if someone doesn't point that out, they don't realize that it needs to be put back. Most people, when they realize their kid is not getting what they got, are upset about it."

Morgan noted that doing both old and new music is necessary to attract and keep audiences. But it's new music that the kids like best, and for that reason he includes it in most of the children's concerts. When the orchestra gets thank-you letters from children, it's the new or newest sounding music that they go for. Morgan remembers putting part of Schoenberg's *Pierrot Lunaire,* composed in 1912 and still beyond the pale for many adult audiences, on one program. The kids loved it, he said. They also love music from the movie *Psycho* and pieces by Charles Ives—the more cacophonous the better. They like to pick out the different tunes in Ives's New England crazy-quilt weave. Morgan has also commissioned pieces especially for young people, including a work for his adult players and the kids' Purple Bamboo Orchestra to play together. How could parents, teachers, and school friends—even City Hall—resist a concert with music like that?

At the age of thirty, Midori has conquered many of the violinist's summits. She regularly performs with the major orchestras of the world (and some of the minor ones) and tours the United States and abroad in recitals with her pianist, Robert McDonald. Her recordings include several of the major concertos performed with such conductors as Zubin Mehta and Claudio Abbado and such orchestras as the Israel and Berlin Philharmonics. Her honors range from Japan's Suntory Hall Award, given in 1988 by the Japanese government to the most promising artist of the year, to the $50,000 Avery Fisher Prize, given in 2001 by the New York arts philanthropist. Television still romances her. She has appeared on the 1992 Winter Olympic Games telecast, various CNN programs, *Sunday Morning, Sesame Street,* the *Tonight Show,* and concert broadcasts around the world, including Carnegie Hall's hundredth-anniversary celebration.

She is also teaching violin performance at the Manhattan School of Music and running a Midori & Friends–type program in Japan. There is no need in Japan for an extensive instrumental program like the one in New York because most Japanese children play instruments anyway, she said. But she wants to counteract the "paper-and-pen" aspects of music education in Japan, which is mostly by rote and offers insufficient exposure to live music.

Unlike some violinists, Midori has no major commissions to her credit. But she has her foundation, which is so well established that she can allow her staff of four to run it. Her involvement consists of an annual round of concerts, participation in interviews of teacher candidates, service as board president, and a financial contribution (she keeps it anonymous and will not say how much it is). Midori & Friends' plans for the immediate future include after-school programs with partner schools and community organizations—the three-tier structure would be maintained—and expansion of existing programs to more schools. Another priority is division of the instrumental instruction into advanced and beginner classes. Schools within neighborhoods would share programs, and the Adventure Concerts would be extended to the public without charge. Already in 2000 a public Adventure Concerts series was taking place for the first time, in a partnership with the Children's Museum of Manhattan.

Long-range plans, Midori said, include development of new programs as well as expansion of existing ones. But she foresees no expansion into private schools; the needs of the public schools are too great. "I can't turn them down and go to schools that can afford it on their own."

As critics never tire of saying, Midori is no longer a child prodigy but a mature artist. In a typical review, Paul Griffiths wrote in the *New York Times,* "When Midori is playing, a very fine line of violin tone—hardly more than brushed off the string and whisper-soft—can contain a huge, bulging quantity of musical character. . . . Though well past her days as a child prodigy, she remains a slight figure. Music, though, has no weight. She can twirl big ideas in the air and send them rushing home to her listeners with tremendous force."[26]

The review was of a Carnegie Hall recital in 1999 with pianist Robert McDonald. Griffiths praised the performance of Mozart's A Major Sonata, K. 526, the sonata by John Corigliano, and Schoenberg's *Phantasy.* But he reserved his highest hosannas for the final offering, Franck's Sonata:

"Midori made the opening melody so gentle, so fragile, you almost did not want to hear it for fear it would break in your ears. But music is tough as well as weightless. For as long as the sonata went on in this vein—and again when it returned to similar material—Midori kept up her fingertip handling, and yet, as in the Mozart, her musical expression was sure and large. There was a touching sense that much more was being implied than could be said, that here was someone smiling through tears—or weeping through laughter. The ambiguity was complete, and right."[27]

Earlier that year another *Times* critic ate his words. Reviewing Midori's performance of the Dvořák Violin Concerto with the Pittsburgh Symphony Orchestra, Bernard Holland wrote that "it was heartening, and a little chastening, to see how she has survived the predictions of doom and destruction (some from this writer) uttered during her years as a child prodigy. The sound is fine and lean and the technique as impregnable as ever."[28]

Isaac Stern has an explanation for this level of accomplishment. "She has all the gifts that one person could possibly have," he has been quoted as saying. "She's beautiful, she's talented, and she has a brilliant, inquisitive mind. But to whom much is given, much is expected—and Midori feels that expectation keenly. The reason for her all-consuming love of children is that she was one of the most extraordinary child prodigies since Mozart. She loves kids because she was never around kids when she was a kid."[29]

But isn't there more to it? Isn't Midori—aren't Yo-Yo Ma, Phyllis Curtin, Gunther Schuller, Robert Spano, the Juilliard String Quartet, and the other voyagers profiled in this book—like Theodore Levin's hundred thousand fools of God in the book that helped to propel Ma on his Silk Road journey? Aren't they all living a life of service to music as a kind of moral calling?

It seems more than coincidence that Midori's wanderings eventually took her to Queens, New York, the same place where Levin ended his pursuit of Asia's fools of God. In the heavily immigrant communities, both discovered ground where vital musical traditions could regenerate and grow.

In *The Hundred Thousand Fools of God,* Levin compares the Asian musicians he met to the *abdâls,* or forty mythical saints of Sufi tradition who live at the highest spiritual plane. During his two decades of travel in Transoxania (as that region of Central Asia was known in pre-Soviet times), Levin found its musicians persevering in their traditions despite Soviet attempts to stamp out authentic styles and replace them with socialist-realism poster-style art. These musicians, he writes, "lived exemplary lives of devotion not only to their art but also to the notion of musicianship as a form of service in which the musician, like the *abdâl,* assumes the moral weight of guiding humankind toward the just and the good." The performers didn't always conform to the Sufi conception, which embodied asceticism, humility, and altruism. For Levin and his Uzbek traveling companion, Otanazar Matyakubov, "what bound all of these fools of God together, however, was their unwavering devotion to a life of service through music, to the notion of music as a moral calling, to the idea of a connection between the way they lived their lives and the moral quality of their art."[30]

Travel in Transoxania was hardly luxurious. On the train from Moscow to Tashkent on one of his earlier trips, Levin was beset by a drunken Georgian who vowed to kill him because Levin had supposedly insulted his honor. After the conductor and other passengers restored order, Levin locked himself in his compartment and thenceforth flew from Moscow, although he could imagine nothing more depressing than the tourist lounge at Domodedovo Airport.

In Queens Levin encountered the musical traditions that Bukharan Jews—Jews from the Silk Road cities of Central Asia—had brought with them when the collapse of the Soviet empire made emigration possible. But these traditions had been watered down by years of Soviet repression and indoctrination. Talking to the émigrés and listening to them perform, Levin concluded that, as one of them, Turgun Alimatov, had told him, the best musicians "might have survived and flourished, but the conditions in which they did so had exacted a formidable price: the long artistic hibernations brought on by the chill of ideological vilification." Immersion in American popular culture had also exacted a price, diluting the traditions further.

Yet in the end Levin is hopeful. For Alimatov, he writes, "the essential condition of good music and good musicianship was *sâz*, harmony; not only harmony in music itself, but harmony between performers and listeners who delight in music of high moral purpose offered in an altruistic spirit of service unfettered by commerce or political ideology." The émigré communities will be scattered in the post-Soviet diaspora, although recordings, radio, concert tours, and music festivals will to some degree unite them. In these conditions, Levin concludes, "the fools of God may not always know the effects of their good works on those they touch. Perhaps, like the forty *abdâls* of Sufi tradition, veiled from public view as they carry out their mission to guide humankind toward the just and good, the musical fools of God will have to serve without the *raxmat*—the "thank you"—that, as Turgun had explained, was remuneration enough when he performed at a *toy* [wedding]. Or perhaps the fools of God can hear our *raxmat*, even from far away.[31]

New York is not Transoxania. But it epitomizes the economic and cultural contradictions that beset America: the extremes of wealth and poverty, the artistic riches amid stunted lives, the glass towers and stretch limos and thousand-dollar pairs of shoes amid the drug dealing and broken homes and poverty-level jobs. The schools become victims of this disparity between private plenty and public want. Starved for funds, they starve the arts, starving children who in turn starve their children and the whole of society, which then starves its schools: a vicious circle. As long as these inequities fester, private initiatives like Midori & Friends can help to keep the arts alive while enriching many lives. The musician becomes a fool of God, passing along music in a spirit of service. Budget cutters will thank these "fools" for sparing them the expense. But the true thank-you comes from children like Kiearra Reynolds, the fifth-grader at P.S. 160 who learned that playing the flute gave her a better understanding of herself and the world.

Classical music is periodically declared to be dead or dying. Sometimes this is said by those who are trying to kill it, if only inadvertently through music that decrees novelty, shock, and titillation to be ultimate values. But in the words of Mark Twain's famous formulation, reports of the death of classical music are greatly exaggerated. The tradition will survive for just the reason that Levin gives: there is a harmony that transcends commerce and ideology, the twin engines driving today's culture-entertainment scene, and there will always be those—a minority, to be sure—who recognize, appreciate, and support quality.

The question isn't whether classical music will survive, but in what form. Will it turn into a museum, trying to preserve the masterpieces of the past regardless of the changes swirling around them? Will it become a kind of fashion runway, with celebrity artists preening before an audience of the well-heeled and well dressed? Will it go the crossover route, with classical and pop musicians exchanging roles and repertoire like cross-dressers? Or will it build on its traditions, exploring new styles to enrich and reinvigorate the old?

The last approach offers the surest way to hold on to the best of the past without making a mindless surrender to the present. The new styles may be as remote as the Silk Road music that Ma is bringing to light, or they may be as close to home as American pop transformed into something richer and more enduring by a composer like John Adams. The music may not take hold, but that's a judgment for posterity to render, as it did when it judged Debussy's and Ravel's dalliances with Asia worth preserving. The experiments will reject the easy answers of fashions and trends, as the best art always has. They will speak to something essential in the human spirit.

Whether through performing, composing, commissioning, publishing, advocacy for the art, or teaching, Midori, Yo-Yo Ma, Phyllis Curtin, Gunther Schuller, Robert Spano, and the Juilliard Quartet have helped to keep this essential spark lit. All make service to music and others not an enhancement of their careers, not a guest room in the mansion, so to speak, but the very bricks and mortar of the mansion itself. Altruism becomes a form of self-interest, and vice versa. At a time when the Western tradition is under assault not by government ideology but by a marketplace juggernaut, these musicians—and hundreds, if not a hundred thousand, like them in cities and towns across the republic—are all workers in a kind of universal Queens, where they seek renewal and transformation.

In her crowded apartment, with Franzie and Willa at her feet, Midori said, "I do this because I love it. I love kids, I love music, and I love how these two are being connected. People think I do it because it's good publicity. But that's not true at all."

So speaks the innocence of a child, the wisdom of the ages.

# NOTES

NOTES: YO-YO MA

1. Quoted in Nat Shapiro, ed., *An Encyclopedia of Quotations about Music* (Garden City, N.Y.: Doubleday, 1978), p. 232.

2. Bernard Holland, "Yo-Yo Ma and Emanuel Ax: After 25 Years, a Symmetry of Soul," *New York Times,* December 13, 2000.

3. Michael White, "Ma, We're Making Eyes at You," *London Telegraph,* September 29, 2000.

4. web.mit.edu/jchang/www/ma2.html (December 31, 2000).

5. www.bn.com (February 2, 2000).

6. John Pitcher, "For He's a Jolly Good Cello," *Washington Post,* June 2, 2000.

7. Janet Tassel, "Yo-Yo Ma's Journeys," *Harvard Magazine,* March–April 2000, p. 47.

8. David Blum, "A Process Larger Than Oneself," *New Yorker,* May 1, 1989, p. 64.

9. Ibid., p. 50.

10. Ibid., p. 52.

11. Tassel, "Yo-Yo Ma's Journeys," p. 47.

12. Blum, "A Process Larger Than Oneself," p. 56.

13. *Hush,* Sony Masterworks, SK 48177.

14. Jamie James, "Yo-Yo Ma May Be a National Institution, but He Continues to Reinvent Himself," *New York Times,* December 31, 1995.

15. Michelle Dulak, "Dipping a Toe into the Early-Music Waters," *New York Times,* August 1, 1999.

16. *New York Times,* August 15, 1999.

17. *New York Times,* September 5, 1999.

18. *Solo,* Sony Classical, SK 64114.

19. *Schubert: "Trout" Quintet, "Arpeggione" Sonata,* Sony Classical, SK 61964.

20. *Yo-Yo Ma Premieres,* Sony Classical, SK 66299.

21. *Boosey and Hawkes Newsletter,* September 2001.

22. Bernard Holland, "A Spirited Argument from a Composer Nearing 93," *New York Times,* October 2, 2001.

23. "Life after 20/20," www.ABCNews.com (June 2, 2000).

24. All citations concerning the recording of the Bach series are taken from *Yo-Yo Ma: The Cello Suites,* Sony Classical, SK 63202-3.

25. Both citations from Tassel, "Yo-Yo Ma's Journeys," p. 48.

26. *Solo,* Sony Classical, SK 64114.

27. E-mails available at www.schirmer.com/silkroad/sheng (August 5, 2000).

28. Tassel, "Yo-Yo Ma's Journeys," p. 107.

29. Shapiro, *Encyclopedia of Quotations about Music,* p. 44.

30. Blum, "A Process Larger Than Oneself," p. 62.

31. Ibid., p. 74.

32. Philip Kennicott, "A Born Idealist," *Gramophone,* April 1996, p. 14.

33. Dulak, "Dipping a Toe into the Early-Music Waters."

34. Ken Smith, "Setting Off on the Silk Road (Project): Yo-Yo Ma Launches His Latest Unconventional Endeavor at the Schleswig-Holstein Music Festival," www.andante.com, September 10, 2001.

35. Edith Eisler, "Yo-Yo Ma: Music from the Soul," *Strings,* May–June 1992, p. 54.

36. Marina Ma, as told to John A. Rallo, *My Son, Yo-Yo* (Hong Kong: Chinese University Press, 1995), p. 84.

NOTES: PHYLLIS CURTIN

1. Beverly Sills (with Lawrence Linderman), *Beverly* (New York: Bantam Books, 1987), pp. 160–61.

2. Ibid., p. 162.

3. Peter G. Davis, *The American Opera Singer: The Lives and Adventures of America's Great Singers in Opera and Concert, From 1825 to the Present* (New York: Doubleday, 1997), p. 499.

4. Ibid., p. 493.

5. Ibid., p. 500.

6. Ned Rorem, *Settling the Score* (New York: Doubleday, 1988), p. 302.

7. Harold C. Schonberg, *The Glorious Ones* (New York: Times Books, 1985), p. 392.

8. Phyllis Curtin, "A Brief Recollection of the *Grimes* Summer, 1946, Tanglewood," Tanglewood program book for *Peter Grimes,* 1996, p. 5.

9. Richard Dyer, "You Only Live Twice," *Opera News,* November 1990, p. 14.

10. *Phyllis Curtin: Opera Arias,* VAI Audio, 1152.

11. Aaron Copland and Vivian Perlis, *Copland since 1943* (New York: St. Martin's Press, 1989), p. 163.

12. Ibid., p. 165.

13. Ibid., p. 166.

14. *Twelve Poems of Emily Dickinson,* VAI Audio, 1194.

15. Andrew L. Pincus, "Dawn Upshaw Gains Stardom Her Own Way," *Berkshire Eagle,* July 1, 1990.

16. Charles McGrath, "Giving Voice to *Gatsby,*" *New York Times Magazine,* November 22, 1999, p. 134.

17. *Simple Daylight,* Elektra Nonesuch, 79189-2.

18. John Ardoin, *Callas at Juilliard: The Master Classes* (New York: Alfred A. Knopf, 1987), p. xv.

19. Dyer, "You Only Live Twice," pp. 10, 12.

20. Claude Kenneson, *Musical Prodigies: Perilous Journeys, Remarkable Lives* (Portland, Ore.: Amadeus Press, 1998), pp. 346–50.

21. Davis, *The American Opera Singer,* p. 581.

22. Anthony Tommasini, "Taking a Look into the Soul of *Susannah,*" *New York Times,* March 31, 1999.

23. Anthony Tommasini, "A Soprano's Life Near the Top," *New York Times,* July 5, 1998.

24. Howard Pollack, *Aaron Copland: The Life and Work of an Uncommon Man* (New York: Henry Holt, 1999), p. 444.

25. *Twelve Poems of Emily Dickinson,* VAI Audio.

26. *Bernstein Live,* set of archival recordings published by New York Philharmonic.

### NOTES: GUNTHER SCHULLER

1. *Transfigured Notes,* GM2060CD.

2. Gunther Schuller, *Musings* (New York: Oxford University Press, 1986), p. ix.

3. Anthony Tommasini, "Preserving New Music Just Because It's There," *New York Times,* December 27, 1998.

4. John Rockwell, *All American Music: Composition in the Late Twentieth Century* (New York: Alfred A. Knopf, 1983), p. 35.

5. Ibid., p. 24.

6. Ibid., p. 94.

7. Ibid., p. 22.

8. Norbert Carnovale, *Gunther Schuller: A Bio-Bibliography* (New York: Greenwood Press, 1987), p. 7.

9. Milton Babbitt, "1995 Composer of the Year: Gunther Schuller," in *Musical America International Directory of the Performing Arts,* 1995.

10. *Musings,* p. 241.

11. Ibid., p. 242.

12. Ibid., p. 259.

13. Bob Blumenthal, "Orchestral Raps: Gunther Schuller & Joe Lovano Discuss 'Rush Hour on 23rd Street,' " *Down Beat,* March 1995.

14. Ben Ratliff, "A Pleasant Swim with Gunther Schuller, the Man Who Named the Third Stream," *New York Times,* March 20, 2001.

15. Ibid.

16. Richard Dyer, "Honoring the Many Strands of a Musical Life," *Boston Globe,* March 20, 2001.

17. Babbitt, "1995 Composer of the Year."

18. Ibid.

19. *The Art of the Rag,* GM3018CD.

20. Discovered by Schuller, who brought him to Tanglewood to study, Marsalis is perhaps the nearest counterpart to Schuller in music today. He composes and plays both classical and jazz, created and heads New York's Jazz at Lincoln Center program, is a controversial figure because of his views, and won the Pulitzer Prize in 1997 for *Blood on the Field,* an oratorio based on slavery. It was the first time the Pulitzer in music went to a jazz composition.

21. *St. Peter: An Oratorio,* GM2027CD-2.

22. John McDonough, " 'Original Intent' Comes to Jazz," *Wall Street Journal,* July 21, 1992.

23. Gunther Schuller, *The Compleat Conductor* (New York: Oxford University Press, 1997), pp. 537–38.

24. Ibid., p. 107.

25. Paul Griffiths, "What's the Score?" *New York Times Book Review,* August 27, 1997.

26. *The Compleat Conductor,* p. 8.

27. Ibid., p. 109.

28. *Gunther Schuller, Conductor,* GM2051CD.

29. *Music of Gunther Schuller,* Bridge 9093.

30. Ibid.

31. *The New Grove Dictionary of Music and Musicians* (London: Macmillan Publishers, 1980), vol. 16, p. 818.

32. *Gunther Schuller: Orchestral Works,* GM2059CD.

33. Ibid.

34. Chapter 10 in *The Orchestral Composer's Point of View,* ed. Robert Stephan Hines (Norman: University of Oklahoma Press, 1970), pp. 191–92.

35. Ibid., p. 202.

36. Ibid., pp. 190–92.

37. Anthony Tommasini, "Out of the Pit and into the Spotlight," *New York Times,* November 9, 1999.

38. Richard Dyer, "Premiere of Schuller Work Expert and Moving," *Boston Globe,* January 3, 1997.

39. *Musings,* pp. 230–32.

40. Ibid., p. 234.

41. Milton R. Bass, "Schuller Leaves Music Center," *Berkshire Eagle,* August 31, 1984.

42. *Musings,* pp. 190–93.

43. Janet Tassel, "Boston's Eclectic Music Man," *Boston Globe Magazine,* December 6, 1981, pp. 92, 94.

44. Anthony Tommasini, "Fear of 12-Tone Repertory: Composer Offers a Remedy," *New York Times,* April 24, 1998.

45. Ibid.

NOTES: ROBERT SPANO

1. Schuman died in 2001, a year after giving this interview.

2. Michael Chipman, "Marilyn McDonald and Robert Spano to Reunite for Violin/Piano Recital," www.oberlin.edu/con/bkstage/199910 (May 15, 2000).

3. "Gregory Fulkerson and Robert Spano to Perform All-Brahms Concert," www.oberlin.edu/con/bkstage/199910 (May 15, 2000).

4. Justin Davidson, "Mr. Spano Takes the Podium," *Newsday,* February 11, 1996.

5. Barbara Jepson, "Finding Maestros for the Podium," *New York Times,* February 11, 1996.

6. Greg Sandow, "Brooklyn's Musical Bridge," *Wall Street Journal,* May 23, 1997.

7. Alex Ross, "New Blood," *New Yorker,* November 24, 1997.

8. Paul Griffiths, "The Future Is Glimpsed through a Mahler Skylight," *New York Times,* November 3, 1997.

9. Leonard Bernstein, *Findings* (New York: Simon and Schuster, 1982), p. 212.

10. Anthony Tommasini, "A Winning Formula for Players and Listeners," *New York Times,* February 2, 2000.

11. Susan Elliott, "Atlanta Selects Brooklyn Conductor," *New York Times,* February 9, 2000.

12. Richard Dyer, "Spano Tries to Hang Out at Tanglewood," *Boston Globe,* July 22, 2001.

13. Justin Davidson, "The Conductor on the Ledge," *Los Angeles Times,* November 4, 2001.

14. Ibid.

15. Ibid.

16. Richard Dyer, "Spano Tries to Hang Out at Tanglewood."

17. Allan Kozinn, " 'Klinghoffer' Composer Fights His Cancellation," *New York Times,* November 14, 2001.

18. *Walt Whitman's New York—From Manhattan to Montauk,* ed. Henry M. Christman (New York: New Amsterdam Books, 1963), p. 61.

19. Quoted on BAM's Web site, www.bam.org/asp/info.org (November 15, 2000).

20. *Walt Whitman's New York—From Manhattan to Mantauk,* p. 61.

21. Paul Griffiths, "Evoking Glories of Heaven in a Rare Messiaen Opera," *New York Times,* May 15, 2000.

22. Allan Kozinn, "Brooklyn Philharmonic: Sober Works Illustrate Sadness' Infinite Variety," *New York Times,* February 27, 2001.

23. David Littlejohn, "A Symphonic Tour through American Music," *Wall Street Journal,* July 11, 1996.

24. Alex Ross, "The Place Genial Chaos Calls Home," *New York Times,* June 30, 1996.

25. David Littlejohn, "A Symphonic Tour through American Music."

26. Anthony Tommasini, "A Pied Piper Lures San Franciscans into the Concert Hall," *New York Times,* June 22, 1999.

27. Richard Taruskin, "Corralling a Herd of Musical Mavericks," *New York Times,* July 23, 2000.

28. Joshua Kosman, "Following Thomas' Lead in 'Mavericks,' " *San Francisco Chronicle,* June 27, 2000.

29. Ibid.

30. James R. Oestreich, "A Festival Is Tackling . . . Did They Say Beethoven?" *New York Times,* August 10, 2000.

31. Bernard Holland, "Soul-Searching, Pyrotechnics, and an Exotic Aviary," *New York Times,* October 4, 2001.

32. Linda Shockley, "The Return of Spano," *Oberlin Conservatory News,* Fall 1999, p. 25.

NOTES: THE JUILLIARD STRING QUARTET

1. Mann refused to be interviewed for this book; he said he was saving his recollections for his memoir.

2. Allan Kozinn, "Quartet Losing Its Leader of Five Decades," *New York Times,* December 11, 1996.

3. Elliott Carter, *The String Quartets,* Associated Music Publishers, 1998.

4. Joseph Wechsberg, *Trifles Make Perfection* (Boston: David R. Godine, 1999), p. 163.

5. Ibid., p. 157.

6. Harriet Gay, *The Juilliard String Quartet* (New York: Vantage, 1974), p. 5.

7. Helen Epstein, *Music Talks: Conversations with Musicians* (New York: McGraw-Hill, 1987), p. 166.

8. Eva Hoffman, "Juilliard: A Renewed Quartet," *New York Times Magazine,* October 5, 1986.

9. Epstein, *Music Talks,* p. 167.

10. Gay, *The Juilliard String Quartet,* p. 7.

11. Carter Harman, "Juilliard Quartet Offers Berg Work," *New York Times,* December 24, 1947.

12. *Musical America,* August 1948, p. 7.

13. Virgil Thomson, "Béla Bartók," *New York Herald Tribune,* March 20, 1949. Reprinted in *A Virgil Thomson Reader* (New York: E. P. Dutton, 1984), p. 324.

14. Carter Harman, "Juilliard Quartet Opens Music Cycle," *New York Times,* January 17, 1950.

15. John von Rhein, "A Final Touch," *Chicago Tribune,* April 13, 1997.

16. Epstein, *Music Talks,* p. 175.

17. Mark Swed, "The Juilliard String Quartet," *Musical America International Directory of the Performing Arts,* 1996 edition, p. 10.

18. Ibid., pp. 13–14.

19. David Schiff, *The Music of Elliott Carter,* 2nd ed. (Ithaca: Cornell University Press, 1998), pp. 1–2.

20. Ibid., pp. 6, 27.

21. Edward Rothstein, "Elliott Carter Quartets Celebrate Juilliard's 45th," *New York Times,* October 14, 1991.

22. Hoffman, "Juilliard: A Renewed Quartet."

23. Epstein, *Music Talks,* pp. 168–69.

24. Andrew L. Pincus, "Tanglewood Connection," *Berkshires Week,* July 25, 1986.

25. Leighton Kerner, "Fifty Years and Counting," *Village Voice,* September 17, 1996.

26. Charles Michener, "The Emerson, Con Brio," *New York Times Magazine,* March 28, 1993.

27. Pincus, "Tanglewood Connection."

28. Joel Smirnoff, "The Juilliard String Quartet: Reflections on Fifty Years," *Juilliard Journal,* February 1996.

29. Philip Kennicott, "Juilliard Strings, Too Wound Up for Anybody's Good," *Washington Post,* December 20, 2000.

30. David Blum, *The Art of Quartet Playing* (New York: Alfred A. Knopf, 1986), p. 16.

31. Gay, *The Juilliard String Quartet,* p. 8.

NOTES: MIDORI

1. Humphrey Burton, *Leonard Bernstein* (New York: Doubleday, 1994), pp. 480–81.

2. She was a classroom celebrity because of another Bernstein-Midori event. A language-arts textbook told how Midori, as a fourteen-year-old, had broken strings on two in-

struments in a row at a Tanglewood concert under Bernstein and needed three violins to get through his *Serenade* for violin, strings, and percussion. It was a legendary night in music history.

3. Nancy A. Ruhling, "Making Beautiful Music," *Newsday,* May 5, 2000.

4. Anthony Tommasini, "A Gifted Young Violinist Gives Something Back," *New York Times,* May 8, 1997.

5. Ibid.

6. Dennis Rooney, "Opening Doors," *The Strad,* April 1997.

7. Quoted in *prelude, fugue & riffs,* newsletter of the Leonard Bernstein Society, spring/summer 2000.

8. Yehudi Menuhin, *Unfinished Journey* (New York: Alfred A. Knopf, 1977), pp. 161–62.

9. Pia Lindstrom, "Itzhak Perlman Discusses Child Prodigies and Handicap Access," *New York Times,* December 1, 1996.

10. Claude Kenneson, *Musical Prodigies: Perilous Journeys, Remarkable Lives* (Portland, Ore.: Amadeus Press, 1998), p. 338.

11. Barbara Lourie Sand, *Teaching Genius: Dorothy DeLay and the Making of a Musician* (Portland, Ore.: Amadeus Press, 2000), p. 155.

12. Ibid., p. 156.

13. Tim Page, "Film Explores a Piano Prodigy's Madness," *Washington Post,* December 22, 1996.

14. Sand, *Teaching Genius,* p. 157, quoted from "Faced with Plunging Sales, Industry Markets Tots; But Are Kids Exploited?" *Wall Street Journal,* July 23, 1996.

15. Edith Eisler, "Coming of Age: A Conversation with Midori," *Strings,* September/October 1995.

16. *Music Education Facts and Figures,* www.musicfriends.org (March 8, 2001).

17. *Growing Up Complete: The Imperative for Music Education,* report of the National Commission on Music Education, March 1991, www.menc.org (March 8, 2001).

18. *The Arts and Academic Improvement: What the Evidence Shows,* pzweb.harvard.edu/Research/REAP.htm (March 8, 2001). An executive summary of a set of articles published in *The Journal of Aesthetic Education,* fall/winter 2000.

19. Judy Eisman and Ann Irerra, "Instrument Instruction Soars to New Heights at P.S. 160," *Flying Together,* educational newsletter of Chamber Music America, February 1999.

20. Ibid.

21. www.leonardbernstein.com/lifeswork/betafund (March 10, 2001).

22. Matthew Gurewitsch, "Bringing a Hero's Welcome to Any Cause," *New York Times,* May 7, 2000.

23. Jeremy Eichler, "Sharing the Wisdom of a Lifetime," *Los Angeles Times,* September 17, 2000.

24. Donald Spoto, "Flicka in 3/4 Time," *Opera News,* March 2000.

25. www.oebs.org (March 10, 2000).

26. Paul Griffiths, "Twirling Big Ideas in the Air and Sending Them Home, Effortlessly," *New York Times,* October 26, 1999.

27. Ibid.

28. Bernard Holland, "Pittsburgh Presents Its New Voice," *New York Times,* February 4, 1999.

29. Stephen Wigler, "Midori's Goodness Reaches beyond Violin," *Baltimore Sun,* October 20, 1999.

30. Theodore Levin, *The Hundred Thousand Fools of God: Musical Travels in Central Asia (and Queens, New York)* (Bloomington: Indiana University Press, 1996), p. 38.

31. Ibid., pp. 286–87.

# INDEX

Babbitt, Milton, 188, 198, 212; Schuller and, 93–95, 102, 106, 117, 120

Bach, Johann Sebastian, 20, 164, 165, 169, 183, 212; Curtin and, 62; Ma and, 30–33; Spano and, 155; spirituality and, 33

*Bach Among the Theologians* (Pelikan), 33

*Ballad of Baby Doe* (Moore), 54

Bando, Tamasaburo, 31

Barbash, Lillian, 23, 26

Barbash, Maurice, 23, 26

Barber, Samuel, 200

Bard College, 179

Barenboim, Daniel, 15, 22, 25, 148

Barraqué, Jean, 116

Bartók, Béla, xi, 204; Juilliard String Quartet and, 187, 188, 190, 194, 196–97, 199, 200, 201, 204, 217–18, 224, 225; Spano and, 164

Baryshnikov, Mikhail, 34, 249

BBC Symphony, 115

Beardslee, Bethany, 66

Beaux Arts Trio, 209

Beethoven, Ludwig van, xi–xii, 20, 164, 203, 204; cello pieces by, 19; Curtin and, 62, 67; God and, 45; Juilliard String Quartet and, 186, 188, 190, 194–96, 197, 199, 216, 225; as maverick, 181; politics and, 160; Schuller and, 95, 122, 126

*Begin Again Again* (Machover), 22

Bell, Joshua, 243

Berg, Alban, xi, 65, 187, 190, 195, 196, 204

Bergsma, William, 200

Berio, Luciano, 163, 165

Berkshire Institute for Theology and the Arts, 33

Berlin Philharmonic, 15, 115

Berlioz, Hector, 165, 166, 168

Bernstein, Leonard, 175, 177, 181, 198, 255; Curtin and, 59, 85; Juilliard String Quartet and, 193, 194; Ma and, 14, 18; Midori and, 230–31, 237, 242–43, 272n2; Schuller and, 121, 134; Spano and, 139, 149; Tilson Thomas and, 172

Bernstein Education Through the Arts Fund, 255

*Beverly* (Sills), 51

Bible, 108, 167

Big Five orchestras, 139

Billings, William, 171

*Billy the Kid* (Copland), 65

Bing, Rudolf, 64

*Birth of the Cool* (Davis), 105

Bis-Quits, 7

*Bitter Melons* (film), 27

Black, Marjorie, 96

Black Caucus, 119

*Black Warrior* (Schuller), 130

Blitzstein, Marc, 100

Bloch, Ernest, 20

Blomstedt, Herbert, 149, 176

*Blood on the Field* (Marsalis), 269n20

*Blue as the Turquoise Night of Neyshabur* (Kalhor), 44

Blum, David, 17, 45–46

Blumenthal, Bob, 110

Bocelli, Andrea, 14

Boccherini, Luigi, 20

Bolcom, William, 24

Boosey and Hawkes, 97

Boston Lyric Opera, 169

Boston Musica Viva, 112, 114

Boston Symphony Orchestra, 25–26, 41, 115, 169, 177, 195, 196, 219; Curtin and, 69; Midori and, 242; Schuller and, 131; Smirnoff and, 218; Spano and, 138, 144–45, 149, 153, 157. *See also* Tanglewood

Boston University, 53, 209, 257

Botstein, Leon, 139, 140, 176, 179

Boulez, Pierre, 177

Brahms, Johannes, 20, 203; Ma and, 9; as maverick, 181; Schuller and, 122; Spano and, 182

*Bridge, The* (Crane), 183

Britten, Benjamin, 20; Curtin and, 52, 59, 69, 89; Spano and, 146

Broadcast Music, Inc., 96

Bronfman, Yefim, 233

Brooklyn Academy of Music, 160–61

Brooklyn Philharmonic, 138–40, 182;

Crosby, John, 56

crossover music, xi

*Crouching Tiger, Hidden Dragon* (film), 21, 47

Crumb, George, 138

Culture of the Cabaret (thematic program), 140

Curtin, Phyllis, ix–xi, 49, 266; Averino and, 58–59; background of, 52–53, 57–61; and Bing, 64; and Boston Symphony, 69; Columbia Artists and, 67–68; composers and, 64–67; and Copland, 59, 64–65, 86–87; Eckert and, 79–80; English and, 67, 75; family and, 60, 63, 88; Floyd and, 53–57; Fu and, 80–82; Goldovsky and, 59–61; individualism and, 52–53; instruction and, 68–84, 257; as Isolde, 66; and Mehta, 82–83, 239; modern trends and, 83–89; and Nelson, 70–71; repertoire of, 50–51, 61–63, 67–68, 85–88; and Rorem, 66–67; and Silber, 72–74; and Sills, 51–52; spirituality and, 89; style of, 78; and Sylvan, 74–77, 84; and Tanglewood, 68–70, 77, 87; and Upshaw, 76–77; vocal register of, 63

*Cycle of Holy Songs* (Rorem), 86

Dalley, John, 226

dance: flamenco, 146, 163; Morris and, 31–34; tango, 2; Torvill and Dean, 31, 33–34

Danielpour, Richard, 23, 36, 44, 155

*Daphnis and Chloé* (Ravel), 146

Dartmouth College, 9–12

Davidson, Justin, 158

Davies, Dennis Russell, 93, 139, 144, 161–62, 163, 168, 178

Davis, Miles, 105, 120

Davis, Peter G., 51, 83

Deadheads, 171–72

Dean, Christopher, 31, 33–34

*Death of Klinghoffer, The* (Adams), 159

Debussy, Claude, 20, 37–38, 124, 169–70, 222, 224

DeGaetani, Jan, 66, 77

Del Tredici, David, 170, 171

DeLay, Dorothy, 16, 239, 241, 243–44

Delius, Frederick, 140

Delta Airlines, 159

*Dervish* (Ali-Zadeh), 42

Deutsche Grammophon, 105

DeVore, Irven, 19

DeYoung, Michelle, 166

Diaghilev, Sergei, 177

Diamond, David, 24, 188

Dickinson, Emily, 49, 64–65

*Distant Echoes: Yo-Yo Ma and the Kalahari Bushmen* (film), 27–28

Dohnány, Christoph von, 121, 148–49

*Don Quixote* (Strauss), 3, 20

donors. *See* funding

Dorati, Antal, 121

*Down Beat* (magazine), 109–10

Downs, Hugh, 26

Dresher, Paul, 80

Drucker, Eugene, 215, 216

Druckman, Jacob, 200

Duffy, Kayla, 234–35

*Duino Elegies* (Rilke), 111

Dulak, Michelle, 21, 46

Dunsmuir Piano Quartet, 221

Dutilleux, Henri, 188, 211, 212

Dvořák, Antonín, xii, 19, 170, 182, 203; Juilliard String Quartet and, 202; Ma and, 3, 26–27

Dyer, Richard, 115, 128

*Early Jazz: Its Roots and Musical Development* (Schuller), 107

*Eating Greens* (Mackey), 148

Eaton, Quaintance, 196–97

Eckert, Rinde, 79–80, 84

education. *See* instruction

Edwards, Ross, 167

Edwards, Ryan, 67–68, 86

Egoyan, Atom, 31

electronic music, 2, 22, 116

Elgar, Edward, 20

Eliot, T. S., 88

elitism, 109

Ellington, Duke, 95, 107, 124, 172

Emerson String Quartet, x, 213, 215–17, 226, 257

Engel, Lehman, 100

*Epitaph* (Mingus), 118

Epstein, Helen, 194, 195, 209

Erb, Donald, 110

Eschenbach, Christoph, 22

ethnic issues, 234, 236, 253–54, 256–57

*Eugene Onegin* (Tchaikovsky), 159

Evans, Bill, 105

Evans, Gil, 105

Faithfull, Marianne, 146, 163

Falla, Manuel de, 146

Fan, Joel, 41

Farwell, Arthur, 99–100

Faull, Ellen, 61

Feldman, Morton, 174, 200

Festival of Contemporary Music (Tanglewood), 115

Figueroa, Guillermo, 215

Finckel, David, 217

Fine, Irving, 200

Fine Arts Quartet, 193

Finns, in music, 140, 158, 164–65

*Fisherman and His Wife, The* (Schuller), 103, 130

*Five Pieces in Folk Style* (Schumann), 34

Flagstad, Kirsten, 59–60

flamenco, 146, 163

Fleisher, Leon, 13

Fleming, Renée, 84

*Flower and Hawk* (Floyd & Curtin), 57

Floyd, Carlisle, 53–57, 64, 84, 86

Fogg, Anthony, 167

Folkman, Marjorie, 34

*Forbidden Childhood* (Slenczynska), 238

Foss, Lukas, 65–66, 139, 161, 163, 172, 200

Franck, César, 262

Frank, Pamela, 22

French Radio Orchestra, 115

Fromm, Paul, 101–2, 103

Fu, Haijing, 80–82

funding, 105–106; Bernstein and, 255; Brooklyn Philharmonic and, 162; community instruction and, 230–32; Juilliard String Quartet and, 214; Midori & Friends and, 232–234, 248–49, 252–53; Schuller and, 93–94, 98, 101; Silk Road Project and, 35–36; U.S. and, 11

Furtwängler, Wilhelm, 103, 121

fusion, 6

Galamian, Ivan, 18, 213

Galimir, Felix, 217

Galimir String Quartet, 210, 217

gamelan, Javanese, 38, 170

Garcia, Jerry, 171–72

Gardner, Howard, 251

Gardner, John Eliot, 120–21

Gay, Harriet, 193, 196, 226

Geller, Timothy, 110–12, 116

Gerhard, Roberto, 146

Gershwin, George, 171, 200

Giamatti, A. Bartlett, 71

Gilbert, Ernest, 85

Gillespie, Dizzy, 105

Ginastera, Alberto, 200, 212, 224

Ginsberg, Allen, 171

Girard, François, 30–31

Giuffre, Jimmy, 105, 120

Glass, Philip, x, 165, 167–68, 169

Glazer, David, 67

globalization, 2–3; fusion and, 6; virtual communication and, 8

*Glorious Ones, The* (Schonberg), 59

GM Recordings, 93, 101, 107, 111–12, 125

Goldmark, Karl, 140

Goldovsky, Boris, 59–61, 88

Goltermann, Georg, 12

gongs, 38

Goodman, Alice, 159

Goto, Midori. *See* Midori

Goto, Setsu, 232, 241

Gould, Glenn, 198, 200

Grateful Dead, 171–72

Greene, Brian, 217

Linden, Judi, 252–53, 255
Ling, Jahja, 26
Lipton, Martha, 87
*Live from Lincoln Center*, 26
Lloyd, David, 61
Los Angeles Piano Quartet, 221
London Symphony Orchestra, 176, 177–78
Los Angeles Philharmonic, 23, 148;
  conductor training, 175
Lovano, Joe, 109, 115
Lully, Jean-Baptiste, 150
*Lyric Suite* (Berg), 190, 196

Ma, Hiao-Tsiun, 17
Ma, Jill Hornor, 3, 19
Ma, Marina, 47
Ma, Nicholas, 19
Ma, Yeou-Cheng, 17
Ma, Yo-Yo, ix, xii, 266; appeal of, 6–8; and
  Ax, 4–5, 15–17, 21–22; background of, 2,
  17–18; charisma of, 14–15; cultural
  boundaries and, 4; Dartmouth and, 9–12;
  and Dvořák, 26–27; eclectic approach of,
  2; electronic music and, 22; fees of, 14;
  globalization and, 2–3; and God, 45; and
  Harbison, 24–25; Harvard and, 3–4, 10,
  18–19; income of, 14; *Inspired by Bach*
  project, 30–33; instruction and, 9–14, 257;
  Kung Bushmen and, 19, 27–30; loneliness
  and, 239; Midori & Friends and, 233;
  online, 8–9; Professional Children's
  School and, 240; religion and, 2–3;
  repertoire of, 19–27; Silk Road Project
  and, 5–6, 9–10, 21, 34–40; slumming
  charges and, 21; style of, 2–4, 10–11, 44–47;
  and Tanglewood, 13, 40–44; travels of,
  27–40; and Williams, 25–26
Maazel, Lorin, 149–50
McBurney, Simon, 216
McDonald, Robert, 244, 261–62
MacDowell Colony, 112
McFerrin, Bobby, 20
Machover, Tod, 22
Mackey, Steven, 148, 172

McNally, Peter, 249–50
Mahler, Gustav, 147, 160, 164, 166, 167, 170,
  218
Mamiya, Michio, 43
Manhattan School of Music, 104
Mann, Robert, 186–87, 193–94, 200, 203, 206,
  207, 208, 213, 215, 227, 271n1; and Rhodes,
  210–11; and Smirnoff, 222; temper of, 198;
  Tokyo Quartet and, 214
Margun Music, 92, 96
marketing, 148, 162–63, 166
Markevich, Igor, 116
Marlboro Music Festival, 16, 18, 210, 221,
  226, 245
Marriner, Neville, 174
Marsalis, Wynton, 118, 269n20
Marshall, Judy, 219
Martin, Frank, 165, 167
Martino, Donald, 98, 212, 225
Massachusetts Institute of Technology, 22
Masur, Kurt, 27, 44, 149–50
Matyakubov, Otanazar, 264
*Meditation* (Schuller), 125
Meet the Moderns (thematic program),
  161
Mehta, Bejun, 82–83, 239
Mehta, Zubin, 242, 243, 261
Meier, Gustav, 157
Mendelssohn, Felix, 203, 227
Mennin, Peter, 200
Menotti, Gian Carlo, 54
Menuhin, Yehudi, 237–38
Meshulum, Idith, 99
Messervy, Julie Moir, 30
Messiaen, Olivier, 140, 165
Metropolitan Opera, 248, 255
Metropolitan Opera Orchestra, 104
Meyer, Edgar, 20, 22, 43
Midori, ix–x, 229, 266; appearances of, 241,
  261; awards of, 261; background of, 235,
  240–41; and Bernstein, 230–31, 237, 242–43,
  272n2; and Chang, 231; commissions and,
  262; composure of, 242–43, 272–73n2;
  crisis of, 241–242; critics and, 236, 242–43,

262–63; and Curtin, 49–89; instruction and, 230–37, 262; media and, 241–43; and Mehta, 242; as own teacher, 244–46; as prodigy, 239, 243–44; Professional Children's School and, 240, 244; psychology studies of, 245–46; repertoire of, 261; sabbatical of, 245

Midori & Friends foundation: beginnings of, 231–32; effects of, 250–52; Explorations in Music program, 233–34, 247; funding and, 232–34, 248–49, 252–53; instruction by, 233–34, 247–61; instruments for, 254; and Japan, 262; and Oakland, 260; progression of, 233–37

Milhaud, Darius, 167, 200

Milnes, Sherrill, 60

Mingus, Charles, 118, 120

Mistral, Gabriela, 57

Mitropoulos, Dimitri, 99

Monette, Paul, 171

Mongolian fiddle, 12

Monk, Meredith, 171, 172

Montagnana cello, 11, 13

*Moon over Guan Mountains* (Zhao-Jiping), 42–43

Moore, Douglas, 54

Morgan, Michael, 258–61, 259

*morin khuur* (fiddle), 12, 42–43

Morris, Mark, 31–34

Mozart, Wolfgang Amadeus, 19, 169, 183, 203, 262; Ma and, 9; as prodigy, 238; Schuller and, 98, 104

Mozart effect, 250–51

Munch, Edvard, 245

Murphy, Heidi Grant, 165

music: advancement of, ix; commercialism and, ix, 131–33; ecclesiatical, 180; fusion and, 6; genres of, xi; modern culture and, 83–84, 180–81; morals and, 263–65; politics and, 159–60; positive effects of, xi–xii, 250–52; prodigies and, 237–39; realization and, 121–22; recorded, 180; specialization and, 108

Music and Religion (thematic program), 164

*Music for the Underdogs of the Orchestra* (Schuller), 128

*Music of the Heart* (movie), 256

*Music Talks* (Epstein), 194, 209–10

*Musical America,* 196

*Musical Prodigies* (Kenneson), 239

*Musings* (Schuller), 94–95, 107, 109, 129, 132

Muti, Riccardo, 149

*My First 79 Years* (Stern), x

*My Son, Yo-Yo* (Ma), 47

Myers, Anne Akiko, 243

*Mystery, The* (Floyd & Curtin), 57


Nagano, Kent, 170

Nakura, Yoshiko, 214

Nancarrow, Conlon, 140, 164

Napoleon, 160

National Commission on Music Education, 251

National Endowment for the Arts, 11

NBC Symphony, 104, 219

Nelson, Philip F., 70–71, 84

New England Conservatory, 96, 97, 107, 113, 128

New England Ragtime Ensemble, 117

*New Grove Dictionary of Music and Musicians, The,* 124

New World record label, 134

New World Symphony, 175, 178

New York City Opera, 51–52, 55, 61; Curtin and, 62–63

New York Philharmonic, 27, 44, 159, 175, 242; instruction and, 255; Spano and, 153

Next Wave Festival, 140, 164

*Nixon in China* (Adams), 140, 164

*Noise of Time, The* (Emerson program), 216–17

Northern Lights (thematic program), 140, 163–64


Oakland East Bay Symphony, 257, 259, 260

O'Connor, Mark, 10, 20

*Of Reminiscences and Reflections* (Schuller), 96, 128, 134

Steiner, Rudolf, 251

Steinhardt, Arnold, 226

Stern, Isaac, x, 16, 17, 22, 224

Stevens, Risë, 59

Stevens, Wallace, 205

Stockhausen, Karlheinz, 116

Stokowski, Leopold, 149, 152, 181

Storace, Nancy, 66

Strauss, Richard, 20, 66, 140, 164, 176, 182

Stravinsky, Igor, xi, 164, 165, 167, 177

Streep, Meryl, 256

*Strictly Baroque* (Ma), 21

Strings of War (thematic program), 140, 163–64

*Struggle for Hope* (dance), 30

Suitner, Otmar, 120

Surinach, Carlos, 146

*Susannah* (Floyd), 53–56, 86

Susman, Robert, 247

Sutherland, Joan, 52

Swed, Mark, 198

Sweete, Barbara Willis, 32

Swieten, Gottfried von, 169, 183

*Swing Era, The: The Development of Jazz* (Schuller), 107

Sylvan, Sanford, 51, 74–76, 84

*Symphony* (Schuller), 127

Symphony for Brass and Percussion (Schuller), 105–6

synthesizers, 2, 22, 116

Takemitsu, Toru, 38, 140, 164

Tan Dun, 24, 3, 57, 169

Tanglewood, x; Bach suites and, 33; Bernstein at, 175; Curtin and, 59–62, 65, 68–70, 77, 87; Juilliard String Quartet and, 186–187, 196, 219–20, 227; Krosnick and, 218–19; Levin and, 41–42; Ma and, 7–8, 13, 25–26, 40–44; Midori and, 242–43; Schuller and, 103, 106–7, 115–16; Spano and, 144, 156–57

*Tango Lesson, The* (film), 20

Taruskin, Richard, 173–74

Tassel, Janet, 18

Taylor, Billy, 212

Taylor, James, 20

Tchaikovsky, Pyotr Ilyich, 20, 159, 179, 203

Tcherepnin, Alexander, 21

teaching. *See* instruction

*Teaching Genius* (Sand), 239

Telarc, 157

television, 147

Tenenbom, Steven, 256

thematic programming, 139–40, 145–46, 163–65

Theofanidis, Christopher, 166, 167, 182

Thibaudet, Jean-Yves, 182

Third Stream style, 107, 114–15, 130, 135

Thomas, Roberta, 175

Thomas, Ted, 175

Thomashefsky, Bessie, 175

Thomashefsky, Boris, 175

Thomson, Virgil, 100, 180, 197, 199, 200

Three Tenors, 84

*Through an Ancient Valley* (Danielpour), 44

Tilson Thomas, Michael, xi, 139, 148–49; background of, 175; critics and, 171–74; London Symphony Orchestra and, 177–78; methods of, 170–77; 181–82; programming of, 173–74, 177; Spectrum concerts and, 177; young audiences and, 178–79

Toho Gakuen School, 214, 240

Tokyo String Quartet, x, 213–15, 226

Tommasini, Anthony, 86, 128, 135, 153, 172, 236

Torvill, Jayne, 31, 33–34

Toscanini, Arturo, 104, 121, 149, 181

Tourel, Jennie, 66

*Transfigured Night* (Schoenberg), 93

*Transfigured Notes* (Babbitt), 93

*Traviata, La* (Verdi), 52, 63–64

Tree, Michael, 226

*Treemonisha* (Joplin), 117–18

Treigle, Norman, 55, 86

*Trial, The* (Kafka), 129

Turina, Joaquin, 146